ANALYSING WITNESS TESTIMONY:
A GUIDE FOR LEGAL PRACTITIONERS AND
OTHER PROFESSIONALS

DEDICATION
To our families

ANALYSING WITNESS TESTIMONY: A GUIDE FOR LEGAL PRACTITIONERS AND OTHER PROFESSIONALS

EDITED BY

Anthony Heaton-Armstrong
of Grays Inn, Barrister

Eric Shepherd
Psychologist, Consultant Forensic Investigative Science

David Wolchover
of Grays Inn, Barrister

BLACKSTONE PRESS LIMITED

First published in Great Britain 1999 by Blackstone Press Limited, Aldine Place, London W12 8AA. Telephone 0181-740 2277

ISBN: 1 85431 731 8

British Library Cataloguing in Publication Data
A CIP catalogue record for this book is available from the British Library

Typeset by Style Photosetting Limited, Mayfield, East Sussex
Printed by Ashford Colour Press, Gosport, Hants

Contents

Part 1   Psychological perspectives

Part 3   Evidential issues

Foreword

Most lawsuits, civil or criminal, turn largely or wholly on questions of fact: what happened? who said what? what did party A know? what did party B believe? what did party C intend? and so on. One of the defining characteristics of the common law has been its abiding concern with such questions, and it has on the whole been successful in developing procedures for testing and assessing oral evidence, to distinguish the honest from the dishonest, the reliable from the unreliable.

But the common law is nothing if not pragmatic. It lives and it learns. So it has learned not only the obvious lessons that some witnesses are honest and others dishonest, some witnesses reliable and others unreliable, but also less obvious lessons: that witnesses may be in part honest and in part dishonest, in part reliable and in part unreliable; that witnesses may be completely honest, entirely confident, very persuasive, but quite wrong; that people may sometimes, for complex psychological reasons, accept or even claim responsiblity for terrible deeds they have never done.

The assessment of evidence is, for all those concerned with the investigation of alleged wrong-doing and the administration of justice, an important subject and this is a challenging book. It challenges many familiar assumptions and habits of thought. It challenges readers to understand and consider the views and arguments of authoritative contributors whose professional and academic disciplines lie outside the law. It challenges us all to think afresh about the elusive but crucial evidential goal of distinguishing the true from the false.

That goal can never be finally and completely reached. But we cannot conscientiously neglect to make what advances we may. So we should be grateful to the editors and authors of this book for making accessible much learning not readily available to lawyers; and we can be confident that these contributions, appropriately tested, properly understood and wisely used, will serve to deepen our understanding and advance the ends of justice.

Bingham of Cornhill
Lord Chief Justice of England and Wales
28 January 1999

Acknowledgements

We are, primarily, grateful to our publisher, Alistair MacQueen, of Blackstone Press, for having faith in this demanding, difficult and controversial project and we feel that it is no coincidence that as well as having recently taken over responsibility for publication of the Journal of the Judicial Studies Board, he is also a member of its editorial board. We have made great demands on our chapter authors, who have complied with our time-consuming requests with patience and fortitude and we express our thanks, particularly, to them for all their efforts. A number of the chapters have been presaged through the delivery of papers on which they are based at seminars organised by the British Academy of Forensic Sciences and we acknowledge the contributions made, albeit indirectly, to the concept of this book by their chairmen and, notably, the late Lord Taylor of Gosforth and Lords Justice Sir Paul Kennedy, Dame Elizabeth Butler-Sloss and Sir Christopher Rose. Other judicial figures, lawyers and police officers have provided us with inspiration during the book's gestation and these include Nicholas Philpot, Jeffrey Gordon, Michael Corkery QC, Alex Carlile QC, Andrew Ashworth QC, James Morton, David Phillips, Chief Constable of the Kent Police and Chairman of the Criminal Committee of the Association of Chief Police Officers, Detective Superintendent Max McClean of the West Yorkshire Police and Detective Inspector Gary Shaw of the Northumbria Police. Finally, we pay special tribute to Gisli Gudjonsson, the forensic psychologist, for advice in the early stages of this endeavour.

Anthony Heaton-Armstrong
Eric Shepherd
David Wolchover

Preface

Some traditionalists consider that the essential issue for those who need to decide if a witness's evidence can be relied upon simply involves whether they are 'telling the truth' or are lying. This wholly simplistic approach to testimony underlines the concerns which led us to conceive this book. For whereas utterances by suspects in criminal cases has long formed the meat of Royal Commissions, significant legislation and, following consideration of expert psychological intervention, judgments of the Appeal Courts, statements by nondefendant witnesses whether prior to the forensic setting or in evidence has been the subject of comparatively scant academic and legal attention. Drawing on a total of 80 years' experience as practising lawyers and, in Eric Shepherd's case, as a criminal and psychological investigator, it has become clear to us that such a naive attitude to witness testimony has been responsible for incorrect analyses which can only have led to miscarriages of justice. Our principal motive in formulating our concept has been to enable those involved in the administration of justice to share in readily available expertise and, thus, to become skilled in recognising what, really, lies behind statements of witnesses.

Thus the project's gestation has been protracted. Much of the contents have been anticipated in or inspired by earlier articles both by the editors and some of the chapter authors. The two legal editors had originally thought that what is now their book on Confession Evidence (Sweet and Maxwell 1996) might usefully include consideration of testimony from all categories of witness but it became apparent that the two topics were sufficiently unique to justify a separate book. Additional impetus has been provided by the success of a series of annual seminars organised by the British Academy of Forensic Sciences between 1992 and 1999 which proved popular with those at whom the book is aimed and comprised lectures by many of those who are now chapter authors. And it was during its lengthy conception that the legal editors had the good fortune to meet and work with Eric Shepherd, the Investigator/Psychologist editor, whose contributions have been essential and important. For whilst a book by lawyers might have prompted a 'teach your grandmother to suck eggs' response, there is no denying that much of the learning summarised and expressed by Eric and his professional colleagues, provides unassailable scientific support for our theories and observations as lawyers.

There has been considerable resistance amongst lawyers to the acceptance of wisdom from scientists as to mental processes. This may have been caused by and is undoubtedly reflected in the absence of reference to learning from other disciplines in professional training courses. Legal education has, understandably, been apt to focus on legal concepts but the drawback of such a narrow approach is that the importance of significant areas of knowledge which might assist lawyers in forensic practice whether as practitioners or members of the judiciary tends to be minimised and even sneered at. And until quite recently judicial education, at least, has concentrated almost exclusively on the mechanics of trial procedures and sentencing policy. Habits collected during professional practice which involve the acceptance of bad practice amongst evidence gatherers are thus perpetuated on the first instance bench and, ultimately, in the Appeal Courts. A particularly striking example of this concerns police officers' collaborative testimony, covered in chapter 14 and on which the legal editors have written extensively in the past. We are not afraid to acknowledge that we have been influenced by the American approach to the use of psychological and psychiatric expertise in the unravelling of issues created by contentious witness testimony. The work of Elizabeth Loftus, the forerunner in her field, has been well known to U.S. jurisdictions for over 20 years but we doubt whether, in spite of the undoubted value of her writings, she is perceived as anything other than an obscure, unimportant and American psychologist, with all that this reputation implies, amongst those few legal practitioners here who have even heard of her.

We do not seek to revolutionise the law on the admissibility of expert evidence concerning the reliability of witness testimony and recognise that change of the kind suggested in the chapter on this subject 18 must, if to be valuable, come slowly and on mature consideration. We have set out, however, to provide some insight into the workings of the human mind to those involved in making decisions and helping others to do so, as to whether testimony is accurate or historically correct and can, thus, be relied upon when decisions as to fact need to be made in the forensic setting.

We anticipate that the book will, primarily, be of use to the judiciary and other practitioners in the criminal justice system, crime investigators, forensic psychiatrists and psychologists as well as to academics and students in the relevant disciplines. Additionally, however, its contents will assist those working in what might be termed the quasi-criminal field, involved in cases where wrong-doing or malfeasance is alleged albeit that the decisions as to fact may lead to the use of Civil Courts' remedies.

The subject matter as reflected in the chapter contents is not intended to be viewed as comprehensive and in some instances it has only been feasible to scratch the surface of highly complex and extensive fields. We have, nonetheless, set out to examine those topics consideration of which we feel to be of greatest importance. The recommended reading lists at the conclusion of each chapter will be of use to those intent on study in greater depth.

Inevitably, the implications of the lessons to be learnt will be unpalatable to status quo traditionalists and far-reaching in cost terms. But in a field where victims' rights and the liberty of the subject are at stake we suggest that a closed mind strait-jacket approach to legal education is not justifiable.

Anthony Heaton-Armstrong
Eric Shepherd
David Wolchover
London/Abingdon 1999

Introduction

In this introduction we explain the layout of the text and summarise its subject matter in a way which will enable the reader to get to grips with the contents easily and with minimal exasperation.

There are three logically sequential parts — focusing on psychological, investigative and evidential aspects — and each are preceded by their own, separate introductions or summaries. Part 1, the psychological section, covers basic mental processes, the risks of corruption of memory caused by outside events, mental and physical disorder and illness and the vulnerabilities of certain categories of witness. Moving on, and assuming the reader's acquaintance with this essential background expertise and knowledge, part 2 focuses on the investigative collation of witnesses' accounts and the means used to obtain them. These two parts will facilitate the identification of factors which, first, may have caused any memory retrieved when providing a historic account to become distorted and second, in the light of any information thus indicated, to examine to what extent investigative methods might have contributed to the provision of factually incorrect information, or have created barriers to its discovery. Finally, the third, evidential, part concentrates on the forensic setting and how awareness of issues discussed in parts 1 and 2 can be put into practice in court and some of the problems that may be faced in efforts to do so.

As we have made clear in our preface, the contents are not intended to be perceived as comprehensive and nor do we pretend that, whereas we have endeavoured to adopt something of a chronological approach to the subject, each and every chapter necessarily fits neatly into place.

The chapters' format will not be familiar to those accustomed to using legal academic textbooks or practitioners' guides for reasons which will become apparent as close acquaintance with the contents increases. And whilst in certain instances, such as the chapter on earwitness testimony, for example, it may be helpful for a chapter to be read in isolation, we do not recommend that this is a book for dipping into. As we have sought to explain, there is a beginning, a middle and an end and we suggest that it is read with this in mind.

Where we have considered it appropriate, we have appended editors' notes to some chapters. These are principally intended to provide some suggestions

as to how the lessons contained therein might be most effectively put to
practical use and to highlight some of the difficulties that might be encountered when endeavours to do so are made.

Editors' list of recommended reading

*Active Defence: a Solicitor's Guide to Police and Defence Investigation and
Prosecution and Defence Disclosure in Criminal Cases.* By Roger Ede and Eric
Shepherd. Law Society, 1997. ISBN 1–85328–442–4.

Anchored Narratives: the Psychology of Criminal Evidence. By Willem
Wagenaar, Peter van Koppen and Hans Crombag. Harvester Wheatsheaf/
St. Martin's Press, 1993. ISBN 0–7450–1459–3.

Eyewitness Testimony: Psychological Perspectives. Edited by Gary Wells and
Elizabeth Loftus. Cambridge University Press, 1987. ISBN
0–521–25564–3.

Eyewitness Testimony. By Elizabeth Loftus. Harvard University Press,
1996. ISBN 0–674–28777–0.

Interpreting Evidence: Evaluating Forensic Science in the Courtroom. By
Bernard Robertson and G.A. Vignaux. John Wiley and Sons, 1995. ISBN
0–471–96026–8.

Psychology and Law: Truthfulness, Accuracy and Credibility. By
Amina Memon, Aldert Vrij and Ray Bull. McGraw Hill, 1998. ISBN
0–7709–316–X.

The Psychology of Interrogation, Confessions and Testimony. By Gisli
Gudjonsson. Wiley, 1992. ISBN 0–471–961–77–9.

Contributors

Janet Boakes is Consultant Psychiatrist in Psychotherapy and Clinical Director for Psychotherapy at Pathfinder NHS Trust, and Honorary Senior Lecturer at St George's Hospital Medical School, London. She is also a group analyst and past Chairman of the Institute of Group Analysis. She was a member of the Royal College of Psychiatrists' Working Party on Reported Recovered Memories of Childhood Sexual Abuse, which led to the publication of College Guidelines. She is co-author of the subsequent review article published in the *British Journal of Psychiatry*. She was formerly the Honorary Secretary of the UK Council for Psychotherapy.

Ray Bull is Professor of Criminological and Legal Psychology at the University of Portsmouth. He has authored or co-authored many papers in referred journals and chapters in edited books (totalling over 95 to date), co-authored five books and co-edited two books, *Handbook of Psychology in Legal Contexts* and *Children's Evidence in Legal Proceedings* (1990). He is co-founding editor of the journal *Expert Evidence*. In 1991, at the invitation of the Home Office, he wrote with a professor of law the first working draft of the *Memorandum of Good Practice on Video Recorded Interviews with Child Witnesses for Criminal Proceedings* (1992).

Noel Clark is a Senior Lecturer in Social Psychology at the University of Kent at Canterbury. He is also a chartered forensic psychologist. His research has focused on psychological aspects of police interrogation and interviewing, and legal decision-making generally. He is currently preparing (with Geoffrey Stephenson and Joanna Adler) a book on the use of narrative models in legal contexts (due for publication in 1999).

Brian R. Clifford is Professor of Cognitive Psychology at the University of East London. His research has focused on the application of memory to everyday events such as processing informational television and texts and eye and earwitnessing. He has written four books including *Person Identification* (with Ray Bull) and edited *Evaluating Witness Evidence* (with Sally Lloyd-Bostock). He has published over 100 academic journal articles, the majority in the eyewitness testimony field.

Gillian Cohen is Professor of Psychology at the Open University and a Fellow of the British Psychological Society. Her research has focused on everyday memory and on the effects of ageing. She recently published the second edition of *Memory in the Real World*. Other books include *Memory for Proper Names* (with D. Burke) and *Psychology of Cognition*.

Andrew M. Colman is Reader in Psychology at the University of Leicester and a Fellow of the British Psychological Society. His most recent books include the *Companion Encyclopaedia of Psychology*, of which he is the editor. He is series editor of the *Longman Essential Psychology Series*.

Graham Davies is Professor of Psychology at the University of Leicester. He is a chartered forensic psychologist and a Fellow of the British Psychological Society. His research interests lie in the eyewitness testimony of adults and children, on which he has published five books and over 100 scientific papers. At the request of the Home Office, he evaluated the special video provisions introduced into the courts for the benefit of child witnesses.

Peter Dunk is a serving officer with the Kent Constabulary. He has recently completed an MSc in criminal justice studies at the Institute of Police and Criminological Studies of the University of Portsmouth. He achieved a distinction in his studies and was the 1997 winner of the Henry Stewart Publications Postgraduate Dissertation Prize for his work on police cautioning.

Peter Fenwick is a consultant neuropsychiatrist and consultant clinical neurophysiologist. He holds honorary appointments at the Maudsley Hospital and at the Institute of Psychiatry. He is the Emeritus Head of the Maudsley Neuropsychiatry Epilepsy Unit, which he ran for 12 years. He is appointed Honorary Research Consultant Clinical Neurophysiologist to Broadmoor Special Hospital and Consultant Neuropsychiatrist to the Radcliffe Infirmary, Oxford. He has wide experience as a medical expert in cases involving automatism. He was involved in the cases of *R* v *Burgess* and *R* v *Sullivan*, which set the law on sleepwalking and on epilepsy.

Chris Fife-Schaw is a Senior Lecturer in Social Psychology at the University of Surrey. He has published in the areas of risk perception, risk-taking and their relationship to decision-making, persuasion and attitude change. He has particular interests in the adequacy of mock-jury methodologies in research and has jointly edited a textbook called *Research Methods in Psychology*.

Gisli H. Gudjonsson is a Reader in Forensic Psychology at the Institute of Psychiatry, University of London, and Head of the Forensic Psychology Services at the Maudsley Hospital. He has published extensively in the areas of psychological vulnerability and false confession. He pioneered the empirical measurement of suggestibility and provided expert evidence in a number of high-profile cases, including those of the 'Guildford Four', the 'Birmingham Six', the 'Tottenham Three', the 'Cardiff Three', Judith Ward, David Mackenzie, Kenneth Erskine (the 'Stockwell strangler'), the 'UDR Four' and Patrick Kane (both in Northern Ireland), and Henry Lee Lucas (in Texas, USA). Gisli Gudjonsson testified at the 'Ashworth Inquiry' and at the arbitration of the Zeebrugge disaster.

Anthony Heaton-Armstrong has been a barrister in independent practice since 1974, specialising in criminal cases and appearing mainly on behalf of defendants. His numerous published articles, many written jointly with David Wolchover, have focused on evidence-gathering methods used by police investigators. He has worked closely with the Home Office on revisions to the Police and Criminal Evidence Act 1984 Codes of Practice and on other issues. He is the joint author, with David Wolchover, of *Confession Evidence*, and is the Meetings Secretary of the British Academy of Forensic Sciences.

Malcolm Lader is an external member of the scientific staff of the Medical Research Council and Professor of Clinical Psychopharmacology at the Institute of Psychiatry, University of London. He is also an Honorary Consultant at the Bethlem and Maudsley Hospitals. He is Chairman of the Home Office's Technical Committee on the Misuse of Drugs. He is a past President of the British Association for Psychopharmacology and the Society for the Study of Addiction. An Honorary Fellow of the American College of Psychiatry, he is a member of the editorial boards of 28 journals and has published 15 books and 600 papers.

R.D. Mackay is Professor of Criminal Policy and Mental Health at the School of Law, De Montfort University in Leicester. He is the author of *Mental Condition Defences in the Criminal Law*.

Ian McKenzie is the Director of the Institute of Police and Criminological Studies of the University of Portsmouth. A former senior officer of the Metropolitan Police Service, he served in police stations in west and south London. He was Chief Instructor of Policing Skills at the Metropolitan Police Training School, Hendon. He holds a PhD from the University of Bath and is a chartered forensic and occupational psychologist.

Amina Memon is a lecturer in social psychology at the University of Southampton. She is currently visiting the University of Texas at Dallas where she completed her first book, *Psychology and Law: Truthfulness Accuracy and Credibility*. Dr Memon has published extensively on the Cognitive Interview and eyewitness memory. Her research has focused on the efficacy of various interviewing techniques, child witnesses and applications of memory research in forensic contexts.

Rebecca (Becky) Milne is a Lecturer at the Institute of Police and Criminological Studies at the University of Portsmouth, where she is the course leader for the BSc in Policing Studies. Her PhD research into cognitive interviewing led to collaborative work in the United States and in Germany. With Colin Clark of the Metropolitan Police Service she is conducting research commissioned by the Police Research Group into witness interviewing following the introduction of the national model of police interviewing. She acts as a consultant to various police forces and social services authorities.

Anna Mortimer is a consultant forensic psychologist and a partner of Investigative Science, an independent forensic psychology consultancy instructed by the defence and by the Crown. She has lectured in the Division of Psychiatry and Psychology, UMDS Guy's and St Thomas's. The former consultant psychologist to Merseyside Police's Interview Development Unit, she specialises in training investigative interviewers in a variety of contexts. She combines a background in computing, knowledge engineering and applied psychology in the development of manual and computer approaches to the fine-grain analysis of recorded and written testimony.

Guy A. Norfolk is a general practitioner and forensic physician. He is a senior member of the Association of Police Surgeons and sits on the British Medical Association's Forensic Medicine Committee. One of his research interests is the fitness for interview of persons detained by the police, a subject on which he was written extensively. He is a contributing author to *Clinical Forensic Medicine* and appears regularly as an expert witness for both the defence and prosecution.

Eric Shepherd is a consultant forensic psychologist, a partner of Investigative Science and honorary senior lecturer and psychotherapist in the Division of Psychiatry and Psychology, Guy's, King's and St Thomas's Medical School. A former intelligence officer specialising in applied language work and interrogation, he trains investigators and develops manual and computer systems for testimony analysis. He is author of the Law Society's series of practitioner texts, *Police Station Skills for Legal Advisers* and (with Roger Ede) *Active Defence*. He was adviser in the production of the NSPCC training film, *A Case for Balance* (1997), which demonstrates to judges and lawyers good practice when dealing with child witnesses in court.

Geoffrey Stephenson is a Professor of Social Psychology at the University of Kent at Canterbury. He is also a chartered forensic psychologist. His research has focused on a variety of aspects of police interviewing and interrogation practice, and on the psychology of addiction. His publications include *The Psychology of Criminal Justice* and the second edition of *An Introduction to Social Psychology* (with M. Hewstone and W. Strobe).

Peter Thornton QC is a criminal defence barrister and Recorder of the Crown Court. He is a contributing editor of *Archbold* and on the editorial board of the *Criminal Law Review*.

Graham Wagstaff is a Reader in Psychology at the University of Liverpool. For more than 20 years he has researched and published widely in most aspects of hypnosis, though he has a particular interest in its forensic aspects. He also researches and publishes in the psychology of justice. He is author of *Hypnosis, Compliance and Belief*, which has been widely cited as an authoritative text on the non-state approach to hypnosis. He is also one of the founder members of the British Society of Experimental and Clinical Hypnosis. In addition to his academic activities, he has acted as an expert witness in cases in which hypnosis has been involved.

David Wolchover was called by Gray's Inn in 1971 and now practises exclusively at the criminal Bar. His works include *The Exclusion of Improperly Obtained Evidence* and *Confession Evidence*, co-authored with Anthony Heaton-Armstrong. He has written extensively on a wide variety of topics relating to criminal evidence and procedure and through his joint authorship with Anthony Heaton-Armstrong of a series of articles and papers on the Police and Criminal Evidence Act 1984 Codes of Practice has been instrumental in securing a number of important revisions to them over the years. He has recently published (1999) with Neil Corre a major new treatise on bail in criminal proceedings.

PART ONE

PSYCHOLOGICAL PERSPECTIVES

To have a qualified psychologist on the team was a bonus: every jury should have one.

The Juryman's Tale, Tevor Grove

SUMMARY

Familiarity with the chapters in part 1 is essential. They detail the workings of human memory and potentially corrupting influences thereon in a way which will enable the reader to make sense of and appreciate the significance of parts 2 and 3. Whether people are 'normal' or 'abnormal', their memories are subject to influence either owing to some inherent psychiatric, psychological or physical defect or due to a variety of external factors.

Chapter 1. Human memory in the real world. Gillian Cohen
The main principles which govern the operation of human memory are summarised. The chapter focuses on the potential failings of memory and the ways in which errors and omissions arise in circumstances which are relevant to the forensic setting. Acquaintance with the principles will, also, facilitate more effective interviewing techniques and useful analysis of the memories that are elicited.

Chapter 2. Contamination of witness memory. Graham Davies
The lessons outlined in chapter 1 are enhanced in a more clinical context and this serves to enable the reader to identify factors which may contaminate accurate memory. Subjects discussed include memory elaboration, memory replacement, memory supplementation and the recovered memories controversy.

Chapter 3. The Influence of drugs on testimony. Malcolm Lader
There are many drugs, illicit or otherwise, which may influence or distort mental processes and put the integrity of witnesses' accounts at risk. The more commonly used drugs, their potential effects and the risks created by their ingestion to memory corruption are detailed in this chapter.

2   Psychological perspectives summary

Chapter 4. The frailty of children's testimony. Anna Mortimer and Eric Shepherd
Children have a potential to endorse, albeit unwittingly, misinforming assertions by an adult, and are particularly at risk of social influences. Attention is drawn to two dimensions of disclosure, motivation to tell and ability to tell. Conversation and relationships directed at obtaining reliable accounts are considered.

Chapter 5. Testimony from persons with mental disorder. Gisli Gudjonsson
Assumptions that those who suffer from mental disorder are, invariably, incapable of providing accurate and reliable testimony are wrong. The potential psychological vulnerabilities of persons with mental disorder are set out. The ways in which these may influence the reliability of a witness's accounts are examined. Effective diagnosis of disorders suffered and appreciation of their effect on the reliability of an account are essential.

Chapter 6. Witness testimony in sleep and dream-related contexts. Peter Fenwick
This study examines the extent to which sleep and dreams can influence the reliability of witness accounts and the conduct of alleged offenders. Difficulties often arise where sexual conduct is said to be involved.

Chapter 7. Physical illnesses and their potential influence. Guy Norfolk
The symptoms and effects of some physical disorders whether accompanied by an underlying psychological vulnerability or inherently likely to affect brain function in any event, have a potentially influential effect on memory and witness behaviour. Categories of relevant illnesses are listed and their potential for corruption of 'normal' thought processes is discussed.

Chapter 8. Complaints of sexual misconduct. Janet Boakes
False, misleading or exaggerated accounts are notorious when sexual misbehaviour is alleged. The circumstances in which dubious claims of sexual misconduct may arise in adults or children are reviewed. The evidence for repression and 'false memory syndrome' are discussed.

CHAPTER ONE

Human memory in the real world

Gillian Cohen

1.1 INTRODUCTION

1.1.1 Human memory and witness testimony

This chapter sets out the main principles that govern the operation of human memory and the conceptual framework that underpins the way psychologists understand memory. The focus is on the fallibility of memory and the ways in which errors and omissions arise because those matters are of particular relevance to witness testimony. Research, which has tended to concentrate on memory failures rather than memory achievements, fails to do justice to the remarkable ability of the memory system to retain the vast quantity of information and experience acquired over a lifetime.

The principles of human memory outlined in this chapter have many practical applications to witness memory. First, they suggest the optimal strategies for interviewing witnesses and methods for inducing witnesses to remember more. Secondly, they should serve to guide interpretations of the memories that are elicited; to understand the kind of circumstances that promote errors and the kind of errors that are likely to arise. An understanding of the strengths and weaknesses of the human memory system allows the interviewer to judge more accurately how much witnesses can be expected to recall and how much weight can be placed on the testimony they produce.

1.1.2 Quantity and quality of remembered information

A particularly important feature of witness memory is that in real-life situations people have a considerable amount of control over their memory reporting in terms of both the quantity and the quality of what they report. There is a tendency for quantity and quality to be inversely related. Witnesses may opt to report only the information they feel very sure about and withhold items of information about which they are uncertain. In this case they are

likely to produce a smaller amount of higher quality information. Or they may
be willing to report memories even when their level of confidence is low, so
that they produce a larger amount of poorer quality information. Quantity
and accuracy are, to some extent, under the strategic control of the witness
and are regulated by factors such as the personal goals of the witness, and
how the witness interprets the goals of the interviewer. Asher Koriat in Israel
is currently studying the way people can vary the 'grain size' of memory
reports depending on the situation so that they may produce very fine-grain
detailed reports or more general coarse-grained ones. The point to note is
that memory is governed by strategies, goals and intentions as well as the
mechanisms of the memory system described in 1.2.

1.1.3 Studying memory in the real world
For many decades the study of human memory was based on experiments
conducted in the laboratory. Such experiments typically consisted of asking
people to study lists of words, syllables or numbers and later testing their
memory. This type of research has the advantage of being rigorously controlled and producing neat quantitative results, but it has the disadvantage that
it seems to have little application to the workings of memory in the real world
outside the laboratory. However, from these experiments psychologists have
derived the basic principles that govern the function of human memory and
have formulated theories and models. Since the late 1970s a great deal of the
research on human memory has moved out of the laboratory and into the real
world. There has been an upsurge of interest in the operation of memory in
practical everyday situations and psychologists currently study how memory
works in the classroom, the street, the home, and in shops, hospitals, factories
and courtrooms. The challenge is to find out how far memory in the real
world still conforms to the general principles discovered in the laboratory.
   The difficulty of studying memory in real, naturally occurring situations, as
opposed to the artificially contrived laboratory tests, arises because it is
influenced by a multiplicity of factors which usually cannot be controlled or
measured or even identified. Take, for example, a relatively simple event like
reading an item in the newspaper. Ability to remember what has been read
depends on the reader's mood, interest in the topic, familiarity with the
context, reading habits and educational level. Age and gender and time of day
might also exert an effect. Memory will also be influenced by the amount of
attention paid while reading, the nature of the events that occurred subsequently and the demands and pressures of the reader's lifestyle. The complex
interactions of many variables like these make it extremely difficult to predict
and explain memory performance in real situations. The general principles
that govern memory can easily be submerged or distorted by all these other
influences.
   These difficulties are all relevant when we come to consider the role of
memory in witness testimony. Suppose that a person who is walking down
the street witnesses or participates in some incident and is later asked to
report what happened. How much information will the witness be able to
report? What level of detail should be expected? How accurate and how

complete will the information be? What kinds of errors, confusions and omissions are likely? Under what conditions is the witness likely to produce more and better information? Questions such as these commonly arise in the evaluation of witness testimony. Theories of human memory cannot provide precise answers in a specific case but an understanding of how memory operates will help practitioners to evaluate the testimony a witness produces and to implement the procedures and conditions that will best facilitate the witness's memory.

1.2   A MODEL OF THE MEMORY SYSTEM

1.2.1   The multi-store model
The multi-store model of memory (figure 1.1), originally proposed by Atkinson and Shiffrin (1968), is somewhat oversimplified but still provides a basic account of the memory system.

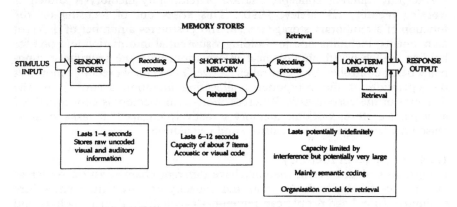

Figure 1.1   The multi-store model of memory

1.2.2   The sensory stores
Atkinson and Shiffrin identified three different memory stores, beginning with a sensory store, which holds raw uninterpreted information perceived by the sense organs for between one second and four seconds. Different sensory stores correspond to each sensory modality (e.g., vision, hearing, smell). A subset of the information that enters the sensory stores is selected and passed on to the short-term store.

1.2.3   Short-term memory
Most people are aware of the distinction between short and long-term memory but may not be familiar with the way psychologists use these terms. Short-term memory corresponds to the current contents of consciousness, that is, what you have in mind at any one moment. It has a brief duration and a strictly limited capacity. It lasts only a few seconds and can only store

about seven items or chunks of information. It is also very fragile in that any distraction or new incoming information will cause items to be bumped out and lost. However, it is possible to maintain the contents of short-term memory by verbally rehearsing information either aloud or subvocally. If you keep repeating the telephone number you are about to dial you are effectively recycling the contents of short-term memory and have a better chance of resisting distractions. However, once attention is diverted away from them, items are rapidly lost. The importance of short-term memory, as far as witness testimony is concerned, is that it is a stage through which information must pass before entering the long-term store. Witness testimony is concerned with information that has passed beyond short-term memory and has been stored in long-term memory but some items may be lost at the earlier stage and never reach long-term memory. For example, a witness may attempt to memorise a licence plate number by repeating it over and over but be distracted by being asked a question. The number is then lost from short-term memory and cannot be recalled.

A slightly different conceptualisation of temporary memory is known as working memory (Baddeley, 1990). This arises out of focusing on the function of a temporary storage system and postulates a number of different components, including one for holding visuospatial information and one for holding speech-based phonological information, with the separate components being controlled by a central executive. The central executive monitors the operation of the components allocating attention according to the demands of the current task. Whereas short-term memory is conceptualised as a passive store, working memory is actively engaged in tasks such as reasoning, language comprehension, and calculation.

1.2.4 Long-term memory

Long-term and short-term memory have different characteristics. As far as can be ascertained, both duration and capacity of long-term memory are unlimited. In old age people can remember events from their early lives and there is no identifiable limit on the amount of information that can be stored, although it cannot always be remembered at will. Long-term memory stores a great diversity of information including knowledge and beliefs, language and music, faces and places, plans and skills. Information in long-term memory only becomes available to conscious awareness through an act of recollection and some long-term memories cannot be recollected and remain inaccessible to consciousness.

1.2.4.1 Episodic and semantic memory Within long-term memory psychologists distinguish between semantic memory and episodic memory (Tulving, 1972). Semantic memory consists of general knowledge about the world, for example, that spring follows winter; that Paris is the capital of France; that BMW is a make of car; that omelettes are made of eggs. Episodic memory is about specific events or episodes that occurred at a specific time and place and have been personally experienced, such as your last birthday party, having supper last night, the journey to work this morning. Witness testimony is primarily concerned with episodic memory — the witness is asked to recall a specific episode. However, the two memory systems are not completely separate. An episodic memory may be filled out and interpreted in the light of knowledge stored in semantic memory. Ask a witness how fast a lorry was travelling when it smashed into a stationary car and the answer may be based on both the episodic memory of its speed and the knowledge drawn from semantic memory that the damage inflicted must have been caused by a high-speed impact. Ask what time of day the incident occurred and the witness may decide it was about 5 p.m. because episodic memory records that it was just getting dark and semantic memory supplies the knowledge that darkness falls at about that time. The episodic/semantic distinction is an important one because, when witness testimony is being evaluated, it is useful to disentangle what aspects of the witness's report are based on direct experience and what are being inferred from previously learned semantic knowledge.

1.2.4.2 Organisation in long-term memory Long-term memory is a highly organised store. Whereas in short-term memory items are held in order of arrival, information in long-term memory is predominantly organised in terms of its meaning. Rather like a library or an office filing system, items that belong to the same category are grouped together so that people can tell you all the jobs they have held or all the houses they have lived in or countries they have visited. Many categories appear to be organised in hierarchies with the most general superordinate category (such as food, or furniture) at the top and lower-level subordinate categories (vegetables, chairs) nested below. This is an economical and efficient system of organisation which makes it relatively easy to access information on demand.

1.3   THREE STAGES OF MEMORY

A useful distinction can be made between three memory processes that form a sequence of stages. These are encoding, storage and retrieval. Information may be lost, discarded or distorted at each of these stages. This section of the chapter will identify the ways in which information is preserved and the ways in which it drops out of the memory system at each stage.

1.3.1   Encoding stage

1.3.1.1 Selective encoding Encoding is the stage at which information is acquired. Before it is encoded, information is perceived by the sense organs and enters the sensory stores. However, only a small fraction of the information that is present in a complex scene is picked up and encoded. Perception is highly selective so that a great deal of information never enters the sensory stores or is discarded almost immediately. This was strikingly demonstrated in a study testing the ability of American subjects to draw the face of a one cent coin from memory. Performance was extremely poor. On average only three of eight features of the coin face were remembered and these were often misplaced. The researchers concluded that people only notice the gross features like size and colour that are necessary to identify a coin and never notice the details.

1.3.1.2   Forms of representation   The information that is selected for encoding is transferred to short-term memory. At this stage an internal, mental representation of the external event is constructed and this may take different forms. In short-term memory the predominant forms of representation are in a visual code or in a speech-based verbal code. A visually perceived event may be encoded as a visual image, or sequence of images, but it is unlikely to be an exact copy of the original event. The image will probably be more sketchy and schematic, retaining the most salient features while many details drop out. The same event may also be encoded verbally in the form of a description. Similarly, when the input has been in the form of words these may give rise to visual images as well as being retained as an acoustic speech-based trace, and it has been shown that memory is powerfully enhanced by this kind of dual (verbal and visual) coding.

When information passes from short-term memory into long-term memory further recoding takes place. In the long-term memory store, although visual and verbal representations may persist, the dominant code is semantic, that is, items are primarily represented in terms of their meaning. They are sorted, categorised, labelled, indexed and linked to related information. Long-term memory is a vast interconnected system in which memories are linked in a rich network of associations and new memories are entered into this mental filing system according to the way they have been interpreted and categorised. It is common for some specific details to be lost at this stage. For example, conversations and written texts are usually not remembered verbatim but the gist is retained. Similarly, the memory of an event such as a party or a journey tends to lose detail over time and become generalised.

1.3.1.3   Level of processing   The way information is encoded determines how robust the memory is and how easily it can be retrieved later. Craik and Lockhart (1972) distinguished between deep and shallow levels of processing. Shallow processing involves encoding inputs in terms of their physical characteristics such as colour or sound. Deep processing involves encoding in terms of meaning and personal significance and there is experimental evidence that deep coding produces more long-lasting memories. If people work through a list of words concentrating on their sounds and finding a rhyming word for each one this constitutes shallow processing and produces poorer recall than if they are asked to attend to their meaning and think of a synonym for each one. Similar results emerge when people try to memorise faces. If they are asked to classify each face by a physical criterion such as face shape, or size of nose, memory is not so good as when they are asked to make deep-level judgments about the person's character.

1.3.1.4   Elaborative encoding   Memory is also strengthened and enhanced by elaborative encoding. Like deep-level processing, this consists of exploring the meaning of what has been experienced, thinking of associations, relating it to previous experiences and stored knowledge. A witness who sees a man come out of a store, thinks that he is looking shifty, that he looks rather like an acquaintance and seems to be having difficulty carrying a heavy suitcase, is likely to remember the episode much better than a witness who simply encodes the man emerging from the store.

When encoding takes the form of deep elaborative processing, and includes encoding of the context in which an event occurred, it is much easier to recall the event subsequently. A good witness recalls not just the event itself but the temporal and situational context in which it was embedded. She remembers what she was doing, where she was going, what she was thinking about, the background scene and the preceding and subsequent events. When a specific memory is encoded with a rich context of this kind it includes numerous cues which, as we shall see in 1.3.3, can aid recall at the retrieval stage.

1.3.1.5 Schemata and schema theory Encoding has been discussed so far as if it consisted entirely in processing information reaching the sense organs from the outside world. Psychologists call this bottom-up, or data-driven processing. However, most encoding also involves some information already stored in semantic memory in the form of prior knowledge derived from past experience and this is known as top-down or conceptually driven processing. In practice the two sorts of processing operate in combination. For example, bottom-up processes may yield sensory data about a fast-moving dark blue object of a particular size and shape while top-down processes based on stored knowledge enable this to be identified as a BMW convertible. Sensory information is often incomplete or ambiguous but stored knowledge helps to guide our expectations, to fill the gaps and to supply an interpretation. These two sources of information, sensory data and stored knowledge, combine so instantaneously and so automatically that it is very difficult to disentangle them and isolate the contribution of each. This is why it may be impossible to decide what witnesses actually saw and what they thought they must have seen.

Schema theory is able to provide a theoretical explanation of considerable generality for many phenomena in everyday memory. It can account for the fact that many of our experiences are forgotten, or are reconstructed in a way that is incomplete, inaccurate, generalised or distorted. Schema theory emphasises the role of prior knowledge and past experience, claiming that what we remember is influenced by what we already know. According to this theory, the knowledge we have stored in semantic memory is organised as a set of schemata, or knowledge structures, which represent the generic knowledge about objects, situations, events or actions that has been acquired from past experience.

Bartlett (1932) introduced the idea of schemata to explain why, when people remember stories, they typically omit some details, introduce rationalisations and distortions, and reconstruct the story so as to make more sense in terms of their own knowledge and experience. According to Bartlett, the story is 'assimilated' to pre-stored schemata based on prior knowledge.

Although for many years Bartlett's idea were neglected, in recent years schemata have been given a central role in memory.

Schemata represent all kinds of knowledge and are linked together into related sets, with superordinate and subordinate schemata. So, for example, the schema for 'table' would be linked to schemata for 'furniture', 'rooms' and 'houses'. A schema has fixed compulsory slots which may be filled with variable optional values. A schema for a picnic has slots for place, food, people and activities as shown in figure 1.2. The slots are filled with the values supplied by a particular experience of a picnic. However, if this information is forgotten or unavailable the general schema supplies default values (e.g., 'sandwiches' for the food slot). Pre-existing schemata operate in a top-down direction influencing the way we encode, interpret and store the new information coming in. According to schema theory, new experiences are not just passively 'copied' or recorded in memory. A memory representation is actively constructed integrating the old generic information in the schema with new information from the current input using processes that are strongly influenced by schemata in a variety of ways:

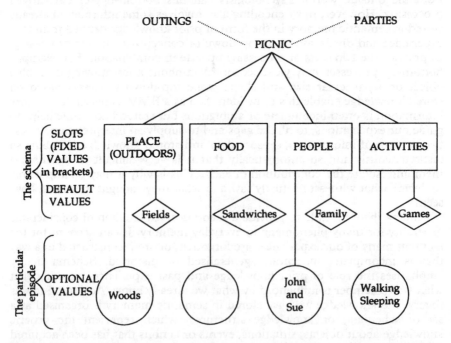

Figure 1.2 A picnic schema: the figure shows how the values supplied by a particular episode mesh with the values supplied by the schema

(a)   Selection: the schema directs attention and guides selection of what is encoded and stored in memory. Information that is relevant to whichever schema is currently activated is more likely to be remembered than information that is irrelevant. In one study (List, 1986) subjects viewed a video showing eight different acts of shoplifting. The acts that were rated as highly probable in a shoplifting scenario were remembered better than those that were less probable. Subjects also falsely 'remembered' some events that were highly probable but had not actually occurred.

(b)   Storage: a schema provides a framework within which current information relevant to that schema can be stored.

(c)   Generalization: information may undergo transformation from the specific form in which it was perceived to a more general form. Specific details of a particular experience (such as going shopping) tend to drop out, while aspects that are common to other similar experiences are incorporated into a general schema and retained.

(d)   Normalisation: memories also tend to be distorted so as to fit in with prior expectations and to be consistent with the schema. They are sometimes transformed toward the most probable or most typical item of that kind. In this way, people may remember what they expected to see rather than what they actually saw. An example of the way schemata may influence memory for common objects by normalisation comes from a study by French and Richards (1993), who found that when subjects were asked to draw a clock with Roman numerals from memory after examining it for one minute, 10 of the 14 subjects represented the four as IV. In fact, all clocks and watches with Roman numerals represent the four as IIII. In this striking example, schema-based memory of the normal form of representation overrode the perceptual experience.

(e)   Inferencing: schemata may also aid retrieval by providing the basis for making inferences. When the information that is sought is not represented in memory directly, it can sometimes be retrieved by schema-based inferences. (If you know that somebody got hit over the head with a bottle, you can infer, from a schema containing knowledge about injuries, that he was hurt.)

The most important prediction from schema theory is that what is normal, typical, relevant or consistent with pre-existing knowledge will be remembered better than what is unexpected, bizarre or irrelevant. However, intuitively, this prediction is not entirely convincing and the results of experimental testing have not always supported it. Critics of schema theory have pointed out that it often seems to be what is odd or unusual that tends to stick in memory. (You might forget that there was a cat in the living room but not that there was a pig in the living room.) This has necessitated a modification of schema theory. The basic principle that the encoded memory representation is formed from an interaction of new sensory information and previously acquired knowledge is still widely accepted, but it is now thought that novel, deviant or irrelevant information is appended to the schema-based memory representation in the form of a pointer or tag.

1.3.2   Storage stage
Psychologists emphasise the important distinction between storage failure and retrieval failure. With storage failure, the information has dropped out of

the memory system and the memory trace is irretrievably lost. This is known as trace-dependent forgetting. With retrieval failure, the information is in memory but cannot be retrieved. These elusive memories are not lost, and, as outlined in 1.3.3, it is often possible to retrieve them if the right cues or hints are supplied so this kind of memory failure is known as cue-dependent forgetting.

1.3.2.1 Causes of forgetting Storage failures can occur even if items have been encoded. In the short-term store items may be bumped out by new inputs which constitute interference. Or, if not maintained by rehearsal, they may simply decay. In either case, information is not transferred from the short-term store into the more permanent long-term memory store. Forgetting in the long-term store can similarly be caused by either interference or decay. However, the idea that information may decay in memory is very difficult to prove. To isolate the effects of pure decay it would be necessary to test memory after a completely blank period during which no other information which might cause interference was being received or thought about. As this situation never occurs (even in sleep the brain is still active) the trace decay theory cannot be proved.

It is much easier to find evidence for interference theory. Proactive interference occurs when previously acquired 'old' information interferes with a new memory. Our old car licence number interferes with remembering the new car's number; a friend's unmarried name is easier to recall than her married name; it's hard to change your golf swing to a more effective one. Retroactive interference operates in the reverse direction so that new information disrupts earlier memories. This is especially true, for example, of repeated experiences. If you make the same journey to work every day, it is hard to remember what happened on the journey last Tuesday. Retroactive interference is particularly relevant in the legal context. As later chapters will illustrate a witness's memory for an event may be changed, confused or contaminated by information acquired subsequently from reading press accounts, by being asked leading questions, or by conferring with others. It can be shown experimentally that the effect of interference is more powerful if the new input is more similar to the original memory. Lists of letters or words that sound similar (p, b, t or mat, bat, hat) are harder to remember than lists of dissimilar items because the similar ones interfere with each other. It is hard to remember the plot of a thriller if you read another with a similar plot and memory for an experience such as a visit to relatives may suffer interference from the memories of other, similar visits. Exactly what happens to stored memories when they are transformed or distorted by later experiences is a controversial issue explored in more detail in later chapters. A recent model (Metcalfe, 1990), known as the composite holographic associative recall model (CHARM) is based on neural models of memory in which memory traces are distributed and form composite patterns. New associations are added into the composite trace and result in blended or integrated memories. The model has been implemented and simulates the kind of blended memories produced by eyewitnesses when they have been exposed to false or misleading information about the witnessed event. The main point to note here is that information that is stored in memory is not in separate watertight compartments and does not remain inert. It exists as part of a dynamic network in which memories interact and modify each other.

1.3.3   Retrieval stage

1.3.3.1   Recognition and recall   There are three different kinds of remembering: free recall, cued recall and recognition. Recognition occurs when something that has been previously encountered (an object, a face, a voice, a scene) is re-encountered and is recognised as familiar. Recognition may include full identification, so that you know whose face or whose voice it is or it may simply be a feeling of familiarity ('I know I've seen it somewhere before'). Tests of recognition may take the form of yes/no questions ('Is this the man you saw leaving the bank?') or forced-choice questions ('Which of these is the man you saw leaving the bank?')

In free recall the target information is not re-encountered. It must be dredged up from memory in response to open-ended questions (e.g. 'What were you doing last Monday evening?') or to a request to recall 'everything you can remember about X'. Essentially no help is given by the questioner. In cued recall information is recalled in response to a specific cue supplied by an interviewer or a memory may come to mind involuntarily when you are reminded of a previous experience by what is going on around you at the moment. Cues function as reminders and may take many forms such as a smell, a piece of music, a scene, a book title. More often in everyday life we remember in response to cues in the form of descriptions ('Do you remember when we were on holiday in France? When we stayed at that old farmhouse? The day there was a terrific storm?') As a general rule, recognition is easier than recall and cued recall is easier than free recall. In tests of recognition the answer is, in effect, supplied and has only to be accepted or rejected; in cued recall a lot of supporting information is supplied and the memory search is guided, whereas in free recall the rememberer has to do all the work. However, recognition tests, and, to some extent, the use of cues, carry the disadvantage that they allow subjects to respond by guessing rather than by remembering.

1.3.3.2   Retrieval failures   Information is often retained in long-term memory but cannot be accessed on demand. In spite of effortful searching there is a retrieval failure. Even target information that is well known, such as the capital city of Finland or the name of your dentist, may be temporarily unavailable. These blocks may persist for long periods and are sometimes resolved by so-called 'pop-up recall', when the answer just comes to mind out of the blue, or sometimes when the right cue is encountered. According to the encoding specificity principle (Tulving and Thomson, 1973) cues are only effective if they have been encoded at the time of the original experience so the 'terrific storm' cue will only succeed in recalling the holiday in France if it was originally encoded as part of the holiday experience. This idea about the effectiveness of cues in aiding recall is instantiated in the principles underlying the cognitive interview described in chapter 10. By this method a witness is encouraged to generate as many cues as possible by recalling all the details of the context in which an event occurred. Even irrelevant cues (like 'I was wearing my new blue shirt at the time') may operate as reminders that produce recall of crucial information.

1.3.3.3 Retrieval failure and the feeling of knowing When people are unable to retrieve a piece of information they often have a feeling-of-knowing (FOK). That is, they are able to produce a graded judgment, ranging from 'definitely do not know' to 'could probably recall it if given time and/or hints'. There is a close relationship between the strength of the FOK judgment and whether successful recall will be achieved and the amount and quality of the information that is recalled. According to Koriat (1993) this is because the FOK is based on partial information about the answer that is below the level of conscious awareness. The findings on the nature of FOK judgments are potentially applicable to witness testimony because the strength of the FOK indicates whether it is worth probing for missing information.

1.3.3.4 Explicit and implicit memory Recently psychologists have made a distinction between explicit memory and implicit memory (Schachter, 1987). Explicit memory is the kind elicited by direct tests of recognition or recall and involves conscious recollection. Implicit memory is not accessible to conscious awareness but can be revealed by indirect tests. In a classic example reported by Claparède (1911) he pricked the hand of an amnesic patient with a pin hidden between his fingers. Later, she did not explicitly remember the incident but nevertheless flinched away when he tried to shake her hand. This kind of implicit memory is revealed by changes in skin conductance when an individual is exposed to a previously encountered item which he or she cannot explicitly recall. It is also evidenced in experiments where subjects who have forgotten some of the words from a previously learned list spontaneously produce these forgotten words when, in a later test, they are required to complete word fragments. In a more mundane example, the young child who has not learned to talk but, on visiting a grandparent, makes straight for the biscuit box, is displaying implicit memory. Implicit memory develops first in children and is more resistant to the effects of ageing and trauma so that in amnesia there is often a dramatic dissociation between impaired explicit memory and intact implicit memory. The kind of witness memory that legal practitioners are concerned with is primarily explicit but it may be useful, in some cases, to consider whether implicit memory could also be probed.

1.4 WHAT MAKES SOME THINGS HARD TO REMEMBER?

What kind of information is particularly difficult to remember and what is likely to be easier? The difference in difficulty between recognition and recall is particularly apparent for information that is hard to verbalise such as faces, music or complex pictures where performance in recognition tests far exceeds performance in tests of recall. Memory for names and dates is notoriously poor, probably because they have fewer and weaker links to the rest of the knowledge network and so lack access pathways. It is also well established that memory for facts is better than memory for the source of those facts, so people will tend to remember a piece of information such as, for example, that hostas grow better in the shade but forget who it was who told them (McIntyre and Craik, 1987). Problems are sometimes encountered when memory for a real event that has actually occurred is confused with the memory of imagining that event. This failure of what is called 'reality monitoring' (Johnson and Raye, 1981) is more likely to happen when the event is one that is often repeated and automatic. Thus witnesses may find it difficult to remember whether they actually locked the car or only thought about locking the car. Memories of real events are usually distinguished by being more vivid than memories of thoughts or imaginings and they are part of a remembered sequence so that, if the memory is a real one, the witness should be able to remember what happened immediately before and after locking the car. More generally, an experience or piece of information that is highly distinctive, unusual, interesting, and emotional is better remembered than what is ordinary and routine.

1.5 COPIES VERSUS RECONSTRUCTIONS

A controversial issue is whether what is retrieved from long-term memory is a copy of the original experience or a reconstruction of it. Schema theory, outlined in 1.3.1.5, is consistent with a partially reconstructive account. The fact that memories contain errors, distortions and confusions based on stored knowledge, or on misleading information received after the event was experienced, suggests that some reconstruction has taken place. Nigro and Neisser (1983) discovered that people can distinguish between memory images seen from the viewpoint from which they were originally experienced (known as 'field memories') and memory images which represent the scene as an external observer might have seen it ('observer memories'). Memories that are recent and memories that are highly emotional are more likely to be reported as field memories. By definition, observer memories must have been reconstructed but field memories may, or may not, be veridical copies of the experience. Evidence for reconstruction also comes from studies of repeated memories. When people are asked to produce the same memory repeatedly it has been shown that their accounts undergo considerable transformation from one occasion to another. Although the core of the memory remains fairly stable, some of the peripheral details tend to drop out and more new details are added (Cohen, Anderson and Taylor, paper presented at the Economic and Social Research Council Seminar, Worcester, July 1998). This finding has particular importance for witness testimony since witnesses are usually interviewed repeatedly. Further evidence in favour of the partial reconstruction account comes from studies of memory for dates. When people are asked to recall the date of an event they commonly reconstruct it by considering its proximity to a landmark event (a birthday, Christmas, starting a new job) for which the date is known.

On the other hand, copy theorists assert that the presence of irrelevant details in a memory is evidence in favour of copy theory because irrelevant details would not be retained in a reconstruction. The so-called 'flashbulb memories' people sometimes retain of the moment when they heard about a dramatic public event are copy-like in that they are very vivid and contain a lot of irrelevant detail. The issue is therefore unresolved, but the most plausible conclusion is that most memories are part copy and part reconstruction, with the proportions varying for different types of memory. Reconstruction allows confusions and errors to be incorporated in a memory. For legal practitioners, a useful rule of thumb is that memories are more likely to be inaccurate when witnesses are pressured to make some response as this will induce more reconstruction and more guessing. When it is acceptable for them to say they don't know the quantity of information yielded is less but the quality is likely to be higher.

1.6 SUMMARY

(a)   Memory in real-life situations is not simply governed by the operating principles of the memory system but is influenced by very many extraneous factors (such as intentions, goals, emotions and the context) interacting with each other in a complex fashion.

(b)   A widely accepted model of memory assumes that there are three separate stores and that incoming information passes through these stages in sequence. The sensory store, short-term memory and long-term memory differ in duration and capacity.

(c)   There are three main processes: encoding, storage and retrieval. Information can be lost at any of these stages. It may be discarded before being encoded; it may be poorly encoded; it may be distorted by processes of generalisation or normalisation; it may be lost through decay or through interference from other inputs; it may be in store but remain inaccessible because the right cues or reminders are not supplied. Reconstructive processes may incorporate false information and confusions into the original memory.

(d)   Recognition is easier than recall, but recall can be helped by supplying cues. When retrieval fails, people can make fairly accurate feeling-of-knowing judgments about whether they might be able to remember. Memories may exist implicitly, below the level of conscious awareness.

(e)   For the interviewer, the challenge is to help the witness to access information that is in memory but is difficult to retrieve, and to do this without inducing false memories or inaccuracies by suggesting additional or alternative accounts.

Key terms
Cues; decay; elaborative encoding; encoding specificity; episodic and semantic memory; explicit and implicit memory; interference; levels of processing; long-term memory; memory representations; reality monitoring; sensory stores; schema theory; short-term memory; top-down and bottom-up processing.

References

Atkinson, R.C. and Shiffrin, R.M. (1968), 'Human memory: a proposed system and in its control processes', in K.W. Spence (ed.), *The Psychology of Learning and Motivation: Advances in Research and Theory*, vol. 2, pp. 89–195. New York: Academic Press.

Baddeley, A. (1990), *Human Memory: Theory and Practice*. Hove and London: Erlbaum, 1990.

Bartlet, F.C. (1932), *Remembering*, Cambridge: Cambridge University Press.

Claparède, E. (1911), 'Recognition et Moité'. *Archives de Psychologie*, 11, pp. 79–90

Cohen, G., Anderson, S. and Taylor, S., Age differences in the stability of memories. In preparation.

Craik, F.I.M. and Lockhart, R.S. (1972), 'Levels of processing: a framework for memory research', *Journal of Verbal Learning and Verbal Behaviour*, vol. 11, pp. 671–84.

French, C.C. and Richards, A. (1993), 'Clock this! An everyday example of a schema-driven error in memory', *British Journal of Psychology*, vol. 84, pp. 249–53.

Koriat, A. (1993), 'How do we know that we know? The accessibility model of feeling of knowing', *Psychological Review*, vol. 100, pp. 609–39.

Johnson, M.K. and Raye, C.L. (1981), 'Reality monitoring', *Psychological Review*, vol. 88, pp. 67–85.

List, J.A. (1986), 'Age and schematic differences in reliability of eyewitness testimony', *Developmental Psychology*, vol. 22, pp. 50–7.

McIntyre, J.S. and Craik, F.I.M. (1987), 'Adult age differences for item and source information', *Canadian Journal of Psychology*, vol. 41, pp. 175–92.

Metcalfe, J. (1990), 'Composite holographic associative recall model (CHARM) and blended memories in eyewitness testimony', *Journal of Experimental Psychology: General*, vol. 119, pp. 145–60.

Nigro, G. and Neisser, U. (1983), 'Point of view in personal memories', *Cognitive Psychology*, vol. 15, pp. 465–82.

Schachter, D.L. (1987), 'Implicit memory: history and current status', *Journal of Experimental Psychology: Learning, Memory and Cognition*, vol. 13, pp. 501–18.

Tulving, E. (1972), 'Episodic and semantic memory', in E. Tulving and W. Donaldson (eds), *Organization of Memory*, London: Academic Press.

Tulving, E. and Thomson, D.M. (1973), 'Encoding specificity and retrieval processes in episodic memory', *Psychological Review*, vol. 80, pp. 352–73.

Recommended reading

Baddeley, A. (1990), *Human Memory: Theory and Practice*. Hove and London: Erlbaum.

Cohen, G. (1996), *Memory in the Real World*, 2nd ed. Hove: Psychology Press.

Editors' notes

It is doubtful whether the material in this chapter could in any circumstances form the basis of expert evidence in a specific case. There is no question, however, that its lessons could be usefully included in training programmes for professional fact-finders, legal practitioners and investigators. In indirect consequence, pre-trial instructions and legal directions to lay fact-finders might be adapted where appropriate to take account of psychological expertise on the workings of human memory as illustrated here.

CHAPTER TWO

Contamination of witness memory

Graham Davies

2.1 INTRODUCTION

2.1.1 Contamination in law and psychology

Contamination of memory is a major concern to both lawyers and psychologists, though the way the process is perceived is rather different. For lawyers, contamination is primarily a social process whereby a witness's clear memories of an event can become clouded through contact with other witnesses, overzealous interviewers or exposure to the news media or other written accounts. Proven instances of contamination serve to undermine the credibility of a witness's statement. For psychologists, contamination is essentially a cognitive process and much research effort has been put in recent years into exploring the mental mechanisms responsible for it. In contrast to law, the emphasis of much of the research to date has been on the theoretical rather than the practical significance of such effects. In this chapter, the three primary explanations for misinformation effects will be outlined and their implications for the legal process explored. To provide a context for this discussion, a case is outlined which raises issues of contamination in its varied forms.

2.1.2 The *Beattie* case

In October 1973, the trial took place at the High Court in Glasgow of George Beattie, who was charged with the murder of Margaret McLaughlin. Miss McLaughlin had been attacked, and stabbed 19 times as she made the short walk from her home to Carluke Station. Beattie's defence was unusual: he claimed to have been present at the scene and forced to watch the crime by the real murderers, but not to have taken part in the murder himself. The police had witnesses who could testify that he was near the scene of the crime at the relevant time (around 8.00 p.m.) but also that he looked outwardly composed and unaffected by the events. No contact traces were found on Beattie's clothing and a search of his home proved fruitless. The only link was provided by a small spot of blood found on a tissue removed from the pocket of his jacket which came from the same blood group as the murdered woman, but as the prosecution admitted, this blood group was common to 43% of the population (and over 50% in the Glasgow area).

The main evidence against Beattie was his own statement to the police, which the prosecution argued contained knowledge which would only have been available to the murderer. Beattie, a man of limited intelligence and a fabled capacity for exaggeration, had come forward voluntarily to say he had passed the crime spot on an errand. Under questioning he alleged that he had been seized by three men, two of whom were wearing top hats with mirrors attached to them. His statement described how the men stabbed the woman and made reference to several exhibits the police had recovered from the scene of the crime which had not been mentioned in newspaper accounts. On being charged with murder, Beattie said, 'I canna say anything more. I didn't do it — it was they six.'

Beattie, a man with no previous convictions for violence, was found guilty and sentenced to life imprisonment. The BBC 'Rough Justice' programme took up his case and uncovered strong circumstantial evidence that Beattie's confession could have been contaminated by a combination of police inter-viewing procedures and the products of his fertile imagination. For instance, when Beattie was brought into the police station, it was alleged that officers were still 'bagging up' exhibits from the crime scene. Police also took Beattie to the murder site in an effort to make more sense of parts of his statement. It subsequently emerged that the last programme Beattie had watched before embarking upon his fateful errand was 'Top of the Pops', which featured the band, Slade, some of whom had worn top hats decorated with mirrors (Hill, Young and Sergeant, 1985).

Beattie is still in prison, an appeal having been unsuccessful (*The Guardian*, 3 December 1994). How plausible is it to argue that his statements could have been contaminated by information acquired prior to or subsequent to the witnessed event? This is a subject to which forensic psychologists have devoted a considerable amount of time and effort in recent years. The psychologist who has made the single largest contribution to exploring contamination effects is Professor Elizabeth Loftus of the University of Washington (Loftus, 1979; Loftus and Ketcham, 1991).

2.2 LABORATORY DEMONSTRATIONS OF CONTAMINATION

2.2.1 Memory elaboration

Loftus was responsible for two of the best known studies demonstrating the influence of what she terms 'post event information' on witness memory. In the first (Loftus and Palmer, 1974), university students viewed a 10 second film of a road traffic accident before answering a series of questions including one concerning vehicle speed. For some participants the question referred to vehicles which 'smashed' into each other while for others the cars were described as having 'hit' one another. The severity of the verb influenced the estimated speed of the target vehicle such that the more impact was implied by the verb, the greater the estimated speed: those who read the word 'smashed' later estimated the speed of the vehicles as some 7 miles per hour faster than those who had 'hit'. Moreover, when participants returned a week later and were asked further questions which included whether broken glass had been present at the locus (it had not), some 32% of those who heard the question as 'smashed' answered affirmatively compared to 14% who understood the vehicles had merely 'hit' each other.

Loftus interpreted her findings in terms of a schema theory of memory, which stands in sharp contrast to the view of memory as a permanent record in which each individual event is taken in and stored and retrieved from memory independently (see chapter 1). According to the schema view, memory involves not the passive reproduction of events, but active reconstruction, based only on fragments of the original together with expectations derived from general knowledge of similar events. When more is learned about an issue, whether it is a car accident or the details of a particular crime, all such information is assimilated into a general store of knowledge from which the origins of a particular fact are rapidly lost.

In the car accident scenario, Loftus argued that when participants searched for details of the accident, they recovered not their original memories but also the information they subsequently acquired regarding the accident's severity. Drawing upon the totality of their information on the topic, including the alleged severity of the impact implied by the verb 'smashed', many were ready to agree that broken glass must have been present. Memory has been elaborated by additional material which serves to contaminate the record.

Subsequent experiments have served to define both the range and constraints of the memory supplementation effect. It is apparent that it is most likely to occur for briefly viewed events involving contexts which are unfamiliar to the witness (Read and Bruce, 1984). It operates on descriptions of people as well as events. In one study (Jenkins and Davies, 1985) participants viewed a videotape of a male shoplifter. Subsequently they viewed a photofit picture allegedly compiled of the man. The photofit was deliberately amended to show curly hair when the man's hair was straight or a moustache when one was not originally present. One week later witnesses provided a description of the shoplifter and attempted to select him from a photographic array. Around 40% of the witnesses incorporated the misleading information into their descriptions and went on to select a person resembling the photofit from the array despite the presence of the actual 'shoplifter'. Similar contamination effects have been observed when the additional misleading information takes the form of a verbal description rather than a facial composite (Loftus and Green, 1980).

2.2.2 Memory replacement

Loftus's second classic study (Loftus, Miller and Burns, 1978) involved volunteers viewing a series of slides depicting a car accident at a road junction. The critical slides showed a vehicle emerging into a main road marked for some participants by a stop sign while for others by a yield (or give-way) sign. Subsequent questions referred to the sign either in a consistent manner or inconsistently (the stop sign was referred to as a yield sign or vice versa). Finally, all observers were asked to select which slides they had seen originally, selecting in each instance between two alternatives. The critical pair of slides were identical except that the sign depicted in one was a stop sign whereas the other showed a yield sign. Where the original slide and the information in the question were consistent, witnesses made correct selections on 75% of occasions. However, when they had been fed misleading information in the interim, this figure dropped to just 41%.

Loftus et al. also discovered that the effect was maximised if a week separated observation and the test and the misleading information immediately preceded the test. This lead them to argue that this phenomenon was yet another type of memory integration: on this occasion, the misleading facts contained in the question eliminated the original memory in much the same way that a correction overwrites original text on a word processor. Such processes were accelerated where the original record was weakened by the passage of time.

2.2.3 Legal impact of research on contamination

Loftus's research has had immense impact both in practical aspects of eyewitness testimony and theoretical debates over the nature of memory. In the United States, where psychologists routinely testify as to the vulnerability of witness testimony to contamination, Loftus has appeared for the defence regularly at trials where eyewitness evidence forms the main plank of the prosecution case, arguing from these and similar experiments for the unreliability of eyewitness statements and their vulnerability to corruption through contact with misleading information supplied wittingly or unwittingly by questioners.

The role of Loftus and others as expert witnesses has excited controversy among their contemporary experimental psychologists, who have argued that the particular conditions provided by a laboratory experiment cannot be reliably generalised to the realities of a criminal case (McCloskey and Egeth, 1983). There is certainly evidence that there are constraints and limitations on the stop sign/yield sign effect; it appears most reliably when misinformation refers to supportive detail rather than the central features of an incident. It is possible to convince someone that the green car he or she saw was actually blue but not that it was a bicycle (Loftus, 1979). Likewise, the authority of the source of misinformation also influences the effect: witnesses are more affected by misinformation supposedly generated by a police officer than an unsighted member of the public (Dodd and Bradshaw, 1980). However, it is on the theoretical interpretation of the misinformation effect which most debate has hinged and this in turn has implications for the practical treatment of contaminated testimony.

2.3 THEORETICAL INTERPRETATIONS AND THEIR PRACTICAL IMPLICATIONS

2.3.1 Destructive updating

Wright (1995) has identified three different interpretations of the stop/yield effect. The first of these, technically known as 'destructive updating', is the one expressed by Loftus: the original memory is actively eroded by later misinformation. According to Loftus some of the best evidence for memory destruction comes from the existence of 'blends', where entirely new memories are created, containing elements from both the original and the misleading information. Thus, a car seen originally which is subsequently referred to as a truck may later be recalled as a station wagon (Loftus and Hoffman, 1989). It is this concept of a blend which perhaps best fits the statement given to the police by Beattie, combining elements both of his actual observations at the crime scene, the content of a TV programme and his incidental observations at the police station and afterwards. Could the concept of blends explain the curious phenomenon sometimes found in genuine victims of child abuse who may offer accounts of their abuse which are in part bizarre or implausible? Dalenberg (1994) has provided an interesting analysis of 'Laura', who as an adult reported extreme physical abuse as a child, but whose body displayed no scars which would corroborate her account. Her father ultimately admitted to physically abusing and terrorising his daughter, but his account did not correspond to her allegations. He then volunteered that he had routinely read her wartime atrocity stories at bedtime and scrutiny of one such story showed strong parallels with her own account. The role of adult influence on children's narratives is a growing area of interest among psychologists (see chapter 4).

2.3.2 Memory supplementation

A second explanation of the stop/yield effect is that destructive updating has not occurred, rather the witness never noticed the vital detail in the first place. Thus, selection of the 'yield' sign is guided purely by the misinformation contained in the question (McCloskey and Zaragoza, 1985): the 'supplementation' viewpoint. In essence, this argument reduces Loftus's two classic experiments to one: both reflect assimilative processes, there is no necessity to assume memories are actively destroyed or damaged. There is currently evidence that any procedure which increases the saliency of the information which is later to suffer contradiction reduces the chance of witnesses being misled.

Davies and Jenkins (1985) repeated their experiment involving the viewing of the shoplifting video followed by a misleading photofit, but on this occasion, witnesses were requested to answer a series of questions about the shoplifter's appearance prior to viewing the photofit. When this procedure was adopted, only 18% chose an incorrect face in the recognition task consistent with the misleading information. This contrasts with a figure of 42% for those who had no prior opportunity to recall the face. Moreover, when the questionnaires were examined for correct mention of the critical features (straight hair, no moustache), none of the observers who answered these questions correctly was subsequently misled, all the errors in the questionnaire group came from those who failed to answer these questions or answered them incorrectly.

Thus, supplementing a deficient or weak memory seems easier to achieve than changing a strong memory confidently held. Moreover, memories can be strengthened in the interval between an event occurring and any subsequent statement by requesting recall in the interim. This immunisation of memory to ensure that it is less vulnerable to contamination and decay over time has been the subject of extensive study. Reyna and Brainerd (1995) summarise the dramatic effects upon children's long-term recall by verbal material when they are given the opportunity of prior recall within a day or two of the original event, a finding which may have interesting implications for the treatment of child witnesses in pre-trial interviews. Likewise, Bennett and Davies (1991) demonstrated that the long-term recall by police officers of a male 'suspect' seen briefly in a lecture theatre could be significantly enhanced over an interval of three months by periodic requests to recall the suspect's appearance in the interim.

2.3.3 The co-existence hypothesis

Returning to Loftus's classic stop/yield study, what of the third possible explanation for the contamination effects? This is that the original information was taken in as was the misleading information, but rather than the new destroying the old, both co-exist in memory with the more recent (and incorrect) information enjoying dominance for the purposes of the recall (Morton, Hammersley and Bekerian, 1985): the 'coexistence' position. One obvious implication of this view is that under some circumstances, it should be possible to retrieve the original correct information and so bypass the more recent contaminating statements. There is evidence that in some circumstances this can occur.

Bekerian and Bowers (1983) were able to eliminate the susceptibility of witnesses to being misled in the Loftus stop/yield experiment by re-creating as far as possible the precise circumstances under which the original stimuli were viewed. Gibling and Davies (1988) were also successful in reducing the proclivity of their subjects to select the person embodying the misleading features derived from the photofit by elaborate procedures designed to reinstate the context of the original event. These included showing the witness slides of the shop where the shoplifting incident took place, prodding them into remembering the precise sequence of events and supplying these details when they had been forgotten. Witnesses were encouraged to imagine themselves revisiting the crime scene and to recall any incidental details concerning the general dress and physical appearance of the 'shoplifter'. This procedure which took between 20 and 25 minutes to conduct had a dramatic effect upon accuracy of recall. Subjects who had undergone the context reinstatement procedure averaged only 8% errors on the misleading picture in the photographic array, a figure not statistically different from those who never viewed the misleading photofit. Those witnesses, by contrast, who received no special instructions selected a face embodying a moustache or curly hair on 38% of occasions.

The use of context reinstatement forms an important element in the 'cognitive interview', a procedure developed by psychologists as an aid to police officers in interviewing witnesses (Fisher and Geiselman, 1992). Careful studies have contrasted the impact of the cognitive interview based on techniques and procedures derived from psychological research on memory with the conventional police interview. These indicate an increase of some 25–30% in correct relevant information when the cognitive interview is employed with no comparable increase in false details. The principles of the cognitive interview figure prominently in the *Guide to Interviewing* (Central Planning and Training Unit, 1992), which is distributed to all police investigative officers to assist them in their duties (see chapter 10).

2.3.4 Some final thoughts on theory

Returning once more to the classic Loftus stop/yield effect, it is evident that a number of psychological mechanisms can be responsible for the contamination effect. I use the word 'can' advisedly, as it has become increasingly clear that no one single mechanism, whether it is destructive updating, memory supplementation or the coexistence of competing memories, can explain all of the effects which research has uncovered. Rather, different factors are likely to be more salient at different times and circumstances. For instance, memories of both the original and the misleading information may coexist for a short interval after the event before giving way to a single recollection based on the more dominant (and frequently misleading) memory trace (Wright, 1995). Further research will no doubt map out the competing effects of these three influences, their erosive impact on witness memory and ways in which their effects may be countered.

2.4 THE RECOVERED MEMORIES CONTROVERSY

Professor Loftus's presence has loomed large in the debate over the status of 'recovered memories', which is the name given to memories of traumatic events from childhood, remembered as an adult and often accompanied with vivid and convincing detail. Such memories can emerge without any previous awareness of the original events beyond, at best, a vague feeling that 'something happened to them' in childhood (Lindsay and Read, 1994). Frequently, these memories can be of sexual abuse and the emergence of such allegations within outwardly settled and happy families invariably lead to denial, bewilderment and schism. Parents who believe themselves wrongly accused by their children have formed pressure groups committed to fighting what they regard as an epidemic of 'false memory syndrome': false allegations planted in the mind of vulnerable adults by doctrinaire therapists committed to the view that the origin of many patients' problems lies in long-repressed memories of abuse. The American False Memory Foundation claims some 5,000 members while its British counterpart has had some 400 contacts.

Professor Loftus found herself at the centre of this controversy through her involvement in the Susan Nason murder case (Loftus, 1993). Eight-year-old Susan had been murdered in 1969 and her killer never traced. However, in 1989, a friend of the murdered girl, Eileen Franklin came forward claiming to have recently recovered a memory of her own father committing the murder and provided police with a vivid account broadly in accord with the known facts. When police raided Mr Franklin's apartment, they found paedophile material and investigations of his past uncovered evidence of involvement in the physical and sexual abuse of children. At his trial, Franklin pleaded not guilty and Professor Loftus appeared as a defence witness, arguing that Eileen Franklin's memories could have been another instance of post-event misinformation, caused by reading newspaper accounts of the murder or by the hypnotic therapy she allegedly underwent prior to recovering the memory, or some combination of these. However, the jury chose to believe Eileen Franklin's dramatic account and her father was sentenced to life imprisonment.

At the trial, the prosecution had made great play with the fact that Loftus's misinformation experiments involved alterations of details in existing memories rather than the manufacture of totally fictitious incidents. Stung by this criticism, Loftus and Coan sought to explore whether complete memories of non-existent events could be implanted through procedures akin to those used by some therapists. Five friends were enlisted and told to try to convince a close relative that, as a five-year-old, they had been lost in a shopping mall and later found by an elderly man who had reunited the child with his mother. Initially, all five denied knowledge of the event (checks had been made to ensure that the person in question had never knowingly been lost in this way). The participants were then encouraged to think repeatedly about the events in the manner of some so-called 'incest therapies'. Within three weeks, four of the five persons involved had 'recovered' a memory of this non-existent event, sometimes accompanied by a wealth of detail. When the four were debriefed as to the nature of the deception, at least one refused to accept that his recovered memory was simply a product of his own imagination and the suggestions offered by his peer (Loftus, 1993). Subsequent studies have used this technique with larger, more representative groups of subjects and a range of fictitious incidents and have reported that around 25% of adults will begin to recover 'memories' of non-existent events after three sessions devoted to intensive reminiscence. Persons who score highly on questionnaires designed to measure experiences of being disassociated from reality appear to be particularly vulnerable to such effects (see Hyman, Husband and Billings, 1995).

It is one thing to show that fabricated memories can be planted in the minds of willing volunteers, quite another to show that all recovered memories are a product of suggestions from therapists and the committed imagination of the client. A survey of British therapists who were members of the British Psychological Society suggested that while the majority might explore their clients' pasts for clues to their current condition, most claimed to be aware of the dangers of suggestive techniques. Nonetheless, around a third reported having a client who had recovered a memory of a previously forgotten traumatic incident in the last year. Of course, to the committed proponent of 'false memory syndrome', this is further evidence of the infinite gullibility of therapists. However, in about a third of the cases reported, the memories involved had been recovered *prior* to the patient encountering the therapist: the reason for entering therapy was to come to terms with the impact of the memory. While sexual abuse was a common theme, other intrusive memories included physical abuse in childhood, witnessing a violent death and periods of wakefulness during operations. Some form of corroboration was available in 41% of cases and only a small minority of reported memories related to bizarre and improbable themes such as abduction by aliens (Andrews et al., 1998). The argument between those who believe that, in general, recovered memories are false memories caused by contamination of the memory record through therapeutic suggestion and those who believe that the majority of such memories recovered in therapy have some basis in fact continues to split professional psychology. Professor Loftus, while leaving the door open that some recovered memories may be genuine, has put her considerable energies behind the view that most such memories are fictitious reconstructions based on post-event misinformation. She is even quoted as saying, 'I feel like Oscar Schindler. There is a desperate drive to work as fast as I can' (Pope, 1996). As for George Franklin, the research demonstrating that memories can be manufactured had a positive outcome: in April 1995, Mr Franklin was freed on appeal over concerns about the admissibility of some of the evidence at his original trial.

2.5 CONCLUSION

(a) Memory contamination, as explored by psychologists, can emerge in a variety of settings: from the witness box to the therapist's couch. In all instances, it appears to reflect the vulnerability of our memory system to distortion from information encountered before, or more frequently after, the key event.

(b) Psychologists have referred to these processes as misinformation effects. They have offered at least three explanations of the causes:

(i) that new information overwrites and eliminates the original memory (destructive updating);

(ii) that the new information has filled in a gap in the witness's memory (supplementation);

(iii) that the new information has not obliterated the original memory so much as supplanted it in the forefront of the witness's mind.

(c) It seems likely that there is no one explanation which will apply in all contexts, but rather each of these three processes will operate in different circumstances. Whatever the theoretical explanations for memory contamination, the result in practical purposes is the same: a more vulnerable and less effective witness who may give misleading testimony.

(d) Psychologists can specify the circumstances when observers are most likely to be vulnerable to being misled. Witnesses are most vulnerable when their memories of the original events are weakened by reason of long delays between observation and report or fleeting glimpses of the original events.

(e) Memories are more vulnerable to erosion on peripheral detail than on central events and when the source of the misleading information is a figure of authority rather than a colleague.

(f)   Memories are at their least vulnerable when witnesses have had good or repeated opportunities to witness and experience events, where delay is minimal or the witness has had the opportunity to rehearse events in response to non-suggestive questioning procedures.

(g)   It is possible to implant a totally fictitious memory of a childhood event through the use of suggestion and repeated requests to recall. This has important implications for the interpretation of the validity of memories recovered through a therapy where such procedures have been employed.

(h)   However, not all recovered memories emerge in therapy and not all therapies include these predisposing elements. It cannot be assumed that, just because a memory emerges after a long delay, it is necessarily false.

(i)   In addition to these procedural and circumstantial factors, there are also factors of personality which may increase or decrease individual vulnerability to these effects (see also chapter 5).

To return to the case of Beattie, in the light of the contaminating factors explored by psychologists, it seems altogether likely that he was potentially vulnerable, both as an individual and by force of circumstances, to producing misleading testimony. Witnesses can and do absorb information provided by others, through questioning and by exposure to news media and adopt and reproduce it as their own. These are not reasons for discarding or discounting witness testimony. Despite the growth of ever more sophisticated surveillance and monitoring systems, we must continue to rely on witness testimony for the foreseeable future. Rather, we must learn to read the signs and symptoms of vulnerability in witnesses and their statements and build in safeguards to our interviewing and interrogation procedures to minimise their pernicious effects.

Key terms
Blends; coexistence hypothesis; context reinstatement; delay; destructive updating; false memories; memory supplementation; post-event information; recovered memories; repeated requests to recall.

References
Andrews, B., Brewin, C.R., Morton, J., Bekerian, D.A., Davies, G.M. and Mollon, P., (1998) 'The nature, context, and consequences of memory recovery among adults in therapy', manuscript under review.

Bekerian, D. and Bowers, J.M. (1983), 'Eyewitness memory: Were we misled?' *Journal of Experimental Psychology: Learning, Memory and Cognition*, vol. 9, pp. 139–45.

Bennett, P. and Davies, G.M. (1991), 'The impact of mental rehearsal and the cognitive interview on memory for a face', Paper presented to the First International Conference on Memory, University of Lancaster, July 1991.

Central Planning and Training Unit (1992), *A Guide to Interviewing*, London: Association of Chiefs of Police Officers/Home Office.

Dalenberg, K. (1994), 'Finding and making memories: a commentary on the "repressed memory" controversy', *Journal of Child Sexual Abuse*, vol. 3 pp. 109–18.

Davies, G.M. and Jenkins, F. (1985), 'Witnesses can be misled by police composite pictures: how and when', in F.L. Denmark (ed.), *Social and Ecological Psychology and the Psychology of Women*, Amsterdam: North Holland, pp. 103–15.

Dodd, D.H. and Bradshaw, J. (1980), 'Leading questions and memory: pragmatic constraints', *Journal of Verbal Learning and Verbal Behaviour*, vol. 19, pp. 695–704.

Fisher, R.P. and Geiselman, R.E. (1992), *Memory Enhancing Techniques for Investigative Interviewing: The Cognitive Interview*. Springfield IL: C.C. Thomas.

Gibling, F. and Davies, G.M. (1988), 'Reinstatement of context following exposure to post-event information', *British Journal of Psychology*, vol. 79, pp. 129–41.

Hill, P., Young, M. and Sargent, T. (1985), *More Rough Justice*, London: Penguin Books.

Hyman, I., Husband, T. and Billings, F. (1995), 'False memories of childhood experiences' *Applied Cognitive Psychology*, vol. 9, pp. 181–97.

Jenkins, F. and Davies, G.M. (1985), 'Contamination of facial memory through exposure to misleading composite pictures', *Journal of Applied Psychology*, vol. 65, pp. 616–22.

Lindsay, S. and Read, J.D. (1994), 'Psychotherapy and memories of childhood sexual abuse: a cognitive perspective', *Applied Cognitive Psychology*, vol. 8, pp. 281–338.

Loftus, E.F. (1979), *Eyewitness Testimony*, Cambridge, MA: Harvard University Press.

Loftus, E.G. (1993), 'The reality of repressed memories', *American Psychologist*, vol. 48, pp. 518–37.

Loftus, E.F. and Green, E. (1980), 'Warning: even memory for faces may be contagious', *Law and Human Behaviour*, vol. 4, pp. 323–34.

Loftus, E.F. and Hoffman, H.G. (1989), 'Misinformation and memory. The creation of memory', *Journal of Experimental Psychology: General*, vol. 118, pp. 100–4.

Loftus, E.F. and Ketcham, K. (1991), *Witness for the Defence*, New York: St Martins Press.

Loftus, E.F., Miller, D.G. and Burns, H.J. (1978), 'Semantic integration of verbal information into visual memory', *Journal of Experimental Psychology: Human Learning and Memory*, vol. 4, pp. 19–31.

Loftus, E.F. and Palmer, J.E. (1974), 'Reconstruction of automobile destruction: an example of the interactions between language and memory', *Journal of Verbal Learning and Verbal Behaviour*, vol. 13, pp. 585–9.

McCloskey, M. and Egeth, H. (1983), 'Eyewitness identification. What can a psychologist tell a jury?' *American Psychologist*, vol. 38, pp. 573–5.

McCloskey, M. and Zaragoza, M. (1985), 'Misleading post-event information and memory for events: arguments for and evidence against the memory impairment hypothesis', *Journal of Experimental Psychology: General*, vol. 114, pp. 1–16.

Morton, J., Hammersley, R.H., and Bekerian, D. (1985), 'Headed records: a model for memory and its failures', *Cognition*, vol. 20, pp. 1–23.

Pope, K.S. (1996), 'Memory, abuse and science', *American Psychologist*, vol. 51, pp. 957–74.

Reyna, V. and Brainerd, C. (1995), 'Fuzzy trace theory: an interim synthesis', *Learning and Individual Differences*, vol. 7, pp. 1–75.

Read, J.D. and Bruce, D. (1984), 'On the general reliability of eyewitness testimony research', *International Review of Applied Psychology*, vol. 33, pp. 33–49.

Wright, D. (1995), 'Misinformation methodologies: explaining the effects of errant information', in G.M. Davies, S. Lloyd-Bostock, M. McMurran and J.C. Wilson (eds), *Psychology, Law and Criminal Justice: International Developments in Research and Practice*, Berlin: De Gruyter, pp. 39–45.

Recommended reading

Gudjonsson, G. (1992), *The Psychology of Interrogations, Confessions and Testimony*, Chichester: Wiley.

Cutler, B.L. and Penrod, S.D. (1995), *Mistaken Identification: The Eyewitness, Psychology and the Law*, Cambridge: Cambridge University Press.

Editors' notes
In America, expert evidence from psychologists such as Elizabeth Loftus is frequently admitted to assist fact-finders in forming reliable conclusions on contentious 'eyewitness' testimony. Familiarity with her writings and this chapter, which draws heavily on them, would explain why, in American jurisdictions, it is thought that psychologists have an important and valid role to play in the fact-finding process. Assumptions that lay fact-finders are capable of understanding the intricacies of the potential for corruption of accurate memory may, in many cases, be misplaced. Loftus's work is supported to a considerable extent by the results of laboratory or scientific research and, thus, is not easily refutable by criticism that it is overly theoretical.

Inclusion of the subject matter of this chapter as with that of Cohen's in training courses is clearly desirable. There may also be circumstances in which expert psychological evidence could appropriately and helpfully be adduced in a particular case — to explain, for example, the risks and dynamics of memory supplementation where 'false memory syndrome' is alleged. Subject to the availability of the source material referred to in part 2 of this book, it may be feasible for a psychologist to identify factors in the investigative process which may have contributed to confabulation and for admissible evidence to be based on any conclusions reached.

CHAPTER THREE

Influence of drugs on testimony

Malcolm Lader

3.1 INTRODUCTION

Modern therapeutics now encompasses an astonishing array of medicines and it must be a very rare individual indeed who has not experienced the effects of some of these substances administered in a therapeutic context. These medicines range from folk remedies whose origins date back millennia to chemically complex molecules developed for highly specific purposes and having clearly defined biochemical actions.

As well as such licit medicines and natural remedies, there is increasing use of illicit drugs, mostly by young people. These substances can be derived from plants such as the opium poppy but can be 'designer drugs' synthesised by capable, if amateur, organic chemists. Effects can be profound.

Doctors and scientists refer to all these substances as drugs. Lay people tend to use the term 'medicine', and many regard a 'drug' as an illicit substance. In this chapter, the scientific convention of using the term 'drug' will be followed.

In much of the Western world, the most important substance affecting the mind is alcohol. It is freely and often inexpensively available, its effects are profound and dose-related, and it can result in a range of psychological effects including the release of hostility. In many ways it is the paradigmatic substance concerning effects on testimony. Much is known about its effects and it provides a useful starting point for any discussion of the effects of substances on mental functioning.

However, some basic principles concerning the properties of drugs in humans need brief rehearsal here.

3.2 PHARMACOKINETICS

This technical term covers detailed and voluminous bodies of knowledge but can be reduced to a few essentials (Preskorn, 1993). Pharmacokinetics concerns itself with what the body does to drugs, for example, how it breaks them down, terminating their action. Thus, an aspirin's effect on a headache will last a few hours only because the body gets rid of the aspirin (chemical name, acetylsalicylic acid). Pharmacodynamics (see 3.3) deals with the effects of drugs on the body and its organs, for example, the brain. Thus, aspirin acts on a set of substances called 'prostaglandins' which, among others, are involved in the control of blood vessels and blood clotting.

The four main processes in pharmacokinetics are absorption, distribution, metabolism and excretion, and each can have an influence on such factors as extent and duration of an effect of a drug on brain function. Drugs can be given by a variety of routes such as by mouth, by inhalation, injection into the bloodstream or a muscle. *Absorption* can be very rapid: for example, puffing on a cigarette can result in nicotine, the active constituent, altering brain function within 15 seconds — hence the 'instant' gratification and reinforcement of the habit of tobacco smoking. Intravenous injections also deliver drugs rapidly to the target organ. Anyone who has had a surgical operation will know that even the relatively slow injection into the vein of the anaesthetic agent results in rapid (and merciful!) loss of consciousness. Oral medication means swallowing the drug, usually as a tablet, capsule or in liquid draught form. Absorption takes place from the stomach or more usually the upper intestine and may be both delayed and spread over several hours.

The next stage is *distribution*. This means that the drug moves from its site of absorption to the various tissues and organs in the body. This includes the entire bloodstream, liver, lungs, muscles and so on. Not all drugs cross into the brain because some do not have the appropriate chemical properties to cross the 'blood–brain barrier'. This is made up of a type of cell which lies between the blood vessels of the brain and the brain fluids and tissues themselves. However, a few drugs which influence brain and mental function do so in a secondary way, that is, by primarily altering function outside the brain, for example, in muscles or heart. Most drugs which alter mental function, so-called 'psychotropic drugs', do so by direct effects on the brain, and these drugs usually enter the brain quite readily. Indeed, some of these drugs, such as antidepressants, are actually concentrated in the brain. This is because this type of drug is highly soluble in fatty (lipid) tissues, and the brain is a highly lipid organ.

The kidney is also a fatty organ so that most drugs which pass through its circulation are reabsorbed and are not excreted in the urine. For example, chlorpromazine, used to treat psychotic symptoms, would stay indefinitely in the body. Therefore, psychotropic drugs (with the exception of lithium which is excreted unchanged) have to be changed ('metabolised') to less fat-soluble substances which the kidney can excrete. The organ primarily responsible for such transformations is the liver, which contains a powerhouse of enzymes which break down drugs and detoxify poisonous substances. Metabolic processes can be very complex in some cases and may vary in efficiency from individual to individual. Thus the drug will persist longer in slow metabolisers than rapid metabolisers. Indeed, in some instances, repeated dosage administrations may lead to the accumulation of some drugs even to toxic levels. The rate of metabolism is exponential, that is, it takes the same time for the concentration of a drug to halve as it does to go from a half to a quarter, a quarter to an eighth, and so on. The exception is alcohol, which is broken down at a constant amount per hour (around 10–15 millilitres). The capacity of the liver to metabolise drugs is finite, and if two drugs are taken at the same time, one may interfere with the breakdown of the other, leading to toxic build-up. Conversely, repeated drug administration may increase the capability of the liver to metabolise that drug ('enzyme induction') and the body concentration of drug drops over time (one form of tolerance).

Finally, the kidney is able to *excrete* the less fat-soluble, more water-soluble metabolite(s) of the active parent drug. The exception is lithium, which as an element is excreted unchanged in competition with sodium and potassium excretion.

3.3 PHARMACODYNAMICS

The pharmacodynamic actions of a drug rely on the drug altering in some way the function of a tissue constituent, usually a protein (Cooper et al., 1991; Stahl, 1996). Sometimes the protein is an enzyme, that is, a specialist catalyst which facilitates some chemical process in the body, for example, the breakdown of sugars to carbon dioxide and water, releasing energy for the body. In many cases, the specialised protein molecule is a 'receptor', that is, a specific site on which a hormone or a transmitter chemical can interact, rather like a key in a lock. The brain has many of these receptor sites, each nerve cell having thousands or even millions. The receptor recognises chemicals released in the brain by nerve cells, which in turn influence other nerve cells, roughly speaking, turning them on (increasing brain activity) or switching them off (decreasing or inhibiting brain activity). A vast array of chemical substances are believed to be transmitters and each transmitter may influence several different types of receptor. Therefore, there is immense scope for developing drugs which act specifically at just one type of receptor. One final point — enzymes and receptors are proteins and proteins are coded by genes. This increases the complexity of possible drug actions as genetic influences may be important.

The upshot is that drug actions can be very complex indeed. Until quite recently, drug actions on the brain were investigated empirically. Subjects were given doses of a chemical substance and effects on the body and on mental function were sought using as sensitive tests as possible. At last, with major advances in both molecular biology and in the neurosciences, a more rational approach is possible with psychotropic drugs being tailor-made to have predetermined actions.

3.4 TYPES OF EFFECT

As outlined above, drugs by and large either increase nervous activity in the brain or they decrease it. However, the effects of a drug may be more complex

(Spiegel, 1989). The best-known example is alcohol. In low doses — a drink or two — it may increase behavioural effects, for example, making individuals more affable, gregarious and expansive. In larger amounts, the drinker becomes withdrawn and less active and eventually lapses into a stupor. However, alcohol is a classic depressant drug at all doses given and all concentrations in the body. The reason for the biphasic, as it is called, response is that the highest functions of the brain are most sensitive to depressant effects of drugs like alcohol, the tranquillisers and other sedatives. The highest functions tend to be inhibitory, that is, they dampen down other excitatory functions of the brain preventing constant overactivity. The depressant drug first decreases this inhibitory activity which has the effect of increasing general brain activity. At higher doses, the excitation of the brain is directly reduced, and at very high doses even the most resistant and fundamental parts of the brain, those controlling the heart, circulation and respiration fail, and the patient may die.

3.4.1 Cognitive and other effects

A wide range of psychological functions may be altered, impaired but sometimes enhanced, by psychotropic drugs. *Sensory function*, the perception of light, sound, heat, touch and smell is not easily altered by such substances although qualitative abnormalities may be induced by hallucinogenic (psychedelic) drugs such as LSD and mescaline.

Central *processing of information* can be profoundly affected by psychotropic drugs. For example, sedative drugs may impair coding ability, converting numbers into symbols, a measure of central processing. Even simple stimuli such as a flickering light may be processed more slowly. So-called 'over-learned' tasks may be less affected, for example, simple addition and subtraction. This can be apparent in much more complex tasks such as driving. The intoxicated driver may just about cope with routine driving but if an emergency arises, the driver's performance is totally inadequate.

Memory and learning are often profoundly upset and this has major implications for the provision of accurate testimony. At high doses of sedatives, total amnesia may occur. The subject may be comatose or asleep but difficult to arouse, but occasionally may appear to be awake and cooperative but have no recollection of events later. This can happen without drugs, as after a head injury or an epileptic fit, but sedative and related drugs may also induce this picture. It is readily observed in heavy drinkers but is also well-known to dentists who use tranquillisers like diazepam (Valium). Occasionally, quite complex effects on memory can be detected using sophisticated tests. Some drugs affect one form of memory more than another. For example, it may be easy to recall the events of the day, or previous experiences, but words are more elusive, and new material may not be learned at all while under the influence of a drug. Meaningful material may be learned more easily than say nonsense syllables. Tests can also distinguish between a drug mainly preventing the learning of new material or interfering with its recall later.

An interesting facet of memory distortions following high doses of sedatives is the 'dentist-chair induced fantasy syndrome' (Dundee, 1990). Women in the dentist's chair heavily sedated with the benzodiazepines midazolam or diazepam, given intravenously, may on occasion report unpleasant experiences, often of a sexual nature. They may accuse the dentist of sexual assault, and litigation may ensue. There is sometimes a relationship between the fantasy and what did occur, for example, insertion of a dental instrument or an oral endoscope into the mouth resulting in fantasies of oral sex. A responsible chaperone should always be present during such manipulations.

3.4.2 Psychomotor effects

Manual and finger *dexterity* can be grossly impaired by drugs, especially if incoordination or a tremor are induced. Both sedative and stimulant drugs may have deleterious effects on fine movements. Gross body movement is also affected; the swaying in drunken individuals is because the fine-tuning of their movements is lost. They try to compensate visually which is why the sway worsens if they close their eyes. Handwriting is another overlearned skill but it is still quite sensitive to various psychotropic drugs. A sample of handwriting is always worth acquiring as it can later be compared with either previous handwriting or later drug-free samples, or both. Speech is also affected so a recording may be helpful for later comparisons.

Reaction time is an important function as it is germane to the investigation of road traffic accidents. Other functions which can be impaired include simulated driving and related computer games requiring accurate perception, rapid processing, and appropriate responses (O'Hanlon and de Gier, 1986).

3.4.3 Subjective effects

As well as all these objective effects, amenable to testing in the laboratory, a huge range of subjective effects can be engendered. These are less easy to investigate as the phenomenon is entirely within the subject's consciousness and experience. The subjective reactions can be roughly divided into the quantitatively abnormal and the qualitatively abnormal. In the former, the subjective experience is within the subject's normal range of experience but is extreme or inappropriate to the circumstances, and is presumed to be induced by the medication or illicit drug which was consumed prior to the reported effect. Sometimes that effect is a wanted one, for example, sleepiness after taking a sleeping tablet. Sometimes, it is an unwanted effect, for example, sleepiness after taking an antidepressant in the morning. The second category of effect is outside the individual's normal experience and may result in uncharacteristic behaviour. The following vignette illustrates this point:

Mr ZJ was an 18-year-old student who obtained 10 dexamphetamine tablets and took them over the course of six hours. After elated, euphoric, and powerful feelings, he began to hear voices threatening that the police would arrest him for taking illicit drugs and then beat him up. The paranoid feeling increased until Mr ZJ left the company of his friends, running out into the street. Here, he encountered a police car with two occupants. He started to kick the car until restrained, shouting that he would not let himself be arrested and tortured. He was restrained and taken to an emergency hospital department where he rapidly settled after being injected with chlorpromazine. He had only a vague recollection of events and was unable to explain his actions.

As well as psychological effects, *bodily effects* commonly accompany psychotropic drug usage. For example, pinpoint pupils are characteristic of narcotic use. A full physical examination can give several clues to the cause of an unexplained behavioural state, but may not be easy to do if the patient is uncooperative, agitated or disturbed.

In the above account, various evaluations have been mentioned such as memory function tests and assessments of motor dexterity. These may resemble commonly used and valid tests to detect brain damage (neuropsychological testing). However, many tests useful in establishing a neuropsychiatric diagnosis or the extent of a mental disability may be insensitive to the short-term changes induced by psychotropic drugs.

3.5 THE INDIVIDUAL

Medicines are given to treat disorders in individuals, a truism which is sometimes overlooked in assessing the effects of drugs on mental functioning such as giving testimony. Individuals vary greatly in their response to most drugs and some of this variation reflects pre-existing pathology. For example, patients suffering from schizophrenia can tolerate doses of antipsychotic drugs such as chlorpromazine and haloperidol which would render normal people semi-conscious, confused or in muscle spasm.

A common example is of the effects of tranquillisers or sedatives on normal subjects and anxious individuals. These medicaments will impair mental functions in normal individuals at all but the lowest doses. Anxious patients are already functioning below their optimum because the anxiety interferes with mental processes such as attention and concentration. A tranquilliser in low to moderate dose will improve such performance because it will lower anxiety levels. Only at high doses will direct depressant effects outweigh indirect anxiety-allaying effects.

A whole range of factors in the individual will affect the drug response. These include the pharmacokinetic factors outlined earlier with genetically determined variation in the rate of metabolism the most important. Physical illness may compound these factors. For example, the problem drinker may be abnormally sensitive to alcohol because of liver damage slowing down its metabolism and alcohol-induced brain damage predisposing to both exaggerated and idiosyncratic responses.

Other factors which may modify drug responses include age and sex, previous experience of that drug and the milieu in which it is taken — whether alone or in company, in a closed environment or in public, and even knowingly or unknowingly. Thus, an experienced LSD user taking the drug in company in a quiet, familiar room will have a very different response from a drug-naive person who has his or her drink 'spiked' in a pub. Expectation is important. An individual who is told by a doctor what effects to expect will tend to have those effects whether they are therapeutic or adverse. Even dummy tablets (placebos) can have marked effects if powerful suggestions of expected properties are given.

The pathological reaction is a concept more legal than medical. It implies that certain individuals will have a very intense and abnormal reaction to, say, alcohol. In practice, it is rare and probably represents not so much a separate drug-response phenomenon but particular circumstances operating at the time, such as dose, physical illness such as brain damage, social and interpersonal factors such as verbal provocation.

3.6 TYPES OF DRUG

Although lay people tend to distinguish between medicines as dispensed or bought in a pharmacy or herbal shop and drugs as illicit substances available on the 'street', the term 'drug' is used by the medical profession to refer to any substance which has effects on the body. Thus, a poison is a highly toxic drug. For our purposes, we can divide prescribed drugs into three main categories:

(a) Those prescribed primarily to treat psychiatric disorders: these will almost inevitably have effects on brain function.

(b) Those prescribed primarily to treat neurological disorders: these will usually enter the brain in order to exert their therapeutic effects and are likely to influence psychological functions as well.

(c) Those, the remainder, which are used to treat disorders of the rest of the body: these may or may not have psychological side effects, usually depending on (i) whether they can enter the brain and (ii) once there, whether they affect nerve cell function.

3.6.1 Drugs used to treat psychiatric disorders and psychological symptoms

Table 3.1 Some hypnotic drugs

Type	Examples	Comment
Barbiturates	Tuinal Soneryl	Obsolete.
Chloral		Obsolescent but still used.
Benzodiazepines	nitrazepam (Mogadon) temazepam lorazepam (Ativan)	Widely used especially in the elderly.
Benzodiazepine-like	zopiclone (Zimovane) zolpidem (Stilnoct)	Increasing usage.

3.6.1.1 Sleeping tablets or draughts ('hypnotics') are medicaments given to treat insomnia by inducing and/or maintaining sleep (Maczaj, 1993). They are widely used and a selection are listed in table 3.1. Some, e.g., zopiclone and zolpidem, are short-acting and few effects persist the next day. Others, particularly nitrazepam, are long-acting, and persist the next day with deleterious effects on psychological and physical functioning, particularly in the elderly.

By their nature, hypnotic medications are meant to induce drowsiness. They will automatically produce sedation before the person falls asleep, which as stated above may persist into the day. In addition, if the individual wakes up in the night, for example, to empty the bladder, marked psychological effects to the point of confusion and physical effects such as staggering gait and slurred speech may be present. However, the right choice of drug in conservative dosage may actually improve psychological functioning the next day because the patient sleeps well and does not feel tired.

Table 3.2 Some anxiolytic drugs

Type	*Examples*	*Comment*
Barbiturates	phenobarbitone	Obsolete.
Benzodiazepines	diazepam (Valium) lorazepam (Ativan) oxazepam (Serenid) alprazolam (Xanax)	Widely used still despite risk of sedation and dependence. Increasingly being abused by drug addicts.
Azapirones	buspirone (Buspar)	Minimal sedation and dependence problems.

3.6.1.2 Tranquillisers are medicines intended to allay anxiety. This class of drugs was originally termed, 'the sedatives', but this term has come to mean drugs inducing drowsiness and torpitude. The widest used by far are benzodiazepines such as diazepam which are long-acting (over, say, 12 hours) and those that are medium-acting (e.g., lorazepam) (table 2). Their usage has been declining because of increased concern amongst prescribers and recipients about sedation, impairment of memory and the risk of dependence on longer-term use (Ghoneim and Mewaldt, 1990). Furthermore, as with alcohol, paradoxical reactions can occur in which the patient becomes more anxious or even angry, hostile or aggressive.

In the right, low dosage, over short periods of time up to a month, anxiolytics can be quite beneficial in allaying symptoms of anxiety and associated behavioural abnormalities such as avoidance of crowded spaces.

Again, such clinical amelioration is often associated with psychological improvements.

Table 3.3 Some antidepressant drugs

Type	Examples	Comment
Stimulants	amphetamine	Not true antidepressants but euphoriants. Many dangers including abuse.
Tricyclics	amitriptyline (Tryptizol) dothiepin (Prothiaden) imipramine (Tofranil) clomipramine (Anafranil)	Widely used. Large range of side effects both bodily (e.g., blurred vision) and psychological (sedation).
Atypicals	trazodone mianserin	Mixed group, mostly sedative side effects.
Selective serotonin reuptake inhibitors (SSRIs)	fluoxetine (Prozac) paroxetine (Seroxat)	Can produce nausea and dizziness. Some are stimulant, some sedative.
Monoamine oxidase inhibitors (MAOIs)	phenelzine (Nardil)	Range of side effects. Can interact dangerously with some other drugs and even some foodstuffs such as cheese.
	moclobemide (Manerix)	Much safer and more selective drug.

3.6.1.3 Antidepressants comprise several groups of compounds used primarily to treat depressive disorders but increasingly other psychiatric disorders such as panic, obsessive-compulsive symptoms and appetite disorders such as anorexia and bulimia. Their pharmacology is complex (table 3.3).

For our purposes, it is important to note that many, but not all, are sedative and induce sleepiness as a side effect. Some also interfere with memory mechanisms (Thompson, 1991). Again, as depression itself is associated with marked psychological impairments, clinical improvement induced by antidepressants may be followed by psychological improvements which outweigh the direct depressant effects of the drugs.

Lithium carbonate is used both to treat mood disturbances and to prevent further episodes of manic-depressive illness. It produces sedation and memory impairment as well as many physical side effects such as tremor, and its use has to be carefully monitored (Jefferson and Greist, 1994).

Table 3.4   Some antipsychotic drugs

Type	Examples	Comment
Phenothiazines	chlorpromazine (Largactil)	Large number of side effects.
	thioridazine (Melleril)	
	fluphenazine	Given by 'depot' injection.
Butyrophenones	haloperidol (Haldol)	Widely used.
Benzamides	sulpiride	
Others	clozapine (Clozaril)	More recent introductions.
	risperidone	Low incidence of
	olanzapine	movement disorders.

3.6.1.4 Antipsychotic drugs are used primarily to treat the symptoms of psychotic conditions such as schizophrenia and mania in which the patient loses contact with reality (table 3.4). They are administered to combat acute major disturbances, to prevent or postpone further episodes of illness, and to alleviate chronic symptoms.

Most are sedative, sometimes intensely so, which may lead to poor compliance (King, 1990). The older compounds also produce a range of bodily side effects of which the most troublesome are movement disorders — spasms, tremors and restlessness. Sometimes these disorders can become permanent. Some preparations are available as 'depots' and are injected deep into the buttock muscles from whence they are absorbed steadily over the subsequent one to four weeks.

3.6.2   Drugs used to treat neurological disorders which have psychological side effects
The main groups are the anticonvulsants, the antiparkinsonian agents, analgesics and drugs used in the treatment of migraine.

3.6.2.1 Anticonvulsants comprise a large number of different types such as barbiturates, benzodiazepines, phenytoin, carbamazepine, valproic acid, and the newer compound, lamotrigine. Although prescribed in this context to prevent epileptic fits of various type, these drugs are also quite widely used as hypnotics, sedatives and 'mood regulators' (see above). A common feature of most of these drugs is that they can produce sedation (Dodrill, 1992).

3.6.2.2 Antiparkinsonian drugs are used to treat the movement disorder, Parkinsonism, whether it occurs spontaneously, mostly in the elderly, or as a side-effect of antipsychotic medication. Some produce sedation but others such as levodopa) can produce activation and occasionally a psychotic disorder.

3.6.2.3 Analgesics cover a range of substances from the very powerful such as morphine and pethidine through weaker compounds such as codeine to common over-the-counter painkillers like aspirin and paracetamol. The powerful opiates will have profound effects on mental functioning inducing sedation, euphoria and even psychotic states. The weak analgesics have mostly undetectable effects. Opiates are dependence-inducing and the withdrawal state is associated with major effects both bodily and psychological.

3.6.2.4 Treatments for *migraine* can affect mental functioning but the attack itself is likely to have a greater effect.

3.6.2.5 Other medications include *antiemetics* to stop vomiting, anti-obesity drugs (appetite suppressants) and stimulants (mostly in children). A variety of secondary effects can occur depending on the individual compound.

3.6.3 Drugs used to treat non-nervous disorders which may affect brain function

A large number of drugs fall into this category. Drugs given for allergies, the antihistaminics, can enter the brain and cause sedation. However, modern drugs of this class do not enter the brain readily and have little or no psychological effect. Similarly, the first histamine–2 blocking agent for ulcers, cimetidine ('Tagamet'), entered the brain and caused psychological effects such as nausea and dizziness. Other drugs of this type enter the brain less readily with lesser psychological effects. Beta blockers such as propranolol can cause nightmares, and hormones can have marked effects on mental functioning, steroids being the most noticeable example. Insulin can induce profound mental changes when given in excess or conversely in insufficient quantities. Drugs given as ointments or eye drops can be absorbed into the bloodstream and produce psychological effects. Even water taken in excess or excreted too slowly (as in 'Ecstasy' poisoning) can induce a delirium, coma and death. Conversely, some medications may improve mental functioning, for example, an antibiotic in a person with infection-induced delirium.

3.7 ILLICIT DRUGS

This is a large and growing group of substances finding increasing usage. The compounds range from the old natural drugs such as opium and hashish to synthetic varieties of these such as methadone and cannabinol, to *de novo* synthetic classes such as LSD and the 'designer drugs' (West and Gossop, 1994). Roughly speaking, three main effects are induced: sedation, stimulation and abnormal perceptions. Various drugs have various combinations of these, depending on dosage and individual susceptibility, but also some additional properties of a different type may be described. An example is repetitive obsessive-compulsive thoughts and actions with high doses of amphetamines. Although some studies have been carried out in laboratory settings under strict controls, much of our knowledge of the effects of these drugs come from anecdotal accounts. Often the dosage or even the identity of the drug taken is unclear.

3.8 DRUG-INDUCED STATES WHICH CAN AFFECT TESTIMONY

It can be seen that psychotropic drugs cover a wide range of different types with almost every conceivable action on mental functioning. In addition, numerous factors both pharmacokinetic and pharmacodynamic affect the intensity and duration of such effects, interacting with factors within the individual and within the context in which the drug is taken. Add to that the common practice of taking more than one medication at a time, licit or illicit or both, and it is hardly surprising that almost any drug-induced state may be encountered. Nevertheless, it is useful to enumerate the characteristics of the four commonest.

3.8.1 Sedation
This is a global term covering various elements of which the common subjective thread is sleepiness, tiredness and inertia. In addition, a wide range of intellectual and performance measures can be impaired including perception of objects, reaction time and ability to carry out cognitive tasks, i.e., the processing of information. Learning of new skills may be particularly affected. Thus, overlearned tasks like driving may be possible, but learning, say, to use a computer may be very difficult after taking a drug with sedative properties.

The effect on testimony may be profound depending on the depth of the sedation. Perception of other people or of objects may be impaired and vision may be blurred. Attention and concentration are disturbed. Thus, details may not be registered. Judgment is usually impaired so the implications of what is seen may be overlooked or misinterpreted. In the most severe instances, for example, in alcohol intoxication with obvious signs such as staggering and slurring of speech, testimony must be regarded as highly suspect.

The following case vignette is typical. Mr VJ was a 41-year-old builder. He was accused of handling a stolen lorry and taken into custody. He complained of severe anxiety and was seen by the police doctor to be trembling and sweating profusely. He was given 10 mg of diazepam ('Valium'), settled and was interviewed within an hour for two hours. He admitted various matters but at a further interview eight days later, drug-free, retracted his confession. Tapes of the interview suggested slurring of speech and incoherence at the first interview, and his signature to the confession was shaky and spidery. The confession was ruled inadmissible and the case dropped.

3.8.2 Disinhibition
This may be a part of sedation or follow the use of stimulant drugs. The individual indulges in excessive, inappropriate behaviour, often an exaggeration or a caricature of his or her usual personality traits. Testimony may be expansive or even fantastical and abnormal, and overactive behaviour may be apparent in the witness. Provocation of the witness may result in overreaction.

3.8.3 Paradoxical reactions
These take the form of drug reactions, the opposite of expected. Thus, a sedative may cause excitement, a stimulant sedation. However, a range of paradoxical reactions can occur, with uncharacteristic actions such as shop-lifting in the law-abiding, aggression or even murder in the meek. Two drugs in particular have received attention in this respect, namely, the sleeping tablet, triazolam ('Halcion'), and the antidepressant, fluoxetine ('Prozac'). Despite the media interest, such severe reactions are rare. Paranoid reactions may follow stimulant use.

3.8.4 Alterations in memory
Deep sedation is associated with memory impairment but other drugs such as LSD can also profoundly influence memory. Manifestly, testimony must be suspect in witnesses known to have been in such a state. Not only may they not remember what did happen, they may fabricate what did not. The latter was most graphically demonstrated by several allegations of sexual assault against their dentists brought by patients given major sedation (see 3.4.1).

3.9 PRACTICAL CONSIDERATIONS

Table 3.5 Some practical considerations

Examinations	—	full drug history
	—	physical including neurological
	—	mental including cognitive tests
	—	rigorous criteria for testamentary capacity
Retrospective	—	contemporary accounts by doctors and nurses
	—	evaluation of content of letters
Documents	—	examine handwriting and signature compare to previous reports to lay people
	—	assessment of general behaviour and condition at that time
	—	pay particular attention to confusion, paranoid feelings, abnormal affect, and (when assessing the validity of a will) relationship to beneficiaries
	—	scrutinise prescription sheet especially what was dispensed and administered
	—	ask about OTCs (non-prescription medicines)

The evaluation of witnesses and of testimony which may have been tainted by psychotropic drug administration requires the use of evidence from as many sources as possible. However, some of these sources, e.g., companions of the witness, may themselves have taken a psychotropic substance. Some of the types of approach are listed in table 3.5.

3.10 SUMMARY

A wide range of drugs (medicines) are in current use of which many are designed to affect brain function. Others do so as a side effect. The effects depend on how the body deals with the drug ('pharmacokinetics') and how the drug affects the body, including the brain ('pharmacodynamics'). An extensive range of effects on the brain and psychological functioning can ensue including effects on intellectual functioning, dexterity, memory, learning and subjective effects. Individual factors are important and can profoundly influence both the type and extent of drug effects.

Relevant drugs can be divided into:

(a) Those prescribed primarily to treat psychiatric disorders. These include sleeping tablets, tranquillisers, antidepressants and antipsychotics.

(b) Those used to treat neurological disorders which have psychological side effects. Examples are anticonvulsants and antiparkinsonian drugs.

(c) Those used to treat non-nervous disorders which may have psychological side effects.

(d) Illicit drugs used in the non-medical context by drug addicts.

Drug-induced states which can influence testimony are mainly sedation, disinhibition, paradoxical reactions and alterations in memory. A list of pointers is given in table 3.5 with respect to practical considerations in assessing the possible effects of drugs on testimony.

Key terms
Antidepressants; antipsychotics; dexterity; disinhibition; effects on cognition; memory; pharmacodynamics; pharmacokinetics; sedation; sleeping tablets; tranquillisers.

References
Cooper, J.R., Bloom, F.E. and Roth, R.H. (1991), *The Biochemical Basis of Neuropharmacology*, New York: Oxford University Press.
Dodrill, C.B. (1992), 'Problems in the assessment of cognitive effects of antiepileptic drugs', *Epilepsia*, vol. 33 (suppl. 6), pp. 29–32.
Dundee, J.W. (1990), 'Fantasies during sedation with intravenous midazolam or diazepam', *Medico-Legal Journal*, vol. 58, pp. 29–34.
Ghoneim, M.M. and Mewaldt, S.P. (1990), 'Benzodiazepines and human memory: a review', *Anesthesiology*, vol. 72, pp. 926–38.
Jefferson, J.W. and Greist, J.H. (1994), 'Lithium in psychiatry. A review', *CNS Drugs*, vol. 1, pp. 448–64.

King, D.J. (1990), 'The Effect of neuroleptics on cognitive and psychomotor function', *British Journal of Psychiatry*, vol. 157, pp. 799–811.

Maczaj, M. (1993), 'Pharmacological treatment of insomnia', *Drugs*, vol. 45, pp. 44–55.

O'Hanlon, J.F. and de Gier, J.J. (eds) (1986), *Drugs and Driving*, London: Taylor and Francis.

Preskorn, S.H. (1993), 'Pharmacokinetics of psychotropic agents: why and how they are relevant', *Journal of Clinical Psychiatry*, vol. 54 (suppl. 9), pp. 3–7.

Spiegel, R. (1989), *Psychopharmacology. An Introduction*, Chichester: John Wiley.

Stahl, S.M. (1996), *Essential Psychopharmacology. Neuroscientific Basis and Practical Applications*, Cambridge: Cambridge University Press.

Thompson, P.J. (1991), 'Antidepressants and memory: a review', *Human Psychopharmacology*, vol. 6, pp. 79–90.

West, R. and Gossop, M. (eds) (1994), 'Comparing drugs of dependence', *Addiction*, vol. 89.

Key references — further reading
Bond, A.J. and Lader, M.H. (1996), *Understanding Drug Treatment in Mental Health Care*, Chichester: John Wiley.

ABPI Data Sheet Compendium, London: Datapharm Publications, issued every 1–2 years.

British National Formulary, London: British Medical Association and Royal Pharmaceutical Society of Great Britain, issued every six months.

Editors' notes

The memory of a witness who is under the influence of drugs at any point during the time from when the relevant incident was first 'witnessed' until evidence is given in court may, subject to the drug's properties, be susceptible to corrupting influence as a result. Where this is reasonably suspected, it is vital that those responsible for causing the witness's evidence to be analysed effectively should establish three matters: first, whether the witness had taken drugs prior to the relevant event — be it original incident, interview with an investigator, the giving of evidence or any intermediate occurrence; second, the properties and potential effects of any drug ingested; and, third, whether the witness displayed any symptoms consistent with the existence of the effects. Medical records will be the most important resource. Where enquiries lead to positive findings, it may be necessary to seek to adduce expert medical evidence relating to the properties and effects of the drug, its potential for memory corruption and the existence of any symptoms identified in the witness which indicate that ingestion of the drug may have distorted perception and memory of the incident said to have been witnessed.

CHAPTER FOUR

The frailty of children's testimony

Anna Mortimer and Eric Shepherd*

With no help from Socrates, children everywhere are schooled to become masters at answering questions and to remain novices at asking them. Normal practice is to induce in the young answers given by others to questions put by others. (Dillon, 1990, p. 7.)

4.1 INTRODUCTION

To the benefit of all, the legal system has become, and continues to become, informed by psychological research and reflective practice. These have demonstrated beyond doubt that when sensible, informed allowances are made, particularly for the very young, children can — and do — give testimony which compares favourably with that of adults in terms of content and accuracy (Goodman and Bottoms, 1993; Spencer and Flin, 1993).

Memory problems may render children suggestible. They have a potential to endorse, unwittingly, misinforming assertions by an adult as being the case. Children are, however, particularly at risk of social influences, 'going along' with what the adult says, or what the child thinks the adult wants to hear (Ceci and Bruck, 1995; Doris, 1991). When this happens it confirms and compounds the frailty of children's testimony in conversations with adults. What they say is distorted, diminished, even destroyed and what they could have said remains unsaid.

In this chapter we examine the frailty of children's testimony by first considering two independent dimensions of disclosure: motivation to tell and ability to tell (Shepherd, 1993). We then examine conversation — the medium for relating experience and for forming relationships between speakers and listeners. We then examine conversation and relationships

---

* We wish to thank David Glasgow for his much valued views, advice, support and friendship over the years.

directed at obtaining evidence within the approach specified in the *Memorandum of Good Practice* (Home Office and Department of Health, 1992).

4.2 TELLING ABOUT EXPERIENCE: THE TWO DIMENSIONS OF DISCLOSURE

4.2.1 Willingness to tell

This dimension reflects the extent to which the child has, or evidences, the desire to tell (or not) about his or her remembrance of an experience — an event in which he or she has been on the receiving end or has observed.

Like adults, even young children may be motivated to tell something which is *not* the case to achieve an instrumental end. Children can, and do, *actively* deceive (Ekman, 1985). They may be moved to make, with apparent willingness, false accusations or false denials that 'nothing happened' — either as spontaneous assertions or as false retractions. They may engage in *passive* deception. They may want to tell but remain silent: they just do not say (Ceci, Leichtman and Putnick, 1992; Ney, 1995).

These decisions may originate from the child. More commonly the deception is compliant behaviour: the child 'going along' with the demands of a significant adult, e.g., the perpetrator, a parent or other family member, threatening or actually wielding coercive power over the child. False denials are much more frequent than false accusations. The greater the dependency and vulnerability of the child, the more likely his or her susceptibility to compliant behaviour.

Willingness to tell does not necessarily increase with age. Older children have been found to be less likely to disclose transgressions to their mothers. Older children have performed as poorly as younger children in reporting details of embarrassing genital examination. In addition to embarrassment, unwillingness to tell may stem from a desire not to upset others close to the child, fear and nervousness occasioned by the interview process, fear of the perpetrator, or fear of the consequences.

Willingness to tell has a temporal aspect. The child will only tell at the 'right' time: when he or she feels confident and it is safe to disclose, despite the fear, anxiety and risks, having weighed up the likely outcomes. Responsibility to tell ultimately rests with the child, not the listener (Westcott, 1993). The listener's responsibility is to create the conditions for telling: a working relationship enabling the child to confide when the time is right.

4.2.2 Ability to tell

The child must have sufficient linguistic, or other non-verbal representational ability, to communicate with another about the child's experience of an event or image. This raises the fundamental issue: ability to tell rests upon the child having witnessed the material event or image. Without this no valid disclosure can be made. However, if there was experience, memorial ability matters in each of its elements — registration of the detail, storage of the information, and retrieval.

Any attempt to summarise children's ability to remember is fraught. This is because: (a) it is a function not only of memory capacity but prior knowledge, techniques used to store, retain and retrieve material, contextual cues, emotional state and motivation, (b) children vary greatly, and (c) there is a wealth of research findings, some of which are contradictory (Ceci and Bruck, 1995; Doris, 1991; Goodman and Bottoms, 1993; Spencer and Flin, 1993; Warren and McGough, 1996).

In research and legal settings there is a two-stage release of information: free recall followed by specific questions. Free recall is a complex task. There are no prompts. This generates the most consistent age differences. Younger children report less information than older children or adults. What they remember is quite accurate but incomplete, often minimal or even cursory.

The second stage involves an intermediate form of memory. In response to prompts — the content of questions — the child has to retrieve information. Research has shown that children best remember:

(a)   personally experienced rather than observed events;
(b)   central, or core, detail (from the child's perspective) rather than peripheral detail;
(c)   event details rather than descriptive information.

Views differ as to the role of stress, although ecologically valid research points to it having a facilitating effect resulting in better recall.

There are problems:

(a)   Younger children are at times less accurate than older children or adults, particularly when questioned about ambiguous, peripheral, or non-salient detail.
(b)   Younger children have difficulty giving details of time, temporal order, or estimates of distance and speed.
(c)   Children find it difficult to differentiate specific instances of a frequently repeated event.
(d)   When describing strangers, questioning generates more detail but also increases errors.

In general children recall less information than adults but what they remember is quite accurate. Their errors tend to be of omission — they leave out detail — rather than commission — reporting erroneous detail. They can report very much more if they are asked appropriate questions. Errors of commission are characteristically the result of inappropriate questions.

Direct, specific questions have 'demand characteristics'. The question's content gives a clue to the 'answer'. Misleading content can give rise to distortion and suggestion. Ability to answer questions reliably and to resist suggestive and leading questions which mislead improves with increasing years and increasing linguistic ability.

Generally children are resistant to accepting the content of misleading questions concerning personally experienced events or core detail (as they see it). Very young children, however, are less resistant and have an increased error rate. Ceci and Bruck (1995) point out a non-trivial number of children are *not* resistant. Furthermore, once detail is implanted children become resistant to subsequent attempts to correct, or remove it.

In contrast to suggestion is compliant responding, a product of social influence rather than any cognitive shortcoming. Children are predisposed to please adults. The risk is of 'going along' with what the adult says, or what the child thinks the adult wants to hear.

Emergent compliance is a reflection of the child's perception of the relationship with the adult. The relationship is defined by their relative conversational performances. It follows that a child's ability to converse, whether compliantly or otherwise, is an important factor. The child, however, needs a listener to manage the conversational exchange sensitively and skilfully, enabling the child to tell as best he or she can, whilst not rendering the child victim to suggestion or responding compliantly.

4.3 THE TELLING MEDIUM: CONVERSATIONS AND RELATIONSHIPS WITH ADULTS

4.3.1 Conversational basics

Conversation is a complex medium demanding mental effort and cognitive, expressive and social skills.

> Talking with another person requires the simultaneous engagement of several interconnecting systems — a transmission system, a tracking and guidance system, and what might be called a facilitation system. The first system operates to assure the sending and reception of messages, the second to identify meanings, and the third to assure that the messages are acceptable and appropriate to the participants. (Garvey, 1984, p. 39.)

The transmission system involves the exchange of turns-at-talking. The one with the *talking turn* 'occupies the floor' and the duration of this constitutes *talking time*. Very often the listener does not wait for the speaker to finish talking, and overtalks (creating parallel talk, both talking at once) or interrupts (occasioning the other person to relinquish the talking turn). Silence between turns is perceived by adults as pressuring even embarrassing. Someone must take the talking turn.

In adult conversations the gaps between turns are extremely short. In the conversation of young children they are typically long. For them this is not a source of pressure. But adults misconstrue the longer pause as indicative of the child not paying attention, not understanding, or disengaging, and they respond dysfunctionally. Rather than wait they feel impelled to say something — typically a question — taking the talking turn away from the child. What the child would or could have said is lost: the powerful, impatient, adult is now talking.

Longer gaps have other causes (Cappella, 1985). Ambiguous and complex questions put pressure on the recipient in terms of additional cognitive load. They have to be worked out as well as an appropriate answer. Misreading the pause the adult jumps in, takes the talking turn and fills the pause. If there is absence of rapport this also adds to the cognitive load, creating longer pauses liable again to be filled by the adult.

Another feature of the transmission system is backchannel feedback, or 'backchannelling'. This comprises the listener's head nods, minimal support-ive sounds, e.g. 'uh-huh', 'hmm', and very short utterances, e.g., 'I see'. These sustain the speaker, encouraging him or her to continue and signalling that the listener is paying attention and 'taking on board' what is being related. This is essential to keeping the speaker going with a long response, such as a narrative, called by linguists an *inform* (Stenström, 1994).

To confirm that meaning is shared backchannelling must be precisely coordinated with the speaker's ongoing message. If it is out of synchrony with the speaker's intended meaning, e.g., nodding in the 'wrong place', the listener risks being construed as not really paying attention or fully com-prehending. Absence of backchannelling leaves even less doubt: the speaker is talking to himself or herself.

Backchannelling develops relatively late towards adolescence. This has major implications for conversations between adults and children. The adult thinks, erroneously, that the child is not listening or does not understand. This construction is all the more likely in conversations with young children for whom, as we have indicated, long pauses are natural.

Adults typically seek feedback, punctuating the conversation with questions to confirm the child *is* paying attention and understands. To be a valid check on attention and comprehension the questions should be open-ended rather than confirmatory yes/no. Adults ask many more of the latter.

Some adults do not bother to check, assuming the child has *not* attended or comprehended. They repeat themselves, often endlessly so, creating a virtual monologue, monopolising the talking turn and dominating the talking time.

4.3.2 Defining the relationship through conversation

Children typically give no feedback. They just accept the adult's behaviour. Their compliance stems from *social desirability*, a basic motivation to be viewed favourably, or at least not unfavourably.

Participants look for conversational clues, indicative of the other person's view of the situation and his or her reactions, intentions, aspirations and attitudes. Critically they adjust their conversational behaviour to accord with their notions of the relationship which exists, or could, should or must exist (or not), between them.

Control of the talking turn, talking most of the time and disruptively listening (interrupting, overtalking, making sounds of minimal interest, and rapidly changing the topic) are perceived as dominant behaviours (Cappella, 1985). In an 'across' relationship neither party is dominant. They relate information as equals. In an 'up-down' relationship, one occupies the superior role and the other the subordinate. The one in the 'up' position determines the course, the conduct and, in very great measure, the content of the exchange. The way he or she converses controls who talks, for how long, on what topic, when, to what extent and how. People assume, are assigned to, or are accepted in, the 'up' position on the basis of status and relative power over the other person.

From early infancy onwards the norm for an adult–child relationship is 'up-down', with the child as the subordinate. Adults typically dominate the conversation, occupy the talking turn most of the time, talk more than the child, and drive the conversation through questions inviting the child to confirm what is in the adult's head.

Children are particularly sensitive to context. Generally they produce shorter utterances in strange settings and with people they do not really know, than when at home with their mothers. The 'up-down' relationship is even more marked, often intensely so, in conversation with strangers. The authority figure tends to talk most of the time, to initiate topics on the basis of a plan of action devised beforehand, to ask questions to which the adult knows the answer and to respond to questions from the child which are relevant to the task as defined by the adult.

Some parents engage in supportive conversation, preparing their children to cope better, giving them confidence to relate more fully and more confidently, in exchanges with other adults, particularly those who are non-familial or strangers (McTear, 1985). Supportive conversation is child-centred and has the discrete defining features (Wells, 1978):

(a)   warm responsiveness to the child's interests;
(b)   recognition of the child as an autonomous individual with valid purposes and ways of seeing things;
(c)   mutual sharing of meaning and purpose, which are skilfully negotiated not imposed by the adult;
(d)   facilitating the child to *think*, particularly in terms of intentions, consequences, feelings and principles.

In supportive conversation the child has relatively greater access to the talking turn since the adult values the child's contribution, encouraging the child to continue relating and to initiate topics spontaneously. This maximises the child's talking time. The minority of children have experience of such supportive conversation.

Practitioners who specialise in working with children are particularly aware of the requirement for 'across' relationships (Jones and McQuiston, 1988) and the necessity for supportive conversation. Shepherd (1987) advocated its use by police officers when obtaining testimony from children. Wilkinson (1998) summarised its essentials:

A general principle is that conversation is satisfying when there is a balanced interplay of mutual control and reward. In other words, the child should be encouraged to have some active control of the conversation rather than simply answering questions, and the practitioner should be responsive and encouraging to the child's contributions. (p. 198.)

Supportive conversation is consonant with the view of Butler-Sloss (1988): the child is a person, not an object of concern.

In the next section we consider the extent to which the *Memorandum of Good Practice* (Home Office and Department of Health, 1992) and actual interviewer behaviours reflect this general principle of conversing with children. We base our assessment on Home Office research (Davies et al., 1995) and shared observations with psychologists, who like ourselves train interviewers and who are instructed to conduct fine-grain analyses of video recordings for court proceedings.

4.4 OBTAINING EVIDENCE FROM CHILDREN

The Memorandum of Good Practice (Home Office and Department of Health, 1992) provides explicit guidance on conducting an interview with a child to enable the child to tell about his or her experience. It presents a recommended protocol for interviewing:

> This treats the interview as a process in which a variety of interviewing techniques are deployed in relatively discrete phases, proceeding from general and open to specific and closed forms of question. It is suggested that this approach is likely to achieve the basic aim of listening to what the child has to say, if anything, about the alleged offence. (para. 3.1, p. 15).

4.4.1 The 'rush to get it wrong'

According to the Memorandum delay is bad, with potentially adverse affects upon the child and the child's testimony:

> Once a plan of action has been agreed upon it is vital to proceed quickly. This will minimise the stress experienced by the child and reduce the risk of him or her forgetting important details, or being influenced by others. (para. 1.7, p. 6.)

> In exceptional cases, for example where any deferment will occasion serious risk to the child, or when the alleged abuser has already been detained by the police, it might be necessary for an interview to be conducted immediately (para. 1.10, p. 6).

Interviewers need to be aware of frailty arising from fatigue and distractibility.

> As a rule of thumb, the team should plan the interview to last for less than an hour (excluding breaks) unless they have good reason to believe the child is mature and strong enough to cope with longer (para. 2.17, p. 12).

The amount of interviewing is constrained, because of the likely reaction of the defence to recordings of two or more interviews. The underlying concern is responses in second or subsequent interviews which may be argued to be indicative of unrecorded interviewing or conversation aimed at improving the child's recorded testimony.

Once the video recorded interview has been recorded no further questioning should take place unless the joint investigating team is fully satisfied, in
consultation as necessary with the Crown Prosecution Service, that it is
essential to elicit further information (para. 1.11, p. 7).

The result is all too apparent: a 'one shot, no more than an hour' mentality
which fundamentally affects the course, conduct and content of interviews.

Bull (in Bull and Davies, 1996) restated his view of the *Memorandum* as
being 'on how to do the easy ones', based on research with children who did
wish to tell. It inadequately prepares interviewers for children who, for
whatever reason, are unwilling, not ready or unable to tell. Interviews of these
children cannot be rushed. More likely than not they need two or more
interviews.

There are no short cuts.

This is particularly so with children who are communicatively or intellectually disadvantaged, or both. They are particularly vulnerable to offenders
who exploit their inability to tell and who, often in collusion with other adults,
render the child unwilling to tell. The testimony of these children is inherently frail. Their expressive burden is increased by unaware adults who misread
any idiosyncratic non-verbal communication. Hence a behaviour which is
'normal' for the child, e.g., avoidance of eye contact, may be construed as
deception.

Teams should be well aware at the planning stage if the child is disadvantaged. We argue that, wherever possible, a child with learning difficulties or
significant communicative problems should *not* be interviewed by a police
officer or social worker who lacks requisite special expertise, endowed by
training *and* extensive experience. The *Memorandum* allows for interviewing
by suitable experts (para. 2.10, p. 10).

4.4.2 The 'rapport' phase

The aim of this phase is to build up a rapport, deemed to have been achieved
when the child is settled and anxiety reduced. As we have indicated above,
relationship is much more than this. The child expects an 'up-down'
relationship, with the child like other subordinates destined to communicate
through answers, typically induced, and which coincide with what the adult
has in mind, believes or knows. The interviewer's task therefore is to redefine
the situation for the child: this is an 'across' relationship with an adult who
wants to listen rather than drive the conversation.

This takes time.

The *Memorandum* points to the necessity 'to go at the pace of the child and
not of the adult' (para. 2.18, p. 12) but cautions against going *too* slowly:

> *Those more used to interviewing adults will need to be especially careful not to go*
> *too fast for the child or to seem impatient.* On the other hand, *those with*
> *experience mainly in child care might go too slowly and, for example, tend to dwell*
> *[sic] in the 'rapport' phase when the child is ready to proceed to the next phase of*
> *the interview (para. 2.18, p. 12; emphasis is original.)*

This guidance is unfortunate. First, notions of 'too slowly' and 'tendency to dwell in the "rapport" stage phase' presume interviewers can judge reliably when time is being wasted which should be devoted to investigation. The *Memorandum* leaves interviewers in the dark concerning clues indicative of an appropriate relationship and a child's readiness to move on: ready acceptance of the talking turn, ease in occupying much of the talking time and spontaneous initiation of topics.

Secondly, it demonstrates a lack of knowledge about establishing rapport with children, particularly those with communicative and intellectual disadvantages. Some children 'hit it off' immediately with the adult. For others, especially the 'difficult ones', the relationship emerges slowly and is particularly fragile. They are particularly sensitive to how something is said (tone of voice), content which raises doubt or distrust, and 'mixed messages' which cause emotional confusion.

Fine-grain examination of recordings reveals how very often the prospects for fostering an appropriate relationship are damaged by the 'one shot, not more than an hour' mentality and the discouragement of 'dwelling' in the rapport phase. In many instances building rapport is ritualised. The interviewer 'goes through the motions', often with almost indecent haste: the child's responses are poorly attended to, with half-hearted or even no sensible attempt to foster longer, fuller responses from the child.

A question, say, about a holiday (Bull, 1992) provides the basis for an inform response, an opportunity for the interviewer to foster (through backchannelling) a pattern of detailed narration. However, too many interviewers nullify the child's attempt to narrate. The tone of voice or facial expressions of some communicate inherent disinterest. Some dismiss the child's view, passing egocentric comments. Some disruptively listen in the way we have described earlier.

Thus unaware interviewers 'rush to get it wrong': adult and child remain locked into an 'up-down' relationship and all this entails.

A closed loop is established as the interviewer's inappropriate behaviour progressively reduces the content and duration of the child's responses. The talking turn reverts quickly back to the adult who, under pressure, reacts quickly, unreflectively and ineptly. The child minimally responds, passing the turn back to the interviewer, who, under pressure . . . and so on.

The child is left in no doubt that this is an adult-driven exchange: a question-and-answer session on topics chosen, probed and then switched according to the desires of the interviewer. This is confirmed when the interviewer switches from talking about neutral topics to necessary 'instructions': to tell the truth, to tell everything the child can remember without leaving anything out, not to make anything up, to say when the child does not know or does not understand.

Establishing in the mind of the child very early on in the interview that this is a typical 'up-down' relationship has another deleterious effect. The *Memorandum* says:

> . . . this phase serves a number of important additional functions. If used
> correctly, it should supplement the interviewer's knowledge about the

child's social, emotional and cognitive development, and particularly his or her communication skills and degree of understanding (for example, the number of words used by the child in sentences might cause the interviewer to revise an earlier judgement about the most suitable length of questions) (para. 3.4, pp. 15–16).

In the absence of guidance or instruction interviewers rely on lay notions of children's receptive ability. Most adults underestimate the ability of children to understand, whether or not the child is learning-disabled. Paradoxically adults overestimate children's ability to understand complex questions, i.e., those which wrap up several questions into one (multiple questions) or offer multiple options. Children struggle to hold all the elements of such questions in working memory, the intellectually disadvantaged even more so. It makes sense, literally, to keep it short but short does not necessarily mean simple. The wording and construction, and thus the sense, must be simple.

If the interviewer's conversational behaviour reduces the length or duration of the child's responses, the interviewer unwittingly undermines his or her ability to gather evidence to perform valid assessment.

4.4.3 The free narrative account
The *Memorandum* says:

> This is the heart of the interview and the interviewer's role is to act as facilitator, not an interrogator (para. 3.12, p. 17).

The Home Office research showed that 28% of interviews examined lacked a heart: there was no free narrative phase. Two explanations were offered. The child may have been reluctant to talk, which could have been proactively managed by: (a) identification and action in the planning stage, or (b) selective interviewing, i.e., not conducting *Memorandum* interviews as a matter of course. Alternatively the interviewer simply chose to omit the phase — an incomprehensible decision given what the *Memorandum* says.

Even when a free narrative account was sought the researchers identified the same pervasive 'rush to get it wrong'. In 43% of the cases 'the child was needlessly rushed on to the questioning phase when they were still in the process of revealing important aspects of the alleged incident(s)' (p. 20). We and others have found this frequently occurs in interviews. It ignores the guidance in the *Memorandum*:

> Provide opportunities to talk about the alleged offence at the child's pace. Use a form [sic] of 'active listening' (p. 22).

There is, of course, only one form of active listening: paying attention and signalling this through backchannelling. Too many interviewers disruptively listen in the way we have described: overtalking, interrupting, showing signs and making sounds indicative of inattention or disinterest, or rapidly changing the topic.

The *Memorandum* advises the use of appropriate open-ended prompts to expand the account, such as 'Did anything else happen?' (para. 3.13, p. 17). It also spells out that many children will feel uncomfortable about recalling some events and will move slowly from peripheral matters and therefore need reassurance, for example, 'I can see you are finding this difficult, but you are being very brave. Just keep telling us about it and we will listen.' (para. 3.14, p. 17.)

Not obtaining a free account or rushing, failing to sustain and expand, failing to listen to and cutting short the child's attempt to tell are all deleterious to the child's testimony. These interviewer behaviours confirm yet again that this is an 'up-down' relationship. The child is primed to respond minimally and discouraged from contributing detail spontaneously, even more so if the rapport stage was rushed and the child not listened to.

4.4.4 Questioning
The *Memorandum* says:

> . . . as with all questions used in the interview, *it should always be clear to the child that to reply 'I can't remember' or 'I don't know' is perfectly acceptable.* The child should also be encouraged to say if he or she does not understand the question (para. 3.17, p. 18; emphasis is original).

> With younger children the interviewer may need to say, in simple terms, that he or she has no idea what has happened to them. Very young children often assume that because one adult knows what has happened to them, other adults are somehow privy to this knowledge. (para. 3.18, p. 18).

This advice demonstrates pure empathy, seeing the 'problem' from the child's perspective. The Home Office research did not indicate whether this advice was followed at the outset, or indeed across, the questioning phase. It has been our experience that, following the free narrative phase, a very large proportion of interviewers do not behave in this empathic manner.

The *Memorandum* says that questioning should be a process of progressively more explicit prompting. The sequence is all the more important when a child has provided very little relevant information in the free narrative phase:

> *It is particularly important in such cases to proceed through this phase step by step and not to be tempted to get to what he or she may consider to be the heart of the matter by asking what a court may later consider to be prejudicial leading questions* (para. 3.19, p. 18; emphasis is original).

Only if it is in the interests of the child should the interviewer proceed to specific yet non-leading questions. These are used to extend and clarify what the child has said in the free narrative phase and in response to open-ended questions. They also enable the interviewer to remind an uncommunicative child, in a non-leading manner, of the purpose of the interview. The issue of not leading is crucial: questions in this stage should not imply the answer.

Significantly the *Memorandum* emphasises the inappropriateness of closed confirmatory (yes/no) and option questions:

> . . . *during this stage questions which require a 'yes' or 'no' answer, or ones which allow only one of two possible responses, should not be asked.* (para. 3.25, p. 19; emphasis is original).

The *Memorandum* says closed questions might be asked if specific but non-leading questions are unproductive. It offers an example of an acceptable closed question: 'Was the man's scarf you mentioned blue or yellow, or another colour, or can't you remember?' From what we have said above it will be clear that this is how *not* to ask a question (it is a multiple question which offers the child four options!).

The *Memorandum* fails to explain that for every closed yes/no and option question there is usually a more evidentially productive open-ended alternative. Here, 'That man's scarf you mentioned.' (Pause.) 'What colour was it?' Having waited at least a couple or three seconds for a reply, if none is forthcoming, the issue of remembering — and not remembering — should be explored sensitively.

The *Memorandum* makes it quite clear that the final stage of questioning — the use of leading questions — is evidentially fraught:

> The greatest care must therefore be taken when questioning the child about central matters which are likely to be disputed (para. 3.33, p. 20).

This is because of the risk of compliant responding:

> In addition to the legal objections, psychological research indicates strongly that interviewees' responses to leading questions tend to be determined by the manner of questioning rather than valid recall. It seems likely that young children in particular may be more willing to respond to 'yes/no' questions with a 'yes' response (para. 3.34, p. 20).

The *Memorandum* therefore recommends counterbalancing, i.e., having posed a leading question and obtained an answer, pose another — mutually exclusive — leading question worded in the opposite direction:

> If, therefore, questions permitting only a 'yes' or 'no' response are asked in this phase, these should be phrased so that those on the same issue sometimes seek a 'yes' response and sometimes a 'no' response (para. 3.34, p. 20).

Saying 'yes' to mutually exclusive questions is acquiescence, i.e., unreflectively agreeing with the interviewer. It must be explored with the child. Yet counterbalancing of questions is uncommon in interviews. Indeed, there is a disinclination to test the child's account systematically. Very common is selective attention to detail which 'fits' the interviewer's case theory. Also common is apparent inability to remember the detail of the child's free narrative and responses to questions across the course of the interview. Hence interviewers fail to detect or choose to ignore anomaly — gaps, ambiguity, vagueness, and contradiction — even different versions of 'what happened' (Shepherd and Mortimer, 1995).

The Home Office research found that only 30% of interviewers followed the *Memorandum* in respect of the staged sequencing of questions. The remaining 70% engaged in questioning wholly at odds with the *Memorandum* guidance.

[They] focused almost exclusively on asking closed, single response type questions. This frequently led to a narrowing of the child's responses to 'yes' or 'no' and discouraged the child from offering more information (Davis et al., 1995, p. 20).

In 40% of the interviews there were questions which breached the rules of evidence. . . . Hearsay was also raised on occasions (p. 21).

A third of the tapes examined in the Home Office research were judged to be of no evidential value. It is not hard to see why. If in 28% of cases no free narrative was requested and in 43% of cases the child was rushed through and questioning began when the child was still attempting give important information, and in 70% questioning was contrary to the *Memorandum's* advice, this means that around three-quarters of interviewers created an interrogative relationship with the child which:

(a) undermined the validity, reliability and evidential status of the child's account;

(b) systematically restricted the child's access to talking time, progressively withdrawing the opportunity to tell;

(c) extinguished the child's desire to tell.

This is persuasive evidence that interviewer-centred conversation confirms and compounds the frailty of children's testimony.

4.5 SUMMARY

(a) Telling about experience of an event or image is an interplay of two psychological dimensions: willingness–unwillingness to tell and ability–inability to tell.

(b) With due allowance made for the very young, children are able to give testimony which compares well with that given by adults in terms of amount and accuracy.

(c) A critical determinant of a child's ability to tell is the conversational behaviour of the adult to whom the child is talking: this signals the type of relationship between them.

(d) Typically adult–child relationships are 'up-down' question-and-answer exchanges.

(e)   Children, like adults, are vulnerable to suggestion and compliant responding, but are at particular risk of 'going along' in 'up-down' relationships.

(f)   Helping a child to tell demands child-centred, supportive conversational behaviour from an interviewer aware of the link between conversational realities and type of relationship.

(g)   Inappropriate conversational behaviour by an interviewer risks confirming and compounding the frailty of children's testimony: introducing error, distorting and even destroying the child's account or rendering the child silent.

Key terms
Suggestibility; compliance; conversation; talking turn; talking time; backchannelling; relationship.

References

Bull, R. (1992), 'Obtaining evidence expertly: The reliability of interviews with child witnesses', *Expert Evidence*, vol. 1, pp. 5–12.

Bull, R. and Davies, G. (1996), 'The effect of child witness research on legislation in Great Britain', in B. Bottoms and G. Goodman (eds), *International Perspectives on Child Abuse and Children's Testimony*. Thousand Oaks, CA: Sage, p. 96.

Butler-Sloss, E. (1988), *Report of the Inquiry into Child Abuse in Cleveland*. London: HMSO.

Capella, J. (1985), 'Controlling the floor in conversation', in A. Siegman and S. Feldstein (eds), *Multichannel Integrations of Non-verbal Behaviour*. Hillsdale, NJ: Erlbaum.

Ceci, S. and Bruck, M. (1995), *Jeopardy in the Courtroom*. Washington: American Psychological Association.

Ceci, S., Leichtman, M. and Putnick, M. (1992), *Cognitive and Social Factors in Early Deception*. Hillsdale, NJ: Erlbaum.

Davies, G., Wilson, C., Mitchell, R. and Milsom, J. (1995), *Videotaping Children's Evidence: An Evaluation*. London: HMSO.

Dillon, J. (1990), *The Practice of Questioning*. London: Routledge.

Doris, J. (1991), *The Suggestibility of Children's Recollections*. Washington: American Psychological Association.

Ekman, P. (1985), *Telling lies*. New York: Norton.

Garvey, C. (1984), *Children's Talk*. London: Fontana.

Goodman, G. and Bottoms, B. (1993) *Child Victims, Child Witnesses*. New York: Guilford.

Home Office and Department of Health (1992), *Memorandum of Good Practice on Video-recorded Interviews with Child Witnesses for Criminal Proceedings*. London: HMSO.

Jones, D. and McQuiston, M. (1988), *Interviewing the Sexually Abused Child*. London: Gaskell.

McTear, M. (1985), *Children's Conversation*. Oxford: Blackwell.

Ney, T. (1995), *True and False Allegations of Child Sexual Abuse*. New York: Brunner/Mazel.

Shepherd, E. (1987), 'Getting children to tell', *Police Review*, 29 May 1987, pp. 1080–1.

Shepherd, E. (1993), 'Resistance in interviews: the contribution of police perceptions and behaviour', in E. Shepherd (ed.), *Aspects of Police Interviewing* (Issues in Criminological and Legal Psychology, No. 18). Leicester: British Psychological Society.

Shepherd, E. and Mortimer, A. (1995), 'Putting testimony to the test', *Practitioners Child Law Bulletin*, vol. 8, pp. 44–6.

Spencer, J. and Flin, R. (1993), *The Evidence of Children*, 2nd ed. London: Blackstone.

Stenström, A. (1994), *An Introduction to Spoken Interaction*. London: Longman.

Warren, A. and McGough, L. (1996), 'Research on children's suggestibility: Implications for the investigative interviews', in B. Bottoms and G. Goodman (eds), *International Perspectives on Child Abuse and Children's Testimony*. Thousand Oaks, CA: Sage, p. 12.

Wells, G. (1978), 'Talking with children: the complementary roles of parents and teachers', *English in Education*, vol. 12, pp. 15–38.

Westcott, J. (1993), *Abuse of Children and Adults with Disabilities*. London: NSPCC.

Wilkinson, I. (1998), *Child and Family Assessment*. London: Routledge.

Recommended reading
Ceci, S. and Bruck, M. (1995), *Jeopardy in the Courtroom*. Washington: American Psychological Association.

Doris, J. (1991), *The Suggestibility of Children's Recollections*. Washington: American Psychological Association.

Garvey, C. (1984), *Children's Talk*. London: Fontana.

Goodman, G. and Bottoms, B. (1993), *Child Victims, Child Witnesses*. New York: Guilford.

McTear, M. (1985), *Children's Conversation*. Oxford: Blackwell.

Ney, T. (1995), *True and False Allegations of Child Sexual Abuse*. New York: Brunner/Mazel.

Spencer, J. and Flin, R. (1993), *The Evidence of Children*, 2nd ed. London: Blackstone.

Editors' notes
The memory of a child, as with that of adult vulnerable witnesses who may be physically ill, under the influence of drugs or mentally disordered, is, notoriously, susceptible to failure through, *inter alia*, inappropriate or improper investigative methods. Where a child is 'abnormal' in the conventional sense, expert evidence is consistent in its basis with that available in relation to adult witnesses is likely to be admissible subject to materiality. More difficult issues may arise when the child has been diagnosed as 'normal' and where fact-finders are likely to be left to draw their own conclusions as to the reliability and credibility of the evidence in the absence of expert evidence thereon.

Nonetheless, even where a child is 'normal' there may be elements of the investigation process which have a potential for memory corruption such that the child may be led to give an unreliable or incredible account. In certain circumstances — where, for example, official guidelines relating to the questioning of children have been breached — it may be feasible for generalised expert evidence to be given about the risks involved, since fact-finders are unlikely to be able to understand them without it (see the judgment of the Court of Appeal in *R* v *Davies* (1995) unreported, transcript No. 94/4098/S2 et al., 3 November, at p. 48E–F).

CHAPTER FIVE

Testimony from persons with mental disorder

Gisli H. Gudjonsson

5.1 INTRODUCTION

It is often assumed that persons who suffer from mental disorder lack the capacity and motivation to give an accurate, complete and reliable account of events. This unfounded view was well highlighted during the Ashworth Inquiry (1992), where the evidence of psychiatric patients about alleged ill-treatment and improper care was challenged by the defendants on the basis of the patients' mental status and their inherent lack of credibility as witnesses.

In this chapter the potential psychological vulnerabilities of persons with mental disorder are set out and it is argued that mental disorder on its own does not usually undermine the credibility of witnesses when interviewed by the police or when giving evidence in court. What is needed is a proper identification of mental problems and psychological vulnerabilities and an explanation of how these factors may influence the reliability of the witness's account to the police and evidence in court. This is what the present chapter aims to do.

5.2 COMPONENTS OF CREDIBILITY

The *credibility* of witnesses refers to the extent to which they are capable of being believed. The related concept of *reliability*, in terms of its legal use, focuses specifically on the trustworthiness of the witness's account (i.e., Is it safe to rely on it as being an accurate and genuine recollection?). Psychologists use the term 'reliability' more technically to indicate the *consistency* of a test or measure. They use the term 'validity' to describe the extent to which a test measures what it is intended to measure. In this chapter the term 'reliability' is used with its legal meaning.

Credibility can be separated into two components (Undeutsch, 1982, Gudjonsson, 1992, and Shepherd, 1991, 1993). The first component involves the *ability* of people to give reliable evidence at any one given point in time. This aspect of credibility is related to the witness's memory of the event in question, cognitive functioning (intelligence, memory capacity, tendency to confabulate), personality (suggestibility, compliance, acquiescence), and mental state (anxiety, depression, feelings of guilt, a state of shock, post-traumatic stress disorder, drug or alcohol intoxication or withdrawal symptoms).

Secondly, there is the *willingness* of witnesses to tell the truth. This is the motivational aspect of credibility and it is influenced by both 'other-deception' (i.e., lying to others) and 'self-deception' (i.e., lying to oneself). Other-deception occurs when people deliberately lie to others in order either to *conceal* or to *falsify* information. Concealing takes place when they intentionally withhold information which may be important and relevant in establishing facts. Falsifying means that people intentionally give false information which they claim is true. Self-deception involves people lying to themselves (usually in order to stabilise mood and self-esteem) and they accordingly give an account of their feelings and behaviour which is incomplete or distorted but they themselves believe it to be true. Both other-deception and self-deception are important in a forensic assessment, but the former is more readily influenced by the context in which the person is being assessed (Gudjonsson, 1990). That is, the way in which the person deceives others is typically under more conscious control and more deliberate than deceiving oneself. Self-deception indicates a lack of insight into one's problems and psychopathology and it is associated with the denial of painful emotional experiences. The consequence is that underlying psychopathology, such as depression and severe emotional problems, may not be readily apparent during the psychological and psychiatric assessment.

There are two kinds of punishment at stake when people lie to others. First, there may be punishment if the lie fails (i.e., punishment associated with people learning about the truth of the matter which is being concealed or falsified). Secondly, the embarrassment and perceived punishment for being caught deceiving is often worse than the punishment that the lie was designed to avoid in the first place. Thus, once people have lied they are often persistent in maintaining the lie, even when confronted with evidence demonstrating the lying. Commonly this serves to protect their pride and self-esteem (Gudjonsson, 1992).

5.3 SUSPECTS, WITNESSES AND VICTIMS

A 'witness' can be defined as any person who is potentially able to provide the police or the court with information about an alleged offence or an offender. 'Suspects' and 'victims' are often important 'witnesses' in that they may provide the police and the court with information which is pertinent to the case.

As far as police interviewing is concerned, there are important differences between victims, witnesses and suspects. One important difference between suspects and other witnesses relates to the circumstances and nature of their interview with the police. Unlike other witnesses, they are suspected of a criminal offence and the likelihood of self-incrimination is high. It is for this reason that they are cautioned against self-incrimination, and if mentally disordered or young persons they are entitled to the presence of an 'appropriate adult' to assist them at the police station. The person acting in this capacity has to be at least 18 years of age and he or she cannot be a police officer or the suspect's solicitor. In the case of a youth, a parent is most commonly called to act as an appropriate adult. In the case of an adult who is suffering from mental disorder, the social services are most commonly approached by the custody officer.

The use of appropriate adults at police stations is intended as a safeguard that protects 'vulnerable' suspects. These include children and adolescents and those suffering from mental disorder or those who are in a disturbed mental state while at the police station.

The role of the appropriate adult is threefold: to give advice, to further communication, and to ensure that the interview is conducted properly and fairly. The nature of the advice given is not specified in the Codes of Practice issued under the Police and Criminal Evidence Act 1984 ('PACE'), but it should not involve legal advice. If the vulnerable suspect is not legally represented, the appropriate adult would be well advised to encourage the suspect to seek legal advice (Pearse and Gudjonsson, 1996). This is particularly important since the implementation in April 1995 of the Criminal Justice and Public Order Act 1994, under which adverse inferences may be drawn by the court if a suspect chooses to remain silent when questioned by the police or he or she chooses not to give evidence in court when the case goes to trial. There is no doubt that modifying the right to silence increases the complexity of the decision-making required of suspects during questioning. This may cause suspects to feel under pressure to make admissions when they do not wish to do so, admissions which may subsequently turn out to be unreliable. In addition, many suspects may not understand the adverse inferences that can be drawn in court from their refusal to answer questions or from their failure to give proper answers. There is evidence that the current caution is very complicated to understand and it is understood fully by only a minority of persons in the general population (Shepherd, Mortimer and Mobasheri, 1995). Persons of low intellectual abilities are particularly disadvantaged in understanding the new caution (Clare, Gudjonsson and Harari, 1998), which is very important to recognise in view of the fact that the majority of suspects detained at police stations for interviewing are of below average intellectual ability. In their study for the Royal Commission on Criminal Justice, Gudjonsson, Clare, Rutter and Pearse (1993) found an average IQ score of 82 for suspects detained for interviewing at two police stations within the Metropolitan Police District. A third of the sample obtained an IQ score of 75 or below, which represents a significant intellectual impairment. This indicates that a substantial proportion of suspects detained at police stations are intellectually disadvantaged.

There are currently many problems with the use of appropriate adults, and the extent to which they provide a safeguard that protects vulnerable suspects has been seriously questioned (Pearse and Gudjonsson, 1996). The problems identified include the vagueness of their role, the lack of availability of suitable persons to act in this capacity, the unsuitability of some of the persons used, and the absence of national guidelines and standards for training. If appropriate adult schemes were shown to provide a good safeguard for vulnerable suspects, then such a facility may also be important to use when mentally disordered witnesses are interviewed by the police. For example, there have been instances when persons with learning disability were first interviewed as witnesses and because of their apparently unsatisfactory or misleading answers during questioning they became suspects and made unreliable confessions (Gudjonsson and MacKeith, 1994; Gudjonsson, 1995).

Another important difference between suspects, victims and witnesses is that the statements of suspects are often more self-serving than those of other witnesses and their motive for being deceptive is therefore stronger. This does not mean that witnesses and victims do not on occasions lie to the police. There are numerous instances where this has occurred due to various motives, including obtaining money under false pretences from insurance companies, revenge, in order to protect the offender, to avoid possible feelings of embarrassment or shame resulting from being truthful, and fear of retaliation or intimidation by the offender, which is not uncommon and may make witnesses reluctant to be forthcoming during police interviewing and testifying in court.

Problems sometimes arise when witnesses are trying to be over helpful to the police. For example, extreme eagerness to assist the police with their enquiries can result in false accounts being given of events and during identification parades.

Special problems may arise when the police are interviewing victims of sexual and violent crimes. Such victims are sometimes so traumatised by the experience that they are unable to recount what happened and fear any discussion about it.

There are many reasons which may prevent suspects from being open, honest and forthcoming during a police interview or when giving evidence in court. The three main reasons are fear of legal sanctions (e.g., being convicted, sentenced), feeling ashamed and embarrassed about the crime, and fear of retaliation by implicating others. Whereas feelings of *shame* inhibit suspects from confessing, feelings of *guilt* facilitate the confession process (Gudjonsson, 1992). Feelings of shame are particularly likely to occur when suspects are interviewed in relation to sexual offending, such as child molestation, which carries strong social stigma. Here the police interview will need to focus on ways of overcoming the feelings of shame associated with such offences. This kind of offender needs to be interviewed particularly sensitively if a reliable confession is to be obtained.

A neglected group of people are those who confess falsely to the police in order to protect a significant person in their life from being prosecuted (e.g., a relative, a friend, a peer). These types of false confession are probably quite common and do not come to the notice of the judiciary because they are typically not retracted (Gudjonsson and Sigurdsson, 1994).

Undoubtedly, one of the most problematic types of case that the police and the courts have to deal with are allegations of childhood sexual abuse. In the United States of America there is currently a large number of cases of alleged childhood sexual abuse which result from so-called 'recovered memories' during therapy (Ofshe and Watters, 1994). Such accusations also occur in the UK and are typically made against a father by a grown-up daughter, who alleges he sexually abused her in childhood, with the memory of the abuse having been 'repressed' until adulthood when the accuser entered therapy for such problems as depression and eating disorder (Gudjonsson, 1997a, 1997b, 1997c). It is often assumed that 'recovered memories' are due to heightened susceptibility to suggestions during therapy (Ofshe and Watters, 1994). Interestingly, this kind of accuser has not been found to be unduly suggestible on psychometric testing (Gudjonsson, 1997d; Leavitt, 1997), which suggests that the beliefs or recovered memories of the alleged childhood abuse are internally generated (i.e., they are not primarily the product of leading questions and interrogative pressure). In one case a low score obtained by a female accuser on the Gudjonsson Suggestibility Scale was used by the Crown as an indication that the 'recovered memories' of childhood sexual abuse were genuine and true. The present author does not believe that a low score on the Gudjonsson Suggestibility Scale can be used as evidence that the allegations are necessarily true, because such beliefs and memories can be due to an internal process of influence rather than as a direct result of suggestions from persons, such as siblings, therapists or social workers. However, low susceptibility to suggestions during questioning, as measured by the Gudjonsson Suggestibility Scales, does not rule out the possibility that recovered memories of childhood sexual abuse could not be true. Each case must be considered on its own merit.

Recovered memories are held by the accuser with very firm conviction, although retractions sometimes do occur (Ofshe and Watter, 1994; Gudjonsson, 1997d). Recent research among members of the British False Memory Society (BFMS) indicates that only a small minority (7%) of their cases proceed to the Crown Court and when the accusation involves alleged recovered memories obtaining a conviction is extremely rare (Gudjonsson, 1997c). It seems that the police, lawyers, judges and jurors are very reluctant to accept the testimony of accusers who claim recovered memories of sexual abuse and as a result such cases are unlikely to succeed in court. A major problem with these cases is the absence of independent corroborative evidence and typically the only evidence presented involves the testimony of the accuser, which is easy to undermine due to its nature.

5.4 PSYCHOLOGICAL VULNERABILITIES

In the context of a police interview and testifying in court, the term 'psychological vulnerabilities' refers to psychological characteristics or mental states which render a witness prone, in certain circumstances, to providing information which is inaccurate, unreliable or misleading. On occasions misleading information can result in witnesses deliberately or unwittingly implicating an innocent person, and in the case of a suspect a false confession may result in a wrongful conviction.

No research has been conducted specifically into differences between suspects, witnesses and victims. These are likely to be overlapping groups in terms of psychological vulnerabilities. There has been a considerable amount of work written on the psychological vulnerabilities of suspects detained at police stations (Gudjonsson, 1992; Gudjonsson, Clare, Rutter and Pearse, 1993). No parallel research has been conducted on psychological vulnerabilities of witnesses and victims.

The forms of psychological vulnerability fall into four distinct groups. The first group can be labelled 'mental disorder', the second, 'abnormal mental state', the third, 'intellectual functioning', and the fourth 'personality characteristics'. Table 5.1 lists the kind of psychological vulnerabilities sometimes found in cases of mental disorder.

Table 5.1 The psychological vulnerabilities of persons with mental illness, learning disability, and personality disorder

Mental illness	Learning disability	Personality disorder
Faulty reality monitoring	Impaired intellectual capacity	Manipulative
Distorted perceptions and beliefs	Poor memory capacity	Lies readily
Guilt feeling proneness	Poor understanding of legal rights	Need for notoriety
Suspiciousness	Heightened suggestibility	Lack of concern about consequences
	Heightened acquiescence	Tendency towards confabulation
	Distorted perception of consequences	

5.4.1 Mental disorder

The term 'mental disorder' implies that the person suffers from diagnosable psychiatric problems, such as mental illness (e.g., schizophrenia, depressive illness), learning disability (also known as 'mental handicap'), and personality disorder.

In cases of mental illness, perceptions, emotions, judgment and self-control may be adversely affected. These factors can result in misleading information being provided to the police or when giving evidence in court. Those suffering from paranoid schizophrenia are sometimes difficult to interview because of their suspiciousness and lack of trust. Breakdown in 'reality monitoring' is an important feature of mental illness. This means that the ability of people to differentiate facts from fantasy is impaired. In extreme cases this may result in people believing that they have committed crimes of which they are totally innocent. Breakdown in reality monitoring also commonly occurs in everyday life in relation to the memory of thoughts, feelings and events and does not require the presence of mental illness. The presence of mental illness makes the breakdown in reality monitoring more pronounced, extensive and frequent.

Severe depressive illness, in extreme cases, can cause people to ruminate and implicate themselves falsely in criminal activity as a way of relieving strong feelings of free-floating guilt.

Persons with learning disability, whether witnesses, victims or suspects, may experience problems when being interviewed by the police and when giving evidence in court. This is due to the fact that their condition may cause inherent problems with regard to their capacity to give clear and detailed accounts of events during police interviewing and when testifying in court. Difficulties often arise because they may find it difficult to remember clearly the material event; they may become easily led and confused when questioned; they may have problems understanding the questions and articulating their answers; they may not fully appreciate the implications and consequences of their answers; and they may feel easily intimidated when questioned and cross-examined by people in authority.

A useful practical paper on identifying witnesses with learning disability and on how to maximise their performance during police interviewing has been produced by Bull and Cullen (1992) for the Scottish Crown Office. However, there has been little research carried out into the psychological vulnerabilities of witnesses who suffer from learning disability. Clare and Gudjonsson (1995) provide a detailed review of the area and conclude that persons with learning disability are disadvantaged in several respects, including the fact that they are less likely to understand their legal rights, they tend to be acquiescent and suggestible, and fail to fully appreciate the consequences of making a misleading statement.

The research of Tully and Cahill (1984), Clare and Gudjonsson (1993), and Perlman, Ericson, Esses, and Isaacs (1994) illustrates the types of problem that witnesses with learning disability have with reporting events by free recall and the extent to which they can be influenced by leading questions.

The studies of Dent (1986), Bull and Cullen (1992), and Perlman, Ericson, Esses and Isaacs (1994) provide useful guidance about the type of question format that is required when interviewing witnesses with learning disability in order to maximise the completeness of the account whilst minimising the amount of inaccurate recall. This includes avoiding the use of leading questions, allowing the witness to give his or her uninterrupted account, and asking open-ended questions.

The 'cognitive interview' techniques (Fisher and Geiselman, 1992) can be used to enhance the recall of witness, victims and cooperative suspects. There is no reason why it could not also be used with witnesses with learning disability. Indeed, Milne and Bull (1996) provide evidence that the cognitive interview is effective for children with learning disability. This is an area where psychological research has had major impact on police practice.

Gudjonsson and Gunn (1982), in a case at the Central Criminal Court, showed how the jury could differentiate between the reliable and unreliable aspects of the evidence of a woman with learning disability who had been a victim of serious sexual assault. The case indicates that persons with severe learning disability may well be capable of providing reliable evidence about factual matters that they clearly remember.

The concept of personality disorder proved to be an important psychiatric diagnosis in connection with disputed confessions in the case of Judith Ward, who was wrongfully convicted of terrorist crimes in 1974 and had her conviction overturned by the Court of Appeal in 1992 (Gudjonsson and MacKeith, 1997). She suffered from a personality disorder with histrionic features. A review of medical records concerning her period on remand prior to the trial revealed evidence of severe mental disorder which had not been disclosed by doctors to the trial court. Psychological assessment indicated a person of average intellectual abilities who scored highly on a test of suggestibility and exhibited a strong tendency to confabulate. (Confabulation refers to the tendency to fill gaps in one's memory by producing imagined material.) Gudjonsson (1992) has discussed the importance of confabulatory tendency in relation to personality disorder. Personality disorder may represent an important psychological vulnerability among some witnesses and suspects in that they appear to have a heightened tendency to confabulate in their memory recall (Smith and Gudjonsson, 1995) and more readily make false confessions as a part of their criminal lifestyle (Sigurdsson and Gudjonsson, 1997).

5.4.2 Abnormal mental state

Witnesses who are interviewed by the police or give evidence in court can suffer from an abnormal mental state, which may adversely influence the reliability of their testimony, without their having had a history of mental disorder. For example, in their recent study for the Royal Commission on Criminal Justice, Gudjonsson et al. (1993) found that about 20% of the suspects were reporting an abnormally high level of anxiety, whilst only about 7% were suffering from mental illness, such as schizophrenia or depressive illness.

In addition to a high level of anxiety witnesses may experience specific phobic symptoms, such as claustrophobia (e.g., irrational fear of being locked up in a confined space such as a police cell) or panic attacks (e.g., victims of crime experiencing a severe panic attack when attempting to describe what happened to them). In the Royal Commission study extreme fear of being locked up in a police cell was very rare (i.e., only one case out of 171), although many detainees complained that they were distressed about being locked up at the police station. The most commonly expressed anxiety was in relation to uncertainties over their predicament. Many of the detainees expressed concern over what was going to happen to them: they kept asking the researchers for information about their detention, and wanted to know when they were going to be interviewed by the police.

Some witnesses are in a state of bereavement when interviewed by the police, because of a loss of a loved one. This may sometimes render them vulnerable to giving unreliable statements because of feelings of guilt and subjective distress that typically accompanies the condition. For example, self-blame associated with a state of bereavement can make suspects unwittingly exaggerate their involvement in an offence.

Since provisions of the Police and Criminal Evidence Act 1984 came into force in January 1986, it is now rare that suspects are interviewed by the police when visibly under the influence of alcohol, although on occasions some alcoholics may be experiencing withdrawal symptoms while in detention. More commonly, suspects who are high on drugs when arrested may be withdrawing from the drugs while in custody and at the time they are interviewed by the police. Some drug addicts may be vulnerable to giving misleading accounts of events when being asked leading questions and placed under interrogative pressure, in addition to saying things in order to expedite their early release from custody.

In a recent study, Sigurdsson and Gudjonsson (1994) found that being interviewed by the police when suspects are under the influence of drugs or withdrawing from drugs causes them to feel confused. This does not mean that they are unfit to be interviewed, only that special care should be taken when interviewing them. Two studies have specifically investigated the effects of drug use and drug withdrawal on interrogative suggestibility, which suggests that opiate users undergoing opiate withdrawal are significantly more suggestible than opiate users who are no longer showing acute withdrawal symptoms (Murakami et al., 1996), and that there is a subgroup of vulnerable drug addicts who may be more suggestible when under the influence of opiates (Davison and Gossop, 1996).

In a follow-up to the Gudjonsson et al. (1993) study for the Royal Commission on Criminal Justice, Pearse et al. (1997) found that whether or not detainees reported taking illicit drugs in the 24 hours before the police interview was the only variable that was significantly associated with making a confession. One possible interpretation of this finding is that withdrawing from drugs encouraged them to make a confession as a way to facilitate their early release.

Some medical conditions (e.g., cardiovascular problems, diabetes, epilepsy) may result in a disturbed or abnormal mental state whilst the person is being interviewed by the police or giving evidence in court. This may adversely influence the accuracy and reliability of the person's account and his or her ability to function in a stressful situation.

5.4.3 Intellectual abilities
Impaired intellectual functioning, even when not amounting to mental handicap, can influence the ability of witnesses to understand questions, articulate their answers, and appreciate the implications of their answers.

There is evidence from our study for the Royal Commission on Criminal Justice (Gudjonsson et al. 1993) that many suspects interviewed at police stations are of low intelligence. The mean IQ for 160 suspects detained at two police stations was only 82, with the range 61–131. Almost 9% of the sample had a prorated IQ score below 70, compared with about 2% of the general population, one third (34%) had a prorated IQ score of 75 or below (i.e., bottom 5% of the general population).

It is probable that, to a certain extent, the IQ scores obtained represent an underestimate of the suspects' intellectual abilities due to the circumstances and context of testing (i.e., many of the suspects were anxiously waiting to be interviewed by the police at the time of testing). However, the findings highlight the fact that the police are commonly interviewing persons of low intellectual abilities.

The average intellectual capacity of witnesses and victims who are being interviewed by the police is not known. Therefore, it is not known how their intellectual functioning compares with that of suspects who are detained for an interview.

5.4.4 Personality characteristics

A number of personality characteristics may be important when evaluating the reliability of witnesses' accounts. The three most extensively researched variables are: suggestibility, acquiescence, and compliance (Gudjonsson, 1992; Clare and Gudjonsson, 1993).

Recently confabulation has been investigated in relation to the reliability of verbal accounts given by witnesses (Clare and Gudjonsson, 1993; Sigurdsson, Gudjonsson, Kolbeinsson and Petursson, 1994). Extreme confabulation has been found in some cases of personality disorder, as it was in the cases of Joe Giarratano (Gudjonsson, 1992) and Judith Ward (Gudjonsson and MacKeith, 1997). However, the study of Clare and Gudjonsson (1993) with subjects of low intelligence, and the recent study of Sigurdsson, Gudjonsson, Kolbeinsson, and Petursson (1994) with severely depressed mental patients, indicate that persons with mental disorder, such as learning disability and severe depression, have impaired memory recall for events, but the accuracy of their accounts is not undermined by a heightened tendency to confabulate.

'Interrogative suggestibility' refers to the tendency of people to yield to leading questions and submit to interrogative pressure. It can be measured by the use of a behavioural test, such as the Gudjonsson Suggestibility Scales. Here subjects are subtly misled in an experimental way and their responses are carefully monitored and compared with those of relative normative groups for the purpose of comparison. If the scores obtained are statistically infrequent, that is, they occur in fewer than 5% of the general population then the person can be described as being abnormally suggestible on the test (Gudjonsson, 1992).

The concept of 'compliance' overlaps, to a certain extent, with suggestibility, but it is more strongly associated with eagerness to please and the tendency to avoid conflict and confrontation. It is more difficult to measure compliance than suggestibility by behavioural observation and it is therefore typically measured by a self-report questionnaire (Gudjonsson, 1989). As a result, it is a measure that is easier to falsify than measures of interrogative suggestibility.

'Acquiescence' refers to the tendency of people, when in doubt, to answer questions in the affirmative irrespective of content. The reason for this tendency appears to be that they answer questions in the affirmative without properly listening to them or fully understanding them. Acquiescence is more strongly correlated with low intelligence then either suggestibility or compliance (Gudjonsson, 1992).

5.5 CONCLUSIONS

This chapter has reviewed the psychological vulnerabilities of persons with mental disorder. A number of factors can influence the reliability and credibility of the accounts given by witnesses, victims and suspects when they are interviewed by the police and when they give evidence in court. These include contextual and environmental factors, which may include the stress of appearing in court, feelings of intimidation, and fear or threat of retaliation. This chapter has focused on the psychological factors that can, under certain circumstances, make witnesses vulnerable to giving unreliable accounts of events. Differences exist between witnesses, victims and suspects, in terms of the nature and circumstances of their evidence, which have a bearing on their *motivation* to be open and truthful. As far as the *ability* to give reliable evidence is concerned, it is not known how these three groups may differ in their mental, intellectual and personality functioning. Within each group there are large individual differences which must not be ignored.

In many cases the courts rely heavily on the accounts of witnesses and victims. Therefore, careful interviewing of these persons is very important as well as the proper recording of the content of the interviews. It is likely that in the future audio or video recordings will be made of interviews of witnesses in major criminal cases, which will make it easier to evaluate properly the reliability and credibility of the accounts given to the police.

Problems sometimes arise when mentally disordered people are interviewed and required to give evidence. Their mental problems are not always easily recognised at the time they are interviewed by the police, and even when they are, police officers and the courts may not be familiar with the kind of factors that may undermine the reliability of their reporting of events.

Psychologists have an important contribution to make in assisting with the identification of factors that influence the reliability of witnesses' information and to develop interviewing techniques and procedures that maximise the reliability of witnesses' reports generally.

Key terms
Police interviewing; psychological vulnerability; mental disorder; suggestibility; compliance; acquiescence; confabulation.

References

Ashworth Inquiry (1992), *Report of the Committee of Inquiry into Complaints about Ashworth Hospital.* London: HMSO.

Bull, R. and Cullen, C. (1992), *Witnesses Who Have Mental Handicaps.* Edinburgh: Crown Office.

Clare, I.C.H. and Gudjonsson, G.H. (1993), 'Interrogative suggestibility, confabulation, and acquiescence in people with mild learning difficulties (mental handicap): implications for reliability during police interrogation', *British Journal of Clinical Psychology,* vol. 32, pp. 295–301.

Clare, I.C.H. and Gudjonsson, G.H. (1995) 'The vulnerability of suspects with intellectual disabilities during police interviews: a review and experimental study of decision-making', *Mental Handicap Research,* vol. 8, pp. 110–28.

Clare, I.C.H., Gudjonsson, G.H. and Harari, P. (1998), 'The current police caution in England and Wales: how easy it is to understand', *Journal of Community and Applied Social Psychology,* vol. 8, 323–29.

Davison, S.E. and Gossop, M. (1996) 'The problem of interviewing drug addicts in custody: a study of interrogative suggestibility and compliance', *Psychology, Crime and Law,* vol. 2, pp. 185–95.

Dent, H. (1986), 'An experimental study of the effectiveness of different techniques of questioning mentally handicapped child witnesses', *British Journal of Clinical Psychology,* vol. 25, pp. 13–17.

Fisher, R.P. and Geiselman, R.E. (1992), *Memory-enhancing Techniques for Investigative Interviewing: The Cognitive Interview.* Springfield, IL: Thomas.

Gudjonsson, G.H. (1989), 'Compliance in an interrogation situation: A new scale', *Personality and Individual Differences,* vol. 10, pp. 535–40.

Gudjonsson, G.H. (1990), 'Self-deception and other-deception in forensic assessment', *Personality and Individual Differences,* vol. 11, pp. 219–25.

Gudjonsson, G.H. (1992), *The Psychology of Interrogations, Confessions and Testimony.* Chichester: John Wiley and Sons.

Gudjonsson, G.H. (1995), '"I'll help you boys as much as I can" — how eagerness to please can result in a false confession', *Journal of Forensic Psychiatry,* vol. 6, 333–42.

Gudjonsson, G.H. (1997a) 'Accusations by adults of childhood sexual abuse: a survey of the members of the British False Memory Society (BFMS)', *Applied Cognitive Psychology,* vol. 11, pp. 3–18.

Gudjonsson, G.H. (1997b), 'The members of the BFMS, the accusers and their siblings', *The Psychologist,* vol. 10, pp. 111–15.

Gudjonsson, G.H. (1997c), 'Members of the British False Memory Society: the legal consequences of the accusations for the families', *Journal of Forensic Psychiatry,* vol. 8, pp. 348–56.

Gudjonsson, G.H. (1997d), 'The false memory syndrome and the retractors. Methodological and theoretical issues', *Psychological Inquiry,* vol. 8, pp. 296–9.

Gudjonsson, G.H., Clare, I., Rutter, S. and Pearse, J. (1993), *Persons at Risk during Interviews in Police Custody: the Identification of Vulnerabilities* (Royal Commission on Criminal Justice). London: HMSO.

Gudjonsson, G.H. and Gunn, J. (1982), 'The competence and reliability of a witness in a criminal court', *British Journal of Psychiatry*, vol. 141, pp. 624–7.

Gudjonsson, G.H. and MacKeith, J. (1994), 'Learning disability and the Police and Criminal Evidence Act 1984. Protection during investigative interviewing: a video-recorded false confession to double murder', *Journal of Forensic Psychiatry*, vol. 5, pp. 35–49.

Gudjonsson, G.H. and MacKeith, J. (1997), *Disputed Confessions and the Criminal Justice System* (Maudsley Discussion Paper No. 2). London: Institute of Psychiatry.

Gudjonsson, G.H. and Sigurdsson, J.F. (1994), 'How frequently do false confessions occur? An empirical study among prison inmates', *Psychology, Crime and Law*, vol. 1, pp. 21–6.

Leavitt, F. (1997), 'False attribution of suggestibility to explain recovered memory of childhood sexual abuse following extended amnesia', *Child Abuse and Neglect*, vol. 21, pp. 265–72.

Milne, R. and Bull, R. (1996), 'Interviewing children with mild learning disability with the cognitive interview', in N.K. Clark and G.M. Stephenson (eds), *Investigative and Forensic Decision Making* (Issues in Criminological and Legal Psychology, No. 26). Leicester: British Psychological Society, pp. 44–51.

Murakami, A.T., Edelman, R.J. and Davis, P.E. (1996), 'Interrogative suggestibility in opiates users'. *Addiction*, vol. 91, pp. 1365–73.

Ofshe, R. and Watters, E. (1994), *Making Monsters. False Memories, Psychotherapy and Sexual Hysteria*. New York: Charles Scribner's Sons.

Pearse, J. and Gudjonsson, G.H. (1996), 'How appropriate are appropriate adults?' *Journal of Forensic Psychiatry*, vol. 7, pp. 570–80.

Pearse, J., Gudjonsson, G.H., Clare, I.C.H. and Rutter, S. (1997) 'Police interviewing and psychological vulnerabilities: predicting the likelihood of a confession', *Journal of Community and Applied Social Psychology*.

Perlman, N.B., Ericson, K.I., Esses, V.M., and Isaacs, B.J. (1994), 'The developmentally handicapped witnesses. Competency as a function of question format', *Law and Human Behavior*, vol. 18, pp. 171–87.

Shepherd, E. (1991), 'Resistance in police interviews: the contribution of police perceptions and behaviour'. Paper presented at the Division of Criminological and Legal Psychology Conference, University of Kent at Canterbury, 3–5 January 1991.

Shepherd, E. (1993), 'Resistance in police interviews: the contribution of police perceptions and behaviour', in E. Shepherd (ed.), *Aspects of Police Interviewing* (Issues in Criminological and Legal Psychology, No. 18). Leicester: British Psychological Society, pp. 5–12.

Shepherd, E.W., Mortimer, A.K., and Mobasheri, R. (1995), 'The police caution: comprehension and perceptions in the general population', *Expert Evidence*, vol. 4, pp. 60–7.

Sigurdsson, J.F. and Gudjonsson, G.H. (1994), 'Alcohol and drug intoxication during police interrogation and the reasons why suspects confess to the police', *Addiction*, vol. 89, pp. 985–97.

Sigurdsson, J. and Gudjonsson, G. (1997), 'The criminal history of "false confessors" and other prison inmates', *Journal of Forensic Psychiatry*, vol. 18, pp. 447–55.

Sigurdsson, E., Gudjonsson, G.H., Kolbeinsson, H., and Petursson, H. (1994), 'The effects of electroconvulsive therapy and depression on confabulation, memory processing, and suggestibility, *Nordic Journal of Psychiatry*, vol. 48, pp. 443–51.

Smith, P. and Gudjonsson, G.H. (1995), 'The relationship of mental disorder to suggestibility and confabulation among forensic inpatients', *Journal of Forensic Psychiatry*, vol. 6, pp. 499–515.

Tully, B. and Cahill, D. (1984), *Police Interviewing of the Mentally Handicapped. An Experimental Study*. London: Police Foundation.

Undeutsch, U. (1992), 'Statement reality analysis', in A. Trankell (ed.), *Reconstructing the Past: The Role of Psychologists in Criminal Trials*. Deventer: Kluwer, pp. 26–56.

Recommended reading

Ashworth Inquiry, *Report of the Committee of Inquiry into Complaints about Ashworth Hospital*. London: HMSO, 1992.

Gudjonsson, G.H. (1992), *The Psychology of Interrogations, Confessions and Testimony*. Chichester: John Wiley and Sons.

Gudjonsson, G.H. and MacKeith, J. (1997), *Disputed Confessions and the Criminal Justice System* (Maudsley Discussion Paper No. 2). London: Institute of Psychiatry.

Gudjonsson, G., Clare, I., Rutter, S. and Pearse, J., *Persons at Risk during Interviews in Police Custody: the Identification of Vulnerabilities* (Royal Commission on Criminal Justice) (1993). London: HMSO.

Editors' notes

'Mental disorder' needs to be widely interpreted. Where a witness has previously been diagnosed as suffering from a mental illness or disorder, the discovery of the relevant history will be comparatively straightforward through conventional disclosure of medical records. Where, however, the condition is suspected but as yet undiscovered the discovery process is likely to be fraught with difficulty, especially when the witness is uncooperative and disinclined to participate in diagnostic endeavours.

In preparing the defence an expert psychologist or psychiatrist will initially be instructed to review any pre-existing history and symptoms shown by the witness during the investigation and to consider whether these factors might have caused the witness during interview to impart, for example, misleading information. If a useful inquiry is to be carried out, much will depend, again, on the integrity of investigators' records. Where a vulnerability is identified and where the expert considers, on scientific criteria, that memory distortion may have occurred, it may be necessary for evidence to be given which explains the implications in relation to the witness's reliability and credibility. This will depend on whether the fact-finding body is capable of comprehending the concepts involved on common knowledge criteria.

CHAPTER SIX

Witness testimony in sleep and dream-related contexts

Peter Fenwick

Allegations of assault and their relationship to sleep can be divided into three categories. In the first the perpetrator of the alleged assault is asleep and during sleep carries out behaviour which is interpreted as being criminal. In the second category the victim is asleep and the perpetrator is awake and commits an alleged sexual assault on the non-consenting partner. A third category includes those alleged sexual assaults in which a disorder of sleep or a psychiatric illness may lead to accusations of sexual assault. These three situations raise quite separate problems at law.

6.1 INCIDENTS IN WHICH THE OFFENDER IS ASLEEP AND THE VICTIM IS AWAKE

In order to understand the significance and likely truthfulness of a defendant's account of such an episode it is necessary to have a detailed knowledge of the structure and physiology of sleep and to obtain an accurate account of the precise timing of events.

6.1.1 Structure of sleep

There are two major stages of sleep, rapid eye movement (REM) sleep, and non-REM sleep. REM sleep is the phase in which dreaming as we normally understand it, occurs. These two stages of sleep have a different physiology and different states of awareness, and follow each other in approximately 90-minute cycles throughout the night.

6.1.1.1 Non-REM sleep Sleep onset is followed by four stages of non-REM sleep as the EEG (electrical activity of the brain as measured by the electroencephalogram) progressively slows and the depth of sleep increases. Light sleep comprises stages 1 and 2, slow wave sleep, stages 3 and 4. In the first cycle of sleep stage 2 is reached after a few minutes, and may persist for 10–20 minutes, after which stage 3 sleep is likely to supervene, with a transition into stage 4. This cycle ends after about 90 minutes. Most stage 3 and 4 sleep occurs in this first cycle. The latter cycles of the night are mainly stage 2 sleep. During non-REM sleep muscle tone decreases, but movements, even complex movements, are possible because the body is not paralysed. Normal sleeping movements are usually simple and stereotyped, but they may become complex as the sleeper awakens. It is thus possible to have sexually responsive movements to sexual stimulation.

Erections rarely occur during non-REM sleep. Sleep talking occurs in stage 2 sleep, and sleepwalking and night terrors in stages 2, 3 and 4 sleep.

Sleep talking usually consists of short phrases which are well-constructed, meaningful and often relating to daytime events. 'John, come over here.' Although often mumbled, sleep talking may be quite loud and sometimes spoken with emotion. In responsive sleep talking it is possible to lead the sleeper with questions and elicit an answer which is usually relevant to the context of the question, and may occasionally be quite detailed. The eyes may be open or opening and closing.

6.1.1.2 REM (dreaming) sleep The first period of dreaming sleep occurs about 90 minutes after sleep onset and usually lasts for about 10 minutes. Subsequent periods of dreaming sleep lengthen as the night progresses. Morning awakening is usually from dreaming sleep.

During dreaming sleep the body is paralysed and movement is limited to small muscle twitches of the extremities. Large body movements may occur but are unusual. Penile erections and ejaculation occur in men and vaginal lubrication in women during REM sleep.

6.1.2 Mentation and awakening during REM and non-REM sleep
Mentation in REM sleep is that of classical dreaming, usually narrative, complex, and frequently containing emotion. This is also the phase of nightmares, during which the sleeper frequently feels he or she is trying to escape but is unable to move. This feeling is due to the true muscle paralysis which occurs in REM sleep. Someone in REM sleep can be awakened easily and rapidly into clear consciousness, without confusion, usually remembering his or her dreams at least for a short time.

Mental content in non-REM sleep is more fragmented than that of REM dreams, with little storyline, usually consisting of feelings of movement or words. It is difficult to arouse people in stage 3 or 4 sleep. They can be pinched, have lights shone in their eyes, shaken or moved without awakening. The awakening from non-REM sleep is slow and confusional. Over a number of minutes the sleeper's level of consciousness gradually lightens and complex responsive movements may occur.

6.1.3 Characteristics of sleepwalking and night terrors
Sleepwalking is known as a state-transition disorder and usually occurs on the transition from stage 3 or 4 sleep to dreaming sleep and thus is most likely to

occur about 90 minutes after sleep onset. It also occurs on the transition between stage 2 and dreaming sleep, in the latter third of the night. Sleepwalking is thought to be genetically determined, most often starts in childhood, occurs during adolescence, and in a few people persists into adulthood. About 1% of the adult population are thought to sleepwalk, although between the ages of 10 and 14 about 8% of the population will sleepwalk. Thus, sleepwalking is mainly a condition of childhood.

Very complex behaviour is possible during sleepwalking. The sleepwalker may get out of bed, dress, open windows, walk round the house, and even go out into the street. The latter part of a sleepwalking episode is similar to a dissociated mental state, and it is probably during this state that the very complex behaviour such as riding motorbikes or driving cars which is reported in the literature takes place.

Case history 6.1   Riding without a licence
A young man with a history of sleepwalking went to a party one freezing February evening, came back and went to bed. About 80 minutes after going to sleep he got out of bed and went out naked into the garden, where he took his motorbike, which was neither insured nor taxed and rode off into the night. A passing police car followed the motorbike with its nude rider for about two miles. The bike then turned into a ditch. When the police asked the rider lying on the ground what had happened he replied, 'Where am I and who are you?'

In night terrors, which have the same features as sleepwalking, there is a very strong emotion of fear, usually unaccompanied by any narrative dream account, although on being awoken the subject will describe an evil blackness or a dark space with closing walls, full of danger and fear. A night terror is frightening for an observer who will see the sleeper sit up in bed, eyes open wide, pupils dilated, and may scream repeatedly. The sleeper may arise from the bed, rush through the house terrified, jump down steps, causing injury, run through plate-glass doors, etc. A sufferer who is not woken during an episode will remember little if anything on awakening subsequently.

6.1.4   Violent behaviour during sleepwalking
Violent behaviour is extremely common during sleepwalking. It is not unusual for the partner of a sleepwalker or a sleeper experiencing a night terror to report kicks, hits, punches or even attempted strangulation. It is thus not surprising that a number of these cases have come to court. The author has appeared for the defence in several cases in which a sleepwalker has carried out a violent offence while asleep which resulted in either death or serious injury.

Case history 6.2   Marital assault
A man with a long history of sleepwalking since childhood started kicking and hitting his wife during his sleep. His wife sought medical help for him but his sleepwalking continued. Unable to stand it any longer she moved out of the marital bedroom, but occasionally he still came into her room and hit her.

Finally she decided to lock the door. On the evening in question he had been asleep for about an hour when his wife became aware of him banging on her bedroom door. The banging became louder until with a crash he broke the door down, rushed into the room and assaulted his wife. The case came to court and it was accepted that this was a sleepwalking episode.

6.1.4 Sexual behaviour during sleepwalking

Sexual behaviour can be carried out during non-REM sleep, and is associated with sleepwalking. The sexual behaviour can be either simple or complex and will typically last for a few minutes. In the simple cases the sleepwalker may caress or stroke a partner's body; these movements may sometimes be more sexually directed, with groping or caressing of the partner's genitals. Sexual intercourse is not reported in sleepwalkers but because it is now accepted that the somnambulistic episode merges into a dissociated state, on theoretical grounds it is perfectly possible for a sleepwalker in the later stages of somnambulism to become sexually aroused and have intercourse. In the more complex cases a sleepwalker will leave the bed and if there are other sleepers in the house may get into bed with them or may interact in a sexual way with other members of the household.

Sometimes the behaviour may appear sexual though it is simply a by-product of the sleepwalking episode. Many people sleep in the nude and so may sleepwalk naked in public, thus offending public decency.

Memory is impaired and dream accounts given by sleepwalkers are usually impoverished because of both the confusion and memory impairment.

Someone accused of a sexual assault during sleepwalking may know nothing of the alleged assault. The accused's memory usually starts after waking, when the episode is over. Tiredness, alcohol and emotional upset are triggers for a sleepwalking episode.

There is only a limited literature on sleepwalking and sexual offending. Accusations of sexual assault by sleepwalkers have been reported in the German literature (Sours et al., 1963; Langeluddeke, 1955). However, in one case reported the defendant had an erection, so it is more likely that this was a straightforward homosexual episode with subsequent denial (see below).

6.1.5 Sleepwalking in the nude

The following three cases illustrate the interaction of the sleepwalker with the social situation in which he finds himself. The outcome of a sleepwalking episode, and whether it leads to a criminal charge, depends not on the sleepwalking behaviour, but on how this is interpreted by those who witness the episode.

Case history 6.3

A 26-year-old woman patient of the author was on a site visit with her company. She suffered from complex sleepwalking episodes and had a family history of sleepwalking. She was tired after her journey and retired to bed at 10.00 p.m. after a drinking session. At 11.00 p.m. she was seen walking naked through the bar, where her colleagues were still drinking, into the adjoining swimming-pool area, where she urinated in a corner. She tells me that her colleagues were very tolerant the next morning. No formal complaint was made to the police.

Case history 6.4
In a similar case, a 36-year-old man, who had a long history of sleepwalking with frequent complex sleepwalking episodes, was sent by his company to a refresher course. He was tired and retired to bed early. He always slept in the nude. At about 11.00 p.m. he arose, opened his first-floor window, and jumped out, fortunately on to the low roof of an outbuilding. He jumped off this and then walked out of the back entrance of the hotel into the main street of the town, quite naked. He reports a confused feeling that aliens of some sort were involved and that their craft had landed with blue flashing lights. He was picked up by the police and taken to the police station, where he explained that he was a sleepwalker and the last thing he knew he was going to sleep. With the confirmation of these facts, the police let him go, loaned him a pair of boxer shorts and returned him to his hotel. No complaint had been made about his behaviour.

Case history 6.5
A quite different outcome occurred in a case in which a formal complaint was made. In 1991 Buchanan reported a case of a 27-year-old single man with a long history of sleepwalking who was charged with indecent exposure. That evening he had consumed 12 single whiskies, and retired to bed at about 10.30 p.m. An hour later he was spotted by a neighbour walking naked up and down their common balcony. The neighbour contacted the police and when they arrived the man was found in bed. He was arrested, taken to a police station and claimed to have no recollection of events. He appeared in court, was convicted of indecent exposure and bound over to keep the peace. This case typically illustrates a sleep automatism, where the sleeper is unaware of his behaviour, which is, however, interpreted as being antisocial.

6.1.6   Sleepwalking with a sexual element
Several cases of sleepwalking with a sexual element in the behaviour have been seen by the author.

Case history 6.6
A young man with a long history of sleepwalking was under considerable stress, had drunk a pint of beer, and came home exhausted at 11.00 p.m. He lived on the third floor of an apartment block, next door to a young woman whom he knew only by sight.

The defendant went to sleep leaving his window open. About one hour later, still asleep, he climbed out along a ledge which led to the open kitchen window of the next-door flat. He walked into the girl's bedroom where she was asleep with her boyfriend. He lay down beside her bed, his hand under the bedclothes against her genitals, and went to sleep.

The girl woke up to feel his hand and saw him asleep beside her. She shouted to her boyfriend, the kerfuffle woke the defendant, who in a confusional state stood up, wandered out of the room and back on to the ledge. He fell three storeys into a flowerbed but survived the fall.

This case has all the major features of a sleepwalking incident. He had a long history of sleepwalking, was tired and stressed and had taken alcohol that evening. The incident occurred about one hour after sleep onset. Most important was his bizarre behaviour in the girl's room and his confusional arousal. However, at the trial the jury had difficulty in understanding how such a complex act could be carried out during sleep and brought in a verdict of guilty.

Case history 6.7

Another case involved an alleged homosexual assault by a young airman who again had a long history of sleepwalking. That evening the defendant was tired and had had several pints of beer. He had been asleep for one hour when his room-mate came to bed, and the alleged assault took place one hour after that. Both men slept naked. The roommate woke to find a hand over his genitals. He turned over several times to avoid the hand, but it reappeared each time. Eventually he grabbed it, pinioned its owner to the ground and found he was kneeling on his fellow officer, who showed evidence of some confusion, repeating, 'What has happened, what's going on?' The room-mate went to report the incident and the defendant immediately went back to sleep.

At the court martial his wife gave evidence of frequent complex sleepwalking episodes, particularly when he was tired, during which he sometimes caressed her genitals. The court accepted that it was highly unlikely that a purposeful, homosexual assault would have taken place without the defendant being sexually aroused. The timing of the event was suggestive of a sleepwalking episode. It was also accepted that during the assault the defendant did not have an erection and this was taken as supportive evidence. The court martial dismissed the case.

6.1.7 Sudden arousals from sleep

The ease of awakening and clarity on awakening will depend on the phase of sleep from which the sleeper is woken. From REM sleep a sleeper usually wakes rapidly into clear consciousness, frequently with dream imagery, while an awakening from slow wave sleep leaves some degree of confusion. Awakenings from stages 1 and 2 sleep leave the feeling that one has slept too long, or not long enough. Awakenings from stages 3 and 4 are quite different. The sleeper may be very difficult to arouse, memory may be impaired and the mental state confused. Thus a sleep-deprived house officer on call may finally awaken to his emergency beep, go to the ward, treat the patient, write up the case, return to bed and to sleep and remember nothing of all this next morning. This is also true of sleepwalking episodes which occur from this phase of sleep.

There is a large literature, dating back to the seventeenth century, describing cases of sudden arousal from sleep which have led to criminal prosecution. The author had one such case. A young clerk had been drinking, though not heavily, and was returning home by train. He had been asleep for half to three-quarters of an hour when some rowdy adolescents entered the carriage, began throwing a cushion and inadvertently struck the sleeping clerk. He stood up, walked into the middle aisle, took a penknife (which he used at work) from his pocket, opened it, slashed the neck of one of the boys quite severely, and went to stand by the door of the moving train. A passenger came up to him and said, 'You shouldn't have done that'. To which he replied, confusedly, 'Done what?' While police were being called the assailant asked the train driver what had happened.

This case illustrates the major points of a sudden confusional arousal. The sleeper must be in slow wave sleep, preferably stages 3 or 4. There should be evidence of confusion, there is seldom if ever dream imagery, and there should be a disorder of memory for the event.

6.2   ALLEGED ASSAULTS IN WHICH THE ASSAILANT IS AWAKE AND THE VICTIM IS ASLEEP

A different category of sleep-related offences are those alleged rapes or sexual assaults in which the assailant is awake and the victim is asleep. If the defendant admits that the victim was unquestionably asleep and did not wake up during intercourse (often because of a high alcohol intake), then the offence is one of rape. The only question is whether or not it is possible for a sleeping person to have intercourse and not wake up. Provided intercourse occurs in stage 3 or 4 sleep it is possible that they may not alert. These offences are medically straightforward and will not be considered further.

6.2.1   Responsive sexual behaviour during sleep

A charge of rape may be brought because the victim claims to have been asleep during intercourse, though the assailant claims that the victim was not asleep and had indicated consent. If consent could reasonably have been assumed by the assailant, then the sexual act would not constitute a rape.

The question of rape will turn, first, on whether the victim was actually asleep, and secondly on the details of the assailant's behaviour and on whether the victim's behavioural responses are part of a sleep behavioural repertoire and could have been carried out during sleep. If the assailant stimulated the victim during REM sleep, the victim would wake immediately and that would be the end of the matter. However, should the approach occur during the deeper stages of non-REM sleep, it is unlikely that the sleeper would awake immediately.

Sexual approaches to sleeping victims entail an initial contact, usually genital stroking, cunnilingus, or talking. Genital stimulation may produce responsive movements in the sleeper, and speech may elicit responsive sleep talking. The sleeper may appear to cooperate in the removal of undergarments by raising his or her hips. By this time the victim will have started to alert and thus his or her bodily movements can become more complex. French kissing can elicit responsive tongue movements by the victim. Spontaneous tongue movements, which occur naturally during sleep, may also be interpreted by the assailant as sexual responsiveness indicating consent. By the time penetration occurs, the victim will usually rouse, and frequently will have simple sexual imagery, usually non-erotic.

Alcohol may play a major part. First, it will speed the descent into stage 3/4 sleep, and prolong this stage. Secondly, in high doses it affects memory recall, the alcoholic blackout. The first of these effects will make arousing the sleeper more difficult, and thus sexual foreplay may continue for a considerable time before arousal. The second effect can lead to a marked discrepancy between the stories of the victim and the assailant. The victim may claim to remember everything till he or she crashed out. There is then a memory gap until he or she came to, either during or wet after intercourse. The assailant reports that during this gap consent was given and after variable foreplay sexual intercourse took place.

Two cases illustrate the intricacies of these issues.

Case history 6.8
The incident occurred in New Zealand at a house party where the guests were sleeping over. The case (*R v Cassidy*) was heard in 1994, went to appeal, and a retrial. The victim, a young woman, had indicated no sexual interest in Cassidy during the evening. She retired to bed, having had a number of drinks, and fell asleep without undressing. She was joined by her flatmate who fell asleep beside her. The victim knew no more till she found herself being struck on the arm by her flatmate, who asked what was going on. She awoke to a non-erotic dream of sexual intercourse, to find a man on top of her. Her flatmate reports that she visibly jumped when spoken to.

The defendant had drunk heavily throughout the evening, and stated that when he entered the room the victim appeared to be awake. He knelt beside her and started talking to her and reports that she answered him and that her eyes were partially opening and closing while they talked. He then kissed her and she responded with tongue movements. He continued kissing her and caressed her breasts, and claimed that she did not move except for the tongue movements. He then removed her underpants, and put his fingers in her vagina. She did not move, but let him do it. He then had cunnilingus with her and felt her moving. He then hopped on top of the woman and placed his penis in her vagina. She placed her hands around his shoulders. It was at this point that her girlfriend awoke and hit her. The victim then became aware of the defendant on top of her and pushed him off. She reported that she remembers coming out of a deep sleep in which she was having a dream of non-erotic sex.

In court it was accepted that had the woman been asleep she could not have responded by complex kissing movements. The jury brought in a verdict of guilty of sexual assault.

The defence appealed on the grounds that the experts involved in the case did not have sufficient knowledge of sleeping behaviour to be able to give an accurate opinion, and no such expert could be found in New Zealand. The appeal was granted.

Assuming both people are telling the truth, the case turns on whether it is possible for a sleeping person to be as strongly stimulated as this woman was, and yet not awaken; also whether a sleeping woman could make responsive movements that could reasonably be interpreted by the assailant as consensual. There was no suggestion that the victim had awoken during the sex play and allowed it to continue voluntarily.

My opinion was that the woman showed no behaviours which were outside the range that could be expected from a sleeping person who was being sexually stimulated. Responsive sleep talking with opening and closing eyes is certainly possible during sleep. Tongue movements are common during sleep and could easily be interpreted as responsive. Movements responsive to sexual stimulation can also occur during sleep.

The jury at the retrial found the defendant guilty of rape, after being told that they could not take alcohol into consideration. The implication of the jury's question is presumably that a sober man would not have attempted sexual intercourse with a girl he did not know when she was sleeping with a partner he could not identify, and possibly that if sober he would not have interpreted sleeping behaviour as consent. It seems reasonable to assume that the jury did accept the medical evidence that complex behaviour in sleep was possible.

Case history 6.9
The second case illustrates the interaction of alcohol with sleep onset. At a party, the victim had a blood alcohol level of over 200 mg per 100 ml. She went voluntarily with the defendant to his room where she sat on one bed and he on the other. They started talking and then the victim admits to 'crashing out'. She knew nothing until she woke up on the other bed having intercourse with the defendant. She had no memory of moving on to the other bed and denied giving consent.

The defendant described the conversation continuing and her coming voluntarily on to his bed. He started to stimulate her sexually and continually asked her if she was enjoying it, to which she always mumbled an affirmative reply. This proceeded through the normal sexual foreplay until he entered her, when she suddenly pushed him away, told him to stop and ran out of the room.

In court, his account of the events was accepted and the case was dismissed.

6.3 ALTERATIONS IN BEHAVIOUR FOLLOWING ABNORMAL DREAMING

There are two conditions associated with dreaming in which the dreamer may confuse dreams with reality. The first of these is a false awakening. In a false awakening the dreamer dreams of having awoken and of having set about his or her day-to-day activities. It is difficult for the dreamer to recognise that this is a dream as false awakenings have a much more real quality than an ordinary dream. It is not uncommon in a sleep laboratory for a sleeping subject to say that he or she got up in the night and went round to talk to the recording technician to pass the time, when the record shows that the subject has not stirred all night. Multiple false awakenings in the same night may also occur: the dreamer awakes into a dream world, realises that he or she is still asleep and has another false awakening, sometimes repeating this process several times before the final real awakening in the morning.

Often associated with false awakenings are lucid dreams. A lucid dream is a dream in which the dreamer knows that he or she is dreaming but has the capacity to control the dream voluntarily. The technique for lucid dreaming can be learnt, but they do occur spontaneously, particularly if the sleep cycle is allowed to continue longer into the morning so the dreams are occurring on a rising level of alertness. A lucid dream can also have the quality of the awakened state, although the dreamer knows it is a dream. Some lucid dreamers find it very difficult to distinguish between the real world and the dream world and have to use strategies of behaviour to reassure themselves that they are not dreaming and are awake. A patient of mine would turn the steering wheel of her car so as to go towards the pavement. She could always tell by the movement of the car if she was dreaming or awake. If she was dreaming she would gently pull back on the steering wheel so the car would rise in the air and fly across the rooftops. Clearly this technique has its risks. As far as the law is concerned it is perfectly possible for a lucid dreamer to make false accusations against other people on the basis of his or her lucid dream life.

6.4 OTHER SLEEP DISORDERS

6.4.1 Narcolepsy
The narcoleptic tetrad (literally meaning 'four symptoms') is a genetic condition with four major symptoms: excessive sleepiness, hypnagogic (on the borders of going to sleep) and/or hypnopompic (on the borders of waking) hallucinations, sleep paralysis, and cataplexy (Lishman, 1987). Sleep paralysis is a condition in which the sleeper 'awakes' into a hallucinatory world in which he or she is paralysed. Cataplexy, which is the sudden loss of muscle tone associated with emotion, is not relevant to this chapter and will be discussed no further.

Narcolepsy is defined as excessive sleepiness. The patient has an overwhelming desire to sleep during the day. The urge is so overwhelming that patients will fall asleep while standing, will have to find a corner to sleep in on the street, or will fall asleep while eating. It is possible that when patients with narcolepsy are asleep in public places they might be victims of assaults. A sufferer may fall asleep during sexual foreplay and so be the unwitting victim of rape.

6.4.2 Hypnagogic imagery
As patients with narcolepsy become sleepy during the day, hypnagogic imagery may become prominent and intrusive. The imagery is usually rich in colour and content and in some patients the strength of these hallucinatory

experiences is such that they can be grafted on to their real experiences. If the hallucinatory experiences are compelling and rich enough then the sufferer may not be able to distinguish between the hallucinatory world and reality. It has only recently been recognised that the syndrome of daytime hallucinations which are prominent and intrusive are sometimes confused with schizophrenia. These prominent experiences only occur in a minority of patients with narcolepsy, but atypical and particularly rich visual hallucinations should always bring the diagnosis of narcolepsy to mind.

Hypnagogic and hypnopompic hallucinations may occur in normal people as well as being part of the narcoleptic tetrad.

6.4.3 Sleep paralysis
During sleep paralysis, a person alerts from sleep or dreaming into a hallucinatory world, unable to move. Imagery is invariably frightening, differs between cultures, and tends to follow fashions. In the middle ages, people were visited by incubi and succubi (male and female malignant presences). The vogue changed to giant rats, and the contemporary night visitor tends to be an alien from outer space. A person suffering sleep paralysis awakes to feel something heavy and evil lying on his or her chest constricting breathing. This has sometimes been called the 'Old Hag' visitation. The sufferer is paralysed and struggles desperately to be free. A sufferer may believe that he or she is the victim of abduction and sexual experimentation. If the patient is sleeping in a room with someone else, this person may become involved in the imagery and accused of sexual assault.

6.4.4 Sexual assault in narcoleptic sufferers
Vivid hallucinations may occur at any time of the day or night in patients with narcolepsy. The excessive drive to sleep leads to decreased alertness, the occurrence of hypnagogic and hypnopompic hallucinations, or often to dreaming sleep (REM) at sleep onset. It is also possible for the sleeping narcoleptic patient to enter a stage of sleep paralysis soon after sleep onset. All these states can lead to the presence of vivid hallucinations with or without paralysis. It is not unusual for a young narcoleptic patient to feel that he or she is being interfered with by another member of the family. Often the accounts are so straightforward that the patient is believed and action may be taken against the wrongfully accused family member (Hayes, 1992). Sometimes the hallucinations may be even more dramatic, the sufferer complaining of being sexually assaulted, drugged, restrained, and sometimes made to walk to waiting cars or even waiting spaceships. They then complain of sexual interference which may vary from simple groping through to orgiastic behaviour. They may feel that members of the family, colleagues at work, unknown strangers, or aliens, take part in these events.

6.4.5 Diagnosis of narcolepsy
If narcolepsy is suspected, its diagnosis is important. A good clinical history is important, and all four symptoms of the tetrad should be sought. There is now a specific genetic profile which should be looked for. The HLA-DR2

genetic marker is present in about 75% of cases. However, its absence does not mean that the patient does not have narcolepsy. A more reliable diagnosis is given by the genetic marker HLA-DRw 15.PQw6: but it has to be stressed that this too is not present in every case. Although sporadic cases of narcolepsy do occur, usually there is a strong family history. The multiple sleep latency test should always be used in diagnosis. Every two hours the patient's EEG is recorded while he or she is lying down, and the time taken to go to sleep is noted. The patient is then woken up and allowed to roam around the laboratory until the next latency test. Patients with narcolepsy will be asleep within five minutes on each occasion. Many narcoleptic patients will go straight into dreaming sleep and this is an additional strong diagnostic feature.

6.4.6 Differential diagnosis

If possible, a careful medical history should be taken from a complainant alleging sexual assault. The exact circumstances of the assault are important and attention should be given to the minute details of the episode. Although it may be difficult for the defence to acquire the victim's medical records, it is important for the previous medical history to be obtained. To illustrate this, I was recently acting for the defence in a case of alleged rape. The victim, who was sleeping in the same room as a young man, claimed that she remembered being woken by him in the early morning. She went back to sleep and awoke to find him on top of her having sexual intercourse. He stated that he had been invited into her bed and invited to have intercourse. The police took blood samples from both, and hers showed some alcohol, but also Valium. The GP's records showed that she had not been prescribed this. In court it became apparent that she was using drugs illicitly and thus was liable to dissociate more easily and not remember her behaviour. More important, the records showed that as a child she had taken a knife to her father during a sleepwalking (dissociative) episode. It was clear that on the occasion of the 'rape' she had acted in a dissociated state and invited the defendant into bed with her.

6.4.7 Other psychiatric conditions

Other psychiatric conditions should be considered if the circumstances suggest that a straightforward explanation is unlikely. Hallucinations from narcolepsy have already been discussed, but hallucinations are common in schizophrenia and in some forms of drug abuse, and these diagnoses should be considered. Patients with the post-traumatic stress disorder may have flashbacks of a particular traumatic episode. This episode may be either so vivid or so changed that it seems to the patient that sexual abuse has occurred. There are a number of psychiatric syndromes unrelated to sleep in which sexual complaints may arise. In schizophrenia it is not unusual for sexual hallucinations and delusions to be present. The patient may feel that his genitals are being interfered with by neighbours or strangers. He may even experience an orgasm induced at some distance by a colleague. In the syndrome of morbid jealousy the husband may complain that his wife is having frequent affairs and accuses her of infidelity. In de Clérambault's syndrome (erotomania) there is a delusional conviction that the person is in a reciprocated amorous relationship. The target of this delusion may be in danger of sexual harassment or even assault.

6.5 ESTABLISHING A DEFENCE OF AUTOMATISM

6.5.1 Medical evidence

It is important in any case involving an offence allegedly committed during a sleepwalking episode that medical evidence should clearly establish that sleep automatism occurred. The following factors are required for the diagnosis of sleepwalking.

6.5.1 History

(a) Family history. It is essential to obtain detailed information about other family members who sleepwalk.

(b) Childhood sleepwalking. It is common for the onset of sleepwalking to be in early childhood.

(c) Adolescent sleepwalking. Although most sleepwalkers start in childhood, a few begin in adolescence. However, most adolescent sleepwalkers will have a childhood history of sleepwalking.

(d) Late onset sleepwalking is rare, and usually only occurs after a precipitating cause, for example, head injury. Regard with some suspicion any episode of sleepwalking which is said to be the first episode, particularly in an adult.

6.5.2 Specific factors

(e) Episodes will occur during stage 2 and 3/4 non-REM sleep, and thus are most likely to occur within two hours of sleep onset, but may occur towards the end of the night.

(f) There must be disorientation on awakening. A straight arousal into clear consciousness is unlikely to occur on awakening from a sleep automatism. Such an arousal usually indicates an arousal from dreaming sleep, unless the automatism is in its late stages, when consciousness return may be abrupt, without confusion.

(g) Any witness to the entire event should report inappropriate automatic behaviour, preferably with an element of confusion.

(h) There must be amnesia for the event. Memories are poorly recorded during stage 4 sleep and equally poorly recalled. It is possible for fragments of distorted memory to be retained.

(i) Trigger factors are important. Drugs, alcohol, excessive fatigue and stress can all precipitate a sleep automatism.

(j) Enquire carefully for sexual arousal (penile tumescence in men); its presence makes a sleep automatism highly unlikely.

(k) The nature and quality of the previous sleep mentation must be that of stage 2, 3 or 4 sleep. It is helpful if it is non-narrative, and non-dream-like with only a vague visual content, and consists mostly of thought and feelings.

(l)   Attempts to conceal the incident are most unusual.

(m) It is helpful if the incident can be shown to be out of character for the individual, but this need not necessarily be so.

6.5.2 Automatism and the law

The current law on sleepwalking in England was defined by the case of *R* v *Burgess* [1991] 1 QB 92. In this case Burgess and his girlfriend both fell asleep on a sofa in her sitting room. She awoke when she was struck on the head by Burgess with a bottle of wine that shattered. Stunned, she recollects Burgess picking up a video tape-recorder with which he then again struck her a further blow on the head. She managed to crawl towards the door when Burgess caught up with her and pinned her to the floor, attempting to throttle her. The attack came to an end when she managed to say, 'I love you, Bar'. Burgess claimed to remember going to sleep on the sofa but to have no memory for the attack until he came to on hearing these words.

At the trial it was argued by the defence that he was sleepwalking, although I put forward the view for the prosecution that Burgess's 'sleepwalking' was more likely to be a dissociated state. Both the defence and the prosecution agreed that sleepwalking had a genetic cause and thus was due to an internal factor. Therefore the judge only allowed the plea of insanity. The jury brought in a verdict of not guilty by reason of insanity and the defence appealed. The Appeal Court agreed with the trial judge that sleepwalking should be considered an insane automatism.

In cases of insane automatism, in accordance with the Criminal Procedure (Insanity and Unfitness to Plead) Act 1991, the judge decides on the disposal. It is to be hoped that judges will give an absolute discharge in cases in which sleepwalkers' behaviour has inadvertently offended public decency. It is unfortunate that sleepwalkers, if found guilty of an offence during a sleep-walking episode, now have the stigma of insanity attached to them, a point which was made in the House of Lords, in *R* v *Sullivan* [1984] AC 156, in the case of epileptic automatism. It would be helpful if Parliament could define another legal category such that a conviction for an offence involving misbehaviour during sleepwalking, or epilepsy for that matter, does not lead to a conviction on the grounds of insanity. The present English law on sleepwalking, which defines sleepwalking as insanity, is also clearly prejudicial to normal citizens and requires changing.

In Canada, following the case of *R* v *Parkes*, sleepwalking is seen as an automatism *simpliciter* and a defendant who has committed an offence during a sleepwalking episode is given an absolute discharge. In my opinion the English law, which requires the judge to decide on the disposal of the sleepwalking offender, is more satisfactory. It provides some protection for the public, particularly in those cases where a sleepwalking defence has been used inappropriately and has received jury approval.

6.6 SUMMARY

Sexual and violent alleged assaults may occur during sleepwalking episodes. A number of specific features, which are related to the structure, physiology and mentation of sleep, should allow the medico-legal expert to decide whether or not the assault truly occurred during sleepwalking.

Sexual assaults on sleeping victims also occur. In these cases it is essential to look at the timing of the assault after sleep onset, the behaviour of the victim as reported by the assailant, the level of alcohol of the victim, and the behaviour on arousal of the victim and his or her mentation at that time.

Although it is theoretically possible for other sleep disorders to be implicated in alleged assaults, these rarely come to court as they are usually dealt with in a medical context.

Key terms
Sleepwalking; sexual assault; violence; sudden arousal; parasomnia.

References
Abbe, K. and Shinakawa, M. (1966), 'Predisposition to sleepwalking', *Psychiatry and Neurology*, vol. 152, pp. 306–12.

Bakwin, H. (1970), 'Sleepwalking in twins', *Lancet*, vol. 2, pp. 446–7.

Bixler, E., Kales, A. and Soldatos, C. (1979), 'Sleep disorders encountered in medical practice: the National Survey of Physicians', *Behavioural Medicine*, vol. 6, pp. 1–6.

Blair, D. (1977), 'The medico-legal aspects of automatism', *Medical Science and the Law*, vol. 17, part 3, pp. 167–82.

Bonkalo, A. (1974), 'Impulsive acts and confusional states during incomplete arousal from sleep: criminological and forensic implications', *Psychiatr. Q.*, vol. 48, part 3, pp. 400–9.

Dement, W.C. (1976), *Some Must Sleep While Others Watch*. San Fransisco Book Co., p. 79.

Dement, W. and Kleitman, N. (1957a) *Electroencephalography and Clinical Neurophysiology*, vol. 9, p. 673.

Dement, W. and Kleitman, N. (1957b), *Journal of Experimental Psychology*, vol. 53, p. 339.

Dement, W. and Kleitman, N. (1957), 'Cyclic variations in EEG during sleep and their relation to eye movements, bodily motility and dreaming', *Electroencephalography and Clinical Neurophysiology*, vol. 9, pp. 673–90.

Fenton, G. (1975), 'Clinical disorders of sleep' (review), *British Journal of Hospital Medicine*, August, pp. 120–45.

Fenwick, P. (1984), 'Epilepsy and the law', *British Medical Journal*, vol. 288, pp. 1938–9.

Fenwick, P. (1986), 'Murdering while asleep', *British Medical Journal*, August.

Fenwick, P. (1990), 'Automatism, medicine and the law', *Psychological Medicine*, monograph suppl. 17, pp. 1–27.

Fenwick, P. and Fenwick, E. (eds) (1985), *Epilepsy and the Law — A Medical Symposium on the Current Law* (Royal Society of Medicine International Congress and Symposium Series, No. 81). London: Royal Society of Medicine, pp. 3–8.

Fenwick, P., Schatzman, M., Worsley, A., et al. (1984), 'Lucid dreaming correspondence between dreamed and actual events in one subject during REM sleep', *Biological Psychology*, vol. 18, pp. 243–52.

Fisher, C., Byrne, J., Edwards, A. and Kahn, E. (1970), 'A psychophysiological study of nightmares', *Journal of the American Psychoanalytical Association*, vol. 18, pp. 747–82.

Fisher, C., Kahn, E., Edwards, A. and Davis, D. (1972), *Psychophysiology*, vol. 9, p. 91.

Fisher, C., Kahn, E., Edwards, A. and Davis, D. (1973), 'A psychophysiological study of nightmares and night terrors. 1. Physiological aspects of the stage 4 night terror', *Journal of Nervous and Mental Disorders*, vol. 157, pp. 75–98.

Fisher, C., Kahn, E., Edwards, A., Davis, D. and Fine, J. (1974), 'A psychophysiological study of nightmares and night terrors', *Journal of Nervous and Mental Disease*, vol. 158, pp. 174–88.

Gaustaut, H. and Broughton, R. (1965), 'A clinical and polygraphic study of episodic phenomena during sleep,' in J. Wortis (ed.), *Recent Advances in Biological Psychiatry*, vol. 7, pp. 197–221. New York: Plenum Press.

Good, M.I. (1976), 'The concept of drug automatism', *American Journal of Psychiatry*, vol. 133, pp. 948–51.

Hartmann, E. (1983), 'Two case reports: night terrors with sleep walking — a potentially lethal disorder', *Journal of Nervous and Mental Disease*, vol. 171, pp. 503–5.

Hayes, P. (1992), 'False but sincere accusations of sexual assault made by [narcoleptic] patients, *J. Medico-Legal*, vol. 60.4.

Hinsie, I.E. and Shatzky, J. (1940), *Psychiatric Dictionary*. London: Oxford Medical Publications.

Huapaya, L. (1979), 'Seven cases of somnambulism induced by drugs' *American Journal of Psychiatry*, vol. 136, pp. 985–6.

Kales, J., Kales, A., Soldatos, C., Chamberlain, K. and Martin, E. (1979), 'Sleepwalking and night terrors related to febrile illness', *American Journal of Psychiatry*, vol. 136, pp. 1214–17.

Kurth, V., Gohler, I. and Knaape, H. (1965), 'Untersuchugen über den Pavor nocturnus bei Kindern', *Psychiatry, Neurology and Medical Psychology*, vol. 17, pp. 1–7.

Jacobson, A., Kales, J. and Kales, A. (1969), 'Clinical and electrophysiological correlates of sleep disorders in children', in Kales, A. (ed.), *Sleep: Physiology and Pathology: A Symposium*, pp. 109–18. Philadelphia: Lipincott.

Kales, A., Soldatos, C., Bixler, E., Ladda, R., Charney, D., Weber, G. and Schweitzer, P. (1980), 'Hereditary factors in sleepwalking and night terrors', *British Journal of Psychiatry*, vol. 137, pp. 111–18.

Klackenberg, G. (1982), 'Somnambulism in childhood — prevalence, course and behavioural correlates', *Acta Paediatrica Scandinavica*, vol. 71, pp. 495–9.

Kleitman, N. (1963), *Sleep and Wakefulness*. University of Chicago Press.

Langeluddeke, A. (1955), *Delikte in Schlafzustande*. Def Nervenarzt. 26: 22–30.

Lishman, W.A. (1987), *Organic Psychiatry*, pp. 617–26. Oxford: Blackwell.

92	Witness testimony in sleep and dream-related contexts

Luchins, D., Sherwood, P., Gillin, C., Mendelson, W. and Wyatt, R. (1978), 'Filicide during psychotropic induced somnambulism', *American Journal of Psychiatry*, vol. 135, pp. 1404–5.
Podolsky, E. (1961), 'Somnambulistic homicide', *Medicine, Science and the Law*, vol. 1, pp. 260–5.
Rechtschaffen, A. (1973), in McGuigan, F. and Schoonover, R. (eds), *The Psychophysiology of Thinking*, p. 153. New York: Academic Press.
Rechtschaffen, A. and Kales, A. (1968), *A Manual of Standardised Terminology, Techniques and Scoring Systems for Sleep Stages of Human Subjects*. BIS/BRI, UCLA.
Schatzman, M. (1986), 'To sleep, perchance to kill', *New Scientist*, 1514, pp. 60–2.
Shirley, A. and Kahn, J. (1958), 'Sleep disturbances in children', *Paediatric Clin. North America*, vol. 5, pp. 629–43.
Soldatos, C.R. and Kales, A. (1982), 'Sleep disorders: research in psychopathology and its practical implications' (review article), *Acta Psychiatrica Scandinavica*, vol. 65, pp. 381–7.
Sours, J., Frumkin, P. and Indermill, R. (1963), 'Somnambulism', *Arch. of General Psychiatry*, p. 400.
Thomas, C. and Pedersen, L. (1963), 'Psychobiological studies: sleep habits of healthy young adults, with observations on levels of cholesterol and circulating eosinophils', *J. Chronic Diseases*, vol. 16, pp. 1099–1114.

Cases
Bratty v *Attorney-General for Northern Ireland* [1961] NI 78 (Northern Ireland Court of Appeal); [1963] AC 386 (House of Lords).
R v *Charlson* [1955] 1 WLR 317.
R v *Joyce* [1970] SASR 184.
R v *Kemp* [1957] 1 QB 399.
R v *Quick* [1973] QB 910.
R v *Sullivan* [1984] AC 156

Recommended reading
Fenwick, P. (1990), 'Automatism, medicine and the law', *Psychological Medicine*, monograph supplement 17, pp. 1–27.
Ferber, R., 'Sleep disorders in children', in R. Cooper (ed.), *Sleep*, Ch. 14. London: Chapman and Hall.

Editors' notes
Where sleep or dreaming behaviour is thought to have contributed to confabulation or the formulation of a false or misleading account, the identification and disclosure of relevant factors is likely to be a severely difficult operation. In many instances, there will be no medically diagnosed condition to rely upon and recourse may need to be had to anecdotal accounts provided by non-professional witnesses who have previously associated with the witness. Sleepwalkers, or those who, suffering from nightmares, are apt to find it difficult to distinguish between real-life and dreamed

events are unlikely to react in a way which makes their condition medically diagnosable. Sufferers from narcolepsy may remain permanently ignorant of their condition.

Proving that an honestly held belief is the product of a sleeping disorder episode may be impossible — particularly if the only available witnesses to the incident are the complainant and the accused. Thus there is considerable scepticism concerning the value of expert evidence in this field.

The witness's cooperation with endeavours to establish whether 'abnormal' sleep behaviour has contributed to the corruption of memory is essential. The boundaries of legitimate expert evidence in this field will, inevitably, remain ill-defined.

CHAPTER SEVEN

Physical illnesses and their potential influence

Guy A. Norfolk

7.1 INTRODUCTION

7.1.1 Physical illness and witness testimony

This chapter considers the effect that physical illness may have on the reliability of witness testimony. In general, the presence of any physical illness renders an individual more vulnerable when having to cope with a stressful situation. Providing a witness statement, which often involves reliving unpleasant or frightening experiences, can impose additional stresses on people who are already coping with physical illness. In these circumstances they are more likely to focus on the short-term consequences of their behaviour than the long-term. For example, patients with angina who find themselves separated from their medication may try to please their interviewers by providing the responses they believe are wanted in order to bring the interview to an early close, thus enabling speedier access to their angina treatment. The long-term consequences of this behaviour may be ignored in preference to the short-term reassurance of having their medication close to hand.

The extent of this vulnerability depends in part on the psychological profile of the individual, something best assessed by a clinical psychologist. As the impact of physical illness on a person's coping strategy is not disease specific, depending more on the actual or perceived severity of the illness rather than the nature of the illness itself, the actual diagnosis is unimportant. By contrast, there are many physical illnesses in which characteristic disturbances in brain function have been recognised. With these illnesses the nature and degree of the mental disturbance produced depends entirely on the diagnosis of the underlying condition. This chapter will concentrate on this group of illnesses, as the mental disturbance they cause has the potential to influence the reliability of witness testimony.

7.1.2 Mental disorder and physical illness

Since the early days of medicine there has been a widely held belief that there are two distinct types of mental illness, those caused by natural or physical illness and those thought to be due to supernatural influences or moral laxity. During the twentieth century these ideas have been challenged, but the distinction is still made between mental disorders in which there is a recognisable physiological abnormality and disorders, such as schizophrenia and depression, in which there are no discernible pathological processes. These latter disorders, often referred to as functional psychiatric illnesses, are discussed in chapter 5: it is the former type of illness that will be discussed here. In fact the distinction between the two groups has been blurred in recent years as advances in neuro-radiological imaging techniques and improved understanding of the complex biochemistry of the brain have suggested the presence of subtle cerebral metabolic and structural abnormalities in patients with functional psychiatric illnesses. Nonetheless, for the purposes of this chapter the distinction will be considered valid.

The list of physical illnesses capable of producing mental disorder is lengthy and classification is not straightforward. One convenient method, which classifies the conditions on the basis of whether the primary abnormality involves the nervous system or not, is shown in table 7.1.

Table 7.1 Conditions giving rise to mental disorders

Neurological conditions

Degenerative diseases	Alzheimer's disease and other dementias, Huntington's disease, Parkinson's disease, Creutzfeldt–Jakob disease, multiple sclerosis, normal pressure hydrocephalus.
Stokes	
Space-occupying lesions	Cerebral tumours, abscesses, intracranial haematomas.
Head injuries	
Epilepsy	
Infections	Encephalitis, meningitis, tertiary syphilis.

Other conditions

Metabolic	Renal failure, liver failure, vitamin deficiencies.
Endocrine	Diabetes, thyroid disorders, Addison's disease, parathyorid disease, hypopituitarism.
Anoxia	Anaemia, heart and lung disease, carbon monoxide poisoning, strangulation.

While the effect on brain function of these conditions is diverse and wide ranging, this chapter will focus primarily on disturbances in cognitive function, particularly memory, as these are crucial in the context of providing reliable witness testimony. Therefore, this chapter will concentrate on the commonly encountered conditions that are capable of causing cognitive impairment and which, thus, have the potential to render testimony unreliable. The discussion of the various conditions is, by necessity, generalist in nature. For more detailed and specific accounts readers are referred to the specialist texts in the bibliography.

7.2 NEUROLOGICAL CONDITIONS

7.2.1 Dementia

Dementia is the term used to describe progressive intellectual deterioration of a degree sufficient to impair functioning in daily living. The condition is a large-scale problem in the elderly. It has been estimated that 10% of patients aged 75 or over suffer from dementia to an appreciable degree, with the proportion probably exceeding 20% in those over 85. However, in many people the dementia is not recognised until there is some form of crisis in their lives, such as sudden illness, bereavement or a change in their environment. People seem able to develop strategies to cope with their daily tasks and thus appear to function normally until the crisis disrupts the status quo and exposes the degree of their dementia. Therefore it is important that the advocate is aware of the possibility that an elderly witness may be suffering from a masked dementia despite reports of apparently normal social functioning. In such circumstances recognition of the dementia can be facilitated by using a standard test of cognitive function such as the Abbreviated Mental Test Score shown in table 7.2. In tests such as these, the patient is asked a series of questions and a poor performance is taken as an indication that there may be a dementing process present. The tests are easy to apply and do not require specialist training.

Table 7.2 Abbreviated mental test score for dementia

Each question scores one mark. Six or fewer correct answers suggests dementia.

1. Age.

2. Time to the nearest hour.

3. An address — e.g., 43 West Street — to be repeated by the patient at the end of the test.

4. The year.

5. Name of hospital, residential institution or home address depending where the patient is situated.

6. Ability to recognise two persons, for example, doctor, nurse, home help, etc.

7. Date of birth.

8. Year First World War started.

9. Name of present monarch.

10. Ability to count backwards from 20 to 1.

7.2.1.1 Causes of dementia There are many different causes of dementia and these tend to vary with the age of onset. While the majority consist of some form of irreversible degenerative process, about 10% of confirmed cases are potentially treatable. Examples of reversible causes of dementia include vitamin B12 deficiency and the dementia associated with an underactive thyroid gland (hypothyroidism). However, the commonest cause of both progressive pre-senile dementia and of severe dementia in old age is Alzheimer's disease, which accounts for about 50% of all cases. Although the diagnosis of Alzheimer's disease is often made on clinical grounds it actually depends on the detection of characteristic histological changes in the brain which can only be confirmed after death.

In Alzheimer's disease the general intellectual decline is steady and progressive, thus distinguishing it from multi-infarct dementia, the second commonest form of the disease. Multi-infarct dementia is a consequence of the accumulated deficits caused by repeated strokes, large or small. The onset is typically abrupt and the deterioration step-like rather than smooth.

7.2.1.2 Clinical features of dementia Despite the many different causes of dementia, the clinical picture shows many basic similarities, although variation is seen depending on the age of onset of the illness, pre-morbid personality, and intelligence.

Three main phases to the disease can often be distinguished. In the first there is a slow development of intellectual deterioration. The slowness of this decline often allows the patient to maintain social functioning until the disease is well advanced. This first phase is characterised by failing memory and spatial disorientation. The memory deficits, which initially affect recent events, gradually extend to include remote memories and orientation. With time patients lose the ability to understand new concepts and no longer learn from past experience. There is a loss of the sense of time and place (so that patients become unable to find the way in familiar surroundings and easily become lost).

The impaired memory, loss of the sense of time and spatial disorientation that characterise this first stage of dementia can all distort a witness's recollection of events. This distortion may be compounded by a lack of judgment that is frequently displayed by those with dementia, and which can cause the witness to misjudge the importance of providing reliable testimony.

The second stage of dementia is associated with a more rapid intellectual deterioration together with a general disintegration and change in the person's personality. Initially, less attractive personality traits are accentuated, but later more serious changes occur. In general, demented patients become more selfish, quarrelsome and inflexible.

The third or terminal stage consists of profound apathetic dementia. The patient, by now usually bedridden and doubly incontinent, appears to have very few thoughts and they tend to be persistent and disconnected. No meaningful testimony can be obtained from such patients.

7.2.2 Epilepsy

Epilepsy should be viewed as a symptom and not as a disease itself. The term represents a set of clinical phenomena rather than a specific cerebral pathology. Indeed, in many cases of epilepsy no definitive pathology can be found to account for the occurrence of the fits. Therefore, classification of the various types of epilepsy tends to be based on the characteristics of the fit rather than on the cause (see table 7.3).

Table 7.3 Classification of epilepsy

1. Generalised epilepsies:

(a) tonic-clonic or grand mal (this is the form of fit instantly recognisable, even to the layperson, as epileptic with loss of consciousness and violent jerking of the limbs);
  (b) tonic;
  (c) atonic;
  (d) absence (petit mal);
  (e) myoclonic.

2. Partial or focal epilepsies:

(a) without impairment of consciousness;
  (b) with impairment of consciousness:

(i) with motor signs (e.g., Jacksonian epilepsy);
    (ii) with sensory symptoms (e.g., olfactory or visual);
    (iii) with autonomic features (such as epigastric sensations);
    (iv) with psychic symptoms (e.g., fear, déjà vu);
    (v) with automatisms.

3. Unclassifiable and mixed forms.

7.2.2.1 Cognitive impairment and epilepsy It is now clear, after long dispute, that a predisposition to epileptic fits does not in itself mean that there will be associated intellectual impairment, personality disorder or mental illness. The majority of epileptic patients remain mentally normal, although this does depend on the presence, site and extent of any brain damage underlying the epilepsy. Epileptics who do have significant brain damage and associated mental symptoms often find the latter more disabling than the epilepsy itself and attention needs to focus as much on the associated psychological problems as on the epilepsy when assessing their reliability as witnesses.

Epileptics without significant brain damage are, though, prone to cognitive impairment, particularly memory impairment, as a result of their epilepsy. It is this cognitive impairment, together with certain other problems encountered with epilepsy, that can potentially affect witness reliability. All these problems are best reviewed by considering those that occur between fits (interictal) and those occurring in close association with the fits themselves (ictal).

7.2.2.2 Interictal problems Difficulties with memory and learning may be found in epileptics who have brain damage underlying their epilepsy. On occasion these difficulties may be obvious, but sometimes will only be revealed on special testing.

Any such difficulties can be further aggravated by the anti-convulsant medication prescribed to the patient. The medical profession is now much more aware that anticonvulsant drugs, when in toxic doses or unsuitable combinations, may lead to problems with concentration, memory and intellectual functioning. In the case of a witness who suffers from epilepsy it is important to obtain a careful history of all prescribed medication and to take advice when appropriate. Blood levels of anticonvulsants can indicate when the drugs are being taken in toxic doses. Sometimes, therefore, it may be prudent to request such blood tests, especially when the witness complains of mental lethargy or appears to be performing below expected levels, as these symptoms are particularly associated with toxicity.

Further problems with the reliability of testimony from epileptics may be related to their personalities. Patients with epilepsy are often overprotected in childhood by concerned parents and, later in life, can be exposed to profound social and occupational discrimination. All these factors can lead to personality problems which include feelings of insecurity, low self-esteem and dependency. Individuals with these personality traits are likely to be highly suggestible and may strive to please interviewing officers by giving answers that seem plausible and consistent with the external cues provided, even though the responses are known to be untrue.

7.2.2.3 Ictal problems The neurophysiological consequences of an epileptic fit can seriously distort an individual's perception of events occurring around the time of the fit, thus rendering any subsequent account of that event potentially unreliable. Complex disturbances of thinking, memory or awareness may feature as part of an aura preceding the actual seizure. These may include distortion of time sense, mental confusion, feelings of depersonalisation or déjà vu. The fit may also be ushered in by distorted perceptions or actual hallucinations of sight, hearing, taste or smell. When the ensuing fit is mild or abortive the connection between these reported experiences and their epileptic causation may be missed.

Certain forms of epilepsy may be barely discernible to the observer and yet have a substantial effect on memory. Typical absences (or petit mal) epilepsy is a disorder that usually starts in childhood, but attacks can continue into adult life. Absence attacks are brief with an abrupt onset and termination. Sufferers cease what they are doing, stare, look a little pale and may flutter their eyelids. The whole attack lasts a few seconds only but several such absences may occur in quick succession producing significant gaps in the sufferer's memory.

Further cognitive disturbances also follow in the wake of seizures, with clouding of consciousness and disorientation lasting for a period of a few minutes up to an hour or more, so that recollection for events occurring during the post-ictal period may also be unreliable.

7.2.3 Cerebral tumours

Brain tumours not unnaturally lead to a high incidence of mental disturbances. Clouding of consciousness can occur as a consequence of the rise in intracranial pressure caused by the tumour growing in the tightly enclosed confines of the cranium, whereas memory impairment is more likely to be due to local brain compression and destruction.

There are many different types of brain tumour and although the extent of any associated mental disturbance will depend to some degree on the type of tumour, the most important factor in determining the nature and extent of the disturbance is the location of the tumour. A simplified list of the major deficits that have traditionally been associated with tumours in the four anatomical lobes of the brain is shown in figure 7.1.

7.2.4 Head injury

Each year about one million head-injured patients attend hospital in the United Kingdom. Whilst the vast majority of these injuries turn out to be mild, with about 80% of patients not having lost consciousness, they are frequently associated with road traffic accidents or assaults and thus may have medico-legal implications. Therefore, the potential for the head injury to affect the person's ability to recall the details of the accident or assault can assume considerable importance.

Memory loss for events occurring around the time of the injury is likely whenever there has been diffuse brain damage of a degree sufficient to cause concussion. In most cases loss of consciousness will accompany the head injury, but this is not invariable and it is possible for patients to display both retrograde and post-traumatic amnesia without losing consciousness.

7.2.4.1 Retrograde amnesia Retrograde amnesia is generally taken to refer to the loss of memory for events that immediately precede the head injury. Patients can often indicate with fair precision the last event that they can clearly recollect. In road traffic accidents the journey may be recalled up to a specific point, and this enables an estimate of the extent of the pre-traumatic gap to be made. Such amnesia is usually short in duration and can usually be counted in minutes or hours rather than days or weeks. Retrograde amnesia for very long periods is often due to hysteria.

Figure 7.1   Mental disturbances caused by cerebral tumours

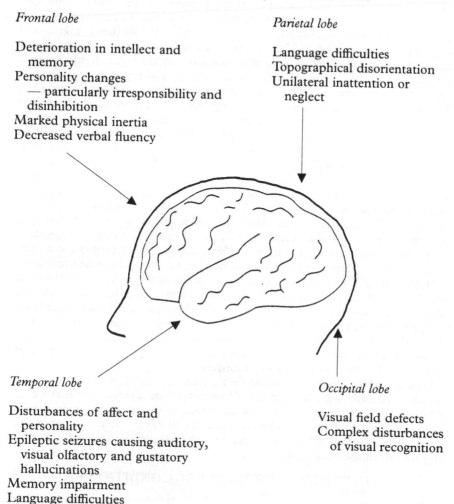

Frontal lobe

Deterioration in intellect and
   memory
Personality changes
   — particularly irresponsibility and
   disinhibition
Marked physical inertia
Decreased verbal fluency

Parietal lobe

Language difficulties
Topographical disorientation
Unilateral inattention or
   neglect

Temporal lobe

Disturbances of affect and
   personality
Epileptic seizures causing auditory,
   visual olfactory and gustatory
   hallucinations
Memory impairment
Language difficulties

Occipital lobe

Visual field defects
Complex disturbances
   of visual recognition

When assessing the reliability of a witness's subsequent account of the
events leading up to an accident it is important not to rely on the extent of
the retrograde amnesia as reported immediately after the accident. At first it
may be very long, but it can then shrink over the next days and weeks
eventually ending up as a matter of minutes only. Recovery from retrograde
amnesia tends to occur in chronological order, with items in the distant past
recovering first. The final estimate of the memory loss should not be made
until the patient has emerged from the period of post-traumatic amnesia and
the fullest possible recovery of cerebral function has occurred.

7.2.4.2 Post-traumatic amnesia (PTA)   The duration of post-traumatic amnesia can be defined as the time from the moment of the injury to the time
normal continuous memory returns, the length of the amnesia providing a
good index, albeit in retrospect, of the severity of the brain damage. It should
be emphasised that PTA only ends when patients become able to give a clear
and consecutive account of what is happening around them. Some patients
will exhibit 'islands of memory' and these should not be taken as indicating
the end of the amnesia. There is a similar danger in underestimating the
duration of PTA in patients who, although aware of things going on around
them, are unable to recall these events at a later date.

Patients may exhibit a variety of behaviours during the period of PTA
ranging from apparent normality to obvious confusion. In general, however,
behaviour is unremarkable and observers may be easily misled into believing
that there is nothing amiss. The patients themselves are usually unaware of
the abnormal memory at the time and can give superficial or made-up
explanations for any defects that are discovered. On occasions the patients
may cover these defects with false memories which at first sight appear
convincing. For example, Whitty and Zangwill report the case of a dispatch
rider who was concussed in a motorcycle accident. After treatment at a local
hospital he was transferred to a special head injury unit where he provided a
clear account of his accident, including its locale, and was able to recount his
journey from the first hospital. Examination showed him to be rational and
fully orientated, the only peculiarity was that he persistently underestimated
his age by two years. It subsequently transpired that he was giving details of
an accident he had had two years earlier and that the description of the
journey from the first hospital was also a false reminiscence. His period of
post-traumatic amnesia was finally assessed as 12 days.

Typically PTA follows on immediately from a period of concussion and
confusion caused by the head injury. However, on occasions there may be no
such period of confusion. The classic example is the rugby player who
receives a blow to the head with no apparent ill effects. It is only after the
game is finished that it becomes clear that the player has no recollection of
the game from the time of the injury.

7.3 OTHER NEUROLOGICAL CONDITIONS

7.3.1 Strokes

A stroke can be loosely defined as a focal neurological disorder of abrupt
onset due to a disruption in the blood supply to the brain. Strokes are the
third commonest cause of death in the Western world and, in the United
Kingdom, are the most frequent cause of severe disability in the community.
This disability is often a mixture of physical and mental problems, the latter
sometimes being directly attributable to the brain damage and sometimes
representing a reaction to the handicaps imposed.

7.3.1.1 Cognitive impairment after strokes   Of all the sequelae of strokes,
defects in intelligence and higher mental functioning are among the most
serious. Whereas the physical disability of having one half of one's body

paralysed (a hemiplegia) will be obvious and easily understood, the more subtle effects on cognition can often prove a greater barrier to recovery and are not infrequently misinterpreted by carers.

Disturbances of language accompany about two thirds of strokes affecting the so-called dominant left cerebral hemisphere and will usually be found in association with a right-sided hemiplegia. These language disturbances, or dysphasias, are a serious handicap. They often outlast recovery in motor function and can be a source of extreme frustration to the patient. There are many different types of dysphasia depending on which part of the dominant hemisphere is damaged but the commonest are: receptive dysphasia, in which the primary deficit is in the comprehension of the spoken word; expressive dysphasia, where comprehension is good but the patient has difficulty in choosing and articulating appropriate words and sentences; and nominal dysphasia, where the patient is unable to evoke names at will, being able, for example, to describe an object and explain its use but finding the name totally elusive.

It is important for all those dealing with patients who have language difficulties to appreciate that the dysphasia is essentially a loss of a linguistic tool and does not necessarily imply that the rest of the intellect has been affected. Many of these patients retain in large degree the automatic and subconscious use of words in their thinking processes and so the presence of a dysphasia does not in itself discredit the reliability of their testimony.

Many other disturbances of higher mental functioning are recognised after strokes, some of which can appear quite bizarre. Disturbed awareness of the self or of space can occur, more commonly when the non-dominant right cerebral hemisphere is affected. Thus a patient may neglect the left half of external space not recognising or registering anything that occurs on this side of his or her body. Agnosia is an impaired ability to recognise objects. In agnosia for colours patients are unable to name or correctly indicate specific colours. However, they are perfectly able to sort coloured objects into appropriately matched groups. Finger agnosia is the loss of ability to recognise, name or select individual fingers. Visuospatial defects may be found and some patients may demonstrate right-left disorientation, being quite unable to distinguish between the two sides.

Specific memory deficits have also been observed in patients with strokes, although in most cases these will be associated with additional cognitive impairment such as visual or language disturbance. Given the wide array of effects on cognition, it is often advisable to obtain a detailed medical report in the case of a witness whose testimony may prove critical if there remains any doubt about residual effects of a stroke.

7.3.2 Migraine

Migraine is a common and sometimes incapacitating disorder, affecting approximately 20% of women and 15% of men at some time in their lives. It is characterised by headaches, which are usually restricted to one side of the head at the outset, associated with nausea and vomiting. The headache is usually preceded or accompanied with visual, sensory, motor or mood

Some degree of mental change is almost universal during attacks. Anxiety and irritability are common early in the attack and are often followed by drowsiness and lethargy. Cognitive impairment may occur. Cerebration is often slowed with poor concentration and there may be marked impairment of memory. Focal disturbance of cerebral functioning may be noted producing similar states to those recognised with strokes, such as dysphasia and agnosia.

A witness who suffered an attack of migraine at or around the time of an event about which he or she is testifying should be questioned closely about previous experience of cognitive impairment during attacks, although it should be recognised that the pattern of any such impairment can change from attack to attack in the same person.

7.3.3 Parkinson's disease

This is a disease characterised by a slowly progressive poverty and slowness of movement associated with rigidity, abnormal posture and tremor. It has an insidious onset usually in the second half of life and affects about 1 in 200 of the elderly population. At the outset of the disease most patients have normal intellectual and cognitive function but with the passage of time a proportion will develop mental changes, with a significant proportion developing slowness of thought and defects of memory. Approximately 20% of patients will finally develop a frank dementia.

7.4 METABOLIC AND RELATED DISEASES

7.4.1 Thyroid diseases

The thyroid gland is responsible for synthesising, storing and secreting thyroxine, the principle thyroid hormone. The physiological effects of thyroxine are widespread, being mediated through influences on the metabolism of cells in all the tissues of the body including the brain. It is hardly surprising then that abnormalities of thyroxine production can lead to disorders of the mental state.

7.4.1.1 Hypothyroidism   Hypothyroidism is the clinical syndrome produced by insufficient secretion of thyroid hormone. The exact clinical presentation depends on the age at which the deficiency occurs. Infantile hypothyroidism leads to cretinism unless recognised and treated early. In older patients the condition is referred to as myxoedema in which mental manifestations are as important as physical. The typical picture is of mental lethargy, general dulling of the personality and slowing of all cognitive functions. Memory is usually affected early in the disease and is often associated with a sense of mental befuddlement.

Hypothyroidism is treated by correcting the deficiency of thyroxine by providing the hormone in tablet form. The treatment is highly effective and rewarding with physical symptoms gradually disappearing and mental processes returning to their usual speed and efficiency. Thus, the only situations in which the condition may have an important effect on the reliability of witness testimony is when the diagnosis has not yet been made or when it is being inadequately treated with insufficient thyroxine. Because of the insidious way in which hypothyroidism develops, and the diffuse and relatively minor nature of the early symptoms, the disease can often be overlooked for some time. Witnesses who exhibit the characteristic features of hypothyroidism should therefore have their thyroid function checked. The appearance is so distinctive as to be almost diagnostic. The face is pale, puffy and expressionless and the eyelids are baggy. The skin feels dry and coarse and body hair is often sparse and short. The voice is croaky, thick and toneless. Diagnosis is confirmed by a simple blood test which will also indicate when treatment is inadequate.

7.4.1.2 Hyperthyroidism This refers to the condition caused by an excessive secretion of thyroid hormone. Sufferers are tense, talkative and restless. They may complain of intolerance to heat, excessive sweating, weight loss and diarrhoea. Psychological disturbance is universal with the attendant over-arousal leading to distractibility and impaired concentration. Memory for recent events may be affected and could have significance for a witness.

7.4.2 Diabetes mellitus

Diabetes mellitus refers to a variety of disorders in which the body either lacks or fails to react to insulin, the hormone which regulates our use of the glucose energy we get from food. Insulin is crucial to health and mental functioning because the brain cannot store glucose and needs a more or less steady supply to run properly. Although confusion is a prominent feature in patients who are slipping into diabetic coma, which is a medical emergency caused by excessively high blood sugar levels, it is more likely that questions regarding witness reliability will involve those with low blood sugar, or hypoglycaemia.

Hypoglycaemia most commonly affects patients receiving treatment for their diabetes, either in the form of injectable insulin or tablets designed to lower the blood sugar (oral hypoglycaemics). Abnormally low blood sugars will occur when patients take their regular medication but then fail to eat sufficient carbohydrate or, alternatively, exercise more than normal, thus burning up more of the body's store of sugar. Episodes of hypoglycaemia are associated with irritability, anxiety and panic in the early stages. As the episode develops patients become disinhibited and may exhibit childish or aggressive behaviour, often mimicking drunkenness. Disorientation and mental confusion are common and, in severe cases, the patient may pass into a coma. Anybody suffering from hypoglycaemia will prove to be a poor witness to events that occur during the episode. Most patients have complete amnesia for the content of the attack and occasionally for an additional period before the attack when their behaviour appeared to be normal. By obtaining a clear history of all prescribed medication taken by a witness, the investigator will be alerted to the possibility of hypoglycaemia in those receiving treatment for their diabetes.

7.4.3   Cerebral anoxia

Cerebral anoxia is defined as a deficient supply of oxygen to the brain. It may occur in a variety of circumstances. First, there may be deficient oxygenation of the arterial blood flowing to the brain. This may occur as a result of respiratory illnesses such as chronic bronchitis and emphysema. Secondly, there may be a disturbance to the oxygen carrying power of the blood such as occurs in severe anaemia or carbon monoxide poisoning. Cerebral anoxia may also be due to arrest or reduction of the blood flow to the brain such as occurs with strangulation. Finally, anoxia may occur when there is ineffective utilisation of oxygen by the brain even though the oxygen supply in the blood is adequate. Such a situation is observed in hypoglycaemia and with poisoning by a variety of substances, including cyanide and carbon disulphide.

The clinical effects of cerebral anoxia depend on its duration and rate of development rather than its cause. Events are usually transient with impaired consciousness, confusion and disorientation. Memory disturbance is common with patients usually exhibiting a dense amnesia for the acute episode. Where the onset of the anoxia is more insidious the memory disturbance may be less obvious and investigators need to be aware of this possibility in patients with medical conditions such as cardiac and pulmonary disease.

7.4.4   Alcohol withdrawal

Alcoholics are prone to develop symptoms of withdrawal whenever they stop or reduce their alcohol intake. The severity of these symptoms will depend mainly on the amount and duration of alcohol taken, although other factors, such as concurrent withdrawal from other drugs, may contribute to the clinical picture. Two distinct clinical presentations are recognised.

Uncomplicated alcohol withdrawal is the most frequent and benign type, occurring some 12–48 hours after reduction in alcohol intake. The essential feature is a coarse tremor of the hands, tongue and eyelids which may be associated with transient hallucinations, usually auditory or visual, and illusions.

The more serious form of alcohol withdrawal is alcohol withdrawal delirium, traditionally referred to as delirium tremens. This typically starts 72 to 96 hours after the last drink and the hallmark is profound disorientation and confusion often accompanied by terrifying hallucinations.

Several complications of alcohol withdrawal have also been recognised, with memory impairment being a prominent feature of one such complication, Korsakoff's psychosis. This is characterised by severe amnesia, usually with a retrograde memory loss extending back for up to one year prior to the onset of the psychosis, in a setting of clear consciousness and intact perception. Loss of short-term memory often leads to confabulation in which the witness, despite clear consciousness, provides a reasonably coherent, perfectly believable but entirely false account of an event or experience which the witness has fabricated in order to cover for memory loss.

The advocate will always face problems in convincing a jury that an alcoholic is a credible witness as confusion, disorientation and memory loss are features of both alcohol intoxication and withdrawal.

7.5 SUMMARY

(a) Any physical illness can render an individual vulnerable when having to cope with stressful situations. The extent of this vulnerability depends on the severity, or perceived severity, of the illness and on the psychological profile of the individual.

(b) Many physical illnesses also produce specific and well recognised disturbances in brain function of a degree sufficient to affect the reliability of witness testimony. In these conditions the reliability of testimony may be adversely affected because of impaired memory or disturbance of other cognitive functions.

(c) It is important that the advocate is aware of the range of physical conditions capable of producing these effects.

(d) Obtaining a brief medical history from a witness, which should include details of any medication being taken, will usually be sufficient to identify potentially relevant illness.

(e) Individuals charged with the responsibility for interviewing witnesses also need to be aware of the potential for physical illness to influence the reliability of testimony. Police surgeons (forensic medical examiners) are available to assist the police in advising when both witnesses and suspects are fit to be interviewed.

References

Gudjonsson, G. H. (1992), *The Psychology of Interrogations, Confessions and Testimony*. Chichester: John Wiley and Sons.

Kapur, N. (1988), *Memory Disorders in Clinical Practice*. London: Butterworths.

Lishman, W. A. (1987), *Organic Psychiatry*, 2nd ed. Oxford: Blackwell Scientific Publications.

Norfolk, G. A. (ed.) (1997), *Fit to be Interviewed by the Police? Proceedings of a Multidisciplinary Symposium*. Harrogate: Association of Police Surgeons.

Weatherall, D. J., Ledingham, J. G. G., Warrell, D. A. (eds) *Oxford Textbook of Medicine*, 2nd ed. Oxford: Oxford University Press.

Whitty, C. W. M. and Zangwill, O. L. (eds) (1977) *Amnesia*. London: Butterworths.

Editors' notes

It will be necessary to seek disclosure of the medical records of a witness who is believed to be suffering from any of the illnesses described in this chapter. This may make it possible to identify factors which will tend to corrupt memory and these may then in turn be identified and considered alongside records of what the witness said in the circumstances of the investigation and the process of gathering evidence. Subject to any conclusions reached, medical evidence may need to be called concerning the illness suffered by the witness, those of its symptoms which have a memory-distorting effect, the signs of the symptoms seen in the witness and the extent to which any investigative methods used may have triggered the effects of the illness in a way which leads to an unreliable account being given.

CHAPTER EIGHT

Complaints of sexual misconduct

Janet Boakes

It is an accusation easily to be made and hard to be proved and harder to be defended by the party accused, tho' never so innocent (Sir Matthew Hale).

8.1   INTRODUCTION

Allegations of sexual misconduct are notorious for the problems they present in discerning the truth. Historically, women who made such allegations were regarded as unreliable witnesses, obsessed by sexual fantasies and prone to exaggeration and invention. In the twentieth century medical jurisprudence, influenced by Freud and his followers, came to view false allegations as arising from a unique condition of women. Women, it was held, secretly desire to be raped and this unconscious wish, in the neurotic individual, renders her unable to tell fact from fantasy. It was therefore recommended that a woman or child who alleged sexual misconduct should be examined by a psychiatrist to establish her credibility.

As a consequence, the sexual abuse of women and children was often disregarded both by medicine and the law. Women's genuine memories of sexual injury were discounted and reports by children dismissed as imagination. Where evidence indicated that a sexual act had occurred there was a tendency to blame the victim. Children were held responsible for leading men on, women and girls accused of 'contributory negligence'. Women became reluctant to talk of their experiences and remained silent.

In the past two decades the extent of actual sexual abuse of children has been recognised. As the women's movement has gained strength, women have spoken out about abuse they suffered as children. The changes they have demanded have resulted in a more sympathetic attitude to the way their stories are investigated.

Nevertheless, unfounded and false allegations of sexual misconduct are periodically made and the description of those making them as 'sexually obsessed' may sometimes be not far from the truth.

As attitudes towards sexual offences against women and children have changed a new phenomenon has emerged. A growing number of adults describe *repressed* memories of previously unknown childhood sexual abuse which those accused deny.

This chapter will review the circumstances in which dubious claims of sexual misconduct may arise in adults or children. It will consider the evidence for repression and the so-called 'false memory syndrome' and will offer some diagnostic pointers. Throughout the female gender is used, reflecting the preponderance of women or girls making allegations of sexual misconduct, but men may occasionally bring similar charges.

8.1.1 Baseline statistics

Most accounts by children of sexual abuse are truthful and children who spontaneously disclose current or recent sexual abuse should be taken seriously. However, children may lie, and may sometimes support a false allegation made by an adult. Several reviews have found that about 2% of allegations by pre-school children are false and the figure rises to 8% for adolescents. Figures are substantially higher in cases of disputed custody. It is also known that about 9% of children withdraw accusations although the evidence points to them being true. Such withdrawal is said to follow pressure from adults, and fears of family break-up.

The base figure for false reports or withdrawals made by adults is not known.

Unfounded allegations in adults and children fall mainly into three categories:

(a) Deliberate deceit.
(b) Psychiatric disturbance of the accuser.
(c) Iatrogenic cases, that is, those caused by medical examination or treatment, including the false memory syndrome.

Many cases show a combination of factors.

8.2 FALSE ALLEGATIONS FROM INTENTION TO DECEIVE

8.2.1 False allegations of rape

A survey (Kanin, 1994) in America looked at all rape allegations made in one police agency within a nine-year period and found that 41% were retracted and declared to be false. This study identified three purposes served by the false allegation — providing an alibi, gaining revenge, or seeking sympathy and attention:

(a) The allegation as an alibi — more than half were invented to account for the unforeseen consequence of a consensual sexual encounter. Amongst the most common reasons given was a pregnancy for which the alleged 'rape' provided a plausible explanation.

(b) The allegation as revenge — slightly over one quarter of the women made allegations against a rejecting man. Usually this followed the breakdown of a relationship but occasionally the accusation was made when the man spurned the woman's advances.

(c) The allegation to gain sympathy — this was the smallest category and occurred within the context of other relationship difficulties.

Were the retractions valid? The allegations were only declared to be false following police investigation and withdrawal by the women. Many women are reluctant to report sexual assault from fear of the police investigation and court procedures, and prefer to withdraw their accusation. In the past the police have tended to be unsympathetic towards women who reported rape. However, in this study all retractions were made early on and did not follow prolonged investigation or police interviewing. Moreover, the women were told they would be charged with filing a false complaint, a felony which carried a heavy fine and possible custodial sentence. None of the women later withdrew their retraction, and it seems likely that the retractions were legitimate.

The women who made false declarations did not differ from women whose complaints were legitimate, but the complaints differed. The fabricated accounts did not include accusations of forced oral or anal rape, in contrast to a quarter of the substantiated rape complaints. None of the women appeared to be deluded or suffering from obvious psychiatric disorder, but were attempting to deal with a personal crisis or social distress.

In a later study of false allegations at two university campuses half of all rape complaints were admitted to be false. Of these, half provided an alibi for the complainant and half were motivated by spite and desire for revenge. Only one was made solely from a wish for attention.

8.2.2 Allegations arising from disputed custody

An allegation of sexual abuse is a potent weapon against a despised spouse and in cases where custody is disputed such allegations have a high probability of being false. That is not to imply that there are no true cases of sexual abuse in custody cases, merely that the context offers peculiar temptations to the adults. Divorce and disputes over custody form the background to about 50% of cases of false allegations of sexual abuse involving children.

Typically, this kind of allegation is a deliberate manipulation by one parent to obtain custody, using the child as an instrument of directed deceit. Most often it is the mother who accuses the father of abusing the child and sometimes coaxes the child to confirm the allegation. Some children come to believe their stories, while others are simply supporting the parent. Not all accusations are as flagrantly dishonest and some arise from anxious misinterpretation of a child's behaviour. Children who are torn between two parents frequently show signs of distress which can be misconstrued as fear of the non-custodial parent. Occasionally, normal events such as soreness around the vulva or rectal irritation have been wrongly construed as evidence of penetration.

8.2.3 Deliberate deceit by children

Deception by the child, not at the bidding of a parent, is unusual. As with adults, when it occurs it is usually opportunistic and motivated by spite or to provide an alibi; for example, an older child may sometimes accuse an adult in order to conceal sexual activity with a peer, and young children have made accusations to avoid being returned to neglecting but not abusing parents.

8.3 FALSE ACCUSATIONS ASSOCIATED WITH PSYCHIATRIC DISTURBANCE

Not all false allegations are deliberately such. Allegations of sexual abuse may occur as part of a psychiatric illness. Such individuals generally show other features of illness and will respond to treatment of the underlying condition. However, some may come to the attention of investigating authorities before the correct diagnosis is made.

The division of mental illness into psychosis and neurosis, though imprecise, remains a useful distinction. As well as mental illness are the various forms of personality disorder which may exist independently of any mental illness but nevertheless cause significant impairment of social functioning.

8.3.1 Psychosis

Psychosis is a mental disorder in which there is gross impairment of mental function to such an extent that insight, judgment and contact with reality are affected. The majority of sufferers experience delusions or hallucinations, have conspicuous social and personality difficulties and generally do not recognise themselves as unwell.

Case example 8.1

A professional woman 'knew' instantly that sexual abuse had taken place when she saw her father comfort his grandchild after a fall. The police and child protection authorities were involved and investigations begun before the case was dropped when it became clear that the mother was hypomanic. After treatment with mood-stabilising drugs she withdrew all her allegations and became severely depressed. Two later relapses were ushered in by further accusations. Now well, the patient is ashamed and embarrassed by her allegations, and when depressed they fuel her sense of herself as irredeemably evil.

Psychiatric illness is rare in young children, but in adolescents an accusation may sometimes be the first indicator of a developing psychosis.

Case example 8.2

A 16-year-old girl accused her father of repeated rape. An extensive social services enquiry found no evidence, but, as a precaution she was rehoused in her own flat. When she later stated that her mother, a music teacher, greeted her pupils topless, doubt was cast on her story. Several years later she had clear symptoms of schizophrenia.

Accusations may arise out of psychological disturbance involving more than one individual. The *folie à deux* is a delusional disorder shared by two people who have close emotional ties. Commonly the stronger, more dominant person develops a delusion and induces it in the other. The condition generally remits if the dominant person is treated. Some custody disputes may be of this kind, in which a child takes on the delusion of the parent. Allegations involving children which are later found to be false often involve mothers with a psychotic illness.

8.3.2 Neurosis
Neurosis is a psychological reaction to stress, expressed through behaviour or emotion which is either excessive or inappropriate. In contrast to psychosis, patients with a neurosis do not strike those around them as out of touch with reality. Rather, their state of mind can be 'understood' and the border between a normal reaction to stress and a neurosis is blurred. Patients may complain of anxiety, phobias, or obsessional-compulsive conditions and some are severely incapacitated by their worries. Their personalities remain relatively intact.

Anxious and 'neurotic' individuals are prone to misperceive cues or misinterpret ordinary actions. It is not uncommon that an immature and sexually naive young woman ignores, or fails to recognise, sexual signals. This may in turn be misconstrued by the man as consent to intercourse. By the time the woman realises what she has got herself into she may not have the social skills to extricate herself. Some women are afraid of upsetting or 'rejecting' the man at this point, recognising that to some extent they are to blame for their own predicament. Others attempt to say 'no' at too late a stage or simply acquiesce as the easiest solution. Guilt and shame may later lead such a woman to reinterpret the event as outside her control and herself as injured. External influences, such as the views of friends and relatives, also exert pressure upon a young woman to regard herself as a victim and minimise her role in the sexual encounter. Women who find themselves in this plight may later 'cry rape'. Some cases of so-called 'date rape' may be of this kind. The woman is not deliberately deceitful so much as deceiving herself.

Some individuals have difficulty in distinguishing fact from fantasy.

Case example 8.3
At the time of a highly publicised murder investigation, a young woman with personal and family stress reported that two men resembling police 'identikit' pictures had attempted to drag her into a green Volkswagen. Within 24 hours she had retracted her statement and later told how she had longed for her husband's attention. As a result she had woven an imaginary story and had come to believe it. Two years later she still said, 'I know it did not happen but it seemed so real. I could see the men and the car so vividly, I can still see them.'

8.3.3 Personality disorders

Personality disorder is an abnormality of personality in which traits are exaggerated to the extent that they cause suffering, either to the individual or to others. The fundamental element is long-standing maladaptive behaviour, originating in adolescence and enduring throughout adult life. However, the distinction between psychiatric illness and personality disorder is not always simple and both frequently coexist. It can be often be difficult to decide whether the disturbed behaviour is due to the personality, the illness, or both.

The paranoid personality disorder is characterised by intense suspiciousness and mistrust of others and is associated with extremes of anger and sometimes circumscribed delusional beliefs. Such people tend to misconstrue others, misunderstand their intentions and often arrive at conspiratorial explanations for events. This condition often lies behind bitter custody disputes in which rage at a hated spouse fuels a delusion. As with neurosis the sufferer may not appear to be unwell and can be extremely convincing.

8.3.4 Munchausen's disease and Munchausen by proxy

Munchausen's disease, also known as factitious illness, is a rare condition in which an adult knowingly fabricates illness seemingly to gain attention. Typically, patients move from hospital to hospital around the country, discharging themselves and moving on as they become known. Most commonly the sufferer claims a physical illness, but there have been instances in which a young woman has made serial false allegations of sexual assault to different social service authorities.

Munchausen by proxy is a variant in which the adult (usually the mother) knowingly creates an illness in her child. As with Munchausen's disease, the claims are usually of physical illness, but false allegations that the child has been sexually abused are also described and may present considerable diagnostic problems. Some mothers may abuse their children as part of the fabrication.

Munchausen by proxy is probably a variant of personality disorder. These women appear to derive pleasure from the drama which attends the involvement of social and legal services. They view themselves as a 'star' in the family trauma, often gaining much sympathy and attention as the courageous parent of a sick or abused child. They are not deterred by any suffering caused to the child. Many have displayed psychiatric disturbance in the past: often they have been troubled teenagers. They must be regarded as mentally unwell.

(A note of caution must be struck. A number of mothers have been incorrectly accused of abusing children who have later been found to be suffering from rare physical conditions. In some cases children have been taken into care and parents prosecuted before the correct diagnosis was made.)

8.4 IATROGENICALLY ASSISTED FALSE ALLEGATIONS

Iatrogenesis, that is, unwittingly creating or extending a patient's illness through treatment or investigation, plays a part in many allegations which turn out to be false. Axioms such as 'Believe the patient' or 'Children never lie' discourage a search for factual accuracy. The beliefs held by individuals influence the way in which reports of sexual misconduct will be received.

8.4.1 Sexual behaviours of children
Behaviours that in an adult would be labelled 'perverse' are part of the normal exploration of small children. Children happily touch any part of their own or another's anatomy, explore with their mouths any object that fits, and smell, lick, suck and taste all manner of substances including excreta. Most children learn, through the normal process of childhood socialisation, that certain behaviours are not acceptable and give them up, but, in a minority of children some behaviours persist beyond the norm for their age group. In recent years there has been a tendency amongst some professionals to construe this persistent behaviour as evidence of premature sexuality, brought about by childhood trauma.

Sexual stimulae in the child's environment can contribute to the overtly sexual behaviour of a small number of children and adolescents. Television and home videos expose children and adolescents to sexually explicit and titillating material and accusations of sexual abuse have followed television programmes with which an impressionable youngster has identified. Although abused children do exhibit sexual play and activity more frequently than non-abused children, there is no behaviour that unequivocally indicates current or previous sexual abuse.

8.4.2 Suggestion and confabulation in children
Surveys show that 25% of cases of demonstrably false allegations of sexual abuse made by children are iatrogenic. These tend to be driven by professionals who have a strong investment in discovering sexual abuse and high belief that certain behaviours are signs of childhood abuse. There is also a naive belief that children do not lie about such matters.

Children are easily influenced by adults. They learn to confabulate to meet the expectations of those around them. This poses problems for fact-finders called in to decide on the truth or falsity of allegations. The professional's belief that abuse has, or has not, taken place is likely to influence the response of the child. Contamination arising from interviewing techniques can contribute to faulty conclusions being reached. The repeated asking of a simple question is enough to persuade a pre-school child to produce stories which serve the presumed expectations of the inquiring adult. In the USA particularly there have been a number of allegations associated with day-care provision which have later proved to be unfounded, but not before they had resulted in costly investigations and wrongful convictions.

It is noticeable that cases of false allegations tend to cluster in some centres and this may well reflect bias on the part of the agency. A few centres appear to support a culture which views allegations or expressions of concern in a naive manner, idealises children, stereotypes circumstances and operates a 'confirmation bias'.

The following factors encourage confabulation in young children:

(a)   When a situation becomes emotionally intense.
(b)   When the child wishes to please an interviewer.

(c)   When the adult repeatedly asks the same question.

(d)   When the adult implies that other children have given information, or that the adult knows what happened.

(e)   When the adult indicates by subtle signs that the answer is the 'right' or 'wrong' one, for example, by grimacing or lavishing praise.

(f)   When the child is pressured by threats, offered bribes, or accused of lying if the expected 'right' answer is not forthcoming.

(g)   When the child is asked to play with so-called 'anatomically correct' dolls. Research comparing play by abused and non-abused shows that they use the dolls in the same manner. A child presented with a peg and a hole will naturally insert the one into the other; when presented with a doll with gaping mouth, anus and vagina, the child will poke its fingers into these openings; and when presented with a male and female doll, the child will put the penis of the male doll into one of the orifices of the female doll. This should never be taken as evidence of sexual abuse.

8.5   FALSE MEMORY SYNDROME

In the 1980s a shift in attitude took place. Growing evidence that the sexual abuse of children was more widespread than previously realised, coupled with the reluctance of women to reveal past abuse, led to a resurgence of belief in Freud's theory of repression. Women (and some men), during counselling or psychotherapy, began to 'recover' apparent 'memories' of previously un-known childhood sexual abuse. This led therapists to believe that the patient had *repressed* the memory of past abuse. Many of these women went on to accuse their often elderly parents of hideous deeds which had taken place years or decades previously. In many cases civil or criminal proceedings followed. Even where legal action was not pursued, many families were disrupted and contact with the accuser completely severed.

The numbers of apparently false allegations were such that accused families formed themselves into societies to raise awareness of the problem. The British False Memory Society, founded in 1993, has had reports from almost 1,000 families. A number of patients subsequently retracted their 'memories', claiming they were the product of imagination and therapist suggestion.

8.5.1   The concept of repression

The belief that memories for past events can be 'blocked out' for many years, even decades, and be recovered intact and unchanged harks back to Freud's 1896 theory of the origins of hysteria. Freud proposed, in his 'seduction theory', that 'repressed', childhood sexual abuse was the cause of most adult psychopathology and must be recalled in its entirety for remediation to occur. He soon repudiated his theory and came to believe that most of his patients were confabulating their memories. In the past two decades Freud's original theories have been revitalised and an increasing number of therapists again believe that traumatic events can be banished from awareness. These thera-pists believe that childhood sexual abuse is especially susceptible to repression and its capacity to create adult psychological distress is unequalled.

Despite widespread acceptance of these ideas there is little solid evidence in support of them. Sixty years of laboratory research has failed to show that repression can occur. More importantly, clinical studies have also failed to give it adequate support. Brains do not work like computers, laying information down for exact duplication. Memory is constructive and reconstructive as well as reproductive. It is known to be fallible, altered by the passage of time and subject to error and distortion. Experiments have shown that expectations and beliefs colour people's recollections, that entirely false 'memories' can be created and held with great conviction, that gaps in memory will be filled to create a satisfying narrative, and that neither confidence in one's memory nor the emotional intensity with which it is held is a guarantee of accuracy.

8.5.1.1 Infantile amnesia Few adults are able to remember events which took place before about the age of three and most have limited memories before age six. This inability to recall very early memories, known as infantile amnesia, is due, in part, to delayed maturation of the brain and a similar amnesia has also been described in animals.

8.5.1.2 Clinical evidence for repression For a clinical study to demonstrate repression it must first prove that sexual abuse actually took place, secondly it must show that the individual developed amnesia which exceeds ordinary forgetting, and thirdly that the amnesia was not caused by brain immaturity or abnormality, such as head injury, intoxication or epilepsy.

There are no research studies which endure these stringent criteria. Most fail to provide any corroboration for sexual abuse and rely on the self-report of the 'victim' after 'memory recovery'. Studies which report apparent loss of memory beyond ordinary forgetting fail to take account of infantile amnesia or the simple failure to report memory, preferring instead to push it aside or not report it to the interviewer.

There are anecdotal accounts of repressed and recovered memory where corroborating evidence seemingly demonstrates the memory to be true. Many of these stories appear at first sight to be believable. But the extent of the 'forgetting' or the reliability of the corroboration often proves to be uncertain. Some 'recovered memories' are often of isolated, relatively minor episodes which would not require extraordinary mechanisms of forgetting and which might quite plausibly be later remembered.

It is not possible to say with absolute confidence that repression cannot occur. It is, however, premature to assert that it has been established beyond doubt. It is a scientific truism that a negative cannot be disproved. The onus of proof rests with those who believe in the concept, it is they who must demonstrate its reality. So far they have not succeeded.

8.5.2 The influence of therapy

Although many scholars and clinicians now conclude that 'recovered memory' should be viewed with a high degree of scepticism, others contend that newly recovered 'memories' should be taken at face value, and that empathic understanding and 'validation' of the trauma are essential in the pursuit of healing. Many practising therapists argue that laboratory findings on repression fail to capture the essence of memory recovery in clinical experience. This leads them to believe that recovered memories are intrinsically accurate. Some believe that acts of extreme violence and brutality are more, not less, likely to be blocked from the memory by 'massive' repression and to remain hidden, sometimes for decades. They have proposed that repeated sexual abuse is recorded by the brain in a unique manner which accounts for total loss of awareness both of the trauma and also of the amnesia.

This contradicts common sense. Everyday experience of memory is that traumatic events are more likely to be remembered than neutral ones. It is not unusual for traumatised people to dwell upon their frightening experiences, rehearsing them in their minds, and to be troubled by intrusive images, or 'flashbacks'. Numerous studies of documented traumatic events have confirmed that subjects do not forget that violent or frightening events befell them though details may fade.

Some therapists believe that certain symptoms are reliable pointers to forgotten sexual abuse and that a diagnosis can be made on the strength of symptoms alone. Others use suggestible techniques to aid their search for suspected childhood sexual abuse. There is in fact no clear evidence that childhood sexual abuse reliably causes any symptoms or behaviour patterns in adults or children, and the best that can be said is that it may be a risk factor for some conditions.

The following practices encourage illusory memory:

(a)   Hypnosis and age regression: memories recalled under hypnosis are unreliable: hypnotic recall increases the confidence with which the memory is held while reducing its reliability. There is no evidence that hypnosis can aid recall of early memory through the technique of age regression and there is compelling evidence of entirely spurious accounts recounted during hypnosis.

(b)   The use of abreactive drugs: 'truth' drugs, like hypnosis, do not increase the accuracy of memory but encourage the creation of illusory recollections.

(c)   Dream interpretation: there is no evidence that dreams can reliably be regarded as recollections of past events. Dreams commonly contain a residue of the previous day's events. If a patient is preoccupied with discerning past sexual abuse it is unsurprising if dreams come to reflect this preoccupation.

(d)   Art work: the same holds for drawing, whether by children or adults: no conclusions can be drawn about the meaning of apparently explicit sexual scenes, or interpretation of apparently sexual symbols.

(e)   Guided imagery: patients are asked to relax and allow the imagination free rein, guided by the prompting of the therapist. The relaxed state fosters an auto-hypnotic state and encourages illusory memories.

(f)   Automatic writing: the individual is asked to write down whatever comes to mind in an uncensored flow and without evaluation. This practice also stimulates imagination and creation of fantasy.

(g)   The use of popular books: a plethora of popular self-help books encourage belief in repression and the search for memories. Many books recommend the above techniques and do not encourage a search for confirmation; some promulgate extreme and irresponsible ideas.

(h)   Massage and 'body memories': the concept of 'body memories' holds that memory is stored in cellular DNA and that physical symptoms are a form of memory which can be released through massage. No evidence supports this belief.

(i)   'Survivor groups': these may be helpful for those who have truly been abused but are hazardous to those who are uncertain because of the danger of peer suggestion and contamination.

8.5.3   Incredible memories
Further evidence for the fabrication of memory is provided by the remarkable 'memories' that some people appear to recover and accept as fact. Individuals have 'remembered' events from earliest infancy, from birth and from within the womb. Accounts range from the foetus as a voyeur of parental intercourse viewed through the cervix, to being an egg stuck in the fallopian tube. People have recounted 'memories' of sexual abuse in previous lives and of abduction by aliens for the purposes of sexual experiments.

While most people would regard 'memories' such as these implausible, one specific set of similarly unlikely 'memories' is often taken at face value and gives cause for concern. Some recollections which begin as 'memories' of sexual abuse progress to accounts of ritual or satanic abuse. Despite the lack of confirming evidence, some therapists continue to believe in ritual satanic abuse as a multi-generation cult conspiracy in which children are programmed from infancy to self-destruct, young women are forcibly impregnated and the foetus or infant later sacrificed in rites that include cannibalism. The lack of any evidence in support of this cult is explained by the extraordinary cunning of its members in concealing evidence, and the belief that the police, judiciary, government and secret services of most Western cultures are themselves deeply involved. Investigations by the FBI in America and by la Fontaine (1994) in this country have failed to find any evidence of such practices, although isolated incidents of 'ritual' abuse have been confirmed.

8.5.4   Retraction of memory
The testament of people who have retracted their 'memories' casts further doubt on 'memory recovery'. Patients often find they are not believed when they retract, whereas statements of the most extraordinary abuse may be accepted without question. Some misguided therapists believe that doubt is proof of the accuracy of a memory which is being overridden by the process of 'denial'. The patient is then caught in a situation in which everything points to past abuse and there is no room for the possibility that a mistake has been made. Similarly, an alleged perpetrator whose repeated denial is taken to be confirming proof that abuse took place is locked into a perverse logic — admission proves guilt and denial also proves guilt.

There are also undoubted occasions when a child, and sometimes an adult, has retracted a truthful account of abuse or assault, under pressure from others. False retractions, like illusory or false memories, may cluster in particular agencies, reflecting bias of the professionals.

8.5.5 Elements which suggest that a memory may be false

(a) The 'memory' is newly recovered and there has been no previous suspicion that abuse took place. A memory which was never forgotten, even if not thought about for long periods, is likely to be true.

(b) A memory occurring before the age of three is almost certainly false and before age six is unreliable. Memories of the first months, or extending back to the womb, are not credible.

(c) The memory arises in the context of a psychological intervention, particularly from a practitioner who accepts the theory of repression.

(d) Memory enhancing techniques have been used.

(e) The patient has been a member of a 'survivors group'.

(f) The memory is stimulated by reading popular literature on recovered memory or exposure to similar suggestive influences.

(g) The patient reports the memory as unlike other memories. The common experience of remembering is that memory returns, with a quality of surprise, 'What made me think of this?', 'How could I have forgotten that?' By contrast, suspect memories are built up over time in the form of a narrative. Subjects often report that memories come in small fragments, and are unlike ordinary memories in being visual, like a film. Suspect memories are also not recognised as having been previously known and forgotten, rather, a distinguishing feature is the complete lack of any knowledge until the recovery occurred.

(h) The patient refers to the memory returning as a 'flashback'.

(i) The memory is inherently improbable or impossible.

(j) The patient expresses doubts about the memory.

(k) Suspect memories frequently show inconsistencies with repetition: frequently they expand with each retelling and become ever more violent and horrifying.

Although the false memory syndrome originally described memories emerging during psychotherapy or counselling it has gradually extended to include disputed memories arising in different ways. About 10% of cases develop during orthodox NHS hospital practice. Other examples have occurred spontaneously and outside the influence of therapy. Increasingly, troubled people speculate that 'something happened' in childhood which has been forgotten, and which accounts for their difficulties. They then set out to 'recover' their memories.

8.6 SUMMARY

Reports of sexual offences against women and children have in the past been minimised or ignored. In recent years the climate has changed and such accounts are regarded more sympathetically and seriously. However, both children and adults sometimes make false allegations of sexual misconduct.

Many of those who do so sincerely believe the truth of what they report. They have become 'honest liars' through illness or following misleading suggestion. Others, however, are opportunistic and are consciously lying for personal gain.

A special type of false allegation, the false memory syndrome, arises typically within therapy. People report the 'recovery' of memories of previously unknown childhood sexual abuse. The influence of practitioners' beliefs and practices in the manufacturing of false memories cannot be overlooked.

Each new case must be approached with an open mind and with an appropriate balance of sympathy and scepticism. External evidence must always be sought and should carry at least as much weight as the testimony of the possibly disturbed accuser. Those who have been at the receiving end of sexual misconduct of any sort, and especially of rape or childhood sexual abuse deserve sympathy and justice but a mistake made in the other direction is abhorrent and those wrongly accused are equally deserving of justice.

Key terms
Child sex abuse; false sex allegation; false memory; false memory syndrome; repression; recovered memory.

References
Kanin, Eugene J. (1994), 'False rape allegations', *Archives of Sexual Behaviour*, vol. 23, pp. 81–93.

la Fontaine, J.S. (1994), *The Extent and Nature of Organised and Ritual Abuse*. London: HMSO.

Recommended reading
Boakes, J.P., (1995), 'False Memory Syndrome', *The Lancet*, vol. 346, pp. 1048–1049.

Brandon, S., Boakes, J.P., Green, R. and Glaser, D., (1998) 'Recovered Memories of Childhood Sexual Abuse: implications for clinical practice', *British Journal of Psychiatry*, vol. 172 pp. 296–307.

Ceci, S. J. and Bruck, M., *Jeopardy in the Courtroom: A Scientific Analysis of Children's Testimony*. American Psychological Association. Washington, 1995.

Loftus, E.F. and Ketcham K.K., (1994), *The Myth of Repressed Memories*, New York: St Martin's Press.

Pendergrast, M. (1996), *Victims of Memory: Incest Accusations and Shattered Lives*, London: Harper Collins.

Pope, H.G. (1997), *Psychology Astray: Fallacies in the Studies of 'Repressed Memory' and Childhood Trauma*. Upton Books.

Pope, H. G. and Hudson, J. I. (1995), 'Can memories of childhood sexual abuse be repressed?', *Psychological Medicine*, vol. 25, pp. 121–6.

Ofshe, R. and Watters, E. (1994), *Making Monsters: False Memories, Psychotherapy and Sexual Hysteria*. New York: Charles Scribner's Sons.

Royal College of Psychiatrists Working Group on Reported Recovered Memories of Childhood Sexual Abuse. (1997) 'Recommendations for good practice and implications for training, continuing professional development and research', *Psychiatric Bulletin*, vol. 21 pp. 663–665.

Yapko, Michael D. (1994), *Suggestions of Abuse*. New York: Simon and Schuster.

Editors' notes

The quality of investigations into allegations of sexual misconduct by the police, social service authorities and even lawyers varies considerably. Often, the focus is on seeking evidence which confirms that misconduct took place and, thus, disconfirming information tends to be ignored or not sought. The lessons of this chapter are ignored at the peril of those wrongly accused.

False complaints involving alleged sexual misconduct are peculiarly phenomenal and may be motivated by forms of mental disorder or syndromes which are unique in this field. Problems involved in diagnosis of conditions which might lead to false complaints being made — Munchausen's syndrome by proxy, for example — are particularly acute. Discovery and disclosure of a complainant's medical records as well as information about previous complaints made by the witness are essential. Fully comprehensive investigative or quasi-investigative records are a crucial resource if an expert, faced with a past diagnosis of disorder, is to be able to analyse effectively the reliability and credibility of the current complaint.

Where an abnormality has been previously diagnosed, the expert analyst's task will, again, be relatively straightforward if the investigative records arising from the current complaint are available. Difficulties will occur, however, where a previously undiagnosed abnormality is suspected but where steps taken to discover it are thwarted as a result of non-cooperation by the witness.

Expert witnesses' reports will frequently be a useful aid during cross-examination of a complainant. Where an abnormality has been detected it will rarely be inappropriate for expert evidence to be given covering its existence and potential effects since fact-finders cannot be guaranteed to know about or be capable of understanding the complex concepts involved.

PART TWO

INVESTIGATIVE PERSPECTIVES

SUMMARY

Using the knowledge available in part 1 of this book concerning the vulner-abilities of those said to be witnessing an incident and when providing subsequent accounts about it, the practitioner now needs to be aware of the mechanics of the methods used to obtain and record statements and the extent to which these may have a tendency to distort 'real' memory or implant false recollections. Obstacles to effective and useful analysis of histories provided are created by the inadequacies of procedures commonly used to record them. Any assessment of whether, due to witness vulnerability, an account has been wrongly influenced or distorted by a questioner will be hampered if the basic crucial raw material needed for this is not available, doctored or otherwise incomplete.

Chapter 9. Full and faithful: ensuring quality practice and integrity of outcome in witness interviews. Eric Shepherd and Rebecca Milne
The role of an investigator's task in facilitating disclosure by a witness is considered alongside identified patterns of witness interviewing techniques which may have the potential for memory distortion. Suggestions are made for improvement which will ensure quality of practice and integrity of outcome in witness interviewing.

Chapter 10. Obtaining detailed testimony: the cognitive interview. Brian Clifford and Amina Memon
Concern that poor-quality investigative interviewing risks the obtaining of undeveloped, partial or otherwise misleading accounts led to the concept of the cognitive interview. The cognitive interview concept is explained and debated thus setting out a process through which reliable and wholesome narratives can be obtained through an integral and sound interview technique.

Chapter 11. Hypnotically induced testimony. Graham Wagstaff

Claims that hypnosis has some special capacity to facilitate memory have led to a belief that it has practical value as an interview procedure tool during police investigations. Modern debate about the value of accounts obtained through hypnosis has led to disquiet over its safety as an investigative procedure. The issues are examined.

Chapter 12. Identification parades: psychological and practical realities. Ian McKenzie and Peter Dunk

Consistent with one of the book's common themes, that memory is frail and susceptible to distortion from outside or inherent influence, this chapter concentrates on visual identification and the extent to which claims of recognition may be fallible owing to hazardous investigative procedures, and other factors.

Chapter 13. Earwitness testimony. Ray Bull and Brian Clifford

The accepted view that correct decisions concerning recognition of a voice, whether the voice of a stranger or that of a person familiar to the witness, can sensibly be made using common knowledge for their basis does not stand up to scientific research on the subject. Available expertise justifies the argument that this is an area where caution is necessary and that earwitness evidence requires more careful analysis than is currently applied in the forensic setting. Additional or different safeguards to those employed over eyewitness evidence are necessary.

Chapter 14. Getting heads together: police collaborative testimony. Noel Clark and Geoffrey Stephenson

Post-event discussions about an event between witnesses during which their primary record about it is written are commonplace amongst police officers and positively encouraged in courts. Whereas collaboration can increase the overall quality and proportion of accurate information, research has shown that the practice leads to errors and the deletion of correct or inconsistent memory. Recommendations are made for improving such investigative practices in a way which will lead to more reliable and comprehensive testimony.

Chapter 15. Recording witness statements. David Wolchover and Anthony Heaton-Armstrong

The obtaining of an unassailable record of what was said both to and by a potential witness during interview by an investigator is of critical importance for the purposes of the later analysis of the account using the lessons learnt in those chapters which centre on the intricacies of human memory and recall. Current investigative practices do not, however, involve procedures which cause comprehensive records of witness interviews to be made. The need for regulation and tape-recording is paramount.

CHAPTER NINE

Full and faithful: ensuring quality practice and integrity of outcome in witness interviews

Eric Shepherd and Rebecca Milne

Information is the lifeblood of criminal investigation and it is the ability of investigators to obtain useful and accurate information from witnesses and victims of crime that is crucial to effective law enforcement (Stewart, 1985, p. 1).

9.1 INTRODUCTION

The investigative process and the judicial system rely fundamentally and predominantly upon accounts given by witnesses. Completeness and fidelity of reporting their accounts are vital determining factors in the solution of a crime. However, police views of witnesses are ambivalent: witnesses are deemed usually to provide central investigative leads but rarely to give as much information as is necessary (Kebbell and Milne, 1998).

These views ignore the pivotal police role in the genesis of witness testimony. Initial interviewing by the first officer attending the scene usually precedes more formal interviewing by the same or another officer at the police station or elsewhere, e.g., the witness's home. The entire process is fraught. Witnesses often struggle to communicate. Their accounts can be incomplete, partially constructed, unreliable, and malleable (see chapters 1 and 2). It demands a particularly professional performance to help a witness recount experience and to ensure that this results in a full account.

Great reliance is placed upon the integrity of police representation of what a witness said. Ill-conceived and ill-judged editing has major implications given the influence of the police record over the direction of investigation and the subsequent interviewing, charging and prosecution of an identified suspect.

Prior to the trial the process of active defence (Ede and Shepherd, 1997) subsumes fine-grain analysis of the police record of witnesses' accounts (see chapter 17). Cross-examination inevitably focuses on anomaly within and between the written statements and subsequent oral testimony (Heaton-Armstrong and Wolchover, 1993). The delay before giving evidence in court is often long. Witnesses (including police officers) typically read their statements to refresh their memories (Gibbons, 1996). An inaccurate record is liable to create the misinformation effect (see chapter 2). Likewise missing information as well as spuriously reported certainty can render the reliability of the individual's testimony extremely vulnerable (Heaton-Armstrong and Wolchover, 1992).

In this chapter we consider in some detail the police officer's task of facilitating witness disclosure in circumstances other than video-recorded interviewing of children (see chapter 4). We review police perceptions and identified patterns in respect of witness interviewing, prior to examining the national model for investigative interviewing (PEACE). We conclude with a proposed method of ensuring quality practice and integrity of outcome in witness interviewing.

9.2   THE POLICE OFFICER'S TASK

The officer's task is to help the witness to give the fullest possible report of his or her experience, enabling the officer to create a mental representation as well as a full and faithful written representation of the witness's disclosures, particularly a statement signed by the witness which is to be used at a criminal trial instead of oral testimony from the witness, under the Criminal Justice Act 1967, s. 9. What the officer has in mind prior to interviewing has the potential to affect his or her entire performance: psychologically, practically and evidentially.

9.2.1   Antecedent knowledge, awareness and aims

9.2.1.1   Offence knowledge   Knowledge is stored as schemata or schemas. These are cognitive structures: abridged, generalised, corrigible, organised stereotypical knowledge derived from first or second-hand experience concerning situations, persons, roles, events, problems, and context-relevant thought and action.

An officer has schematic knowledge for different offences, typically subsuming points to prove or disprove the offence. For many officers this knowledge is extremely limited (Mortimer, 1993).

9.2.1.2   Procedural knowledge   Through formal and 'on the job' training officers learn how to apply offence knowledge when interviewing and creating written evidential texts, i.e., notes, notebook entries, incident record books, crime reports and statements. They implement 'how to do it' 'scripts', which are formulaic sequences of action to elicit and to edit disclosures:

  (a)   within the context of the officer's awareness of the case;
  (b)   with a view to generating a 'good' statement.

9.2.1.3   Awareness of the case   Colman (1989, p. 75) indicated it was 'of prime importance that the interviewing officer be in possession of as many of the facts of the case as possible, before commencing an interview'. This knowledge typically includes accounts and details given by (or even obtained by the officer from) other witnesses, briefings, awareness of objective evidence and the results of forensic analyses, and the identity, arrest, detention and interviewing of any suspect.

The prevailing 'case theory', constructed either by the interviewing officer or another officer, is of particular significance. A case theory brings together offence knowledge, experience of investigating similar cases, selected salient detail from testimony and the scene, and speculation. The theory is deemed to account plausibly for 'what happened' or 'who did what to whom, how and why'. Although pure conjecture, case theories are potent guides to police decision-making and action (Ede and Shepherd, 1997).

Officers are advised to prepare a written list of questions before the interview and to have this to hand as an aide-mémoire together, wherever possible, with statements from other witnesses. Preparing the list ensures awareness of all aspects of the case (Colman, 1989).

There are a number of risks when processing case information.

(a)   *Premature closure.* Premature closure is the disposition to draw pre-emptive conclusions from information processed prior to conducting an interview. It involves selective attention to, and placing significance upon, available and representative information (Tversky and Kahneman, 1974) which 'fits' the individual's views or preconceptions whilst ignoring or actively discounting that which does not. A case theory is an instance of premature closure.

Premature closure creates an illusory, unjustified sense of already 'knowing the answer'. This gives rise to confirmation bias.

(b)   *Confirmation bias.* Confirmation bias is the disposition to seek and to note information which accords with prior assessment (Evans, 1989). Disconfirmatory information is ignored, dismissed or discarded, lending spurious salience and significance to detail which apparently confirms, or does not damage, beliefs about the case.

(c)   *Ironing out and selective synthesis.* Ironing out can occur at any stage prior to or during the interview. It involves wittingly or unwittingly ignoring and glossing over inconvenient contradictory detail, unwanted uncertainty, gaps, vagueness, ambiguity and anomaly. These features typically reflect poor or inadequate investigation, particularly in interviews with witnesses. The officer knows something should be done but the informal code of conduct in the service says 'Do not rock the boat' and 'Do not criticise the work of fellow officers' (Reuss-Ianni, 1983). Mortimer (1994) found officers working on case files prior to interviewing a suspect resolved this stressful dilemma by 'defensive avoidance': around half of the forensically significant detail, particularly that which did not 'fit', was just not registered.

Selective synthesis is a variation of ironing out. Detail is selectively drawn from two or more accounts and integrated into a representation by the officer of what 'witnesses are saying'. However, it is an instrumental, synthetic construction, attributable to no one witness.

9.2.1.4 The evidential aim: a 'good' statement A 'good' statement is the ultimate goal. This aim potentially influences how the officer defines his or her task. It affects information processing. It determines what detail is sought, registered, recorded and represented in the final document. The officer is de facto the arbiter of what representation of the witness's disclosures will be introduced into the investigative process and the judicial system.

9.2.2 Asking questions

Traditionally officers have received highly programmatic guidance (Colman, 1989; Levie and Ballard, 1978) on how to question, particularly with a view to producing or completing a formal document, such as a crime report or a written statement. Typically this guidance tells officers:

(a) to apply the 7-WH mnemonic: what, when, where, how, who, which and why;
(b) to keep questions short and simple;
(c) to avoid marathon and multiple questions;
(d) not to suggest answers — whether by content or inflection.

Since words inadequately communicate visual imagery the witness should be:

(a) encouraged to illustrate non-verbally through gesture, enactment (mini-role-play), drawings or sketches;
(b) if possible and appropriate taken back to the scene — which may additionally assist recall.

9.2.2.1 The appropriate interviewing style Interviewing style is determined by the degree of directiveness exercised by the interviewer, i.e., the latitude given to the interviewee to take the initiative, to speak spontaneously and to select a topic. Table 9.1 summarises the roles, relationships and characteristic behaviours of three styles on a dimension of directiveness.

The interviewer who already 'knows the answer' uses a directive style, asking questions to confirm the 'answer'. It is inappropriate for witness interviewing because only the witness has the 'answer'. A directive style, influenced by preconceptions and the pursuit of a 'good' statement, risks distorting or displacing the witness's representation with that of the officer.

A combination of patterned and non-directive styles facilitates the witness in the difficult task of communicating his or her experience. This approach is effective and ethical, characterised by respect, empathy, supportiveness, positiveness, non-judgmental behaviour, and straightforward talk with an individual perceived as an equal (Shepherd, 1994a).

	Directive	*Patterned*	*Non-directive*
Interviewer's role	Interrogator	Conversational guide	Counsellor
Relations with interviewee	Superior–subordinate	Equals	Helper
Latitude given to interviewee to influence the interview	Very little	Some	A great deal
Plan/agenda	Rigid adherence	Flexible	Free
Flow	Interviewer sets the pace and interrupts the interviewee	Interviewer supports and steers the interviewee's flow	Interviewer supports the interviewee's flow, builds upon replies and waits out pauses
Sharing the talking	A great deal, perhaps most, talking done by the interviewer	Evenly shared, with perhaps most talking done by interviewee	Most talking done by interviewee
Types of question	A high proportion of closed and leading questions	A high proportion of open-ended, with some reflecting back questions	A high proportion of reflecting back, with some open-ended, questions

Table 9.1   Styles of interviewing (after Biddle and Evenden, 1980)

9.2.2.2   A two-phase process   To minimise the risk of preventing, obstructing, influencing, distorting or displacing the witness's account interviewing should be a two-phase process:

(a)   uninterrupted free narration by the witness;
(b)   probing by the officer to expand and to test the detail of narration and subsequent responses.

9.2.2.3   Obtaining free narration   It makes sense to invite the witness to give the fullest possible account at his or her own pace, reporting everything in his or her mind or mind's eye, editing out nothing and including even the apparently inconsequential. Good manners and common sense also argue that the witness should not be interrupted when narrating.

A free-narrative phase elicits approximately 35% of the total accurate information gained from the interview as a whole (Lipton, 1977; Stone and DeLuca, 1980). Interruption is therefore counter-productive. Valuable information could be lost because interruption:

(a)   prevents completion of what the witness wanted to say (Fisher and Price-Roush, 1986);

(b) disrupts concentration, the essential requirement for effective and fuller retrieval;

(c) discourages concerted effort at retrieval, resulting in more superficial responses.

Repeated interruption may be construed as the pattern for the remainder of the interview, leading the witness to give shorter, less detailed, responses to fit the reduced talking time.

In the narration phase there are real benefits to obtaining a first account and then second and subsequent accounts (e.g., a selected episode, or episodes) before the probing phase.

(a) Second and subsequent accounts give even more latitude to expand, modify and qualify preceding versions.

(b) More accounts permit comparison of original and subsequent versions, enabling detection of consistency and anomaly.

9.2.2.4 Probing Probing should fulfil common-sense criteria.

(a) *Appropriate pacing.* Rapid-fire questioning is pressuring and alienating. Pausing after each question and after the witness's answer removes pressure, helps collection of thoughts and facilitates retrieval.

(b) *Questions born of answers.* An answer gives an insight into what the witness has in mind or in his or her mind's eye, i.e., imagery. Logically the next question should be born of the detail in the preceding answer. Hence the question should be mindful of the image the witness is trying to verbalise, i.e., be image-compatible (Fisher and Geiselman, 1992). If the officer 'topic hops', i.e., moves prematurely to another image or changes the topic altogether, this disrupts the witness's retrieval and, cumulatively, discourages further effort (Shepherd, 1986).

Methodical answer-focused questioning permits the witness's attention to be brought to identified anomalies — gaps, vagueness, ambiguity, contrasting degrees of detail, and contradiction.

(c) *Systematic probing and topic progression.* The officer should move logically from one topic to another, not leaving a topic until it has been exhaustively probed. This can be achieved by implementing the *questioning spiral* (Shepherd, 1986): open up the topic, systematically probe this topic, summarise the responses, move to the next topic.

(d) *Use productive questions.* Open-ended and invitational questions, echo and mirror probes, and minimal supportive prompts (e.g., 'And then' . . .) give maximum latitude for responding. They encourage expansion, creating more detail for probing.

(e) *Avoid counter-productive questions.* Leading, option, or multiple questions are all directive and counter-productive. They trigger short, frequently affirmative, answers and thus involve less concentrated retrieval. They signal the officer's knowledge and beliefs about 'facts of the matter'. If they incorporate misinformation, speculation or conjecture, they risk contaminating the witness's recollection (see chapter 2; Loftus, 1979).

Counter-productive questions occur in the technique of 'oblique questioning', which is 'often used by interviewing officers in cases where they believe they already know the answer (sic) to a particular question' (Colman, 1989, p. 86). In Colman's example the officer is aware that a 21-year-old suspect has been arrested:

Q. *Can you describe the intruder?*
A. *Not very well, he was a young man.*
Q. *What age?*
A. *I don't know, quite young.*
Q. *How young, 20s, 30s, 40s?*
A. *Twenty to thirty I would say.*
Q. *Early 20s or late 20s.*
A. *More early 20s.*
Q. *Can you be more specific?*
A. *No that's the best I can do.*

Counter-productive questioning is particularly likely to shape the responses of witnesses engaged in *social desirability* responding (wanting to create a favourable impression) and monitoring the *demand characteristics* of questions (content indicative of the 'right' response).

Especially at risk are those whose psychological make-up, or current emotional or mental state render them excessively compliant (disposed to occupy the submissive role and to 'go along' with the officer), acquiescent (agreeing unreflectively to mutually exclusive questions on the same matter), and suggestible (problems with recall and memory distrust leading to acceptance of what is suggested in the question).

(f) *Use risky questions circumspectly.* Closed confirmatory questions are risky. They notionally reduce the witness's response options to a 'yes' or 'no'. They are, however, very common in everyday conversation. The duration of the response signals how the respondent feels about the relationship. Confidence, trust and a belief that the questioner is genuinely interested motivate the respondent to treat closed questions as if they were open-ended.

A preponderance of 'yes' or 'no' responses suggests reservations about the relationship. More productive questions are required. Furthermore asking closed confirmatory questions too early on in an interview is likely to 'close down' the witness, resulting in increasingly shorter responses.

9.2.3 Processing disclosed detail

9.2.3.1 Creating a mental representation Reduction and reconstruction are fundamental processes in creating a mental representation of something listened to and observed (Singer, 1990). There is always a risk of:

(a) altering what was actually said, in word and even sense;
(b) adding material through inferencing and inclusion of detail known only to the listener.

Spoken text conveys *propositions*: assertions about circumstances, events, episodes, actors, actions, reactions, causes, effects, intentions, and implications. The way things are said (i.e. vocal non-verbal behaviour, called *paralanguage*, e.g., tone of voice) and physical non-verbal behaviour (e.g., facial and bodily movements) transmit more subtle propositions: feelings, attitudes, disposition, and perceptions about the exchange, the topic and the other person.

Antecedent knowledge enables the officer to reduce the mass of incoming material and to create a mental representation in working memory. At the most general level this is the 'gist' of what the witness has said. 'Gist' is underpinned by a framework of *macro-propositions* (van Dijk and Kintsch, 1983): key bits of information, ideas, themes, or 'bullet points' derived from the stream of propositions by:

(a) *deletion* — discarding irrelevant or redundant detail;
(b) *integration* — combining two or more distinct ideas into a single idea;
(c) *generalisation* — reducing two or more similar ideas into one;
(d) *construction* — 'going beyond the evidence', creating through inference an idea not stated explicitly by the witness.

'Going beyond the evidence' is precarious. We think four to six times faster than the speed of everyday spoken speech. This excess capacity enables an officer to attend concurrently to antecedent information, his or her agenda, what he or she thinks about the topic and the witness *and* to anticipate what the witness is about to say, as well as preparing to say what the officer wants to say.

9.2.3.2 Disruptive listening   Spare capacity gives rise to three disruptive styles of listening:

(a) a *non-attender:* antecedent knowledge and the officer's agenda lead the officer to 'tune out' the witness;
(b) an *assumer:* the officer believes he or she knows what the witness really has in mind, typically leading to pre-emptive judgement or jumping in, answering for the witness;
(c) a *word-picker*, a severe form of assumer, who homes in on, and frequently misinterprets and misrepresents, the witness's replies and intentions.

Typical disruptive behaviours are minimal supporting feedback (*backchannelling*, indicative of lack of following or even interest — see chapter 4), overtalking, interrupting, and rapid changing of topic. They are all directive and counter-productive, resulting in:

(a) the officer being seen as dominant, driving the conversation in the direction the officer wants;
(b) increasing likelihood of social-desirability responding and monitoring questions for demand characteristics;
(c) increased risk of compliance, acquiescence and suggestibility.

9.2.3.3 Active listening Active listening means wholehearted commitment to understand what the witness has in mind. It requires the officer (Shepherd, 1986):

(a) to *concentrate* — intently listening;
(b) to *comprehend* — identifying failure to understand or to follow and, at the right time, asking the witness to explain;
(c) to *sustain* — keeping the witness talking, using backchannelling and other non-verbal supportive behaviour;
(d) to *summarise* — communicating the product of intent listening, inviting feedback on the accuracy of the summary and, crucially, facilitating further recall and disclosure of detail. Summarising also helps to consolidate the detail in memory, as well as facilitating accurate note-taking and subsequent statement construction.

9.2.4 Capturing the detail

Police training concentrates on the procedural aspects of note-taking, i.e., to enable form completion and statement composition. It is impossible to listen intently (for detail) and attentively (for paralanguage and non-verbal behaviour) *and* at the same time to make a faithful written record of what is being said and how. Psychologists call this dilemma *response competition*.

Applying speed-writing techniques (e.g., shorthand, abbreviations and symbols) eases the task but this record will:

(a) typically omit paralanguage and non-verbal behaviour;
(b) be essentially gist, with only selected verbatim fragments;
(c) be predominantly one-sided, with little or no detail of the officer's contribution: his or her explanations, own account, observations, commentary, and efforts at facilitating the witness's recall *in addition* to the content and form of questions actually asked.

If other officers were present they are likely to put their heads together but not make a note of doing this. Such collaborative recall has major shortcomings (see chapter 14).

Limited note-taking and note-taking ability deny other officers and the courts knowledge of what the witness *really* said and in what way. Furthermore no one knows to what extent the officer influenced the emergence and content of the witness's account and responses (Heaton-Armstrong and Wolchover, 1992).

9.2.5 Creating a statement

9.2.5.1 Drafting the statement Few witnesses write their own statements for use under the Criminal Justice Act 1967, s. 9. The officer, as amanuensis, relies upon his or her recall and notes, together with any interpretations he or she has made (Fisher, 1995; Gibbons, 1996), editing these to construct a 'good' statement.

For many officers a 'warts and all' statement (Heaton-Armstrong and Wolchover, 1992; 1993) is a waste of time or worse, counter-productive. For them a statement should satisfy, or at least not damage, the police case and the other prosecution evidence (Ede and Shepherd, 1997). Its contents should be plausible and raise no doubt about the validity and certainty of the assertions attributed to the witness.

9.2.5.2 Checking back with the witness   Checking back for accuracy permits further potential expansion. The motivation to do this is created by the extent to which the officer has inspired confidence, trust and commitment:

(a)   to give the fullest possible account;
(b)   to point out *across the course of the interview* instances when the officer has misapprehended, misunderstood or misrepresented what the witness said or meant.

A directive style is unlikely to create this motivation. A demotivated witness will say little or nothing, wanting 'to get it over and done with' quickly. The excessively compliant, acquiescent or suggestible will just agree.

9.3   POLICE PERCEPTIONS AND PRACTICES

9.3.1   Prevalent perceptions
Interviewing witnesses is a high-frequency activity. Witnesses are presumed to be cooperative, unlike suspects who resist. Traditionally interviewing has been seen as a low-status activity: a routine process requiring low-level skills and abilities possessed by everyone and anyone. In contrast suspect interviewing is high-status. Suspects are seen as difficult one-offs, requiring high-level persuasive skills and abilities possessed by the few (Shepherd, 1986).

9.3.2   Observed practices
Witness interviewing is a closed world, beyond the scrutiny of other officers and the courts. Three significant studies recorded what goes on.

Fisher et al. (1987)
Fisher et al. analysed the tape-recorded witness interviewing of eight experienced American detectives. All requested a free narrative, which they interrupted on average after only 7.5 seconds.

Not one interviewee completed the free-narrative account without interruption.

Subsequent questioning revealed pervasive problems.

(a)   The officers were agenda-driven. Their questioning was manifestly directed at their investigative needs, particularly the requirement for a derived statement. This imperative deflected witnesses away from complete recollection.
(b)   Witnesses who went off track were interrupted to return them to the set of questions conjured up to prove the officer's hypotheses (i.e., case theory).

(c)   Many officers asked formulaic questions about suspects, consistent with completion of a final written report but incompatible with the witness's efforts at representation.

(d)   Questioning was rapid-fire and pressuring. On average only one second separated an answer from the next question.

(e)   Questions were predominantly directive, constraining and obstructed retrieval. Inappropriate short-answer questions outnumbered open-ended questions nine to one.

(f)   Judgmental comments were common. Questions often had negative phraseology, implying the witness did not know the answer to the question. This discouraged concerted retrieval and evoked a high frequency of 'I don't know' responses.

(g)   Questions often focused on perceptually and memorially unrelated features.

(h)   Some questions switched witnesses from one modality to another. Such switching is known to reduce recall by approximately 19% (Fisher and Price-Roush, 1986).

(i)   Questioning was not image-compatible, again hindering recall.

(j)   Officers disrupted retrieval by interjecting with questions on other matters.

(k)   Officers did not follow up potential leads, indicating the officers had problems holding detail in working memory.

(l)   Officers interrupted the witness's disclosures and train of thought to probe earlier responses on a different matter. This lagging was associated with inability to keep up with the witness when taking notes.

The officers impeded the process by using formal, stylised language, often beyond the intellectual capabilities of the witness, and by using technical terms and jargon.

George (1991)
In the UK George, a detective, asked 28 experienced officers to tape-record three witness interviews, one being randomly selected for analysis.

Common witness interviewing schemata emerged, akin to those identified by Fisher et al. (1987). Closed questions and extension/clarification questions predominated with more leading questions than open-ended questions being used. Pauses were almost non-existent.

McLean (1992)
McLean, another UK detective, asked 16 experienced officers to tape their witness interviews and to give him copies of section 9 statements which they prepared.

The officers typically talked more than the witnesses. They filled the pause taking the talking turn before the witness had time to speak and listened disruptively, overtalking, interrupting and rapidly changing the topic.

Nearly half their questions were counter-productive, one in five were risky and only one in three productive. Questioning was much more directive than interviews of suspects (McLean, 1990), where only a quarter of questions were counter-productive, a quarter risky and the remainder productive.

Comparing the statements with the interview recordings showed that whilst errors of commission in the document were relatively few, there were serious errors of omission. Evidentially significant detail, some of it vital, did not appear in the statements.

These three studies served to confirm what everyone in the police service knows. Biased by antecedent case information and mindful of the requirement to complete reports and to compose statements, officers obstruct, shape and even prevent disclosure of detail. Were they interviewing suspects in this manner on tape, their grossly directive behaviour would occasion intervention by any legal adviser present and attract adverse judicial comment at trial.

The dominant interviewing style is paradoxical. It is counter to common sense because it actually hinders rather than helps the giving of a complete account and puts pressure on the officer. The officers' memory and note-taking problems are compounded if not created by them doing most of the talking. Mental resource is directed more on what to say next than on registering the answer to the last question.

The net result of these behaviours is statements which are illusory, inadequate and inaccurate: a forensic fiction being the officer's instrumental representation rather than a full and faithful record of that given by the witness.

9.4 PROFESSIONALISING WITNESS INTERVIEWING

9.4.1 Prior to 1992
Before 1992 there were no training courses specifically dedicated to witness interviewing. Two developments pointed to ways of improvement.

9.4.1.1 The conversation management model In 1983 Merseyside Police requested Shepherd to develop an approach to interviewing consonant with the spirit and letter of the Police and Criminal Evidence Act 1984 (PACE). The result, *conversation management*, was a patterned/counselling approach applicable when interviewing witnesses as well as suspects, whom he considered to be a special category of witness.

Conversation management is founded on simple assumptions and principles:

(a) Although potentially more manifest from a suspect, resistance can also undermine the 'finding out' process with a witness. It is an interplay of two dimensions: *ability to tell* and a motivational, decision-making dimension — *willingness to tell* (see chapter 4; Shepherd, 1993).

(b) Key behaviours inspire the confidence, trust and respect essential to facilitate disclosure and to overcome resistance:

(i) Send relationship messages of *equality* by paying attention to form of address at initial **greeting** and thereafter across the interview.

(ii) At the outset define the working relationship: a concept central to counselling and psychotherapy, not least with resistant individuals. This is done by considered **explanation**, i.e., spelling out:

(1)   the *reason* for the interview;
(2)   the *route map* (a flexible agenda of actions and topics to be covered in the interview);
(3)   the *routines* (e.g., the interviewer's note-taking, reference to notes and exhibits);
(4)   *expectations* (i.e., preparing the interviewee to view silence as constructive rather than pressuring — the interviewer will not fill pauses or interrupt and give the interviewee plenty of time to think about questions and about his or her answers; inviting the interviewee to ask questions at any time).

(iii) Put the emphasis on registering, noting and analysing the fine-grain detail of what is said (and how), as the essential antecedent to further finding out. This involves managing the course of the interview by the **mutual activities** of:

(1)   *monitoring* — intent, non-disruptive, active listening (*concentrate, comprehend, sustain* and *summarise*) and focused observation of fine-grain non-verbal (vocal and non-vocal) behaviours;
(2)   *assertion* — using productive questioning and the interview spiral to obtain multiple accounts and to probe these systematically.

This approach gives the initial responsibility for narration, expansion and correction to the witness. This allows the interviewer simultaneously to engage in more efficient registration in memory, collation and comparison of the detail of successive versions.

(iv) Pay particular attention to the *close* of the interview, summarising to check back derived detail with a motivated witness.

The mnemonic GEMAC — greeting, explanation, mutual activity (monitor/assert), close — summarises the effective, ethical steps to facilitate maximum disclosure from someone treated as an equal, placed 'in the picture' and who feels able to influence the course of events.

9.4.1.2 Cognitive interviewing Clifford and Memon (see chapter 10) describe how Geiselman and Fisher developed cognitive interviewing (CI) in response to requests from police forces for a method of improving witness interviews. Like conversation management CI centres upon obtaining an uninterrupted account or accounts in which the individual is asked to report everything, even the seemingly inconsequential. The enhanced form of the CI incorporates interview-management behaviours reminiscent of conversation management.

However, the CI is unique for its focus on memory-enhancing techniques: inviting the interviewee to reinstate the context of the experience, to adopt a different perspective, and to recall in reverse order, and activating and probing the interviewee's mental image, accessing different modalities, and using other memory-jogging methods (Fisher and Geiselman, 1992; Milne and Bull, 1999).

9.4.2   The PEACE model

9.4.2.1   A Guide to Interviewing and the equal emphasis model   In September 1990 the Association of Chief Police Officers (ACPO), with Home Office backing, formed a working party to establish investigative interviewing principles and practices to be applied by all officers. The group recognised the imperative to improve witness as well as suspect interviewing. In due course a project team of officers with substantial training and operational experience abridged and incorporated GEMAC into a five-stage model summarised by the mnemonic PEACE: planning and preparation; engage and explain; account; closure; evaluate.

The model was described in a pamphlet *A Guide to Interviewing* (Central Planning and Training Unit, 1992a) supported by a second pamphlet *The Interviewer's Rule Book* (Central Planning and Training Unit, 1992b). These were issued to all officers in advance of attending a five-day training course: one day covering basic issues and then equal emphasis on witness interviewing and suspect interviewing — two days each. In early 1993 a costly programme of training began, aimed at officers across the entire career span.

The *Guide* gave clear and comprehensive guidance and explanation of 'best practice' and essential psychological issues, i.e., memory and human communication.

In the account phase officers were able to choose between:

(a) *conversation management* (the GEMAC multiple-account/systematic-probing approach) deemed to be applicable to resistant suspects and witnesses, and

(b) the *cognitive approach* (a programmatic form of CI) deemed to be applicable to willing interviewees, both witnesses and suspects.

In respect of capturing detail and creating a full and faithful record of disclosures by witnesses and victims the *Guide* said:

> In more serious cases, such as a fatal road accident or a serious assault, you may find it beneficial to support your note taking by tape-recording the interviews. If you do use a tape recorder, as with your notes, the tapes must be kept with the case papers and their existence disclosed in the event of a prosecution. (p. 29.)

Fisher and Geiselman (1992) argued that wherever possible cognitive interviews should be tape-recorded, because CI techniques generate a very large amount of detail. The CI makes substantial mental demands: to concentrate for prolonged periods, to hold a large amount of detail in working memory, and to make a comprehensive note of this information, including significant non-verbal behaviour, e.g., observable indicators of imaging. Köhnken et al.

(1994) found that information gets lost: statements composed by interviewers who used CI contained only two-thirds of the information recalled by interviewees.

The *Guide* (p. 29) also drew attention to the necessity for full investigation, i.e., asking questions to establish the validity of a witness's account.

> When obtaining information from eye witnesses or victims it is essential to consider the points made in the case of *R* v *Turnbull* in 1976. These points are outlined below:
> A   Amount of time under observation
> D   Distance
> V   Visibility
> O   Obstruction
> K   Known or seen before
> A   Any reason to remember
> T   Time lapse
> E   Error or material discrepancy

Officers were required to make a faithful record, including all the AD-VOKATE elements and any discrepancies in the witness's written statement.

9.4.2.2 Investigative Interviewing and the primacy of suspect interviewing
Three developments led to a revision of the PEACE model with increased emphasis on suspect interviewing:

(a)   Since February 1994 legal advisers in police stations have increasingly followed the Law Society's professional texts (Shepherd, 1994a, 1994b, 1996a, 1996b), requiring the service to give officers guidance on disclosure of evidence.

(b)   The provisions of the Criminal Justice and Public Order Act (CJPOA) 1994, particularly the timely administration of special warnings, have significant implications for the management of the interview and of information within the interview.

(c)   The cognitive approach had assumed 'problem' status. There was growing ambivalence about its use (Croft, 1995; Kebbell, Milne and Wagstaff, in press). Most considered it useful but time-consuming. Some felt the extra time was worthwhile in terms of fuller outcomes (Longford, 1996). Many felt operational demands for expeditious investigation precluded its use.

There were concerns about its value in that anxiety might distort the experience of victims such that events may be reorganised and placed into a different order. This distortion was a particular source of frustration for officers who had heard a description of the event in another order from other sources, so that what they heard from an interviewee did not square with antecedent knowledge (Croft, 1995).

Context reinstatement was considered inappropriate for potentially traumatised victims (Croft, 1995). The technique of reverse-order recall was difficult to apply and its underlying logic, and therefore benefit, was not apparent. The only widely used element of the approach was the 'report everything' (Boon and Noon, 1994). Officers mistakenly thought that issuing this instruction and listening without interruption constituted CI.

CI was being restricted more and more to serious offences, being implemented by those who were confident and competent in its application.

A revised model was published in *Investigative Interviewing: A Practical Guide* (1996. A subsequent second edition (1998) comprises four parts (principles of investigative interviewing, interview skills, the PEACE model, interviewing law and procedure). It is rounded off by a case reference index, six appendices, reference information and feedback information).

A chapter on *conversational techniques* explains questioning but in lesser detail than the *Guide*. The new model retains the GEMAC concepts. The account phase has three stages: *account, clarification* and *challenge*. This notion of challenge reflects the shift in emphasis towards suspect interviewing, and the tactical use of special warnings.

There is no conversation management/cognitive approach distinction. Officers are guided not to rush, to set the scene ('reinstate the context', p. 54), to obtain an uninterrupted account (p. 56), to encourage repeated attempts at recall ('from different points of view or with different goals in mind' bearing in mind that 'information is received through all five senses', p. 57), to expand and clarify disclosures by selecting topics for probing, rounding each off by summarising.

Unlike its predecessor the new text gives no explanation of memory or explicit advice on memory-enhancement methods. However, on data capture and tape-recording it says:

> Note-taking will also help you later to write a report, statement or summary of the interview. This is particularly important with witness and victim interviews as it can be difficult to retain all that they have to say in your memory. In these circumstances notes will help you retain valuable information and enable you to use the interviewee's own words rather than police jargon. In some cases it may be useful to record the victim and witness interviews on audio or videotape. (p. 33.)

The revised text also requires attention to ADVOKATE issues, stressing that 'These points must be recorded as part of a witness statement' (p. 58).

The shift in emphasis towards suspect interviewing is reflected in the new five-day course: three days tend to be devoted to interviewing suspects, with only one to witnesses.

9.5   THE CASE FOR TRANSPARENCY OF WITNESS INTERVIEWING

9.5.1   Tape-recording of suspect interviews: the impact of technology on police behaviour

Tape-recording has rendered the process of suspect interviewing transparent. There was substantial opposition. Many thought it would prevent officers engaging in persuasive questioning and inhibit suspects who wished others not to know what they said. Central government reservations centred on the cost of equipment, tapes and storage.

The PACE requirement to tape-record opened up the previously closed world of the interview room to scrutiny. Lawyers, judges and juries learned what really went on. As more and more tapes were played in court, it became clear that the police service desperately needed to professionalise. Interviewing of suspects was frequently ineffective, unethical or both. Written records of tape-recorded interviews (ROTIs) emerged as distorted and distorting representations of questions and replies. Research (e.g., Baldwin, 1992) only confirmed what the courts had learned.

Williamson (1993), now an ACPO officer, commented upon the tremendous impact of technology. The transparency of tape-recording brought in to protect the suspect, as a by-product, motivated the service to change investigative behaviour. Had there been no tape-recording there would not now be a national model, training, and the recognition that supervision is the key to ensuring the transfer of learning to the workplace.

9.5.2 Tape-recording of witness interviews
Tape-recording would allow fellow officers in charge of investigations as well as the courts to identify and do something about:

(a)   instances where the officer prevented, shaped, distorted or displaced disclosure by the witness;

(b)   shortcomings in the witness's account — gaps, vagueness, ambiguity, contradiction, uncertainty, doubt and different versions in what the witness said.

Although PEACE invited officers to consider tape-recording witness interviews, there has been a marked disinclination to do so. This reluctance is resonant of the resistance to tape-recording of suspect interviews. Those who have always questioned witnesses directively, even more persuasively than suspects, to obtain disclosure confirming the officer's preconceptions and to generate a 'good' statement, cannot conceive things being any other way. In a similar vein all too many statements do not report the elements of ADVOKATE, and leave out discrepancy. Those who do not want witness interviews recorded remain unconvinced that detail which raises doubt should be made public.

When Heaton-Armstrong and Wolchover (1997) advocated tape-recording a key official objection was the problem of selection: which interviews should be recorded? To date only a few forces have a specified procedure regarding the tape-recording of witness interviews. However, the Northumbria Police have a policy requiring interviews to be tape-recorded (Milne and Shaw 1999). The Kent Police routinely video record witnesses concerning grave allegations. In addition, a working party at the National Crime Faculty under the aegis of the ACPO Crime Committee has recently produced a manual for best practice in the investigation of crime, using the offence of murder as a model. This indicates that tape-recording of *significant witnesses* is a key aspect of best practice. We applaud this development but it raises fundamental, thorny, questions.

What are the defining criteria of witness significance in a given case? In many, if not the majority, of instances the significance of a witness's account will not be apparent until he or she is actually being, or has been, interviewed. Furthermore significance may not emerge until some time after section 9 statements have been constructed and signed by a large number of witnesses. The decision to record someone deemed to be significant at this later stage may be well justified, but there will be major implications in terms of the quality of his or her testimony (see chapter 2). *Post hoc* decisions concerning significance strike us as inherently problematic — practically and psychologically.

We differ from Heaton-Armstrong and Wolchover only in terms of the extent to which we argue tape-recording should take place. There are overwhelming arguments that it should be a commonplace not something reserved for the exceptional. So long as the decision to tape-record rests upon subjective perceptions of seriousness and *post hoc* judgments concerning witness significance and seriousness of offence the quality of witness interviewing will continue to prejudice the effectiveness of police investigation.

If tape-recording of witness interviews remains a matter of discretion, the vast majority will go unrecorded. Officers will continue to interview in the way they always have, safe in the knowledge that no one will ever know what really went on, the officer's performance and its effects, what the witness really said or was prevented from saying, and the fidelity of the statement constructed by the officer.

Sustaining officers in this behaviour involves a terrible cost to victims and witnesses. Frustrated in their attempts to disclose in interview, they may fail subsequently to 'come up to proof', giving an account at odds with what the officer wrote down. There is a cost to the service and our system of justice. Every obstructive inappropriate interview and every 'failure' at court contributes to a loss in public confidence. When shortcomings in evidence lead to wrongful conviction, when revealed at successful appeal there is yet more loss.

Those who are likely to object to recording anything other than witnesses deemed to be significant in serious offences, however defined, are likely to raise the issue of cost. Yet the machinery and the tapes are already inexpensive and would be even more so given economies of scale. Cost must be considered relative to benefit. Tape-recording is the *only* way of assessing the cost-effectiveness of expensive PEACE training directed at improving the quality of witness interviewing. Furthermore, tape-recording is the *cheapest* means of supervising large numbers of officers, as well as being an objective basis for bringing about *real* behaviour change. Listening to tape-recordings and subsequently mentoring the officer is the most economical, effective and efficient means of ensuring the transfer of learning from the PEACE classroom to the workplace.

Other official objections have included witness concerns about confidentiality and tampering.

The notion of a witness not wanting to be recorded on grounds of confidentiality is remarkably akin to earlier arguments about suspects being similarly inhibited. No witness can be given assurance of 'special relationship' or threaten not to proceed if confidentiality cannot be guaranteed. PACE Code C, note 1B, points to the civic duty of all citizens to help police officers to prevent crime and to discover offenders.

Similarly specious and readily dispatched is the notion of tampering. To tamper with audio-cassette tape with a view to avoiding detection demands technical skill and appropriate technology. Furthermore forensic methods easily reveal tampering (Shepherd, in preparation).

The overriding argument for transparency is public faith in the police and the courts. Without tape-recording as a matter of everyday procedure the witness interview will continue to be a source of frustration and fiction: investigation and the administration of justice will continue to be prejudiced by the absence of full and faithful accounts from all-important witnesses.

9.6 SUMMARY

(a)   Witness testimony is essential to effective and ethical police investigation and administration of justice.

(b)   Investigators and the courts rely upon officers to be professional in the process of interviewing witnesses and in producing a record of what the witness disclosed.

(c)   Preconceptions, case theories, notions of knowing the 'answer', premature closure, confirmation bias, and ironing out predispose officers to interview directively to produce a 'good' written statement, i.e., a trimmed-down, plausible, unequivocal account attributed to the witness.

(d)   To obtain a full account and to produce a faithful record of a witness's disclosures requires a patterned/non-directive style of interviewing, in which constructive questioning and active listening are used to obtain multiple uninterrupted accounts which can be systematically analysed and probed.

(e)   The current PEACE model endorses this style, notwithstanding the demise of cognitive techniques and the de-emphasis of witness interviewing.

(f)   Only the transparency of tape-recording will ensure change in police behaviour such that full and faithful accounts emerge from the professional interviewing of witnesses.

Key terms
Interviewing; witness; case theory; premature closure; confirmation bias; active listening; conversation management; cognitive interviewing; cognitive approach; tape-recording.

References
Baldwin, J. (1992), *Preparing Records of Taped Interviews* (Royal Commission on Criminal Justice Research Study No. 2). London: HMSO.
Biddle, D. and Evenden, R. (1980), *Human Aspects of Management*. London: Institute of Personnel Management.

Boon, J. and Noon, E. (1994), 'Changing perspectives in cognitive interviewing', *Psychology, Crime and Law*, vol. 1, pp. 59–69.

Central Planning and Training Unit (1992a), *A Guide to Interviewing*. Pannal Ash: Home Office.

Central Planning and Training Unit (1992b), *The Interviewer's Rule Book*. Pannal Ash: Home Office.

Colman, T. (1989), *Incident into Evidence*. Maidenhead: McGraw-Hill.

Croft, S. (1995), 'Helping victims to remember', *Police*, November 1995, pp. 13–14.

Ede, R. and Shepherd, E. (1997), *Active Defence*. London: Law Society.

Evans, J. (1989), *Bias in Human Reasoning: Causes and Consequences*. Hove: Erlbaum.

Fisher, R. (1995), 'Interviewing victims and witnesses of crime', *Psychology, Public Policy and Law*, vol. 1, pp. 732–64.

Fisher, R. and Geiselman, R. (1992), *Memory-enhancing Techniques for Investigative Interviewing: The Cognitive Interview*. Springfield, Ill: Charles Thomas.

Fisher, R., Geiselman, R. and Raymond, D. (1987), 'Critical analysis of police interviewing techniques', *Journal of Police Science and Administration*, vol. 15, pp. 177–85.

Fisher, R. and Price-Roush, J. (1986), *Question Order and Eyewitness Memory*. Unpublished manuscript.

George, R. (1991), *A Field Evaluation of the Cognitive Interview*. Unpublished master's thesis, Polytechnic of East London.

Gibbons, S. (1996), 'Extracting the best', *Police Review*, March 1996, pp. 18–20.

Heaton-Armstrong, A. and Wolchover, D. (1992), 'The eyes have it', *Police Review*, 28 August 1992, pp. 1594–5.

Heaton-Armstrong, A. and Wolchover, D. (1993), 'Warts and all', *Police Review*, 5 February 1993, pp. 22–3.

Heaton-Armstrong, A. and Wolchover, D. (1997), 'Tape-recording witness statements', *New Law Journal*, pp. 855–7 and 894–6.

Kebbell, M. and Milne, R. (1998), 'Police officers' perception of eyewitness factors in forensic investigations', *Journal of Social Psychology*, vol. 138, pp. 323–30.

Kebbell, M., Milne, R., and Wagstaff, G., 'The cognitive interview: a survey of its forensic effectiveness', *Psychology, Crime and Law*, in press.

Köhnken, G., Thürer, C. and Zoberbier, D. (1994), 'The cognitive interview: Are the interviewers' memories enhanced too?' *Applied Cognitive Psychology*, vol. 8, pp. 13–24.

Levie, R. and Ballard, L. (1978), *Writing Effective Reports on Police Investigation*. Boston: Holbrook Press.

Lipton, J. (1977), 'On the psychology of eyewitness testimony', *Journal of Applied Psychology*, vol. 62, pp. 90–3.

Loftus, E. (1979), *Eyewitness Testimony*. Cambridge, Mass: Harvard University Press.

144   Ensuring quality practice and integrity of outcome in witness interviews

Longford, G. (1996), *The Use of the Cognitive Interview by Police Officers Trained on the National Investigative Interviewing Course*. Unpublished MSc dissertation, Institute of Police and Criminological Studies, University of Portsmouth.

McLean, M. (1990), *Identifying Patterns in Police and Criminal Evidence Act Interviews*. Unpublished report, Bradford and Ilkley College.

McLean, M. (1992), 'Quality investigation? Police interviewing of witnesses', *Medicine, Science and the Law*, vol. 35, pp. 116–22.

Milne, R. and Bull, R. (1999), *Investigative Interviewing: Psychology and Practice*, Chichester: John Wiley & Sons Ltd.

Milne, R. and Shaw G., Obtaining Witness Statements: best practice and proposals for innovation, *Medicine, Science and the Law*, in press.

Mortimer, A. (1993), '"A case of . . .": patterns in police officers' perceptions of offences', in E. Shepherd (ed.), *Aspects of police interviewing*. Leicester: British Psychological Society.

Mortimer, A. (1994), 'Asking the right questions', *Policing*, vol. 10, pp. 111–24.

National Crime Faculty (1996), *Investigative Interviewing: A Practical Guide*, Bramshill: Police Staff College.

National Crime Faculty (1998), *Investigative Interviewing: A Practical Guide*, 2nd ed., Bramshill: Police Staff College.

Reuss-Ianni, E. (1983), *Two Cultures of Policing: Street Cops and Management Cops*. New Brunswick, Conn: Transaction Books.

Shepherd, E. (1986), 'The conversational core of policing', *Policing*, vol. 2, pp. 294–303.

Shepherd, E. (1993), 'Resistance in police interviews: the contribution of police perceptions and behaviour', in E. Shepherd (ed.), *Aspects of Police Interviewing* (Issues in Criminological and Legal Psychology, No. 18), Leicester: British Psychological Society, pp. 5–12.

Shepherd, E. (1994a), *Becoming Skilled*. London: Law Society.

Shepherd, E. (1994b), *A Pocket Reference*. London: Law Society.

Shepherd, E. (1996a), *Becoming Skilled*, 2nd ed. London: Law Society.

Shepherd, E. (1996b), *A Pocket Reference*, 2nd ed. London: Law Society.

Shepherd, E., *Testing Testimony*. London: Law Society, in preparation.

Singer, M. (1990), *Psychology of Language: an Introduction to Sentence and Discourse Processes*. Hillsdale, NJ: Erlbaum.

Stewart, J. (1985). Cited in R. Geiselman, 'Interviewing victims and witnesses of crime', *Research in Brief* (US Department of Justice, National Institute of Justice), vol. 1.

Stone, A. and DeLuca, S. (1980), *Investigating Crimes*. Boston: Houghton Mifflin.

Tversky, A. and Kahneman, D. (1974), Judgements under uncertainty: heuristics and biases', *Science*, vol. 185, pp. 1124–31.

van Dijk, T. and Kintsch, W. (1983), *Strategies of Discourse Comprehension*. New York: Academic.

Williamson, T. (1993), 'Review and prospect', in E. Shepherd (ed.), *Aspects of Police Interviewing* (Issues in Criminological and Legal Psychology, No. 18). Leicester: British Psychological Society, pp. 5–12.

Recommended reading
Ede, R. and Shepherd, E. (1997), *Active Defence*, London: Law Society.
Fisher, R. and Geiselman, R. (1992), *Memory-enhancing Techniques for Investigative Interviewing: The Cognitive Interview*, Springfield, Ill: Charles Thomas.
Heaton-Armstrong, A., and Wolchover, D., 'The eyes have it', *Police Review*, 28 August 1992, pp. 1594–5.
Heaton-Armstrong, A. and Wolchover, D., 'Warts and all', *Police Review*, 5 February 1993, pp. 22–3.
Heaton-Armstrong, A. and Wolchover, D., 'Tape recording witness statements', *New Law Journal*, 1997, pp. 855–7 and 894–6.
Milne, R. and Bull, R. (1999) *Investigative Interviewing: Psychology and Practice*, Chichester: John Wiley and sons Ltd.
National Crime Faculty (1998), *Investigative Interviewing: A Practical Guide*, 2nd ed., Bramshill: Police Staff College.
Ord, B. and Shaw, G. (1999), *Investigative Interviewing explained. The operational guide to practical interviewing skills*, The New Police Bookshop.

Editors' notes
Where, at least, a vulnerability has been identified, perhaps for one of the reasons set out in part 1, the forensic desirability for fully recording an investigative interview with the witness appears to be overwhelming when considered in the light of this chapter. In the absence of a 'full' interview record and where there are any reasonable grounds for suspecting that a witness's pre-trial written statement may not provide the complete investigative picture, it is doubtful whether a witness's testimony can be effectively examined in court. An application for the witness's evidence to be excluded in accordance with s. 78 of the Police and Criminal Evidence Act 1984 might need to be made — using similar criteria to those which would be employed if incomplete or expurgated records were made of an interview with a suspect. There is no shortage of examples of cases of proven miscarriages of justice involving memory corruption or subornment of prosecution witnesses by investigators, the details and recognition of which emerge only years after the event.

At the time of writing, the Youth Justice and Criminal Evidence Bill is being debated in Parliament. In its present draft it contains provision for video-recorded interviews with restricted categories of 'vulnerable' witness (those under 17, the mentally or physically disordered, the frightened or distressed and complainants in sex cases) to be used in substitution for their evidence in chief. We consider it unfortunate that this radical change in the law has not been extended to *all* witnesses, since *all* witnesses are potentially vulnerable to the corrupting influence of improper investigative methods. (See also chapter 15.)

CHAPTER TEN

Obtaining detailed testimony: the cognitive interview

Brian R. Clifford and Amina Memon

10.1 INTRODUCTION

The ability to obtain full and accurate information is critical in many aspects of the criminal justice system: a good interview with a key witness may determine whether or not a case is advanced or solved by the police or prosecuted by lawyers. Yet the eyewitness literature reveals that memory for witnessed events is generally poor. The cognitive interview (CI) was initially developed in the United States of America by psychologists Ed Geiselman and Ron Fisher in 1984 as a response to the many requests they received from police officers and legal professionals for a method of improving witness interviews. Fisher et al. (1987a) found certain fundamental problems in the conduct of 'standard' police interviews that were leading to ineffective communication and limiting interviewer and witness performance. They documented several characteristics of the 'standard police interview', among which were constant interruptions (when an eyewitness was giving an account), excessive use of question-and-answer format and inappropriate sequencing of questions. This led to the characterisation of a 'standard police interview' as being one of poor quality and stressed the need for an alternative procedure for interviewing witnesses.

In this chapter we will show how the CI has met the demand for an effective interview technique in police interviews and evolved into a powerful investigative tool for eliciting information from witnesses and victims, having stood up to empirical tests in the field and in the laboratory. While not discussed directly, we believe these findings can be transferred to other investigative areas inhabited by lawyers and social workers. The chapter is divided into a number of parts. We will begin with a description and evaluation of the original CI procedure and its various components. We will then review field and laboratory tests of the enhanced cognitive interview. Finally we will indicate the applicability of the CI in the criminal justice system and certain areas that require further investigation to maximise the CI's efficiency.

10.2   THE CI

The original CI drew heavily upon what psychologists knew about the way in which we remember things. The revised version (the enhanced CI) focused on considerations for managing a potentially difficult social interaction and was motivated by a desire to improve communication in police interviews and alleviate some of the problems described above.

10.2.1   The original CI

The 'cognitive' components of the CI draw upon two theoretical principles. First, that a retrieval cue is effective to the extent that there is an overlap between the encoded information and the retrieval cue and that reinstatement of the original encoding context increases the accessibility of stored information (the encoding specificity hypothesis). Secondly, the multiple trace theory, which suggests that rather than having memories of discrete and unconnected incidents, our memories are made up of a network of associations and consequently there are several means by which a memory could be cued. It follows from this that information not accessible with one retrieval technique may be accessible with another. These two theoretical principles issued in four cognitive mnemonics of the CI.

10.2.1.1   Context reinstatement   The first cognitive technique is to elicit in the witness a mental reconstruction of the physical and personal contexts which existed at the time an event was experienced, by asking the witness to form an image or impression of:

(a)   the environmental aspects of the original scene (e.g., the location of objects in a room),
(b)   the witnesses' emotional reactions and feelings (surprise, anger, etc.) and
(c)   the physical conditions (hot, humid, smoky, etc.) that were present.

While many researchers have agonised about the transient nature, or even reality, of context reinstatement (Memon and Bruce, 1985) it does appear to be the most effective component of the CI. While Clifford and Gwyer (1999) showed context reinstatement effects to have little or no impact on person identification they consistently found positive effects on recall of event details. Context reinstatement is also the key element of the guided memory interview, in which eyewitnesses are guided through each step of the incident and probed for a full description of the environment in which the incident took place and their emotional reactions to it (Malpass and Devine, 1981).

10.2.1.2 Report everything A second technique is to ask the witness to report everything without screening out anything considered to be irrelevant or for which there is only partial recall. This may well facilitate the recall of additional information, perhaps by shifting criteria for reporting information. In addition, this technique may yield information that may be valuable in putting together details from different witnesses to the same crime.

10.2.1.3 Change perspective The third retrieval aid is to ask for recall from a variety of perspectives by encouraging witnesses to place themselves in the shoes of the victim (if a bystander) or of another witness and to report what *they* would have seen. The theoretical assumption here is that a change in perspective forces a change in retrieval description, thus allowing additional information to be recalled from the new perspective. There are, however, several concerns about the use of this instruction, in particular the possibility that it could lead to fabricated details and confuse the witness (Memon et al., 1996a). Police officers have tended not to use this instruction and some have expressed a concern about the possibility of it misleading the witness (Clifford and George, 1996). However, there is some recent evidence that suggests the change-perspective instruction can produce as accurate information as the other CI techniques (Milne, 1997).

10.2.1.4 Reverse order The fourth component of the CI is the instruction to make retrieval attempts from different starting points — from the end or from the middle of the incident, or from the most memorable event — thereby encouraging extra focused and extensive retrieval. Witnesses usually feel they have to start at the beginning and are usually asked to do so. This technique, like the change-perspective instruction, is assumed to change the retrieval description, resulting in the recall of additional details. Geiselman and Callot (1990) found that it was more effective to recall in forward order once followed by reverse order than to make two attempts to recall from the beginning. So far there is little evidence that this technique yields any more information than a second retrieval attempt when used in a cognitive interview although Milne (1997) has found the instruction to be of some benefit when applied with specific prompts.

10.2.2 Tests of the original CI procedure

Between 1984 and 1990 several 'simulation' studies of CI were undertaken employing staged and filmed scenarios of forensic relevance. Geiselman et al. (1985) compared the cognitive interview with the interviews more usually conducted by experienced police officers (the 'standard' interview procedure described earlier). The participants (witnesses) were undergraduate students and the interviewers were experienced law enforcement professionals (e.g., police investigators, members of the CIA, and private detectives). Witnesses were interviewed approximately 48 hours after viewing the films. Three weeks prior to the interview the interviewers received instructions to follow one of two procedures: (a) standard interview or (b) the cognitive interview.

Geiselman et al (1985) coded the witnesses' recall information as pertaining to information about 'persons' or 'objects' or 'events', and scored it for the number of correct, incorrect and confabulated items of information recalled. The CI elicited 35% more correct information than did the standard interview but the two types did not differ on incorrect items or confabulations. Scoring of critical items from the film showed that the CI not only enhanced recall of ancillary facts but also key information.

There are several points that should be noted here: (a) the means by which the CI group were trained is not specified; (b) there were no apparent checks on whether or not interviewers and witnesses understood the CI techniques and the frequency with which the instructions were applied; (c) the control group were not trained and there was no monitoring of the techniques they used. However, since these original studies, numerous replications of CI superiority over the standard interview have been recorded.

10.2.3 Application of the CI by British police forces
Until 1992 training of the British police forces in witness and victim interviewing was unsystematic and ad hoc. With the production of *A Guide to Interviewing* (1992) a national system for such training was put in place. However, as figure 10.1 shows, the police approach to the CI was overly formalistic. The CI was never intended to be applied like a recipe, with particular mnemonics applied to particular phases of the interview. The guidelines to which all forces in England and Wales were exposed can thus be seen to be too rigid.

GET INTERVIEWEE INTO CONTEXT

Mentally relive
Edit nothing

FREE RECALL

SECOND RECALL

Change order

THIRD FREE RECALL

Change perspective

PROBE

REVIEW

WRITTEN STATEMENT

Figure 10.1   The CI as presented by the text *A Guide to Interviewing*

10.2.4 The enhanced CI

In order to be able to implement effectively the use of the 'cognitive' components of the CI, it is necessary to provide interviewers with the social skills and communication strategies that are required to build rapport with a witness. As indicated earlier, research with police officers suggested this was something they lacked. The revised version of the CI is often referred to as the enhanced CI because it is even more effective than the original version of the CI (Fisher et al., 1987b).

The enhanced version combines the four cognitive techniques described above with strategies for improving interviewer–witness communication and flow of information in the interview. These techniques include the 'transfer of control' of the interview from the interviewer to the witness. This technique is put into place during the rapport-building phase in several ways; initially by telling the witness that as he or she was present at the incident only he or she knows what really happened, and subsequently, through the use of open questions which request an elaborated response from the witness (thereby allowing the witness to do most of the talking), by not interrupting the witness, and by timing questions carefully so that they are related to the witness's retrieval patterns and not to a protocol that an interviewer may be using.

The various elements of the enhanced CI work interactively. For example, building rapport with the witness renders the witness more relaxed and open to using the various cognitive techniques and by not interrupting and pausing after questions, the interviewer can facilitate contextual reinstatement.

Further refinements of the CI also include additional cognitive techniques for activating and probing a witness's mental image of the various parts of an event, such as a suspect's face, clothing, objects. The instructions to form an image are used in conjunction with the context reinstatement technique during the questioning phase of the interview (see Memon et al., 1997a). Given that witnessing is predominantly a visual process, imaging should be a powerful technique. However, when contextual reinstatement is accompanied by instructions to image and the images are probed with questions, further details which are both correct and incorrect may be elicited. In addition some research in the source monitoring tradition suggests that imaging could be problematic to accurate memory performance. Thus, despite its intuitive appropriateness, it is suggested that imagery instructions should be used with some caution until we have a better understanding of how they influence source monitoring and corresponding decision processes.

This more fluid enhanced CI is represented in figure 10.2, where it can be seen that the cognitive mnemonics are applied at any stage of a highly interactive and spontaneous exchange, being deployed if and when felt to be required to elicit maximum recall.

GREET AND ESTABLISH RAPPORT

EXPLAIN INTERVIEW

> *Report everything*
> *Concentrate*
> *No fabrication or guessing*

OPEN-ENDED NARRATION (Free recall)

> *Context reinstatement*

PROBE MEMORY CODES (Questioning)

> *Re-emphasise concentration*
> *Report everything*
> *Reinstate specific context*
> *Recall in varied order*
> *Witness-compatible questioning*

REVIEW

> Probe new information if
> volunteered by appropriate
> CI mnemonics

Figure 10.2   The enchanced CI showing flexible application of retrieval mnemonics

10.2.5   Empirical tests of the enhanced CI

10.2.5.1   Field studies   To date there have been only two field tests of the cognitive interview. The first involved police detectives in Miami, Florida (Fisher et al., 1989), the second involved the Hertfordshire police in the UK (George, 1991; George and Clifford, 1995; Clifford and George, 1996.)

The aim of the Fisher et al. (1989) field study was to examine the use of the enhanced CI by trained and 'control' police detectives when questioning real-life victims and witnesses. The pre-training phase of the study involved the collection of tape recordings of interviews from a sample of detectives using their usual, standard techniques. Half of the group underwent enhanced CI training over four 60-minute sessions. After the fourth training session each detective tape-recorded a practice interview in the field and received individual feedback from psychologists on the quality of the interview. The detectives then followed the enhanced CI procedure or 'standard interview' procedure (as defined earlier) during the course of their interviews with real witnesses over a period of time. Two measures of the effects of training were taken: the number of facts elicited before training versus after training; and facts elicited by trained versus untrained officers.

Trained detectives elicited 47% more information after training and significantly more information than detectives not trained in CI. In addition the CI did not appear to increase the amount of incorrect information, as indicated by corroboration rates.

While the results of this CI field study are promising, given the relatively small sample size, the representativeness of the trained group is questionable. The officers were selected for training rather than being randomly assigned to conditions and this is of some concern especially in light of evidence that police officers may not be so open to the use of new techniques (Memon et al., 1995). Finally, there was no trained control group in this field study and data are not provided on the techniques used by interviewers.

George (1991) reported a UK field study involving 32 experienced British police officers (George and Clifford, 1995; Clifford and George, 1996). Officers were randomly assigned to one of four conditions: CI (with two days' training), conversation management (with seven days' training), CI and conversation management (seven days' training) and a no-training control group. Conversation management is a procedure which resembles the structured interview described earlier and includes training in planning the interview, listening skills, conversational styles, question types and summarising. Prior to training, each subject provided a tape recording of an interview he or she had conducted with a real-life witness or victim. Following training each police officer tape-recorded three more interviews with victims or witnesses of street crimes and one of these tapes was selected at random to serve as the 'after-training' tape. Both sets of tape recordings before and after training were transcribed and evaluated for the amount of information provided by the interviewee. The results showed that the CI elicited significantly more information than the standard police interview (25% more than the no-training control group). A comparison before and after training showed an increase in information elicited of 55% for the CI group. There were no significant differences between conversation management and the untrained control, and the CI plus conversation management group fared worst of all, possibly as a result of training overload, or incompatible techniques.

10.2.5.2 Laboratory studies From a practical perspective, it is important to show that the CI is more effective than the techniques currently in use by police officers and others. The selection of untrained police interviewers in the field studies discussed in 10.2.5.1 was a sensible control. From a theoretical perspective, however, an experimental control is needed to demonstrate that the techniques themselves are causing the effects and not some aspect related to training such as motivation, quality of questioning or rapport building skills.

More recent tests of the CI have addressed this question by comparing the CI with a procedure known as the structured interview (SI) procedure, where the quality of training in communication and questioning techniques is comparable to the CI procedure. The training of the structured group follows a procedure that is recommended to professionals who interview children (the *Home Office Memorandum of Good Practice*, Home Office and Department of Health, 1992; see Bull, 1992, 1995). The essence of the *Memorandum* is to treat the interview as a procedure in which a variety of interviewing techniques are deployed in relatively discrete phases proceeding from general to open, to specific, to closed-form questions. Rapport building, through open questions and active listening, is an important component.

So is it possible for an interviewer, armed with a range of 'good' interviewing techniques and effective communication skills, to achieve the same effects as a CI-trained interviewer? The answer is somewhat ambiguous.

The question has been addressed in Germany (Köhnken et al., 1994; Mantwill et al., 1995) and in the UK by Memon et al., (1997a, 1997b) and Gwyer and Clifford (1997). In all these studies the cognitive interview was compared with a structured interview in which the structured interviewers received training of comparable quality and length in terms of basic communication skills, rapport building, use of various types of questioning, discussion of transcripts and videotaped interview, and practice in roleplaying. The training of the cognitive group in addition uniquely involved the use of the various cognitive techniques. The training session lasted four to five hours.

In the German studies, the to-be-remembered event was a videotape showing a blood donation. Participants were tested a week after viewing the event. In the Köhnken et al. (1994) study the CI resulted in an average of 52% more correctly recalled information without increasing the number of errors and confabulated (made-up) details. In the Mantwill et al. (1995) study the enhanced CI yielded 25% more correct information without any differences in errors and confabulations.

These results suggest that the enhanced CI effects are due to the use of the cognitive techniques rather than merely a result of enhanced communication. However, this conclusion does not fit with the results of a series of studies conducted by Memon. Memon et al. (1997b) directly examined whether the source of the CI advantage was due to facilitated communication arising from the use of the 'communication' components of the enhanced CI or a result of the 'cognitive' components of the enhanced CI (context reinstatement, imagery, reverse order and reporting in detail). Following Köhnken, CI and SI interviewers received a similar quality of training, with all interviewers being trained separately over a period of two days in basic communication techniques, building rapport, types of questions to ask, role-plays and receiving feedback on practice interviews. In order to examine the effects of training and motivation, an untrained group was also included in their study.

It was found that the CI and SI did not differ in terms of the overall amount recalled, the accuracy of recall, the number of errors or the number of confabulations. Both groups of trained interviewers elicited more in the way of overall information and amount of correct information than did the untrained group. However, this was offset by their producing a significantly higher number of errors and confabulations than the untrained group. These findings are important in themselves but they also raise the question of what is the appropriate control group. Clearly, in this study, if the CI is compared to an untrained group it produces some advantages. However, if the CI is compared to a group matched for everything but the cognitive techniques (namely the SI) then the advantage of the CI is reduced. This finding is at odds with the studies conducted in Germany and suggests that the effects of the cognitive interview depend on the standard of comparison that is used (Memon and Stevenage, 1996).

However, in line with the German studies, Gwyer and Clifford (1997) found that enhanced CI training did produce significantly greater correct and total recall, but no greater error, than a suitably trained SI comparison group. Tentatively, then, it could be concluded that the effect of the enhanced CI is due to more than just enhanced communication.

10.3 AREAS OF FUTURE DEVELOPMENT

10.3.1 Developmental variables

The vast majority of studies on the CI have focused on the performance of adults. Where children have been considered as witnesses, the general finding has been that children do somewhat less well with the CI than adults. However, to date, there has not been a comparison of children and adult performance in a single study using the same incident, comparable versions of the CI interview and the same interviewers.

Several problems in applying the CI with children have been identified. First, younger children (6–7 years of age) may have difficulty understanding the CI techniques in the form developed for adults (e.g., Memon et al., 1997b). Secondly, the CI, when used with children, can increase the number of errors and confabulations. Thirdly, the CI interview results may be affected by demand characteristics in that children respond in a way they think may please the interviewer.

Notwithstanding these caveats, research has shown that the CI can be used to good effect with children. Geiselman and Padilla (1988) found 7–12-year-olds interviewed by the CI produced 21% more correct information than a group interviewed by the SI. Likewise Saywitz, Geiselman and Bornstein (1992) found 7–8 and 10–11-year-olds interviewed by the CI recalled 26% more correct facts than an SI group, and McCauley and Fisher (1992) found a CI-interviewed group of children recalled twice as many facts as an SI group, and 64% more facts in a later study (McCauley and Fisher, 1995). Confirmation of the CI's usefulness with children is not confined to American studies. Finger, Nitschke and Köhnken (1992) found CI-interviewed children recalled 93% more correct details than an SI control, while Loohs (1996) showed that the CI elicited more recall than the SI with 6-year-olds. Akehurst, Milne and Köhnken (submitted) investigated 8–9 and 11–12-year-olds and found CI-interviewed children recalled more detail than SI, and Chapman and Perry (1995) found CI-interviewed children reported more correct information than SI-interviewed children, at all ages.

In addition to these studies with 'normal' children, Milne (1997) has demonstrated the beneficial effects of CI with children who have learning disabilities. Clearly, then, children can benefit from being interviewed by the CI method. However, even greater benefit could accrue by future examination of the parts of the extant CI discussed above which are thought or are known to be troubling for children.

The utility of the CI with an elderly population may be an interesting question to explore, as research from allied fields (e.g., face recognition) would predict that older adults would benefit more than younger adults from procedures that enhance the recollection of contextual information. To date, however, there has been only one published study comparing the recall performance of college students and older adults with the CI and no age-related differences were found (Mello and Fisher, 1996).

10.3.2 Interviewer variables
Although it is clearly the case that interviewer differences are an important source of variance in the CI, there have been only a few attempts to systematically investigate such variability. Memon et al. (1996b) examined interviewer differences in the use of the cognitive and communication techniques that form the enhanced CI. They compared the CI with the SI in a study of children's memory for a staged event (magic show) and found differences amongst the individual CI interviewers in the number and type of questions asked (e.g., open-ended versus closed), and in the use of the various CI techniques. This was also found by George (1991) and Clifford and George (1996) with police officers.

It is likely that differences in the attitudes, motivation and prior experience of the interviewers may play a large role in determining the kind of results obtained with the CI. Thus while Memon et al. (1994) found that the police showed considerable resistance to the training, failed to follow instructions and used poor questioning techniques in both the CI and SI, George (George and Clifford, 1995; Clifford and George, 1996), a senior police officer, found officers were more than happy to receive instruction from him, but still showed great variability in the use of the various mnemonics. Pre-training measures may establish how motivated and interested candidates are about embarking on a training programme (see Memon, Bull and Smith, 1995 for an extended discussion).

It is important to note also that the use of the CI techniques is likely to vary with characteristics of the *interviewee*. As Fisher (1995) has pointed out, an interview is an interactive process, and an interviewer's questions and instructions are responses to interviewee behaviour.

10.3.3 Training in CI techniques
The success of the CI depends upon adequate training of interviewers in the techniques described above. To date it is not clear how much training is required. Some studies report effects with relatively brief training. Fisher et al. (1989) report benefits after four 60-minute sessions, while George (1991) trained officers over two to seven days. Memon et al. (1994) trained officers over a more limited period of time (four hours) and found this was insufficient to motivate officers to use the new techniques. Turtle (1995) has

evaluated several one-week training courses on the CI for Canadian police officers and found that training has relatively little effect on the use of CI techniques. An extensive study in the UK still to be published found that 23 UK constabularies reported that they spent a mean of only 8.6 hours during probationary training on the CI.

But it is not just quantity of training that is important — quality matters also. The 1992 *A Guide to Interviewing* booklet, from which all police were trained, presented a somewhat strange depiction of the CI. Although this booklet has now been replaced by *A Practical Guide to Investigative Interviewing* 1998 2nd ed.) it has to be said that this revision blurs the distinction between the CI and conversational management, and does not use the term CI or even 'the cognitive approach' to interviewing. This blurring is unfortunate because it tends to equate a suspect who wishes to keep matters of fact concealed from the police (to which conversational management may apply but to which the CI does not) and a witness and/or victim who wishes to recall as much detail as possible but cannot because of memory difficulties (to which the CI most definitely applies but conversational management may not). Only the CI has inbuilt mnemonic aids to overcome these memory blocks. To play down or even exclude the CI's mnemonics is to prevent the interviewer from using tried and tested methods for maximising witness or victim recall. And yet the exclusion of the CI from the revised training guide may be more apparent than real because in that guide there is talk of 'Tell all without editing anything out' (p. 49), 'memory-enhancing techniques' (p. 28), 'reinstating the context' (p. 54), recalling from 'different perspectives, i.e. what the interviewee heard' (p. 57), and recruiting imagery ('visual scenes') and witness-compatible questioning ('systematically examining each episode or topic' p. 57). However, the question remains, to quote Juvenal, *'quis custodiet ipsos custodes'*? At present there are now two specific training packages but it is felt by the police that those trained on the 1992 guidelines (which included the CI explicitly) need not be retrained on the revised guidelines (which explicitly eschew the concept of a cognitive approach and the CI specifically). This seems to be a recipe for disaster at the coal face, as the work of Memon et al. (1994) suggests that unless they are provided with continuing feedback on their interview methods, police officers will continue to slip into bad practice. Geiselman and Fisher (1997), in a review of 10 years of research on cognitive interviewing, also stress the importance of providing feedback on interviewers' performance. The question must now be raised, in the light of two sets of extant guidelines, just what form of feedback and guidance will be offered.

10.4   CURRENT APPLICATION OF THE CI BY THE CRIMINAL JUSTICE SYSTEM AND THE WAY FORWARD

Until 1996 all probationary police officers in the UK were trained in the CI. However, there is some evidence that operational officers do not use all the CI techniques and when they are used they are often used inappropriately. Longford (1996) found officers believed that the CI was a useful tool but interview logistics prevented its extensive use. Kebbell et al. (submitted 1997) and Croft (1995) both found time was the biggest prohibitor of its use by serving officers, while Boon and Noon (1994) report that only the 'recall everything' component is widely used. To the extent that police officers are not using the CI in its most robust form, and yet claiming that they are, the credibility of the CI is in danger of being lost.

In addition to evidence that the CI is used by operational officers (albeit sporadically and selectively) the courts seem to have accepted its validity also. In a recent Court of Appeal case (*R* v *Hill* — the Bordon baseball bat murder) the CI was used by Eric Shepherd to interview a person claiming to have committed the murder (rather than the man imprisoned for the offence — Hill). The upshot was that Hill was released.

The CI, then, appears to be a case where psychology and legal personnel have come together for the betterment of justice. Many questions still remain to be addressed by empirical research but the major hurdles of replicability, generalisability, applicability and acceptance seem to have been overcome. Further progress can now be ensured by focusing on customising the CI in terms of field-friendliness and utilisation of only the most productive of the CI components in order to ensure the best and most productive use of time by hard-pressed officers. This in turn calls for both accelerated componential research on the different mnemonics and the investigation of the interactive nature of these cognitive components with the social and communicative aspects of the CI. Also in need of clarification are the reasons why some studies show increased errors and confabulations with the CI while other studies do not.

Over and above these research-led developments there is also the question of maximising the return on investment in the CI. Everyone agrees that the application of the CI mnemonics within a carefully planned and conducted interview result in the production of a mass of *potentially* useful data. However, the data-capturing techniques of the police leave much to be desired. Research shows that the use of a CI not only makes the witness or victim work harder, but also the interviewer. Wherever and whenever possible the police officer's data-capturing techniques should be enhanced by the aid of technology and training in order to improve both on-line and off-line interviewing performance. Better data-capturing techniques could aid officers in noting significant imaging points, keeping track of the stages of the interview and establishing, off-line, any associations between specific questioning techniques and specific recall of details.

There can be little doubt that if these developments are pursued then this demonstrably useful technique for witness and victim interviewing can be strengthened yet further.

Key terms
Children; cognitive interview; context reinstatement; imagery; report everything; reverse order recall; structured interview; training.

References
Akehurst, L., Milne, R. and Köhnken, G., 'The effects of age and delay on recall in a cognitive interview', *Journal of Applied Psychology*. In submission.

Bekerian, D.A. and Dennett, J.L. (1993), 'The cognitive interview technique: reviving the issues', *Applied Cognitive Psychology*, vol. 7, pp. 275–97.

Boon, J.C. and Noon, E. (1994), 'Changing perspectives in cognitive interviewing', *Psychology, Crime and Law*, vol. 1, pp. 59–69.

Bull, R. (1992), Obtaining evidence expertly: the reliability of interviews with child witnesses', *Expert Evidence: The International Digest of Human Behaviour, Science and Law*, vol. 1, pp. 5–12.

Bull, R. (1995), 'Innovative techniques for the questioning of child witnesses especially those who are young and those with learning disability', in M. Zaragoza, J.R. Graham, G.C.N. Hall, R. Hirschman and Y.S. Ben-Porath (eds), *Memory and testimony in the child witness*. Thousand Oaks, CA: Sage.

Central Planning and Training Unit (1992), *A Guide to Interviewing*. Pannal Ash: Home Office.

Chapman, A.J. and Perry, D.J. (1995), 'Applying the cognitive interview procedure to children and adult eyewitnesses of road accidents', *Applied Psychology: An International Review*, vol. 44, pp. 283–94.

Clifford, B.R. and George, R. (1996) 'A field investigation of training in three methods of witness/victim investigative interviewing', *Psychology, Crime and Law*, vol. 2, pp. 231–48.

Clifford, B.R. and Gwyer, P. (1999), 'The effect of context reinstatement and other methods of context manipulation on identification', *Psychology Crime and Law* (in press).

Croft, S. (1995), 'Helping victims to remember', *Police*, November 1995, pp. 13–14.

Finger, M., Nitschke, N. and Köhnken, G. (1992), *Criteria-based Content Analysis and the cognitive interview*. Poster presented at the NATO Advanced Study Institute: The Child Witness in Context: Cognitive, Social and Legal Perspectives, La Lucca.

Fisher, R.P. (1995), 'Interviewing victims and witnesses of crime', *Psychology, Public Policy and Law*, vol. 1, pp. 732–64.

Fisher, R.P. and Geiselman, R.E. (1992), *Memory Enhancing Techniques for Investigative Interviewing: The Cognitive Interview*. Springfield Ill: Charles C. Thomas.

Fisher, R.P., Geiselman, R.E. and Amador, M. (1989), 'Field test of the cognitive interview: enhancing the recollection of actual victims and witnesses of crime', *Journal of Applied Psychology*, vol. 74, pp. 722–7.

Fisher, R.P., Geiselman, R.E. and Raymond, D.S. (1987a), 'Critical analysis of police interviewing techniques', *Journal of Police Science and Administration*, vol. 15, pp. 177–85.

Fisher, R.P., Geiselman, R.E., Raymond, D.S., Jurkevich, L.M. and Warhaftig, M.L. (1987b), 'Enhancing eyewitness memory: refining the cognitive interview', *Journal of Police Science and Administration*, vol. 15, pp. 291–7.

Geiselman, R.E. and Callot, R. (1990), 'Reverse versus forward recall of script based texts', *Applied Cognitive Psychology*, vol. 4, pp. 141–4.

Geiselman, R.E. and Fisher, R.P. (1997), 'Ten years of cognitive interviewing', in D. Payne and F. Conrad (eds), *Intersections in Basic and Applied Memory Research*, Mahwah, NJ: Lawrence Erlbaum Associates, pp. 291–310.

Geiselman, R.E., Fisher, R.P., MacKinnon, D.P. and Holland, H.L. (1985), 'Eyewitness memory enhancement in the police interview: cognitive retrieval mnemonics versus hypnosis', *Journal of Applied Psychology*, vol. 70, pp. 401–12.

Geiselman, R. E. and Padilla, J. (1988), 'Cognitive interviewing with child witnesses', *Journal of Police Science and Administration*, vol. 16, pp. 236–42.

George, R. (1991), *A Field Evaluation of the Cognitive Interview*. Unpublished master's thesis, Polytechnic of East London.

George, R. and Clifford, B.R. (1995), 'The cognitive interview — Does it work?', in G. Davies, S. Lloyd-Bostock, M. McMurran and C. Wilson (eds), *Psychology, Law and Criminal Justice*. New York: Walter de Gruyter, pp. 146–54.

Gwyer, P. and Clifford, B.R. (1997), 'The Effects of the Cognitive Interview on Recall, Identification, Confidence and the Confidence/Accuracy relationship', *Applied Cognitive Psychology*, vol. 11, pp. 121–45.

Home Office and Department of Health (1992), *Memorandum of Good Practice on Video-recorded Interviews with Child Witnesses for Criminal Proceedings*. London: HMSO.

Kebbell, M.R., Milne, R. and Wagstaff, G. (1997), 'The cognitive interview: a survey of its forensic effectiveness', *Psychology, Crime and Law*, submitted 1997.

Köhnken, G., Thurer, C. and Zorberbier, D. (1994), 'The cognitive interview: Are interviewers' memories enhanced too?' *Applied Cognitive Psychology*, vol. 8, pp. 13–24.

Longford, G. (1996), *The Use of the Cognitive Interview by Police Officers Trained on the National Investigative Interviewing Course*. Unpublished master's dissertation, Institute of Police and Criminological Studies, University of Portsmouth.

Loohs, S. (1996), *Mnemonic Aids in Questioning Children: Misleading, Useless or Helpful?* Paper presented at the Sixth European Conference of Law and Psychology, Sienna.

Malpass, R. and Devine, P. (1981), 'Guided memory in eyewitness identification', *Journal of Applied Psychology*, vol. 66, pp. 343–50.

Mantwill, M., Köhnken, G. and Aschermann, E. (1995), 'Effects of the cognitive interview on the recall of familiar and unfamiliar events', *Journal of Applied Psychology*, vol. 80, pp. 68–78.

McCauley, M. and Fisher, R.P. (1992), *Improving Children's Recall of Action with the Cognitive Interview*. Paper presented at the American Psychology-Law Society, San Diego.

McCauley, M. and Fisher, R.P. (1995), 'Facilitating children's eyewitness recall with the revised cognitive interview', *Journal of Applied Psychology*, vol. 80, pp. 510–17.

Mello, E.W. and Fisher, R.P. (1996), 'Enhancing older adult eyewitness memory with the cognitive interview', *Applied Cognitive Psychology*, vol. 10, pp. 403–18.

Memon, A. and Bruce, V. (1985), 'Context effects in episodic studies of verbal and facial memory: a review', *Current Psychological Research and Reviews*, pp. 349–69.

Memon, A., Bull, R. and Smith, M. (1995), 'Improving the quality of the police interview: can training in the use of cognitive techniques help?', *Policing and Society*, vol. 5, pp. 32–40.

Memon, A., Cronin, O., Eaves, R. and Bull, R. (1996a), 'An empirical test of the mnemonic components of the cognitive interview', in G.M. Davies, S. Lloyd-Bostock, M. McMurran and C. Wilson (eds), *Psychology and Law: Advances in Research*. Berlin: De Gruyter.

Memon, A. and Köhnken, G. (1992), 'Helping witnesses to remember more: the cognitive interview', *Expert Evidence: The International Digest of Human Behaviour, Science and Law*, vol. 1, pp. 39–48.

Memon, A., Milne, R., Holley, A., Bull, R. and Köhnken, G. (1994), 'Towards understanding the effects of interviewer training in evaluating the cognitive interview', *Applied Cognitive Psychology*, vol. 8, pp. 641–59.

Memon, A. and Stevenage, S.V. (1996), 'Interviewing witnesses: what works and what doesn't?', *Psycholoquy*, 7(6), witness memory.1.memon.

Memon, A., Wark, L., Bull, R. and Köhnken, G. (1997a), 'Isolating the effects of the cognitive interview techniques', *British Journal of Psychology*, in press.

Memon, A., Wark, L., Holley, A., Bull, R. and Köhnken, G. (1997b), 'Eyewitness performance in cognitive and structured interviews', *Memory*, in press.

Memon, A., Wark, L., Holley, A., Köhnken, G. and Bull, R. (1996b), 'Interviewer behaviour in structured and cognitive interviews', *Psychology, Crime and the Law*, vol. 3, pp. 181–201.

Milne, R. (1997), *Application and Analysis of the Cognitive Interview*. Doctoral Dissertation. University of Portsmouth.

National Crime Faculty (1992), *A Practical Guide to Investigative Interviewing*, 2nd ed. Bramshill: Police Staff College.

Saywitz, K.J., Geiselman, R.E. and Bornstein, G.K. (1992), 'Effects of cognitive interviewing and practice on children's recall performance', *Journal of Applied Psychology*, vol. 77, pp. 744–56.

Turtle, J. (1995), *Officers: What Do They Want? What Have They Got?* Paper presented at the 1st biennial meeting of the Society for Applied Research in Memory and Cognition, University of British Columbia.

Recommended reading
Bekerian, D.A. and Dennett, J.L., 'The cognitive interview technique: reviving the issues', *Applied Cognitive Psychology*, vol. 7 (1993), pp. 275–97.

Fisher, R.P. and Geiselman, R.E. (1992), *Memory Enhancing Techniques for Investigative Interviewing: the Cognitive Interview*. Springfield Ill: Charles C. Thomas. 1992.

Memon, A. and Bull, R. (1999), *Handbook of the Psychology of Interviewing*, Chichester: John Wiley and Sons Ltd.

Memon, A., and Köehnken, G. 'Helping witnesses to remember more: The 'cognitive interview', *Expert Evidence: The International Digest of Human Behaviour, Science and Law*, vol. 1 (1992), pp. 39–48.

National Crime Faculty (1992), *A Practical Guide to Investigative Interviewing*, 2nd ed. Bramshill: Police Staff College.

Editors' notes

Where cognitive interviews are conducted professionally and with integrity there is obviously much to be said for them. However, not all investigator trainees are enthusiastic about attending courses on witness interviewing skills, appreciate the importance of their instructions, or are capable of putting them into effective practice. This chapter provides useful guidance for those intending to get the best, and the truth, out of a witness but there are pitfalls where the technique is abused and, unless cognitive interviews are comprehensively recorded on tape, there is no means of discovering whether they are conducted with propriety or what risks to memory corruption may have been created.

CHAPTER ELEVEN

Hypnotically induced testimony

Graham F. Wagstaff

11.1 INTRODUCTION

11.1.1 Public conceptions of hypnosis

Survey research from Britain, the USA and Australia, indicates that the popular public conception of hypnosis is similar to that held by many nineteenth-century writers and practitioners. Hence hypnosis is viewed as a mysterious sleep-like state or 'trance', that enables people to transcend their normal waking capacities. Given this background, it is not surprising that claims have been made that hypnosis has some special capacity to facilitate memory, and may, therefore, have practical value in police investigations as an interview procedure. Indeed, in the late 1970s and early 1980s a number of books and articles were published describing the extraordinary capacities of hypnosis to enhance memory in police investigations, and up until the late 1980s there were many reports of the use of hypnosis by the police in countries including the UK, USA and Australia (Wagstaff, 1993; McConkey and Sheehan, 1995). For instance, Haward (1988) reports that he used hypnosis in 17 cases in Britain in one week, and says another colleague used it on 50 occasions.

However, on first consideration all of this would seem to be at odds with the views of many modern researchers who now question the idea that 'hypnosis' enables one to transcend so-called 'waking' or 'non-hypnotic' abilities, including memory performance. Indeed, the status of hypnosis as a special altered state of consciousness has itself been a source of considerable controversy amongst academics and clinicians. Therefore, as the background to the nature and status of hypnotically induced testimony, it may be informative to outline briefly some of the general debate about the nature of hypnosis.

11.1.2 The state versus non-state debate

What is frequently referred to as the 'state–non-state' debate is one of the longest-standing academic controversies in the area of hypnosis (Wagstaff,

1981, 1996a). Modern supporters of the 'state' school continue to argue that central to the concept of hypnosis are profound alterations in the subject's state or condition. Perhaps the most popular modern version of the state approach is Hilgard's 'neodissociation' theory (Hilgard, 1986, 1991). According to this theory, when individuals enter the hypnotic state they surrender to the hypnotist some of the normal control and monitoring they have of their experiences. As a result, in response to suggestion, motor movements (such as arm lowering) are experienced as involuntary (because the part of the mind responding to the hypnotist and actually controlling the movement is 'dissociated' from awareness), pain is reduced or eliminated (because the painful sensations are dissociated from awareness) and memory and perception are distorted such that, for instance, suggested hallucinations and false memories are perceived as 'real as real' (because the part that would normally monitor and detect distortion is dissociated from awareness).

In contrast, contemporary supporters of the non-state view reject the traditional notion of hypnosis as an altered state of consciousness and contend that various hypnotic phenomena are more readily explicable in terms of interactions between more mundane psychological processes such as imagination, attention, relaxation, role-enactment, compliance, conformity, attention, attitudes and expectancies. Non-state theorists see hypnosis as primarily a strategic role enactment. In other words, individuals enact the role of a hypnotised person as defined by cultural expectations, cues provided by the immediate situation, and their role-taking skills. So whilst hypnotised individuals may, for example, depending on instructions, feel very relaxed, or focused in their attention, they do not fall into a special altered state of consciousness. In effect then, to non-state theorists, terms such as 'hypnosis' and 'hypnotic' are simply labels that refer to situations defined by participants or observers as such (because, for example, the situations contain what are called 'hypnotic induction' rituals); they do not refer to the existence of some kind of special state or process (Spanos and Chaves, 1989; Wagstaff, 1991).

More recently, however, the debate has been complicated somewhat by a tendency for some of those who have adopted a dissociationist perspective on hypnosis to place less emphasis on the idea of a hypnotic 'state' or 'trance'; hence the demarcation lines between the various perspectives are perhaps less clear than they used to be (Kirsch and Lynn, 1995; Lynn and Rhue, 1991).

To test hypotheses derived from these different approaches, researchers have often compared groups of subjects given hypnotic induction procedures and suggestions with other usually 'non-hypnotic' control groups (that is, groups not given hypnotic induction procedures, but who may simply be instructed to relax, try hard, imagine, etc.); the logic being that if the behaviour of hypnotic subjects can be produced by non-hypnotic subjects, then there is no necessity to invoke the concept of an hypnotic state or special dissociative process to explain the behaviour of the hypnotic subjects. Other studies have looked at the effects of varying instructions and cues on hypnotic behaviour. Although studies using such designs have not enabled researchers to agree on the utility of the state and dissociationist concepts of hypnosis, nevertheless, these studies have told us a lot about the capacities of ordinary, non-hypnotised individuals, and have done much to dispel the myth of the hypnotic subject as a helpless automaton possessed of abnormal powers. For instance, there is mounting evidence that hypnotic subjects are active, goal-directed agents, not passive respondents with no control over their actions; that most hypnotic behaviour is comparatively easy to simulate, and non-hypnotic control groups can equal or even surpass the hypnotic groups on a variety of performance measures including feats of strength and endurance, and pain tolerance (Spanos and Chaves, 1989; Wagstaff, 1981, 1994, 1996a).

Largely as a consequence of this research, most modern academic theorists and researchers claim to have abandoned the idea that hypnosis has mysterious properties that can miraculously increase performance, and there have been calls from those of all theoretical persuasions to counter popular misconceptions about hypnosis (Perry, 1992). Instead, therefore, debate on hypnosis tends to centre round more mundane issues such as the utility of terms such as 'state' and 'dissociation' in the explanation and description of hypnotic behaviour and experience, rather than the transcendent properties of hypnosis (Wagstaff, 1994, 1996a).

11.2 MEMORY FACILITATION WITH HYPNOSIS

11.2.1 Hypnosis, memory and the transcendence tradition

The recognition that hypnosis does not improve performance dramatically has obvious implications for how we assess hypnotically induced testimony. For example, there now seems to be general agreement amongst academic researchers that hypnosis cannot somehow act as a 'truth serum'; people can lie in hypnosis situations just as well as in other contexts.

Nevertheless, one might be forgiven for thinking that some other aspects of the legacy of the nineteenth-century 'transcendence' tradition live on, not only in the minds of the general public, but also in the minds of some professional practitioners of hypnosis. In a recent survey of 10 'experts' on forensic hypnosis conducted by Vingoe (1995), all 10 agreed with the statement, 'A witness to a crime may be helped by hypnosis to remember details of the crime which were observed at the time the crime took place'. And in a recent book on interviewing with hypnosis, McConkey and Sheehan adopt the position that 'hypnosis is useful' as an investigative procedure (1995, p. 217). At the same time, however, this view seems to contrast rather dramatically with that held by a number of authorities in the USA who have argued that the testimony of any witness who has been hypnotised to improve memory should be banned on the grounds that hypnosis renders a witness incompetent to testify. Indeed, so persuasively has this argument been used, that a number of states have enacted such a ban (Anderton, 1986; Laurence and Perry, 1988).

To any newcomer to the area, therefore, views on the status of hypnotically induced testimony seem contradictory and confusing. In the rest of this chapter, however, I will attempt to make some sense of the conflicting literature on this issue.

Supporters of what is often termed 'forensic hypnosis' have based their arguments on three main sources of evidence; studies of hypnotic age regression; experimental studies of the effects of hypnosis on learning and memory; and case reports where hypnosis has allegedly been helpful in facilitating memory. So let us briefly examine each of these areas.

11.2.2 Studies of hypnotic age regression

Those who believe that hypnosis possesses a special capacity to improve memory sometimes refer to classic experiments on age regression in which subjects have allegedly been able, through hypnosis, to recall events from childhood and enact childlike behaviours with amazing accuracy. However, the claims of these studies have been hotly disputed by other researchers in the area. For instance, in one famous study, True (1949) reported that some hypnotic subjects when given suggestions for age regression managed to recall the day of the week on which their birthday fell 81% of the time. However, by 1974 there had been no less than eight failures to replicate this finding, and it was concluded that somehow True's subjects knew the formula for calculating the days, or had picked up cues from the way the experimenter had asked the questions (Barber, Spanos and Chaves, 1974).

The modern consensus view on this topic is little different from that formed over 25 years ago by O'Connell, Shor and Orne (1970), who demonstrated that subjects directed to fake hypnosis (hypnotic simulators) were indistinguishable from so-called 'real' hypnotic subjects on a variety of age regression tasks. Interestingly, it has also been noted that subjects good at age regression also tend to be the ones good at age 'progression'; they will give a vivid and detailed account of their anticipated future behaviour. To most modern researchers, therefore, the phenomenon of hypnotic age regression, including alleged hypnotic 'regression to past lives', is more testament to the imaginative capacities of hypnotic subjects, and their abilities to gather relevant information, than their powers of memory.

11.2.3 Experimental laboratory studies of hypnosis and memory

Supporters of hypnosis as an interview procedure have also drawn attention to a number of other laboratory studies that have purported to demonstrate hypermnesia (improved powers of memory) with hypnosis for more recently learned materials. However, these studies have also been criticised on a number of grounds.

From the viewpoint of psychological methodology, in order to demonstrate that 'hypnosis' has some special capacity to improve memory it is necessary to rule out alternative explanations in terms of other, more mundane, psychological processes. For example, it could be the case that asking people to remember information in a context defined as 'hypnosis' simply motivates them to try harder; so it is 'motivation' that is the key variable not a special state or dissociative process. There are also problems associated with testing the same subjects with and without hypnosis procedures. It is well known, for example, that, in accordance with experimental demands, subjects can sometimes 'hold back' their responses in the non-hypnotic condition so that their performance when they are supposedly hypnotised will look better. A number of earlier studies have been criticised for these reasons (Wagstaff, 1981, 1984).

As an illustration of the problems, in a more recent attempt to test whether hypnosis improves memory, Shields and Knox (1986) reported that hypnosis improved recall and recognition of 'deep-processed' words (that is, words processed in terms of their meaning, rather than at a more superficial or 'shallow' level in terms of their visual or phonological characteristics). However, everyone in the experiment, including the control groups, knew that the study was about hypnosis, and might have biased their responses to fit the experimenter's expectations. Wagstaff and Mercer (1993), therefore, repeated this study, but did not inform the control group that hypnosis was involved. We found no improvement with hypnosis on the recall and recognition of either shallow or deep-processed stimuli, compared to a relaxed/motivated control group.

Indeed, our results accord with what now seems to be a fairly overwhelming body of experimental evidence to indicate that hypnotic procedures do not improve the accuracy of memory to a level above that achievable in motivated non-hypnotic conditions. The absence of any superiority for hypnotic procedures is evident regardless of the nature of the hypnotic materials (objects, faces, people, words), the way they are presented (incidentally, intentionally, on slides, films, or 'real-like' staged events) or the method of recall (forced-choice recognition or free recall) (Erdelyi, 1994; McConkey and Sheehan, 1995; Smith, 1983; Wagstaff, 1984, 1989, 1993).

Nevertheless, in a detailed breakdown of this literature Erdelyi (1994) has detected an interesting pattern in the findings. He categorised the experimental studies into four types according to the nature of the stimuli presented to participants and the method of testing. Thus stimulus materials were categorised as either 'low-sense' (ink blots, nonsense syllables, etc.) or 'high-sense' (filmed crimes, staged incidents, etc.). Testing was then categorised either as recognition (identifying the materials from a film or word list) or recall (freely reporting with no reference materials). Using these categories to distinguish between different studies, a broad pattern emerges. Significant memory improvements with hypnosis are more or less confined to situations that require free recall of high-sense materials. However, problematically, this enhanced recall is invariably accompanied by an increase in the report of inaccurate information. Hence, although there can be an increase in recall for correct items, overall accuracy as determined by the proportion of correct to incorrect responses is not improved; in fact, it can deteriorate (see, for example, Dywan and Bowers, 1983).

There is also some research to suggest that hypnosis also encourages subjects to incorporate more misleading information into their reports, and to be more confident in their reports generally, including their reports of incorrect information; resulting in a 'false confidence' effect. It has also been suggested that these distorting effects are most prevalent for those subjects who are most responsive to hypnotic procedures; that is, those who score high on 'hypnotic susceptibility' (Wagstaff, 1989, 1993; McConkey and Sheehan, 1995).

If we view hypnosis in terms of normal social and cognitive processes, it is not difficult to see why hypnotic procedures might enhance both accurate and distorted testimony in this manner. If an interviewee is given lengthy induction and memory facilitation procedures, it will be fairly obvious that these 'hypnotic' procedures are expected to enhance recall (indeed, in many experiments explicit instructions are given to this effect). Interviewees may, therefore, attempt to fulfil this requirement by giving some additional details about which they were previously unsure (that is, adopt a lax criterion for report), resulting in increases in both correct and incorrect information. In addition, because of a belief that hypnosis improves memory, some interviewees may report vague details or imaginings as confident memories, believing that, because they are created in the hypnotic context, they must be accurate.

11.2.4   Hypnosis and memory distortion in the legal arena

As a response to findings of this kind there has been a tendency amongst some involved in research on hypnosis and memory to change their emphasis; hence, instead of viewing hypnosis as a potentially valuable tool for uncovering accurate memories, they consider it to be a liability in that it increases the probability of inaccurate reporting (Diamond, 1980; Orne, 1979). In fact, it was as a result of expert evidence on this subject that a number of states in the USA enacted the per se exclusion rule, and banned victims and witnesses who have been interviewed with hypnosis from giving evidence in court. However, it has since been found necessary to exclude defendants from this ban, as this would affect the defendant's constitutional right to testify and call witnesses on his or her behalf (Laurence and Perry, 1988; Perry and Laurence, 1990).

In Britain, the problem of the admissibility of hypnotically elicited testimony first arose in the case of *R* v *Coster* (1980) *Police Review*, July 1987, at Maidstone Crown Court. In this the evidence from prosecution witnesses who had previously been hypnotised for the police by a lay hypnotist was deemed inadmissible in court. One of the factors in this case was that the Home Office suggested guidelines for the use of hypnosis in interviews had not been followed (Home Office Circular No. 66/1988); these guidelines include, for example, the stipulation that the interview should be videotaped. Had they been followed the outcome might have been different (Marwood, 1987).

Rather more bizarre, however, is the more recent case in 1994 in the Court of Appeal of *R* v *Browning* [1995] Crim LR 227. Browning had been convicted of murdering a woman by the M50 motorway. Some time after his conviction, it was revealed that the police had called in a hypnotist to interview a key prosecution witness to help him remember details of the event. However, when the evidence that the witness produced turned out to be, if anything, prejudicial to the prosecution case, the police failed to inform the defence or the court that this interview had taken place. When these events came to light, ironically, the prosecution then attempted to construct a case for dismissing the evidence of their own witness as 'contaminated' by hypnosis. Browning's conviction was subsequently quashed on appeal, on the grounds that the jury might have decided differently had they known of this evidence. This case illustrates well the problems created by the kinds of views promulgated by those who argue for the special status of hypnosis; some argue that hypnosis has a special capacity to enhance memory, others that it has a special capacity to distort memory, and some that it has both (Wagstaff, 1996b).

Given the results of such cases, and the rather negative picture painted by the experimental picture one can perhaps see the case for limiting, if not banning, the use of hypnosis in forensic investigations. So why, given all these considerations, have the police in so many countries continued to use hypnosis for memory enhancement purposes? It is notable that, despite the negative publicity attached to hypnosis, hypnotically induced testimony is, in principle, still allowed as evidence in English courts; and even the Home Office guidelines for conducting hypnotic interviews are just that, guidelines; they are not mandatory (Wagstaff, 1988).

The main reason why some continue to endorse hypnosis as an interview procedure is that, the experimental literature apart, anecdotal cases have purportedly shown it to be effective. Indeed, the Association of Chief Police Officers have alluded to cases in which hypnosis has been useful, and have suggested that hypnosis might be applicable in some serious cases where leads are few; a view obviously endorsed by some other professionals including McConkey and Sheehan (1995), and those interviewed by Vingoe (1995). So why should 'case studies' of the effects of hypnotic interviewing look so much more impressive than the experimental research findings?

11.2.5 Hypnotic interviews in the field
A number of factors might lead investigators to form a favourable yet quite spurious impression of the efficacy of hypnotic interviewing in the field. For example, the experimental research suggests that when hypnotic procedures are used, both the amount of information (correct and incorrect), and confidence in that information, may sometimes be increased. These factors may be important because other studies suggest that the amount of information that witnesses provide, even if it is trivial, and confidence in that information, tend to be used by people to estimate the accuracy of witness testimony. Furthermore, if hypnosis increases susceptibility to leading questions, replies to such questions are more likely to be consistent with the expectations of the interviewers. Also, the belief among hypnotists, police officers and the public that hypnosis improves memory may become a self-fulfilling prophecy. For instance, Wagstaff, Vella and Perfect (1992) found that subjects put in the role of jurors were more likely to find a defendant guilty if they were led to believe that the evidence against him had been obtained through hypnosis.

Nevertheless, supporters of hypnotic interviewing will still point to cases in which hypnosis appears to have revealed important new evidence of considerable forensic relevance and which are not obviously explicable in these ways. However, once again, if we view hypnotic interviewing in terms of ordinary processes from mainstream psychology it may be possible to understand the disparity between the results obtained in experimental research and anecdotal case studies.

Perhaps the most important point to make is that, whilst the experimental evidence suggests that memory enhancement instructions delivered in the context of hypnosis do not produce memory increments above those obtainable by non-hypnotic instructions, they may sometimes (though not always) work better than no memory enhancement instructions at all (see for example, Geiselman et al., 1985). And, indeed, there are a number of techniques that hypnotists have employed in forensic investigations that might produce better results than *routine* police interviews, but none necessarily has anything to do with the introduction of a special hypnotic state or process (Wagstaff, 1982b). To understand this problem it may be useful first to outline briefly what goes on in a hypnotic interview.

Although hypnotic interviews for forensic purposes vary from situation to situation, in most cases a similar general procedure is used (see for example, Hibbard and Worring, 1981; Reiser, 1980). First, the hypnotist establishes rapport with the witness, and explains what will happen in a way that will alleviate fears and make the witness feel comfortable. Next the hypnotist uses a hypnotic induction procedure. Typically the witness is asked to concentrate on a particular physical or mental activity (such as staring at a target affixed to a wall) while suggestions are given (such as, 'Your eyelids are becoming heavy'). After this initial stage the hypnotist attempts allegedly to 'deepen' the witness's level of hypnosis. So, for example, the hypnotist may count and suggest that with each count the witness will go into a deeper and deeper state of relaxation. Another method is to ask the witness to imagine that he or she is in a very relaxing setting, for example, lying on a beach in the sun. On completion of the induction procedure the hypnotist introduces a variety of instructions intended to enhance recall. Two commonly used techniques are 'age regression' and the 'television technique'. Age regression involves asking the witness to go back in time and re-experience the original event in every detail. The television technique involves asking the witness to imagine that he or she is watching an imaginary television screen on which the events to be described can be seen, focused in upon and replayed. After the witness has finished recalling the event, further instructions may be given to the witness to suggest that his or her memory will improve in time and over future sessions. Then the witness is 'woken'; typically the hypnotist does this by counting whilst suggesting that the witness becomes more awake.

Clearly, this kind of procedure differs markedly in many respects from a standard police interview, and in many ways could be considered an improvement. Researchers have identified a number of problems with standard police interviewing procedures that may impair witness performance. For example, police interviewers frequently interrupt the witnesses, thus breaking their concentration. Such interruptions may impair the ability to remember information, and result in short responses that may exclude important details. Most police interviewers also rely heavily on the use of closed questions (such as, 'What colour was his shirt?') rather than open-ended ones (such as,

'Describe your attacker'). Closed questions tend to result in short, truncated answers and the only information elicited is that which is requested. Moreover, the interview is directed by the interviewer rather than the witness, thus preventing the active involvement necessary for the retrieval of detailed information.

Other problems that may impair witness reports include inappropriate language and judgmental comments. Police interviewers sometimes use formal sentences or words which are difficult for the witness to understand. Authoritarian judgmental comments are sometimes made about the witness's role in an incident (such as, 'That was a stupid thing to do'). Such comments may make the witness defensive or feel offended, and prevent accurate and detailed report. These problems are likely to be exacerbated in cases where the victim has been traumatised by an embarrassing or humiliating event, such as rape, and do nothing to aid a witness who is confused and unable to recall because of anxiety.

In contrast, hypnotic interviewers often have a clinical background, may possess good interpersonal skills and be more sensitive to the psychological needs and fears of witnesses. Moreover, the characteristics of the hypnosis ritual, and the manner in which the witness is questioned as a consequence, may alter the style of interviewing so that it is more compatible with optimal recall; the interviewer automatically adopts a softer, less aggressive and authoritarian tone, encouraging the witness to relax, concentrate and report fully and openly, without interruption.

Hypnotic interviews may possess a number of other characteristics not associated with conventional police interviews. For instance, the hypnotic induction procedure encourages focused attention and the use of imagery. The hypnotist may give instructions to focus mental reinstatement of context; this may involve asking a witness to remember not only what happened during a crime but also to 'relive' the event, describing experiences of how he or she felt at the time, and visualising incidental details such as clothes worn at the time and the physical environment in which the crime occurred. Also instructions may be given to report everything, and recall events in different orders. These are all techniques that, in non-hypnotic contexts, have been reputed to enhance witness recall: even simple repeated questioning has been shown to increase correct reports (Bekerian and Dennett, 1993; Erdelyi, 1994; Fisher and Geiselman, 1992; Nogrady, McConkey and Perry, 1985; Wagstaff, 1982a).

The obvious conclusion to be drawn from all this is that, in real-life situations, so-called 'hypnotic interviews' might achieve genuine improvements in memory and reporting, but as a result of ordinary psychological factors that do not necessitate postulating some special hypnotic process.

11.2.6 Hypnosis as a face-saving device

Another reason why case studies of hypnosis may look impressive, is that any new testimony may reflect a lifting of restraints on reporting rather than actual memory enhancement, or hypermnesia. It is not uncommon for witnesses to claim that they cannot remember details of an event, when in fact they remember perfectly well what happened. Reasons for not providing information initially can include fear of reprisals for telling the police, a reluctance to talk about abhorrent acts, or the fact that the witness feels partly responsible for the crime committed. In these situations, some witnesses may subsequently wish to change their testimony and provide details. However, to do so would mean admitting to having lied previously about their inability to remember details of an event, or having to justify why they did not volunteer the information earlier. When this happens, hypnosis procedures might conceivably act as a face-saving device to explain the sudden recall of information; thus, in the guise of a special memory facilitation technique, hypnosis could be construed as providing 'permission' to report previously undisclosed information.

Such an analysis might be particularly relevant to the 'repressed memory' versus 'false memory' issue that has been the source of much heated controversy recently, especially in relation to accusations of sexual abuse in childhood. Thus some have argued that hypnosis may be especially useful for uncovering repressed or 'dissociated' childhood memories of abuse, whilst others have argued that hypnosis can serve to create pseudo-memories of abuse (Ofshe and Watters, 1996). In fact, as we have seen, the literature on hypnosis could be construed as being supportive of both sides of this debate, but without postulating the involvement of special hypnotic processes that uncover 'repressed memories'. There is ample evidence to suggest that subjects put through hypnotic procedures (as well as non-hypnotic interviewing procedures) may sometimes report false information, or pseudo-memories, if led to do so; but there are also good reasons to suggest that the procedures employed by hypnosis interviewers may involve techniques that can both aid the retrieval of details from memory, and provide permission for interviewees to talk about events that they would otherwise be reluctant to mention. The latter might help to explain a sudden emergence of (independently corroborated) reports of extensive periods of abuse that people would not normally be expected to forget. However, there is as yet no evidence to suggest that it would not be possible to achieve comparable results in non-hypnotic situations with a sufficiently sensitive and skilled interviewer.

11.3 THE STATUS OF HYPNOTICALLY INDUCED TESTIMONY

11.3.1 Should hypnosis be used to interview witnesses?
Given these considerations, there seems to be little point in using hypnosis as an interviewing procedure (or more correctly, hypnotic induction as an adjunct to an interviewing procedure). The evidence suggests that any advantages to be gained from hypnosis over standard interviewing procedures in terms of rapport and memory facilitation mnemonics such as context reinstatement, can be found with alternative memory enhancement techniques such as the cognitive interview. Indeed, a direct comparison between the cognitive interview and hypnosis has shown no differences in effectiveness between the two techniques (Geiselman et al., 1985); though on balance the evidence suggests that, in terms of the production of incorrect information,

the potential distorting effects of the cognitive interview may be less (Bekerian and Dennett, 1993). Also, at present there is a very real danger of hypnotically elicited testimony being thrown out of court simply because hypnosis has been employed.

11.3.2 Should hypnotised witnesses be banned from testifying?

Although there is clearly a case for advising the police not to use hypnosis as an interview technique, the case for a blanket ban on allowing the witnesses who have been interviewed using hypnotic procedures from testifying in court could be seen as something of an overreaction. If we view the problems of memory distortion with hypnosis in terms of ordinary psychological processes, there is no reason why the use of hypnosis in interviewing should *inevitably* result in distorted and biased reports. Whether or not a hypnotic procedure produces adverse effects will depend on the particular social demands and expectations, and individual characteristics of the interviewees, present in the particular situation. And, indeed, the empirical evidence suggests only that hypnotic procedures can produce adverse effects on testimony, not that they will inevitably do so.

For example, whilst finding no superiority for hypnosis in facilitating memory, some investigators have failed to find that hypnotic subjects incorporate more misleading information, produce more information both accurate and inaccurate, or express inflated confidence in incorrect information (see Wagstaff, 1993; McConkey and Sheehan, 1995). Spanos et al. (1989) also found that hypnotic procedures per se were not more likely to produce memory distortions, but subjects classified as highly susceptible were generally more likely than other subjects to produce memory distortions in both hypnotic and non-hypnotic conditions.

Other research suggests that hypnotically induced inaccuracies may often reflect reporting biases rather than genuine irreversible memory distortions (that is, subjects report false information because they think the situation requires it of them, rather than because their memories are impaired). Thus hypnotically created pseudo-memories and false confidence effects can be significantly reversed if hypnotised subjects are told, for example, that a 'hidden part' of them can describe their 'real' memories, or are cross-examined under oath, or are given a financial incentive for accurate reporting, or are given an opportunity to deny being in a trance. Under these circumstances errors are not completely eliminated, but the errors that accompany hypnotic procedures are no greater than those produced by non-hypnotic procedures (see, for example, Murray, Cross and Whipple, 1992; Spanos and McLean, 1986; Spanos et al., 1989; Spanos et al., 1991; Wagstaff and Frost, 1996).

Thus instead of dismissing the whole of the testimony of the witness who has previously been hypnotised, perhaps we might more usefully ask, what might be the effect on *particular* statements, made by this *particular* witness, of this *particular* hypnosis session? Moreover, in principle, it should be possible to apply some fairly commonsense guidelines about how to evaluate such testimony. Some obvious points are: Did the witness obviously respond to the hypnosis procedure? Were leading questions asked and did the witness respond to them; and was anything said during the hypnosis interview a simple reiteration of something said before? If the witness did not respond to the induction procedure, was not asked leading questions, or did not respond to them, or simply reiterated what was said before the hypnosis session, there seems little point in discarding everything said simply because the witness has been subjected to a hypnosis procedure (Wagstaff, 1996b).

11.4 SUMMARY

(a) Research indicates that the public image that hypnosis has some special capacity to facilitate the recall of accurate memory, and that hypnotically induced testimony is to be accorded a special status, is outmoded and inaccurate. If anything the evidence suggests that the addition of hypnosis to an interview procedure can sometimes lead to an increase in inaccurate and distorted testimony.

(b) At present the evidence suggests that any benefits that apparently accrue from using hypnotic techniques to interview witnesses arise from social and mnemonic factors that hypnotic interviews share with other interview procedures such as the cognitive interview. Moreover, although the cognitive interview may not be perfect, compared to hypnosis, it may run less risk of producing distorted and biased testimony, and may lead to fewer problems when testimony is to be presented in court.

(c) Whilst hypnosis may lead to distorted testimony, this distortion is not inevitable and will depend on the particular circumstances. Nevertheless, perhaps the best general advice that can be offered to the police regarding the use of hypnosis procedures to interview witnesses is: Don't bother; use a cognitive interview instead.

Key terms
Admissibility of hypnosis; age regression; cognitive interview; conceptions of hypnosis; face-saving device; false confidence; forensic hypnosis; hypnotic memory facilitation; hypnotic state versus non-state debate; hypnotic susceptibility; hypnotic transcendence; memory distortion; pseudo-memories; recall; routine interviews.

References
Anderton, C.H. (1986), 'The forensic use of hypnosis', in F.A. De Piano and H.C. Salzberg (eds), *Clinical Applications of Hypnosis*. Norwood, NJ: Ablex, pp. 197–223.
Barber, T.X. (1969), *Hypnosis: A Scientific Approach*. New York: Van Nostrand.
Barber, T.X., Spanos, N.P. and Chaves, J.F. (1974), *Hypnotism, Imagination and Human Potentialities*. New York: Pergamon.
Bekerian, D.A. and Dennett, J.L. (1993), 'The cognitive interview technique: reviving the issues', *Applied Cognitive Psychology*, vol. 7, pp. 275–97.
Diamond, B.L. (1980), 'Inherent problems in the use of pre-trial hypnosis on a prospective witness', *California Law Review*, vol. 68, pp. 313–49.

Dywan, J. and Bowers, K. (1983), 'The use of hypnosis to enhance recall', *Science*, vol. 22, pp. 184–5.

Erdelyi, M.W. (1994), 'The empty set of hypermnesia', *International Journal of Clinical and Experimental Hypnosis*, vol. 42, pp. 379–90.

Fellows, B.J. (1990), 'Current theories of hypnosis: a critical review', *British Journal of Experimental and Clinical Hypnosis*, vol. 7, pp. 81–92.

Fisher, R.P. and Geiselman, R.E. (1992), *Memory Enhancing Techniques for Investigative Interviewing: The Cognitive Interview*. Springfield, Ill: Charles C. Thomas.

Fisher, R.P., Geiselman, R.E., and Amador, M. (1989), 'Field test of the cognitive interview: enhancing the recollection of actual victims and witnesses of crime', *Journal of Applied Psychology*, vol. 74, pp. 722–7.

Fisher, R.P., Geiselman, R.E., and Raymond, D.S. (1987), 'Critical analysis of police interview techniques', *Journal of Police Science and Administration*, vol. 15, pp. 177–85.

Geiselman, R.E., Fisher, R.P., MacKinnon, D.P. and Holland, H.L. (1985), 'Eyewitness memory enhancement in the police interview: cognitive retrieval mnemonics versus hypnosis', *Journal of Applied Psychology*, vol. 70, pp. 401–12.

Haward, L.R.C. (1988), 'Hypnosis by the police', *British Journal of Experimental and Clinical Hypnosis*, vol. 5, pp. 33–5.

Hibbard, W.S. and Worring, R.W. (1981), *Forensic Hypnosis: the Practical Application of Hypnosis in Criminal Investigation*, Springfield, Ill: C.C. Thomas.

Hilgard, E.R. (1986), *Divided Consciousness: Multiple Controls in Human Thought and Action*. New York: Wiley.

Hilgard, E.R. (1991), 'A neodissociation interpretation of hypnosis', in S.J. Lynn and J.W. Rhue (eds), *Theories of Hypnosis: Current Models and Perspectives*. New York: Guilford, pp. 83–104.

Kirsch, I. and Lynn, S.J. (1995), 'Altered state of hypnosis: changes in the theoretical landscape', *American Psychologist*, vol. 50, pp. 846–58.

Laurence, J.R. and Perry, C.W. (1988), *Hypnosis, Will and Memory: a Psycho-legal History*. New York: Guilford.

Lynn, S.J. and Rhue, J.W. (eds) (1991), *Theories of Hypnosis: Current Models and Perspectives*. New York: Guilford.

Marwood, W. (1987), 'In a daze over hypnosis', *Police Review*, July 1987, pp. 1335–6.

McConkey, K.M. and Sheehan, P.W. (1995), *Hypnosis, Memory, and Behavior in Criminal Investigation*. New York: Guilford.

Murray, G.J., Cross, H.J. and Whipple, J. (1992), 'Hypnotically created pseudomemories: further investigation into the "memory distortion or response bias" question', *Journal of Abnormal Psychology*, vol. 101, pp. 75–7.

Nogrady, H., McConkey, K.M. and Perry, C. (1985), 'Enhancing visual memory: trying hypnosis, trying imagination, and trying again', *Journal of Abnormal Psychology*, vol. 2, pp. 194–204.

O'Connell, C.N., Shor, R.E. and Orne, M.T. (1970), 'Hypnotic age regression: an empirical and methodological analysis', *Journal of Abnormal and Social Psychology*, monograph supplement, vol. 76, pp. 1–32.

Ofshe, R. and Watters, E. (1995), *Making Monsters: False Memories, Psychotherapy and Sexual Hysteria*. London: Andre Deutsch.

Orne, M.T. (1979), 'The use and misuse of hypnosis in court', *International Journal of Clinical and Experimental Hypnosis*, vol. 27, pp. 311–41.

Perry, C. (1992), 'Countering the stereotypes of hypnosis', *Contemporary Hypnosis*, vol. 9, p. 150.

Perry, C. and Laurence, J.R. (1990), 'Hypnosis with a criminal defendant and a crime witness: two recent related cases', *International Journal of Clinical and Experimental Hypnosis*, vol. 38, pp. 266–82.

Reiser, M. (1980), *Handbook of Investigative Hypnosis*, Los Angeles: Lehi.

Shields, I.W. and Knox, J. (1986), 'Level of processing as a determinant of hypnotic hypermnesia', *Journal of Abnormal Psychology*, vol. 95, pp. 358–64.

Smith, M.C. (1983), 'Hypnotic memory enhancement of witnesses: Does it work?', *Psychological Bulletin*, vol. 94, pp. 387–407.

Spanos, N.P. and Chaves, J.F. (eds) (1989), *Hypnosis: the Cognitive Behavioral Perspective*. Buffalo, NY: Prometheus, pp. 149–74.

Spanos, N.P., Gwynn, M.I., Comer, S.L., Baltruweit, W.J. and de Groh, M. (1989), 'Are hypnotically induced pseudomemories resistant to cross-examination?', *Law and Human Behavior*, vol. 13, pp. 271–89.

Spanos, N.P. and McLean, J. (1986), 'Hypnotically created pseudomemories: Memory distortions or reporting biases?', *British Journal of Experimental and Clinical Hypnosis*, vol. 3, pp. 155–9.

Spanos, N.P., Quigley, C.A., Gwynn, M.I., Glatt, R.L. and Perlini, A.H. (1991), 'Hypnotic interrogation, pretrial preparation, and witness testimony during direct and indirect cross-examination', *Law and Human Behavior*, vol. 15, pp. 639–53.

True, R.M. (1949), 'Experimental control in hypnotic age regression states', *Science*, vol. 110, pp. 583–4.

Vingoe, F.J. (1995), 'Beliefs of British law and medical students compared to an expert criterion group on forensic hypnosis', *Contemporary Hypnosis*, vol. 12, pp. 173–87.

Wagstaff, G.F. (1981), *Hypnosis, Compliance, and Belief*, Brighton: Harvester.

Wagstaff, G.F. (1982a), 'Helping a witness remember — a project in forensic psychology', *Police Research Bulletin*, vol. 38, pp. 56–8.

Wagstaff, G.F. (1982b), 'Hypnosis and witness recall: a discussion paper', *Journal of the Royal Society of Medicine*, vol. 75, pp. 793–7.

Wagstaff, G.F. (1983), 'Hypnosis and the law: a critical review of some recent proposals', *Criminal Law Review*, pp. 152–7.

Wagstaff, G.F. (1984), 'The enhancement of witness memory by hypnosis: a review and methodological critique of the experimental literature', *British Journal of Experimental and Clinical Hypnosis*, vol. 2, pp. 3–12.

Wagstaff, G.F. (1988), 'Comments on the 1987 Home Office Draft circular: a response to the comments of Gibson, Haward and Orne', *British Journal of Experimental and Clinical Hypnosis*, vol. 5, pp. 145–9.

Wagstaff, G.F. (1989), 'Forensic aspects of hypnosis', in N.P. Spanos and J.F. Chaves (eds), *Hypnosis: the Cognitive Behavioral Perspective*. Buffalo, NY: Prometheus, pp. 340–57.

Wagstaff, G.F. (1991), 'Compliance, belief and semantics in hypnosis: a non-state, sociocognitive perspective', in S.J. Lynn and J.W. Rhue (eds), *Theories of Hypnosis: Current Models and Perspectives*, New York: Guilford, pp. 362–96.

Wagstaff, G.F. (1993), 'What expert witnesses can tell the courts about hypnosis: a review of the association between hypnosis and the law', *Expert Evidence*, vol. 2, pp. 60–70.

Wagstaff, G.F. (1994), 'Hypnosis', in A. Colman (ed.), *Companion Encyclopaedia of Psychology*. London: Routledge, vol. 2, pp. 991–1006.

Wagstaff, G.F. (1996a), 'Methodological issues in hypnosis', in J. Haworth (ed.), *Psychological Research: Innovative Methods and Strategies*. London: Routledge, pp. 202–20.

Wagstaff, G.F. (1996b), 'Should hypnotised witnesses be banned from testifying in court? The role of hypnosis in the M50 murder case', *Contemporary Hypnosis*, vol. 13, pp. 186–90.

Wagstaff, G.F. and Frost, R. (1996), 'Reversing and breaching posthypnotic amnesia and hypnotically created pseudo-memories', *Contemporary Hypnosis*, vol. 13, pp. 191–7.

Wagstaff, G.F. and Mercer, K. (1993), 'Does hypnosis facilitate memory for deep processed stimuli?', *Contemporary Hypnosis*, vol. 10, pp. 59–66.

Wagstaff, G.F., Vella, M. and Perfect, T.J. (1992), 'The effect of hypnotically elicited testimony on jurors' judgments of guilt and innocence', *Journal of Social Psychology*, vol. 31, pp. 69–77.

Yuille, J.C. (1984), 'Research and teaching with the police: a Canadian example', *International Review of Applied Psychology*, vol. 33, pp. 5–23.

Recommended reading
Wagstaff, G.F., 'Hypnosis and the law: a critical review of some recent proposals', *Criminal Law Review*, 1983, pp. 152–7.

Wagstaff, G.F., 'What expert witnesses can tell the courts about hypnosis: a review of the association between hypnosis and the law', *Expert Evidence*, vol. 2 (1993), pp. 60–70.

Editors' notes
At first sight, the inclusion of what many may consider to be an obscure and marginalised subject might seem to be incongruous. However, the observations by the authors and others about hypnosis have wide implications. A properly conducted hypnotic interview may have the potential for drawing out the witness's real and accurate memory in a more effective and reliable way than a 'botched' cognitive interview by a poorly trained police officer who interrupts and leads the witness during what is supposed to be free recall. Yet whereas police officers are left to get on with it when interviewing witnesses, free of the requirements relating to recording which they have to comply with when interviewing suspects, hypnotists are viewed with such suspicion by Parliament and the courts that their activities are, by comparison, very strictly regulated. Thus the Home Office Circular 66/1988 suggests that hypnotic interviews with potential witnesses should be video recorded and in *R* v

Browning [1995] Crim LR 227, the Court of Appeal emphasised the desirability of hypnotic interviews with witnesses being video-recorded as a prerequisite to admissibility (although the questioned interviews in *Browning* had not, in fact, infringed this principle). The Court's ultra-cautious approach to hypnotic interviews might be said to contrast most remarkably with that to those by police officers whose questioning of witnesses in unrecorded circumstances has been shown to be considerably more dangerous (see chapters 9 and 15).

CHAPTER TWELVE

Identification parades: psychological and practical realities

Ian McKenzie and Peter Dunk

12.1 INTRODUCTION

The problem peculiar to evidence of visual identification is that this evidence, because of its type and not because of its quality, has a latent defect that may not be detected by the usual tests. The highly reputable, absolutely sincere, perfectly coherent and apparently convincing witness, may, as experience has quite often shown, be mistaken.

With those words, Lord Devlin introduced one of the key texts (Shepherd et al., 1982), in what must, despite lay perceptions of the position, be one of the most contentious areas of the interface between psychology and the criminal justice system: the psychology of person identification.

Put simply, an eyewitness is a person who experiences an event and is later required to remember the episode. The widely held belief of the general public is that people store visual and sound memories rather like a video recorder. However, general research on memory, and more specific research on eyewitness identification, have shown that human memory and perception do not work like that.

Psychologists have established that the processes of memory (including the processes of memory for faces) consists of three separate but linked stages: encoding, storage and retrieval (see chapter 1). The process of facial identification (and identification of things seen before) is summarised as the operation of recall leading to recognition, but, as we shall see, depends upon the effective operation of 'normal' memory processes, some of which are rendered more problematic as a result of their relationship to other human functions such as language or the skill (or otherwise) of those gathering information, or to the legal procedures which exist to gather and present evidence to a court. It is the purpose of this chapter to examine some of those problematic areas.

12.2 PSYCHOLOGICAL RESEARCH

Throughout this century, and especially during the past two decades, psychologists have studied eyewitness identification with great vigour. The majority of research has been completed under laboratory conditions, a fact which has given rise to some legitimate questions about whether results are biased or relevant to real life (Tollestrup, Turtle and Yuille, 1994; Clifford and Bull, 1978).

A few observers have felt that for too long the judiciary, the police and juries have adopted a naive belief in the total accuracy of eyewitness identification. This problem is exacerbated, as we shall see, by the nature of the rules and regulations under which formal identification for the court must take place. These rules are said to exist in order to ensure that such identifications are both reliable and admissible. Nevertheless, emphasising the importance placed upon the proper identification of a suspect, the Code for Crown Prosecutors suggests that, 'Reliable and admissible identification evidence is an essential feature in every case, no matter how minor'.

Thus, particularly for legal purposes, the extent to which identification is properly conducted (i.e., is admissible) *and* is held to be something which the court can accept as legitimate and accurate (i.e., is reliable) is of core concern. The problem is that numerous experimental studies based on staged crimes have resulted in a surprisingly large number of false identifications. In the USA, Wells (1993, p. 554) undertook an analysis of 1,000 convictions of innocent people and concluded that the single most important factor that led to the false convictions was eyewitness error. One consequence of these studies has been that some authors who have studied individual cases of misidentification, have suggested that people are quite incapable of remembering a face and that as a consequence, identification evidence is 'virtually useless' (Coles and Pringle, 1974 cited in Bull et al., 1983, pp. 21–2). This is a view which is both far too pessimistic and too simplistic.

Bull and his colleagues (Bull et al., 1983) have, for example, suggested that, rather than assuming identification evidence is virtually useless or that positive bias (the naive belief) in the courts is a problem, the true position is that: 'Psychological research has shown that witnesses' identification performance can range from total accuracy to total inaccuracy depending upon a multitude of factors'.

However, such a statement is a tacit acknowledgement of the *possibility* of the unreliability in the testimony of *some* eyewitnesses, and psychologists have suggested that eyewitness error is a joint product of inherent human cognitive limitations (i.e., the innate or learned ability — or otherwise — of a witness accurately to identify the person they saw committing or at or near the scene of a crime) and of the methods that are used to obtain information from eyewitnesses.

12.2.1 Estimator variables and system variables

Wells (1993) discusses two basic variables which are said affect eyewitnesses' accuracy: estimator and system variables. Estimator variables are the elements which affect the eyewitness's accuracy but are beyond the control of legislation, and system variables are matters that are controllable by legislation, by the police and by the judiciary (Shepherd et al., 1982, p. 46).

ESTIMATOR VARIABLES		SYSTEM VARIABLES
Situational Factors	Witness Factors	Parade Factors
Physical conditions	Race	Composition
Type of crime	Confidence	Functional size
Stress and arousal	Sex	Instructions
Duration of incident	Age	Parallel parades
Delay effects	Intelligence	Social dynamics
Interpolated activity	Personality	Mode of presentation
Extraneous information		

Table 12.1 Estimator and system variables which affect the accuracy of eyewitness identification together with their associated factors (after Wells, 1993 and Ellis, 1984)

It is, of course, essential for the police and judiciary to know something about situational and witness factors, most of which are almost impossible to regulate, if only because of their effect on the overall identification process. Research has shown that memory processing may be affected by any or all of the situational and witness factors shown in table 12.1, and that, for example, encoding of memory may be adversely affected:

(a) if the witness experiences physical or psychological trauma (stress, arousal, physical conditions, type of crime);
(b) if there is delay between the event and the identification procedure;
(c) if the target is of a different race from the witness (cross-race identifications have been shown to be more problematic than intra-race identifications).

Accuracy may also depend upon the gender, age or personality of the witness. Brief explosure to the target may reduce identifiability, as may 'interference' with encoding of memory if another 'memorable' event follows it. Finally, although this may be hard for the lay person to accept, there is substantial evidence that there is *no consistent and enduring relationship* between the post hoc confidence of a witness that he or she will be able to make an identification and the accuracy of a later identification. Neither is there any satisfactory evidence that ante hoc confidence signifies accurate identification (see Cutler and Penrod (1995) for a full description of the foregoing research findings).

However, it is the principal aim of this chapter to examine the effects on identification of the system variables. Thus it is to the requirements of legislation, etc., the things 'controllable by legislation, by the police and by the judiciary', to which we now turn.

12.3 PROCESSES OF IDENTIFICATION

Historically, the first reference to the organisation and management of an identity parade may be found in a set of Metropolitan Police Orders, dated March 1880. Although the regulations were fairly rudimentary, they were adequate in the context of contemporary psychological knowledge. However, throughout the next 106 years, identification procedures were refined, usually in attempt to prevent miscarriages of justice rather than in response to psychological studies. Such refinements, it has been observed, normally coincided with particular *cause célèbres* which involved identification issues.

Until the implementation in 1986 of the Police and Criminal Evidence Act 1984 (PACE), the control of identification procedures was through Home Office Circulars which were merely advisory and not binding on the police service. The Act put in place a number of Codes of Practice, one of which, Code D, provides detailed procedures relating to identification. Adherence to the contents of all the Codes was made mandatory by section 67 of PACE, which makes failure to comply with them a disciplinary offence and makes a breach of the requirements of the Codes something that must be taken into consideration in any criminal or civil proceedings, if thought relevant by the judge. The main aim of Code D is to ensure a common approach to identification procedures throughout England and Wales, and, at the same time, to attempt to ensure that false identifications are kept to a minimum.

The legislation permits four types of procedure, correct use of which results in admissible identification: the identification (ID) parade, a group identification, a video film identification and a confrontation (Code D, para. 2.1).

The principal purpose of the remainder of this chapter is to examine psychological research in three key areas: the gathering of evidence, the 'construction' and management of an identification parade, and the post-event processes.

12.4 AFTER THE CRIME

12.4.1 At the scene of the crime: first description

It is important, at this stage, to draw attention to the distinction to be made between the suspect and the culprit. For research purposes psychologists have developed the practice of referring to the person who actually committed the offence as the culprit, whilst the person later arrested and put up for ID is called the suspect. This distinction, as we shall see, has much relevance when considering the appropriate structure of the later identification parade. Suffice it to say at this stage, that the aim of an identification parade may, using this distinction, be said to be to assess whether or not the suspect and the culprit are one and the same. However, in most, if not all of the regulatory documents, this distinction is not made.

Thus, the revised Code of Practice, effective from 10 April 1995, requires that:

> A record shall be made of the description of the suspect as first given by a potential witness. This must be done before the witness takes part in the forms of identification. . . . A copy shall be provided to the suspect or his solicitor before any procedures. (Code of Practice D, para. 2.0.)

Some have argued that records of first description should be made as soon as possible, and in the first draft revision of the Code such wording was used. However, the words were amended in the final version. It is, at this stage, a moot point as to whether the removal of this phrase will or will not present a problem. Although some forces takes a different view, Kent Police have interpreted the instruction to mean as soon as possible. Therefore, in that force, the computerised incident handling and recording system has 'first description' details placed on it together with a label such as 'description verbatim'. These records are disclosable to the defence and would provide the details of first description which should be provided at any identification procedure.

An example of a recent first description in Kent came from a witness to a burglary. Much research on general descriptions appears to indicate that witnesses usually provide information based upon six or seven characteristics (e.g., age, height, weight, gender, race and hair) expressed in broad terms (25 to 30, $10\frac{1}{2}$ to 11 stone, etc.). In the case in question, however, only three descriptive characteristics were provided and they were quite specific. The person was described as 'male, six foot, rough dress, brown hair with earring'. It will be noted that the only *facial* element of the characteristics mentioned is the hair of the suspect. What is of importance here is the paucity of the description and of the 'common' variables, when one bears in mind the implicit requirement of the 'procedures' to identify the *face* of the culprit.

One might expect that if the suspect had a large moustache or beard that would probably be mentioned at first description stage, but it is not surprising that first descriptions do not contain much facial information or description. This is because psychologists argue that, as a rule, faces are very difficult to describe and descriptions when required are brief. Ellis (1984) outlines the situation clearly:

> It would seem that language is much too imprecise to be of much use in acquiring the subtle information regarding each face we encounter. When asked to describe faces, people usually resort to simple general labels (e.g. crafty looking) or select a few salient features (e.g. large nose and red hair).

However, *sometimes*, as Wells (1993) has indicated, facial descriptions can be highly diagnostic.

Thus, a second example, also taken from a witness statement made in Kent, and recorded about an hour after an armed robbery in December 1995, contains the following:

> [He had] a chubby face, which as he got closer, I saw had three scars on the right cheek of his face. Two of the scars were lines down his right cheek approximately two inches long and the third was a line running under these two, again two inches long. Although he was unshaven these scars were prominent through the stubble.

Were an arrest to be made on the basis of this description, such detail would suggest a high probability that the suspect and culprit are the same.

It is very unusual for this degree of detail to be available and recalled, but this case can be used to illustrate further a number of 'estimator variables'. The culprit was of the same race as the witness. Although the witness was observing an armed robbery, he never saw a gun nor was he involved in any way in observing the actual robbery, which took place inside a shop. In view of this, his arousal level (and level of trauma) can be regarded as moderate. Both the culprit and witness were in telephone kiosks that overlooked each other and the observation period was well in excess of two minutes, a long time for most such observations. At this point the witness was unaware of the man's intentions but he made the interesting comment that when they made eye contact it made '. . . me feel uncomfortable and I looked away'. But, one may legitimately wonder, if the scars to the culprit's face had not been present, whether the facial description would have descended to the simple general labels mentioned by Ellis?

Research has shown that witnesses are usually accurate in their account and identification if they are interviewed as soon as possible after the event (Stern and Dunning, 1994, p. 275). There has been a great deal of debate about whether it is best to allow witnesses freely to recall events (narrative report) or for them to be questioned and then respond (interrogative report). The development of the cognitive interview (CI), discussed elsewhere in this book, is based on the idea that the former process produces more and more accurate information (see, for example, Bull et al., 1983, pp. 29–30).

However, whilst the proper application of the CI requires the luxury of time, there is more of a dilemma for a police operations room operator than for a police officer who interacts with a witness face to face. The operations room operator needs information quickly to aid patrol officers to apprehend offenders. Furthermore, the witness wants to provide information so that tangible assistance from the police can arrive. In such a situation which type of report is best at eliciting description and facial details? Is is possible to destroy or alter a witness's encoding, storage and later recognition if this initial police contact is bungled?

This Code of Practice requirement is so recent that it is doubtful whether any serious thought has been given to police telephone operators' techniques and the impact of them on a witness's ability to store and then successfully (and accurately) recognise a suspect. This is an issue worthy of further research, particularly in the light of the research on overshadowing.

12.4.2 Overshadowing

Eyewitnesses are often interviewed by more than one police officer. This is especially true in the more serious crimes. As a result of these interviews, a wealth of information is provided which includes details of the suspect. Whilst it is obviously necessary to obtain a description of an offender, Lindsay (1994, pp. 45–6) discusses research which found that when eyewitnesses provided a verbal description of the suspect, their performance at a subsequent identification test was impaired. This effect is known as 'verbal overshadowing'.

The effect occurs because people possess both memories of their verbal description and an additional memory trace of the actual culprit; the former interferes with (overshadows) the latter and identification ability is impaired.[1]

Not surprisingly, people differ in their ability to describe faces, and some faces may be more easily described than others. Unfortunately, research shows that, '. . . better describers were not better identifiers, but faces that were better described were more accurately identified'. Regrettably, as Cutler and Penrod (1995, p. 93) note, '. . . in a forensic situation we have no way of knowing which faces lend themselves to accurate description'.

12.4.3 Intervening images

Some crimes are so heinous, or are regarded as so important, that the police appeal direct to the public at large by means of national and local media. With the increasing use of closed-circuit television in most town centres and shops, it is likely that this trend will increase. The revised Code of Practice acknowledges this is an important means of recognising and tracing a suspect. However, safeguards have been included so that suspects (or their solicitors) can review this media material prior to any identification process. Also, investigating officers[2] are expected to ask each witness after they have completed the identification process whether they have seen any broadcast, published film or photographs related to the offence (Code D, para. 2.21A and 2.21B; annex A, paras 2A and 17A; annex B, paras 8A and 12A; annex C, paras 2A and 5; annex E, paras 11 and 12).

---

[1] Similar problems were experienced according to research by Cornish on the use of Identikit. It was found that persons who had attempted an Identikit of a suspect did not perform as well as a control group at a later identification parade. The latest method is E-fit (electronic-fit). It takes about two hours to create a facial picture of a culprit (a 'type likeness'). In that time, an immense amount of 'verbal overshadowing' could have occurred and thus might cause the witness grave problems at any future identification parade.

[2] A strange element of this part of the Code is the emphasis on the 'investigating officer' asking witnesses if they have seen any witness material. The Code of Practice precludes the investigating officer from taking part in the organisation and management of any part of the identification process, so why give him or her this task? For the psychological reasons discussed herein and in order to ensure fairness, the fact that a witness has seen a media item or an 'E' fit, etc., must be covered by the course of the identification process and the questions should logically be asked by the independent identification officer (inspector in charge of the process), who has the responsibility for the organisation and management of the ID parade.

The principal psychological dynamic here is that psychologists (see Ross et al., 1994) have, for many years, researched and discussed the notion of 'unconscious transference'. This phenomenon can be defined as the inability of an eyewitness to distinguish between a familiar but innocent person and a culprit (or some other relevant person) observed at the scene of a crime or in some other context.

This means that it is possible that a picture of a possible suspect, who is in fact totally innocent, which is shown in the local media, could blend and merge with the actual culprit's face stored in the memory of the witnesses. At any subsequent identification process, it may become impossible for the witness to differentiate the images. Thus a misidentification and a possible miscarriage of justice might occur. It is therefore both sensible and prudent that all media material should be studied before and during a trial to ensure the probity of any identification.

12.5 IDENTIFICATION PARADES

Although, as indicated above, Code of Practice D allows other methods of identification, the principal method is the identification parade, and it is to this we now turn. However, it is important to bear in mind that many of the research findings outlined here relate to all or some of the alternative methods (although each method has its own research literature). However, for reasons of space and parsimony, these similarities (and differences) will not specifically be addressed but will be referred to in passing. For additional information, the interested reader should examine one or more of the recommended texts listed at the end of this chapter.

Around the world there are many variations in the way in which ID parades are permitted to be constructed. In some states in the USA, for example, it is quite permissible for the police to put together a parade in which all of the suspects of a crime might be placed together and the witness is invited to select the culprit — a procedure which has been referred to as similar to a multiple-choice examination question with no wrong answer.

However, in England and Wales, the process is very specific. The Code of Practice requires that:

> The parade shall consist of at least eight people (in addition to the suspect) who so far as possible resemble the suspect in age, height, general appearance and position in life (Code D, annex A, para. 8).

This process, which is, on the surface, reasonable and apparently sound, is clearly aimed, as one would expect in a legal system which is essentially adversarial in its structure', at ensuring that the suspect — the person arrested, who may or may not be the culprit — is protected. It is designed to ensure that it is as difficult as possible for the witness to select *the suspect* from the line-up. It is a process which is accustorial in its structure and impact and is far removed from any inquisitorial (investigatory) process. From that point of view, although on the surface it appears to be fair to the suspect, it is, in practice, the reverse. The selection of the suspect as the culprit, in such circumstances, is tantamount to a, 'Get out of that, you can't, can you?' statement by the prosecution, *even if an error has been made*.

From a psychological point of view, a witness, at any parade, should be relying on a memory of initial contact with the culprit, and should therefore be looking for the features he or she saw and later described to the police. In the case where a parade consists of people who are similar in appearance to the suspect and in which the suspect does not match the description of the culprit, the witness is faced with an exclusionary process. He or she must eliminate from the 'possibles' those who do not match the memory trace. In other words, this intellectual process is one of elimination such that the rejection of 'possibles' may lead to the selection of a person (possibly the suspect) on the basis of the worst possible criterion — 'relative judgment', that is, the selection of the person 'who is *most like* my culprit memory' — even if none of them match it to any significant degree.[3] As Cutler and Penrod (1995, p. 124) put it: 'The suspect in a line-up of clones, is protected from mistaken identity, but there is little chance of correct identification because the witness cannot discriminate among line-up members'.

On the other hand, if the parade consists of people who match the culprit description, the psychological process is very different. Given that, as before, the witness is attempting to fit a memory trace to a person, the witness will be faced with a line-up of people who are similar to the first description. The process of selection then becomes one of saying, as each face is encountered, 'How similar is this person to my recollection?' The list of possibles becomes therefore those that are the best fit to the trace — not on the grounds of exclusion, but of *inclusion*. A final decision, the selection of a single person from the line-up, is made on the basis of similarity to the memory, rather than on the basis of 'What is left after I've rejected all the others?'

It is therefore the case that, as has been argued by Wells and others, an ID parade should be constructed of people who look like the culprit as described to the police. The aim of parade construction should therefore be to obtain 'distractors' on a parade who are similar in appearance to the actual culprit (or, more correctly, to the first description of the culprit), in order to make the witness think very carefully about his or her choice.[4]

Wells has argued convincingly that 'culprit description strategy' is superior to a 'suspect resemblance strategy'. Furthermore, it has an added investigatory advantage. If it should transpire that the suspect is not selected, but that some other person is — on the basis of similarity to the culprit — such a

---

[3] Some eyewitnesses, when faced with an identification parade, will complete what has been termed a relative judgment process. This means that a witness will choose one of the parade participants who is closest to the witness's memory of the offender, relative to the other members of the parade (Wells, 1993, p. 560). For instance, an armed robbery in a Canadian supermarket in 1973 resulted in a female cashier describing one of the two offenders as simply 'rather good-looking' (Bull et al., 1983, p. 26). It would be possible for her to choose the most good-looking person on the parade, relative to the other members, and he would not necessarily be the offender.

[4] Good distractors in this case would be people who match the verbal description of the culprit but vary in details not mentioned in the initial description.

selection will give the investigators a wealth of information about the appearance of the culprit (McKenzie, 1995). Furthermore, as Wells (1993) suggests, '. . . the culprit-description strategy offers the same level of protection for the innocent suspect that the suspect-resemblance strategy offers and yet the culprit-description strategy is more likely to produce an accurate identification of the actual culprit than is the suspect resemblance strategy'.

Lawyers in England and Wales, including two of the editors of this book (Wolchover and Heaton-Armstrong, 1995) suggest that the new Codes of Practice, through the requirement, discussed earlier, to record the first description, 'tacitly acknowledge' the option of using 'foils' who fit the original description, 'whether or not the defendant himself also bore similar features'. We dispute this observation. The Codes are very specific and this interpretation appears to be wrong. Nevertheless, by the inclusion of the 'first description' requirement, the groundwork appears to have been laid for some dispute. With the requirement that all identification parades are photographed or video recordings made, the issue of suspect or culprit-based participants will probably be debated in court. As with other changes based upon case law (e.g. *R* v *Turnbull* — see 12.5.1), it is our expectation that judicial guidance will eventually dictate the move to a 'culprit description strategy' because it appears fairest *for all concerned.*

12.5.1 The *Turnbull* warning
In an effort to deal with the 'relative judgment problem', and following a number of cases in which disputes about identification had become a cause for concern, psychologists recommend that witnesses should be told that the culprit may or may not be present on a parade; Lord Devlin so recommended (Devlin, 1976). Although there was some delay in its incorporation into practice, the requirement was first incorporated into case law (*R* v *Turnbull* [1977] QB 224) and is now embedded in the Codes of Practice, with some minor refinement (Code D, annex A, para. 14). It remains unclear whether the direction that before being introduced to the parade, a witness is to be told that, '. . . the person he saw may or may not be on the parade', is of itself sufficient to control the making of relative judgments.

12.5.2 Two bites of the cherry
After the requirement to give the *Turnbull* warning, the Code requires that the identification officer shall tell the witness that:

> . . . if he cannot make a positive identification he should say so but that he should not make a decision before looking at each member of the parade at least twice (Code D, annex A, para. 14).

The incorporation of the requirement to look at each member of the line-up twice, is in the face of the current 'suspect resemblance' strategy, rather strange. It may represent an ongoing tendency for those involved in the drafting of Codes and so on, to use pop-psychology, rather than research, to inform their drafting — a kind of 'two looks are better than one' notion. Research which has examined the abilities of accurate witnesses has found that '. . . faces are represented as holistic gestalts', that is, the face is viewed as a whole structure rather than concentrating on individual features (Stern and Dunning, 1994). In practice this means that:

> . . . recognition could involve *an immediate and automatic one-to-one matching* between a stored gestalt and the external stimulus face . . . it seems unlikely that successful facial identification requires much reflective thought (Stern and Dunning, 1994, p. 279, emphasis added).

It is the experience of both authors that witnesses do not require a second look if their recognition has been instantaneous. When told to look twice, many witnesses regard the exercise as futile. Our impression has been similar to the findings of Stern and Dunning (1994), who found that accurate witnesses could not give a specific reason for their choice: they 'just recognised' the individual. Stern and Dunning came to the conclusion that inaccurate witnesses used an elimination strategy which appears to closely resemble the relative judgment process mentioned above (i.e., they seemed to choose a person who was closest to their memory of the offender).

Stern and Dunning's study also found that accurate witnesses took less time to identify someone than those who were inaccurate. Throughout the Code of Practice, instructions appear which give witnesses 'two bites of the cherry'. Not only are witnesses to be told to look twice at ID parade members, but the Code indicates that in the case of video identification, '. . . there is no limit on how many times he can view the whole tape or any part of it' (Code D, annex B, para. 10). One concern that arises is whether the 'two bites' process, where there is more chance to compare and contrast pictures, might lead to inaccurate identification due to the elimination strategy mentioned above.

It should be borne in mind, however, that viewing the parade twice might have the effect of *limiting* the situation which occurs when a witness wrongly identifies a person because that person shares the features detailed in the witness's original statement (the relative judgment problem). It could be said that this second view might require the witness to look twice at a minimum of eight people, all of whom share, except possibly the suspect, similar features to those originally described by the witness. But this is *only* true when the parade is constructed using the culprit description strategy. In the current suspect resemblance process, the second bite of the cherry may, at best be time-consuming and at worst, pointless.

12.5.3 Line-ups: one by one or all at once?
Experiments conducted by Lindsay and Wells (1985) illustrated that sequential procedures (i.e., the showing of individual foils, or photographs, with no other foil or photograph present at the time of viewing) rather than the usual simultaneous identity parade method (i.e., the expectation that all foils and the suspect will be in view — if not actually looked at — at one time) led to

fewer false identifications when the culprit was not present and no reduction in accurate identification when present (Wells, 1993, p. 561). A sequential, live ID parade would mean that each member (volunteers and suspect) would be introduced separately to the witness and he or she would be asked to decide whether the person is the culprit or not, after seeing the entire sequence. Unfortunately, although the words 'The witness shall be asked to walk along the parade . . .' (by inference obviating the possibility of a sequential viewing of a live parade, since the line itself implies a simultaneous presentation) have been removed from the latest edition of the Code of Practice (they were included in Code D, first version, annex A, para. 14) the code remains silent about the possibility of sequential presentation of a live parade. Certainly there is no overt approval of a situation in which, for example, each person on the parade (including the suspect) is viewed as an individual in the absence of any other. Formal live identifications will, it appears, continue to be a simultaneous showing of all participants, if only because (despite the removal of the words noted above) the witness may still be expected to walk the line.[5]

However, there is confusion here. The Code allows (Code D, para. 2.1 and annex B) the use of video in identification. The video film must include the suspect and at least eight other people who as far as possible resemble the suspect, in age, height, general appearance and position in life. But the nature of video film does produce a sequential presentation, if only because, each person on the 'parade' may be shown in exclusive single shot format.[6]

Furthermore, although the Code D, apparently unambiguously, declares at annex D, that:

The witness shall be shown not less than twelve photographs *at a time*

seeming to suggest what American psychologists refer to as 'photo spread', (i.e., a simultaneous presentation of photographic images) the water is muddied by the use of electronic media and an apparently different approach. (Confusingly the first version of the Code, annex D, at para. 3 spoke of a *sequence* of photographs.)

The use of photographs stored on optical disks is a permitted form of presentation to a witness of images, including that of a suspect, for the purposes of identification. By their very nature images stored on disks are presented in a sequential form. Thus, save in situations in which live parades are conducted in a sequential manner (we think an unlikely event) many

---

[5] However, there is a method of producing a form of sequential process using live participants and that is by means of a group identification (Code D, annex E). A group identification can take place in any location but it should be in an area where 'other people are either passing by, or waiting around informally, in groups such that the suspect is able to join them and be capable of being seen by the witness at the same time as others in the group' (Code D, annex E, para. 3). By using the moving group identification format, an identification officer can get closest to Wells's ideal of a sequential line-up.

[6] Heaton-Armstrong (1997, personal communication) describes his own experience in a recent case in which a video line-up consisting of '. . . the filmed live images of a suspect plus at least seven volunteers in sequential format' was used.

other forms of presentation *are* sequential in their format. As noted above, psychological research has suggested that those viewing sequential presentations (i.e., principally video or materials from an optical disk) are less likely to be inaccurate when the culprit is not present and will achieve a similar degree of accuracy to those who view simultaneous presentations when he or she is present. In the interests of equity, accuracy and psychology, should not the conducting of a live sequential parade be formally declared to be legitimate, or at a minimum, should not the distinction between simultaneous and sequential presentation be acknowledged and spelled out for the benefit of identification officers, suspects (and culprits) as well as for lawyers and the courts?

12.6   AFTER THE PARADE

It was indicated in 12.2.1 that, contrary to common belief, research has shown that there is a very weak and often non-existent relationship between the confidence of a witness about the accuracy of his or her selection following a parade and the extent to which (in experiments) the witness has been accurate in selecting the culprit (Deffenbacher, 1983/1989). To be sure, part of the problem here might be that such experiments in controlled conditions are far removed from witnessing a real crime, attending a real ID parade and giving evidence in a real court. People who are real witnesses may employ different strategies for encoding, storing and recalling memories. However, there is, even in this context, a cause for concern to be found in research findings.

12.6.1   Bolstering
Professor Elizabeth Loftus (1979, 1993, and others) has shown that confidence may be increased even when a wrong identification has been made, if people experience 'bolstering', which is the term used to describe the type of things that happen following a identification when, not unnaturally, the witness asks, 'How did I do?' A police officer may, under current rules, quite legitimately respond, 'Yes, that was our suspect', or even, 'Well, let's put it like this, we found a mass of stolen property at her house', or make some such remark which confirms to the witness the 'correctness' of his or her decision.

Despite the fact that bolstering can affect confidence and that a witness's stated confidence can affect a jury, the Code of Practice is silent about the possibility of such remarks having an unintended, and possibly negative outcome. Although we would wish to see any form of bolstering rendered unacceptable through a specific Code of Practice prohibition, in its absence we would recommend counsel, magistrates and judges carefully to consider whether such events have occurred and to investigate the likely import of them.

Following statements made by several Crown Court judges, it is policy in Kent, and some other areas, not to confirm or deny any identification made by a witness. Although it appears that the psychological dynamics of bolstering exceed mere confirmation and denial, this is undoubtedly a step in the right direction.

12.7 SUMMARY AND CONCLUSIONS

Despite the fact that many people believe themselves to be good at recognising others, research shows that in many staged events witnesses are poor at recognising those they have seen. The processes through which the culprit in a real crime is declared to be one and the same person as the suspect held by the police is an amalgam of pop-psychology and pragmatism, both firmly based in the crime-control/adversarial system of English law. Although we would not wish to be seen as arguing in favour of a change in that tradition, it is clear that a number of research studies tend to suggest that the interests of suspects, witnesses, the police and the legal system itself are not best served by the current requirements of the Code of Practice on Identification. There is, we believe, a very real need for the procedures we have discussed to be readdressed in future revisions of the Code, if only to remove some of the rigidity.

12.7.1 Bolstering
For example, as a matter of considerable urgency, the problem of bolstering must be addressed formally. The Code of Practice must be amended to include a prohibition on investigating officers (and others) openly discussing the success (or otherwise) of a witness in selecting the suspect and on statements being made from which inferences of accuracy can be construed. Counsel must be encouraged to investigate bolstering in cross-examination and to call expert evidence about the effect of it.

12.7.2 Culprit description
In addition to changing the Code of Practice clearly to allow such a course in the police construction of the ID parade, defence solicitors should be encouraged to ensure that parades are constructed from volunteers whose appearance is similar to the description of the culprit given to police at the time of the incident. If this is not feasible, because, perhaps, of unusual facial features described, all the parties, including the suspect, should (as well as matching on more general features) be disguised by the wearing of a hat or by placing a sticking plaster over the place where a scar or facial blemish is or was described to be.

12.7.3 Warnings
The existing *Turnbull* warning should be extended so that witnesses are warned, not only that the culprit may or may not be present, but also that a person should not be picked out simply because he or she shares some of the features of the culprit. Witnesses should be cautioned against choosing the person in the parade who most resembles the culprit. Only if the witness clearly recognises a person on the parade *as the culprit* should that person be *identified as the culprit*.

12.7.4 Sequential presentations
Some thought should be given to relaxing the expectation that all members of a live ID parade will simultaneously be present when the witness is

introduced. Alternatively rules should be developed to ensure that *all* methods of identification are in the form of simultaneous presentation. However, it should be borne in mind that such a course would fly in the face of empirical research.

12.7.5 Conclusion

Some police forces in the UK have established dedicated identification suites as the only locations at which ID parades may be conducted. The principal strength of this practice is that such suites tend to become 'centres of excellence', managed by specially trained and dedicated staff. If such suites were required rather than recommended, the expectation would be of a degree of standardisation and, at the same time, a removal of the (occasional) ad hoc arrangements currently to be found.

Finally, the aim must be to produce clearly defined processes and practices leading to *admissible* identification which are, at one and the same time, fair to witnesses, to suspects and to the police. It is high time that the gathering of evidence, the construction of identification processes and the examination of the propriety of them in courts of law are based more on empirical research than upon wishful thinking about the capacity of eyewitnesses or upon outdated ideas about human nature.

References

Bull, R., Bustin, B., Evans, P. and Gahagan, D. (eds) (1983), *Psychology for Police Officer*. Chichester: Wiley.

Clifford B. and Bull, R. (1978), *The Psychology of Person Identification*. London: Routledge and Kegan Paul.

Cutler B. and Penrod, S.D. (1995), *Mistaken Identification — the Eyewitness, Psychology and the Law*. Cambridge: Cambridge University Press.

Deffenbacher, K.A. (1983), Eyewitness accuracy and confidence: can we infer anything about their relationship? *Law and Human Behaviour*, vol. 4, pp. 243–60.

Deffenbacher, K.A. (1989), *Forensic Facial Memory: Time Is of the Essence*. New York: Elsevier Science Publishers.

Devlin, L.J. (1976), *Report to the Secretary of State for the Home Department of the Departmental Committee on Evidence of Identification in Criminal Cases*. London: HMSO.

Ellis, H.D. (1984), 'Practical aspects of face memory', in C.L. Wells and E.D. Loftus (eds), *Eyewitness Testimony — Psychological Perspectives*. Cambridge University Press, pp. 12–37.

Lindsay, R.C.L. and Wells, G.L. (1985), Improving eyewitness identification from line-ups, simultaneous versus sequential line-up presentation, *Journal of Applied Psychology*, vol. 70, pp. 556–64.

Lindsay, S. (1994), 'Memory source monitoring and eyewitness testimony', in D. Ross et al. (eds), *Adult Eyewitness Testimony*. Cambridge: Cambridge University Press, pp. 27–55.

Loftus, E.F. (1979), *Eyewitness Testimony*. Harvard, Conn: Harvard University Press.

Loftus, E.F. (1993), 'Psychologist in the eyewitness world', *American Psychologist*, vol. 48, pp. 550–2.

McKenzie, I. (1995), 'Psychology and legal practice, fairness and accuracy in identification parades', *Criminal Law Review*, pp. 200–8.

Ross, D., Ceci, S.J., Dunning, D., and Toglia, M. (1994), 'Unconscious transference and line up identification, toward a memory blending approach', in D. Ross et al. (eds), *Adult Eyewitness Testimony*. Cambridge: Cambridge University Press, pp. 80–100.

Shepherd, J., Ellis, H. and Davies, G. (1982), *Identification Evidence — A Psychological Evaluation*. Aberdeen University Press.

Stern, L.B. and Dunning, D. (1994), 'Distinguishing accurate from inaccurate eyewitness identifications: a reality monitoring approach', in D. Ross et al. (eds), *Adult Eyewitness Testimony*, Cambridge: Cambridge University Press, pp. 273–99.

Tollestrup, P.A., Turtle, J.W. and Yuille, J.C. (1994), 'Actual victims and eyewitnesses to robbery and fraud: an archival analysis', in D. Ross et al. (eds), *Adult Eyewitness Testimony*, Cambridge: Cambridge University Press, pp. 144–60.

Wolchover, D. and Heaton-Armstrong, A. (1995), 'Questioning and identification changes under PACE', *Criminal Law Review*, pp. 356–70.

Wells, G.L. (1993), 'What do we know about eyewitness identification?', *American Psychologist*, vol. 48, pp. 553–71.

Key terms

Bolstering; culprit description; estimator variables; eyewitnesses; first description; holistic gestalts; intervening images; line-ups; overshadowing; recall; recognition; suspect description; system variables.

Recommended reading

Cutler, B. and Penrod, S.D. (1995), *Mistaken Identification — The Eyewitness Psychology and the Law*. Cambridge: Cambridge University Press.

Ross, D., Ceci, S.J., Dunning, D. and Toglia, M. (eds), (1994), *Adult Eyewitness Testimony*, Cambridge: Cambridge University Press.

Shepherd, J., Ellis, H. and Davies, G. (1982), *Identification Evidence — A Psychological Evaluation*. Aberdeen University Press.

Editors' notes

It seems that no matter what lengths are gone to in regulating the conduct and composition of identification parades, significant errors will continue to be made and there will always be scope for improvement in the mechanics of procedures used. The importance of the role of the lawyer assigned to represent a suspect at an identification parade cannot be overemphasised. Legal representatives may need to take expert psychological advice before contributing to any decision concerning the identity and appearance of those who are to compose the parade line-up. The use of video equipment and libraries of video images of 'volunteers' may reduce the difficulties presented to identification officers and defence lawyers where a suspect's appearance is unusual.

CHAPTER THIRTEEN

Earwitness testimony

Ray Bull and Brian Clifford

13.1 INTRODUCTION

In December 1996 almost the entire front page of a daily newspaper was devoted to the report of a court case involving earwitness testimony. The headline in the *Portsmouth News* stated, 'Landmark case as attacker jailed by "ear-witness" evidence', and the article began with the sentence: 'A Portsmouth armed robber was convicted by the sound of his voice alone in the first case of its kind in England'.

It was pointed out in the article that the defendant, whose voice was picked by the robbery victim from an audio-taped voice identification parade, was sentenced to seven years in prison. While the article's claim that 'an aural identification parade has never been used in England and Wales' is inaccurate, it is relatively rare for a defendant to be convicted solely on the basis of voice identification. The article noted that, 'The result of the taped ID parade which involved 12 men repeating the same 10-second snatch of conversation was the only evidence against' the defendant. The victim reported that when he was robbed in his shop he at that time recognised one of the robbers by his voice as being a regular customer. Later he picked out this man's voice from the voice parade.

The first author of the present chapter was asked by the defence solicitor to advise on the veracity of the voice identification evidence. In his report he pointed out that there exists little direct, written guidance on how properly to conduct a voice parade though in several countries there do exist guidelines or rules about the conduct of visual identification parades. In the Portsmouth case the police claimed that they had chosen as the non-suspect voices in the parade voices which were similar to the suspect's. However, the police officers who did this appeared to have no special training or skill which could inform their choice of voices for inclusion in the parade. In his report Ray Bull pointed out that it was now possible for an appropriate expert (e.g., a phonetician) to determine the similarity of the voices in the parade. The account above stated that 'During legal argument before the trial a phonetics expert for the defence claimed the voice identification parade had been biased because' the defendant's 'was only one of two unusually deep voices on the tape'. However, the judge ruled that this evidence was inadmissible. Ray Bull also pointed out in his report that because the victim had stated prior to the voice parade that he recognised the robber's voice as that of a regular customer, all he may have done (consciously or non-consciously) at the time of the parade was to pick out the voice of that customer (who may or may not have been the robber).

Although cases such as this are relatively rare compared to those involving visual identification, earwitness testimony inevitably plays a crucial role in such situations. Earwitness testimony can also, of course, play a role alongside other evidence when this is available, such as eyewitness testimony. In some countries legal proceedings now require that the fact-finders be warned and made aware that eyewitnesses giving evidence may well be mistaken. For example, in England and Wales judges are required to give a *Turnbull* warning to the jury. However, requirements such as this do not necessarily formally apply to earwitness evidence. This is surprising given that many of those who have conducted research on earwitnessing have concluded that, by and large, earwitness performance is poorer than eyewitness performance. In December 1997 the Court of Appeal made it clear, in the case *R v Hersey* (mentioned above), that a suitably adapted *Turnbull* warning should be given regarding earwitness testimony.

Why should such judicial caution be necessary? In our daily lives voice recognition mostly concerns people we already know. From such situations most of us form the impression that we are fairly good at voice identification. However, these situations rarely involve the identification of a stranger's voice that we have heard only once or infrequently before. The general impression that voice identification is reliable may not be correct in such circumstances. Indeed, the cognitive processes or the representations underlying the recognition of familiar voices may differ from those concerning unfamiliar voices (e.g., Hollein et al., 1995). What, then, does the relevant research tell us about people's ability to recognise a stranger's voice?

One of the most recent overviews of research on voice identification is by Yarmey (1995a). In this review Yarmey states, that 'One of the myths still held by many laypersons and officials in the criminal justice system is the belief that eyewitness memory, including voice recognition, is merely common knowledge' (p. 263). Yarmey notes that, over a decade ago, he stated that long-term speaker identification for unfamiliar voices must be treated with caution (Saslove and Yarmey, 1980), and 'more recent evidence reinforces this conclusion' (Yarmey, 1995a, p. 264). Thus Yarmey is of the view that evidence based on witness voice identification of a stranger should be treated with caution.

The present chapter will briefly review research on earwitness testimony, especially that published since our earlier literature reviews (Bull, 1981; Bull

and Clifford, 1984; Clifford, 1980, 1983) which stemmed from a substantial
research project which was funded by the Home Office (Clifford, Bull and
Rathborn, 1980) following the publication of the Devlin Report in 1976. The
chapter will focus first on matters to do with the voice samples, then on
factors to do with witnesses, and then on issues to do with the identification
procedures. (Considerably lengthier reviews are available in Bull and Clifford,
1984; Hammersley and Read, 1996; Yarmey, 1995a, 1995b.)

13.2   VOICE SAMPLES

13.2.1   Unfamiliar speaking styles

The voice(s) that a crime witness hears at the time of the offence may not
always involve an accent or language with which the witness is familiar. Does
this make a difference to identification ability?

Thompson (1987) pointed out that in a variety of locations, particularly
large cities, a witness to or victim of a crime may not be familiar with the
language or accent used by the perpetrator. He found that people who only
spoke English identified the voices of bilingual individuals better when these
individuals spoke normal English than when they spoke English with a strong
Spanish accent, which was better than when they spoke Spanish. By contrast,
Goldstein et al. (1981) found no evidence that accent or the language used
by speakers (Spanish) affected identification performance. However, the
identifications of the voices in this latter study were attempted immediately
after hearing the target voice or with a few minutes' delay, whereas Thompson's (1987) study employed a forensically more relevant delay interval of a
week between the hearing of a voice and later trying to recognise it.

Groggin et al. (1991) also found that people who only spoke English
identified the voices of bilingual individuals better when these individuals
spoke English than when they spoke German or Spanish. Similarly, people
who only spoke German were better at identifying voices speaking German
than English. People who were bilingual in English and Spanish could
recognise English and Spanish speaking voices equally well. They also found
that making a spoken English passage progressively less similar to normal
English by rearranging the passage (e.g., in terms of word order and syllables)
led to a deterioration in voice recognition. These researchers concluded that
their experiments 'confirm that language familiarity plays an important role
in voice identification' (p. 448). To this we should add the point made by
Yarmey (1995a) that an unfamiliar speaking style of the perpetrator and/or
the suspect may create problems for those attempting to construct fair voice
parades.

13.2.2   Change in voice tone

Read and Craik (1995) conducted a number of experiments which were
informed by earwitness testimony given in a Canadian murder trial. In this
trial the witness claimed to have recognised a voice based on an initial
eight-word sample (of a duration between four and five seconds). In their first
experiment Read and Craik found that when the recorded voice sample at

test 17 days later was absolutely identical (the very same recording) to that at initial hearing, recognition performance concerning picking out the voice from a voice line-up was significantly better than would be expected by chance (i.e., mere guessing), but was far from 100%. However, if the initially heard speaker was heard at test saying something different in tone and content from the initial sample then performance was no better than chance. In their second study they also found that if the recorded target voice at test was the same voice uttering the same words in the same tone as at initial hearing, but was a different recording, then correct recognition was 43% for the identical recording, 30% for a re-recorded 'identical' voice, and 19% for the same voice but different content and tone — chance being 17%. Earlier work by Saslove and Yarmey (1980) also found that a change in voice tone (e.g., from angry to normal voice) reduced identification performance.

13.2.3 Disguise
Disguise or alteration in voice quality has a crippling effect upon identification. Perpetrators can disguise their voice either at crime commission or (less likely) at the voice line-up. In addition to this we have to consider the fact that during the commission of a crime a perpetrator's voice may be different from normal because of a variety of possible involuntary factors, for example, stress or emotion or because of the presence of something over the mouth such as a scarf (which occurred in one criminal case upon which the first author was asked to write a report).

Read and Craik (1995) found that disguised voices were more difficult to identify, and that such identification was almost at chance level. Likewise, Reich and Duke (1979) and ourselves (Bull and Clifford, 1984) have found that recognition accuracy for a disguised voice is much lower than for a non-disguised voice. Similarly, Orchard and Yarmey (1995) found that, overall, whispered voices were more difficult to identify than normal voices. Thus, the few studies presently available on the effects of the target voice being disguised or changed in tone do suggest that this has a profound negative effect on earwitness performance.

13.2.4 Effects of the telephone
In our report to the Home Office (Clifford, Bull and Rathborn, 1980) we noted that some criminal events involved the perpetrator speaking to the witness over the telephone. Because telephones distort voices, can they reduce the likelihood of voice identification compared to the direct hearing of a voice not involving the telephone? Our study of this (Rathborn, Bull and Clifford, 1981) suggests that they do. We also found that constructing voice line-ups from voice samples using the telephone did not redress the loss caused by the target voice initially being heard over the telephone.

13.2.5 Conclusion
From the above brief overview of some of the research on the effects of voice type alteration we can conclude that changes in a voice between its initial hearing and later trying to recognise it are likely seriously to impair recognition.

13.2.6 Voice sample size

In a landmark case in the United States, the Supreme Court held that the longer the interval of time a witness is visually exposed to a perpetrator the greater the likelihood that an identification would be accurate (*Neil* v *Biggers* (1972) 409 US 188). Does the same hold true for voice?

In one of our own studies with unfamiliar voices we found that increasing the voice sample initially heard from one to two to four sentences occasioned very small and statistically non-significant improvements in recognition performance. However, reducing the sample (in a separate study) to half a sentence reduced performance compared to a two-sentence sample. In this second study performance with a two-sentence sample was better than with a one-sentence sample. In our third study we found performance with an eight-word voice sample to be better than with a one-word sample (Bull and Clifford, 1984). Other researchers have found equally conflicting results.

Legge, Grossman and Pieper (1984) found that increasing the voice sample from six to 60 seconds improved voice recognition performance but that a 120-second sample led to poorer performance than did the 60-second samples. The six-second voice samples produced performance at chance level. Yarmey (1991) found that voice identification was better for eight-minute samples than for four-minute samples. However, the longer samples also led to more incorrect decisions for the six-voice line-ups when the target voice was present but not when it was absent from the line-up, and the number of participants saying 'don't know' decreased with increased voice sample both in the target-present and target-absent line-ups.

Orchard and Yarmey (1995) found that listening to a target voice for eight minutes compared to half a minute led to significantly better subsequent recognition, but in this study, unlike in the 1991 study, the false alarm rate (i.e., choosing an incorrect voice) did not increase with the longer voice sample. Finally, Yarmey and Matthys (1992) found correct identification to be better with initial voice samples of two or six minutes 'duration than of 18 or 36 seconds' duration. This applied to line-ups in which the perpetrator's voice was present. However, for line-ups from which the perpetrator's voice was absent the duration of initial exposure to the perpetrator's voice had no effect on the frequency with which people correctly said that his voice was not present. For the two and six-minute initial voice samples as many people incorrectly picked out a voice from the perpetrator-absent line-ups as correct-ly picked out a voice from the perpetrator present line-up! For the 18 and 36-second voice samples more people incorrectly picked out a voice from the perpetrator-absent line-ups than correctly chose a voice from the perpetrator present line-ups!

The effect of the size of the voice sample may not merely involve the time duration of the sample but the variety in the speech sample which typically increases with time. Roebuck and Wilding (1993) found that accuracy of speaker identification improved significantly the more vowel sounds heard but that increased voice sample duration alone had no significant effect on performance. A similar finding was noted over 40 years ago by Pollack, Pickett and Sumby (1954), who found that repetition of short samples did not increase the number of correct identifications, although later Haggard (1973) did find a positive effect of repetition.

What all these research studies seem to add up to is that the greater the variety of a perpetrator's voice that is initially heard the more likely is an earwitness later correctly to recognise the voice. What has not yet clearly been established by research is how short the sample needs to be before subsequent correct recognition is unlikely. Hammersley and Read's (1996) review of the relevant literature suggested to them that what is important is not solely the type of voice sample heard but that the voice (to be later identified) needs to be heard at least twice, on two different occasions.

But the question of speech duration exposure is more complicated still. In many situations information about the duration of the initial exposure to a perpetrator's voice may only be available from the actual witness, who may be a poor estimator of the duration of a voice sample. Yarmey and Matthys (1992) found that 98% of the participants in their study overestimated the duration of 72-second speech sample. In fact the average time estimation was 312 seconds. This error rate is quite alarming. Not surprisingly, then, Yarmey and Matthys concluded that 'time estimates in forensic situations should be accepted with great caution' (p. 233). Orchard and Yarmey (1995) came to a similar conclusion.

13.3 WITNESS FACTORS

13.3.1 Gender and age
Although there is no doubt that people differ from each other in many important ways these individual difference factors have rarely been found to relate significantly to witness identification performance in a consistent way. Yarmey (1995b) noted that 'recent studies have not found gender differences in voice recognition' (p. 802), and recent work by the second author has shown both children and adults to be equally poor at voice identification (e.g., Clifford, 1997; Clifford and Toplis, 1996). Of course, as people age many develop hearing loss, some relatively early in adulthood, and children and adults do differ in attention deployment and perception of social situations. This could explain why in our own studies (see Bull and Clifford, 1984) we found young adults to perform better than adults over 40 years of age.

13.3.2 Blindness
Sight loss could, perhaps, lead to compensatory enhanced performance regarding voices. We found that blind people were superior to sighted people in correctly picking out a voice from a voice line-up, but we found no effect of degree of blindness (Bull, Rathborn and Clifford, 1983). However, Winograd, Kerr and Spence (1984) did not find a difference between blind and sighted people.

13.3.3 Witness confidence
A witness who seems confident about his or her identification may have more impact on the fact-finding process than one who is not so confident.

Psychologists have conducted many studies on the possible relationship between witness confidence and objective accuracy (e.g., Hollins and Perfect, 1997). The overall conclusion presently emerging from such studies is that a highly confident witness is by no means necessarily more accurate than a less confident witness.

Most of the studies investigating the relationship between witness confidence and accuracy have involved eyewitnesses rather than earwitnesses. In our studies for the Home Office (Clifford, Bull and Rathborn, 1980; Bull and Clifford, 1984) we found within-subject positive relationships between earwitness confidence and accuracy except for voice line-ups which did not contain the target. However, most earwitness studies on this topic have sought to determine if confident earwitnesses are, in fact, more accurate than witnesses who are not so confident (i.e., across witnesses). Yarmey's (1995b) overview of these studies led him to the conclusion that 'earwitness confidence is an unreliable criterion to judge speaker identification accuracy' (p. 803) and Clifford and Bulloch (1999) reinforce this assertion with children.

This lack of relationship may exist especially when the true culprit is not, in fact, in the voice line-up. One likely reason for this is that witnesses in research studies (and probably in real life) are prone (incorrectly) to pick out a voice even when they are explicitly told that the perpetrator's voice may or may not be present. It may be difficult for witnesses to believe that the perpetrator's voice is unlikely to be present in a voice line-up that the police have taken the trouble to construct.

It could be that there only exists a substantial positive relationship across the earwitnesses between confidence and accuracy if the task is easy (Read and Craik, 1995; but cf. Clifford and Gwyer, 1999) or encoding is optimal (Bothwell, Deffenbacher and Brigham, 1987).

At the present time the conclusion has to be that earwitness confidence should not be taken to indicate that one witness is more likely to be correct than another witness.

13.4 VOICE IDENTIFICATION PROCEDURES

13.4.1 Delay

In many earwitness testimony situations there will have been a delay, sometimes considerable, between the witnessed event and the subsequent attempt to identify the stranger. One of the first studies of the effect of delay found performance to be relatively stable with delays of up to a week but then to deteriorate across intervals of two or three weeks and three to five months when performance was very poor (McGehee, 1937). In a second study McGehee (1944) again found an effect of a two-week delay compared to a two-day delay but no further effect of delays of four or eight weeks. Clifford and Denot (1982) found performance to be poorer after a three-week delay than after delays of 14 or seven days and Clifford, Rathborn and Bull (1981) found no difference between delays of 10 minutes and two hours but a difference between 10 minutes and one, seven or 14 days (the latter three delays not differing in terms of performance). However, this was for 'easy-to-recognise' voices (as found in a previous study). For 'difficult-to-recognise' voices there was a straightforward decrease in performance with increasing delay.

Yarmey (1991) found overall that delays of two to three days or two hours did not lead to poorer performance than no delay, but with no delay there were also more false alarms (i.e., incorrectly choosing a voice) for the target-absent voice line-up. Perhaps the effect of delay depends on whether the target voice is present in the line-up. If it is present and is not an easy-to-recognise voice then delay may lead to a drop in performance.

The conclusion we draw from these studies is that earwitness performance may well be poorer with delays of months but may not necessarily be poorer with delays of a few days (Yarmey and Matthys, 1992). However, the various research studies on this topic have used different voice durations, different administration and test procedures. Thus, comparing outcomes across studies is neither easy nor particularly valid, especially since few studies have used perpetrator-absent line-ups a well as perpetrator-present ones.

13.4.2 Number of voices in the line-ups

Few studies have examined the question of how many voices should normally be in a fair voice line-up. Yarmey, Yarmey and Yarmey (1994) found that non-perpetrators were more likely to be falsely identified in one-person line-ups (i.e., show-ups) than in six-person line-ups. In our own experimental studies we have found that, when the target voice is present in the line-up, increasing the number of other voices in the line-up from four to six has an effect on how accurately people choose the target voice. However, increasing the number from six to eight does not affect performance. Therefore, we concluded (Bull and Clifford, 1984) that in our optional testing situations six other appropriate voices were all that was required for a parade. In contrast, Hammersley and Reid (1996) argue that 20 voices should be used!

The question of 'how many voices' presumes that each of the non-suspects' voices in the line-up (called 'foils') stands some chance of being picked out: i.e., the foils must be similar to the suspect. In the recent criminal case with which this chapter commenced there was concern on this point. In another case the first author was asked by the defence solicitor to provide an opinion concerning (a) the particular voice evidence and (b) 'the whole question of the value of voice identification evidence' which would be forwarded to the Court of Appeal. Police officers had constructed a voice line-up of voices which they claimed spoke 'with a London-type accent'. An important question was whether the police officers had the expertise to do this successfully. For a number of reasons the appeal was successful.

The first author testified in another criminal trial (and in the retrial) concerning this issue, the history of which demonstrates the complexity of the whole voice identification issue. The defendant was being tried (and was eventually convicted) for rape. Soon after the rape the defendant was spotted by the police in that part of the city where the rape occurred. Later a voice line-up was held and the victim picked out the defendant's voice. The police took the trouble to try to make the voice line-up fair and asked a respected phonetician to assist them in the choice of appropriate foils in terms of aspects of the speakers' voices. The eight-person line-up did seem to me to contain similar voices. However, the voices each said different things. Only one of them, the defendant's, mentioned the city in which the rape took place and the defence team were, quite rightly, concerned about this, even though this word was barely audible.

The first author conducted a study in which listeners were told that a serious crime had been committed in a particular city and they were to try to say which of the eight voices was of a person who lived in that city. Only one eighth of the listeners picked out the defendant's voice (i.e., exactly what would be expected by chance). When each of the people who had chosen the defendant's voice was asked why he or she had chosen that voice one of them said that only his voice sample contained information that sounded as if it had been extracted from a question-and-answer interview whereas the other speakers spoke in monologue. Another of them said that the defendant's voice sample was the only one which contained information indicating the presence of another person. A second study was then conducted in which other listeners were asked to indicate which one of the eight voice samples had been taken from a police interview with a suspect (but from which the interviewer's voice and any incriminating words had been removed). No fewer than 70% of the listeners chose the defendant's voice sample. The first author's evidence on this was deemed admissible by the judge.

13.5 CONCLUSION

In connection with a number of criminal cases the first author has been asked to write reports not only relating to the specific circumstances in each case but also on the general likely reliability (i.e., accuracy) of earwitnesses. Even though there has been a steady, if slow, accumulation of research evidence since our 1984 overview of the topic the opinion given has been similar to that we offered in 1984 when we said that we would recommend that prosecutions based solely on a witness's identification of a suspect's voice ought not to proceed, or if they do proceed, they should fail. We said this because the literature available at that time demonstrated that earwitnessing is considerably error-prone. Contrary to what individuals may believe, people are not usually good at identifying the voices of strangers.

Five years later a group of highly respected psychologists from North America overviewed the relevant literature and came to a very similar conclusion (Deffenbacher et al., 1989). More recently still another group of researchers (McAllister et al., 1993) came to a similar conclusion when they stated that, 'For the criminal justice system, the current findings suggest that police and courts should treat voice identifications made by auditory-visual witnesses with caution' (p. 169). They said this partly because they found the presence of visual identification information reduced earwitness performance. Legge, Grossman and Pieper (1984) noted that voice recognition is more difficult than face recognition as did McAllister, Dale and Keay (1993), who also found that people (e.g., mock jurors) nevertheless seem as willing to rely on earwitness identifications as on eyewitness identifications.

In the opening section of this chapter we noted that in some countries it is now required that the fact-finders in legal proceedings be warned and made aware that eyewitnesses giving evidence may well be mistaken. In our view this is even more important regarding earwitness evidence. In their review paper Hollein et al. (1995) suggested that 'the witness who uses auditory perception for identification purposes does not do as well as an eyewitness' (p. 145). Yarmey and Matthys (1992) concluded that 'speaker identification for a stranger's voice is a very difficult task even when opportunities to listen are relatively good and witnesses are prepared to study the individual's voice' (p. 376).

We concur with this view. The weight of currently available research evidence clearly supports the view of Deffenbacher et al. (1989) that 'earwitnessing is so error-prone as to suggest that no case should be prosecuted solely on identification evidence involving an unfamiliar voice' (p. 118). In their review Hammersley and Read (1996) stated that 'earwitness identification evidence should never be taken alone to be incontrovertible evidence of personal identity' (p. 118). They do, however, opine that it would be wrong to exclude earwitness identification from the fact-finding process so long as the identification procedures were conducted properly and, presumably, some other types of quality evidence were available.

13.6 SUMMARY

(a) Voice identification is poorer than visual identification and hence more unreliable.

(b) Many factors are known to contribute to voice identification unreliability and a sample of these have been presented in the current chapter.

(c) As with eyewitness evidence, practice cannot be informed by theory because the latter has not yet been developed.

(d) Notwithstanding this fact, consensual, considered, opinion both in the UK and the USA advises great caution in prosecuting cases based solely or mainly on voice identification.

(e) While expert evidence may have a role in disputed voice identification trials the cases cited in this chapter demonstrate that while such testimony can be illuminating it may also have to be developed by quite tortuous means.

Key terms
Blind listeners; confidence and accuracy; delay; disguise; expert evidence; gender and age; judicial caution; number of line-up voice foils; perpetrator-absent and present line-ups; speech variety; telephone voice identification; unfamiliar speech samples; voice change; voice identification procedures; voice sample size; witness estimates of speech duration.

References
Bothwell, R., Deffenbacher, K. and Brigham, J. (1987), 'Correlation of eyewitness accuracy and confidence: optimality hypothesis revisited', *Journal of Applied Psychology*, vol. 72, pp. 691–5.

Bull, R. (1981), 'Voice identification by man and machine: a review of research', in S. Lloyd-Bostock (ed.), *Psychology in Legal Contexts*. London: Macmillan.

Bull, R. and Clifford, B.R. (1984), 'Earwitness voice recognition accuracy', in G. Wells and E. Loftus (eds), *Eyewitness Testimony: Psychological Perspectives*. New York: Cambridge University Press.

Bull, R., Rathborn, H. and Clifford, B.R. (1983), 'The voice recognition accuracy of blind listeners', *Perception*, vol. 12, pp. 223–6.

Clifford, B.R. (1980), 'Voice identification by human listeners: on earwitness reliability', *Law and Human Behavior*, vol. 4, pp. 373–94.

Clifford, B.R. (1983), 'Memory for voices: the feasibility and quality of earwitness evidence', in S. Lloyd-Bostock and B.R. Clifford (eds), *Evaluating Witness Evidence* (pp. 189–218). Chichester: Wiley.

Clifford, B.R. (1997), *A Comparison of Adults' and Children's Face and Voice Identification*. Paper presented at the 5th European Congress of Psychology, 6–11 July 1997, Dublin, Ireland.

Clifford, B.R., Bull, R. and Rathborn, H. (1980), *Voice identification*. Report (Res. 741/1/1) to the Home Office.

Clifford, B.R. and Bulloch, G. (1999), 'Face and voice identification by children under sequential and simultaneous lineups' (under review).

Clifford, B.R. and Denot, H. (1982), *Visual and Verbal Testimony and Identification under Conditions of Stress*. Unpublished manuscript, North East London Polytechnic.

Clifford, B.R. and Gwyer, P. (1999), 'Is the confidence-accuracy relationship a function of "easy items"?' (under review).

Clifford, B.R., Rathborn, H. and Bull, R. (1981), 'The effects of delay on voice recognition accuracy', *Law and Human Behavior*, vol. 5, pp. 201–5.

Clifford, B.R. and Toplis, R. (1996), 'A comparison of adults' and children's witnessing abilities', in N. Clark and G. Stephenson (eds), *Investigative and Forensic Decision Making: Issues in Criminological and Legal Psychology*. Leicester: British Psychological Society.

Deffenbacher, K., Cross J., Handkins, R., Chance, J., Goldstein, A., Hammersley, R. and Read, J.D. (1989), 'Relevance of voice identification research to criteria for evaluating reliability of an identification', *Journal of Psychology*, vol. 123, pp. 109–19.

Devlin, Lord (1976), *Report to the Secretary of State for the Home Department of the Departmental Committee on Evidence of Identification in Criminal Cases*. London: Her Majesty's Stationery Office.

Goldstein, A., Knight, P., Bailis, K. and Conover, J. (1981), 'Recognition memory for accented and unaccented voices', *Bulletin of the Psychonomic Society*, vol. 17, pp. 217–20.

Groggin, J., Thompson, C., Strube, G. and Simental, L. (1991), 'The role of language familiarity in voice identification, *Memory and Cognition*, vol. 19, pp. 448–58.

Haggard, M. (1973), 'Selectivity versus summation in multiple observation tasks: evidence with spectrum parameter noise in speech', *Acta Psychologica*, vol. 37, pp. 285–99.

Hammersley, R. and Read, J.D. (1996), 'Voice identification by humans and computers', in S. Sporer, R. Malpass and G. Koehnken (eds), *Psychological Issues in Eyewitness Identification*. Manwah, NJ: Erlbaum.

Hollein, H., Huntley, R., Kunzel, H. and Hollein, P. (1995), 'Criteria for earwitness lineups', *Forensic Linguistics*, vol. 2, pp. 143–53.

Hollins, T. and Perfect, T. (1997), 'Methodological differences make a difference when evaluating eyewitness confidence', *Expert Evidence*, vol. 5, pp. 43–8.

Legge, G., Grossman, C. and Pieper, C. (1984), 'Learning unfamiliar voices', *Journal of Experimental Psychology: Learning, Memory and Cognition*, vol. 10, pp. 298–303.

McAllister, H., Dale, R., Bregman, N., McCabe, A. and Cotton, C. (1993), 'When eyewitnesses are also earwitnesses: effects on visual and voice identification', *Basic and Applied Social Psychology*, vol. 14, pp. 161–70.

McAllister, H., Dale, R. and Keay, C. (1993), 'Effects of lineup modality on witness credibility', *Journal of Social Psychology*, vol. 133, pp. 365–6.

McGehee, F. (1937), 'The reliability of the identification of the human voice', *Journal of General Psychology*, vol. 17, pp. 249–71.

McGehee, F. (1944), 'An experimental investigation of voice recognition', *Journal of General Psychology*, vol. 31, pp. 53–65.

Orchard, T. and Yarmey, A.D. (1995), 'The effects of whispers, voice-sample duration, and voice distinctiveness on criminal speaker identification', *Applied Cognitive Psychology*, vol. 9, pp. 249–60.

Pollack, I., Pickett, J. and Sumby, W. (1954), 'On the identification of speakers by voice', *Journal of the Acoustical Society of America*, vol. 26, pp. 403–6.

Rathborn, H., Bull, R., and Clifford, B.R. (1981), 'Voice recognition over the telephone', *Journal of Police Science and Administration*, vol. 9, pp. 280–4.

Read, D. and Craik, F. (1995), 'Earwitness identification: some influences on voice recognition', *Journal of Experimental Psychology: Applied*, vol. 1, pp. 6–18.

Reich, A. and Duke, J. (1979), 'Effects of selected vocal disguises upon speaker identification by listening', *Journal of the Acoustical Society of America*, vol. 66, pp. 1023–8.

Roebuck, R. and Wilding, J. (1993), 'Effects of vowel variety and sample length on identification of a speaker in a line-up', *Applied Cognitive Psychology*, vol. 7, pp. 475–1.

Saslove, H. and Yarmey, A. (1980), 'Long term auditory memory: speaker identification', *Journal of Applied Psychology*, vol. 65, pp. 111–16.

Thompson, C. (1987), 'A language effect in voice identification', *Applied Cognitive Psychology*, vol. 1, pp. 121–31.

Winograd, E., Kerr, N. and Spence, M. (1984), 'Voice recognition: effect of orienting task, and a test of blind versus sighted listeners', *American Journal of Psychology*, vol. 97, pp. 57–70.

Yarmey, A.D. (1991), 'Voice identification over the telephone', *Journal of Applied Social Psychology*, vol. 21, pp. 1868–76.

Yarmey, A.D. (1995a), 'Earwitness and evidence obtained by other senses', in R. Bull and D. Carson (eds), *Handbook of psychology in legal contexts*. Chichester: Wiley.

Yarmey, A.D. (1995b), 'Earwitness speaker identification', *Psychology, Public Policy and Law*, vol. 1, pp. 792–816.

Yarmey, A.D. and Matthys, E. (1992), 'Voice identification of an abductor', *Applied Cognitive Psychology*, vol. 6, pp. 367–77.

Yarney, A.D., Yarmey, L. and Yarmey, M. (1994), 'Face and voice identifications in showups and lineups', *Applied Cognitive Psychology*, vol. 8, pp. 453–64.

Recommended reading

Bull, R. and Clifford, B.R. (1984), 'Earwitness voice recognition accuracy', in G. Wells and E. Loftus (eds), *Eyewitness Testimony: Psychological Perspectives*. New York: Cambridge University Press.

Hammersley, R. and Read, J. (1996), 'Voice identification by human and computers,' in S. Sporer, R. Malpass and G. Koehnken (eds), *Psychological Issues in Eyewitness Identification*. Manwah, NJ: Erlbaum.

Editors' notes

The Court of Appeal's contribution to the understanding of the fallibilities of earwitness or voice recognition testimony could be said to be at a nascent stage, apparently uninfluenced to any noticeable extent by the wealth of scientific research which indicates that it needs to be treated with great caution by fact-finders — more so than its eyewitness counterpart. The current leading case, whose judgment concerns a number of relevant issues including the composition of earwitness parade line-ups and the admissibility of expert evidence on this topic, is *R v Hersey*, Court of Appeal reference 96/8495/Y3, judgment 1 December 1997, briefly reported in [1998] Crim LR 281 but with a useful editorial commentary. This is the case referred to by the authors at the commencement of the chapter.

CHAPTER FOURTEEN

Getting heads together: police collaborative testimony

Noel K. Clark and Geoffrey M. Stephenson

14.1 INTRODUCTION

14.1.1 Overview

Imagine the scene . . . a criminal trial in the Crown Court or a magistrates' court. The defence counsel's case relies on the testimony of two *civilian* witnesses who provide highly consistent alibi accounts of the defendant's whereabouts at the time that the alleged offence was committed. How would you view the reliability and fairness of their testimony if it were revealed that, prior to making their original statements, the witnesses had met and discussed what they would include in their statements? Would you believe that their statements following the meeting would be more reliable, accurate, comprehensive and fair, or so tainted by the fact that they had discussed the situation prior to making their statements that their testimony was likely to be worthless? It is very likely that most (if not all) judges, magistrates and prosecution counsel would react very negatively to such a disclosure. Indeed, as Heaton-Armstrong and Wolchover (1993, p. 15) note:

> One of us conducted a case which was stopped by the trial judge when it emerged that two civilian prosecution witnesses had been present together when each in turn gave eyewitness section 9 statements to a police officer. The judge's justification for the decision was that this fact alone so tainted the quality of their evidence as to make a fair trial impossible. Where two or more defence witnesses give evidence covering the same ground, most prosecution counsel will expect juries to view denials of collusion with disdain — often without objection from the judge.

Although the criminal justice system views with great suspicion any hint that civilian witnesses might have discussed their experiences, statements or testimony with each other, this is not the case when police officers are witnesses. Indeed, it is not uncommon for police witnesses to admit discussing a case with other officers involved in an investigation, preparing their own (sometimes identical) individual notebook entries together and, subsequently, presenting testimony in court which is the product of such discussion and collaboration. As Heaton-Armstrong and Wolchover (1993, p. 15) comment:

> Far from showing any reluctance to accept the word of an officer who asserts that his notes, although containing exactly the same series of factual assertions as a colleague's, are the product of his own recollections only, most judges unquestioningly welcome 'collaborative testimony' from police officers.

The willingness of courts in England and Wales to accept the collaborative testimony of two or more police officers as being both reliable and fair, whilst refusing to accept collaborative testimony from civilian witnesses, suggests that the judiciary views police officers as in some way immune to the potential dangers that apparently are inherent in the collaborative testimony of civilian witnesses.

In this chapter we will review research evidence for the effects of collaboration on (a) the preparation of statements — specifically on the preparation of notes from memory and (b) answering direct questions. In doing this, we shall attempt to answer the following general questions:

(a)   Are the judiciary justified in their confidence that the collaborative production of statements by police officers is acceptable, while the collaborative production of statements by civilians is unacceptable?

(b)   What are the potential benefits and risks inherent in accepting collaborative testimony in courts of law, whether from police or civilians?

Our review will also outline the comparisons that we have made in our own research between the performance of police officers and civilians (university students) in producing individual and collaborative accounts in relation to the following issues:

(a)   the accuracy of what is recalled in notes, and in answers to specific questions;

(b)   the reported confidence with which answers to specific questions are held;

(c)   errors made in notes;

(d)   the completeness of notes.

Our discussion will be limited to situations where police officers (and civilians) are instructed to try to produce the most *accurate collaborative* notes and answers possible. We do not address situations where police or civilians collaborate with the intention of producing individual notes or answers with a greater regard for consistency between accounts than accuracy.

14.2 COLLABORATIVE REMEMBERING

14.2.1 Discussion and collaboration

Discussing our recollections with others who experienced the same event is a common part of everyday life. Indeed, we may often feel that our understanding of an event is made clearer or more complete by such conversations. Similarly, we might expect two or more police officers who attended the same incident or interview to discuss the event afterwards, either before, during, or after, the compilation of their individual notes or statements. However, while the accuracy and reliability of our recollections of a social event may be of little consequence, accuracy and reliability are most certainly at issue when police officers discuss an incident prior to, or during the compilation of, their notes or statements (Stephenson, 1990).

Currently, there is no available research evidence which directly addresses the effects of discussion on subsequent individual note and statement compilation by police officers. However, Heaton-Armstrong and Wolchover (1993, p. 15) suggest that such discussions are a potential source of miscarriages of justice because the content of the discussions is neither recorded nor disclosed to the defence. For example, factual assertions may be made, or disagreements between officers become apparent, which did not feature in subsequent testimony.

14.2.2 Collaborating to produce notes or statements

Although we have all enjoyed collaborative discussions of shared experiences as a common part of our social lives, it is very unlikely that we will have ever been in a situation where we are required to produce an agreed account of an event with those who experienced it with us or, indeed, to reach agreed answers to questions regarding the event. Our everyday experiences of collaboration as members of task-oriented groups generally involve reaching a group decision, judgment or product based on the verifiable information presented to us — such decisions do not require us to compare our own and others' remembrances of an event in order to produce an accurate agreed account of 'what happened'. The fact that police officers are allowed or even encouraged to produce such collaborative accounts is therefore a matter for concern — particularly as no police force in England or Wales has ever to our knowledge provided officers with any training in the production of such accounts.

14.2.3 The legal status of collaborative notes and statements

It is a common occurrence for more than one police officer to be present during an incident, or to be present when a suspect is interrogated, or a witness interviewed. As noted above, in such situations it is possible, and indeed likely, that officers will discuss the case together afterwards. They may also produce a joint report of the event, either in their notes or as a formal statement.

The effects of collaboration on remembering have generally been neglected as a research area by psychologists, although there have been occasional psycho-legal studies (for example) of jurors' collaborative recall (Hartwick, Sheppard and Davis, 1982), and collaborative eyewitness testimony (Hollin and Clifford, 1983). However, we were surprised to discover that no systematic comparisons of individual and collaborative remembering by police officers had been reported in the literature until we began our research programme.

The ability to recall information about incidents accurately and reliably is an essential requirement for all operational police officers, as they may often be called upon to recall full and specific details about an incident some time after it occurred. This requirement is particularly important with respect to incidents where there is no 'objective' record (e.g., audio or video recordings) of what took place.

One of the most reliable findings in the general memory literature is that the greater the delay between the presentation of information and its subsequent recall, the greater is the likelihood that people will recall the information incompletely, inaccurately or both (see Wells and Loftus (1984) for a review of the experimental literature). One unexpected consequence of the introduction of the Police and Criminal Evidence Act 1984 was a trend towards increasing delays in the time between an incident and police officers' completion of their notes and statements (Baines, 1987).

Section 9 statements (that is, written statements to be given in evidence instead of oral testimony, under the Criminal Justice Act 1967, s. 9) and police officers' notes, usually made in their own notebooks, frequently form the basis of an officer's testimony, and officers often declare under oath that they wrote their notes or made their statement 'as soon as possible' after an incident. Officers also often claim that they did not collaborate with other officers in the preparation of their notes. However, such claims have occasionally led to incredulity from judges and defence lawyers when several officers have presented the same evidence, almost word for word, while swearing that they compiled their notes and statements separately.

Collaboratively based testimony raises legal problems (Stephenson, 1990). For example, if testimony is based on the collaborative recollections of two or more officers, how did the officers resolve disagreements on matters of fact? If an officer agrees to include facts in a collaborative account because others assert them, although he or she believes them to be inaccurate or incorrect, a jury would be deprived of its right to decide the case on *all* the available facts. Moreover, if an officer agrees to a joint account that he or she does not know to be true from the evidence of his or her senses, it is, strictly, only hearsay evidence. Finally, if an officer presents testimony on behalf of him or herself and other officers, and some of the testimony originates from the observations of the other officers, how can such a witness be fully cross-examined in court as to the truth of those observations?

In England and Wales the police have had the option of presenting collaborative testimony in court since an Appeal Court ruling in 1953 (*R* v *Bass* [1953] 1 All ER 1064). Although the two key police officers in the case testified that they had compiled their notes of an interview with the suspect independently, the defence argued that the police accounts appeared to be identical and accused them of collaboration. The defendant was, however, convicted and subsequently appealed. The Court of Appeal commented (before dismissing the appeal) that:

> It was suggested to the officers that they had collaborated. They denied that suggestion. This court has observed that police officers nearly always deny that they have collaborated in the making of notes and we cannot help wondering why they are the only class of society who do not collaborate in such a manner. It seems to us that nothing could be more natural and proper when two persons have been present at an interview with a third person, that they should afterwards make sure that they have a correct version of what was said. Collaboration would appear to be a better explanation of almost identical notes than the possession of a superhuman memory. (p. 1067.)

A strict interpretation of the *R* v *Bass* ruling (Heaton-Armstrong, 1987) is that police officers should be able to produce collaborative testimony relating to what a person *said* during an interview (i.e., reports of verbal statements), but *not* of anything else (e.g., reports of a suspect's behaviour during an incident). However, the use of collaborative testimony was extended by a second Court of Appeal ruling in 1985 (*R* v *Owen* (1986) 83 Cr App R 100), where collaborative testimony of the accused's utterances and actions were approved without criticism by the Court and the conviction was sustained.

The use of collaboratively produced police testimony in court has not gone unchallenged. Heaton-Armstrong (1987, p. 472), in a swingeing critique of the acceptability of collaborative testimony, '*condemned uncompromisingly the insidious and dangerous practice of pre-note making collaboration by police officers over anything other than the spoken word*'.

Heaton-Armstrong's concerns were related to, first, the nature of the collaborative notes and statements themselves; secondly, that one motivation for the police to present collaborative notes and statements was that their production allowed the officers involved an opportunity to 'iron out' any inconsistencies between their individual recollections, ensuring that key aspects of the police case will be fully corroborated.

In contrast, Baines (1987, p. 1869), a serving police officer, presented a different view:

> Collaboration is designed to produce a clear overall picture of what has occurred and not as . . . [Heaton-Armstrong] suggests — that the officers should agree a 'common version' of the incident. . . . A clear overall picture of the incident will assist not only the prosecution case but can also assist the defence in that, as far as possible, no particulars will be left out of the officers' records, particulars which could assist one or more of the defendants at a subsequent trial.

Heaton-Armstrong (1995, p. 140) has documented a more recent judgment by the Court of Appeal which appears to limit the police's scope for producing collaboratively 'improved' statements:

In *R* v *Vincent* the CPS were criticised for sending a memorandum to police officer witnesses which pointed out inconsistencies in their statements and asked for observations. Predictably, further statements were made in which the inconsistencies were tidied up. Commenting on this practice, the court said:

> There is plainly no objection to a solicitor or police officer who is not a witness interviewing witnesses individually after committal in order to seek clarification of points arising from their witness statements. But there can be no justification for sending a memorandum such as this to a Crime Support Unit containing most of the police officers concerned in an alleged affray in the expectation that further statements would be procured from them by the police sergeant who was himself a witness and who was alleged to have been assaulted in the incident to which the document referred. The obvious risk was that the officers would be encouraged, even if they were not invited, to attempt to agree with each other a reconciliation of their various and sometimes conflicting recollections.

The rhetoric of both the police and lawyers is profuse, at odds, but consistently short on hard facts. Are collaboratively produced statements by their very nature unreliable, or untestable? Can collaborative testimony both threaten the legal process and offer potential benefits to the prosecution and the defence? The research that we have conducted to date has attempted to provide at least some indications of the potential benefits and dangers which appear to be inherent when collaboratively prepared accounts are accepted as evidence in the courts.

14.3 WHEN ARE TWO (OR MORE) HEADS BETTER THAN ONE?

14.3.1 Design overview

The majority of our studies have investigated the recall of a particular type of interaction: a fictional police interview of a woman who alleged that she had been raped, using two presentation formats: a dramatised audio recording (Clark, 1987; Stephenson et. al., 1986b), and a slide presentation of a transcript of the interview (Clark, 1987; Clark et al., 1990). We have also used a video excerpt from a real police interview of a woman alleging rape (Stephenson et al., 1986a; Stephenson and Wagner, 1989), and transcribed slides of that interview (Stephenson et al., 1991).

Both university undergraduate students and experienced serving police officers participated in our studies. After exposure to the stimulus interview and a distractor task, participants were randomly assigned to either individual or dyadic recall condition, and sometimes additionally to a four-person group condition (Clark, 1987; Clark et al., 1986; Clark et al., 1990; Stephenson et al., 1986b). Both individuals and groups were then required to produce a free-recall account of the interview, and then to complete questionnaires containing factual questions about the interview. Participants were also asked to rate their confidence in each answer they gave on a four-point scale (guessing — doubtful — fairly certain — certain). In dyads and four-person groups all group members had to agree on the material included in their free-recall protocol, answers to questions and confidence ratings.

14.3.2 Free-recall measures

Two studies analysed free recall in detail. Stephenson et al. (1986b) compared individual, dyadic and four-person group accuracy using student participants, while Clark et al. (1990) compared the performance of students against that of serving police officers.

14.3.2.1 Quantity of recall Reproductive recall refers to the quantity of material in a free-recall protocol which accurately reproduces, or is semantically equivalent to, what was said during the interview. In one study (Stephenson et al., 1986b) we found that the quantity of accurately recalled material increased significantly from individual, to dyad to four-person group, and this was true for both the content of what was said and for identifying who said it. On average, dyads accurately reproduced some 43% more of the original than individuals, and four-person groups 37% more than dyads and 96% more than individuals. However, although four-person groups reproduced almost twice as much as did individuals, on average they still only managed to include approximately one-fifth of the content of the original.

In a further study (Clark et al., 1990), although individual students recalled significantly more of the original interview accurately than did police officers, in the two group recall conditions the police outperformed students by a considerable margin (dyad 36% more; four-person groups 31% more reproductive recall). For police participants, dyads produced some 80% more reproductive recall than did individual police officers, while four-person groups reproduced 61% more than individuals (but some 7% *less* than dyads). In contrast, students in both group conditions reproduced only marginally more of the original than did individuals.

In terms of identifying who said what during the interview, police participants generally identified more speakers, both correctly and incorrectly, than did students across all conditions. Although police in the group conditions identified significantly more speakers correctly than did individuals, the number of correctly identified speakers by students did not vary across conditions. Similarly to the first study, the participants who produced the greatest reproductive recall (in this case, police dyads) on average still only reproduced less than 25% of the total content of the original interview.

14.3.2.2 Quality and consistency of recall It is important to be able to distinguish between the *quantity* of reproductive recall produced, and the *quality* of that recall. This issue is of particular concern when, at one extreme, a witness may recall a substantial amount of accurate but peripheral detail, while another witness may accurately recall far less in terms of quantity, but accurately describes the main actions which took place (i.e., high quality). Obviously, in terms of the value of the testimony of these two witnesses, the testimony of the latter may be far more significant than that of the former, despite the fact that the quantity of accurate recall is less.

Clark (1987) reported a qualitative analysis of the accurate recall of individuals and groups, using data from Stephenson et al.'s (1986) study. The important issue was whether or not the quality of what was recalled by groups was systematically different to that of individuals. Clark (1987) reported differences in the quality of recall for both student and police participants in terms of the *consistency* with which items of information were reported (to measure consistency, Clark calculated the number of items from the original interview which were reported by 50% or more individuals, dyads and groups). Overall, participants who recalled individually were the least consistent, dyads included more than twice as much consistent information, and four-person groups were marginally more consistent than dyads. In addition, police participants were far more consistent than their student counterparts within each recall condition.

In summary, while collaboration does not appear to influence the general quality of what is recalled, it clearly influences the consistency with which particular items of information from the original interview are included in protocols. Group remembering, then, leads to consistency in quality, but not to enhanced quality.

14.3.2.3 Reconstructive or implicational errors Reconstructive or implicational errors were defined by Stephenson et al. (1986b, p. 1115) as errors 'giving either (a) the addition of normal properties and plausible detail, (b) particularisation, or (c) specification of normal conditions, components, or consequences of events', in other words, material which did not appear in the original, but which did not contradict anything in the original. Both of our studies found similar patterns of error for students: those who recalled individually included a significantly greater number of reconstructions than did those in the group conditions, but there was no difference in the number of reconstructions included by dyads and four-person groups. In both studies group recall led to the suppression of reconstructive errors for students. In contrast, for police participants, group recall led to an increase in the number of reconstructions included, with police dyads producing some 44% more reconstructions than individuals, and four-person groups some 21% more.

A further comparison of student and police recall revealed an important stylistic difference between the two (Clark et al., 1987). Regardless of recall condition, when students were asked to recall the interview they consistently reported it as a *story*. In contrast, although approximately half of the police individual participants also recalled the interview as a story, the remainder recalled it in direct speech as a *script*. We compared the numbers of reconstructional errors made by police individual scriptwriters and storytellers, and found that the number of reconstructions made by scriptwriters was similar to that made by police participants in the dyadic and four-person conditions (who were all scriptwriters), while the number of reconstructions by individual police storytellers was far lower, and similar to the number made by student individuals (who were all storytellers).

These studies indicate that the amount of reconstructive error included in free recall of an interview may be significantly influenced by two factors: (a) whether participants recall as individuals or in groups, and (b) whether they recall the interaction as a story or as a script.

14.3.2.4 Confusional errors Confusional errors are recalled items which clearly contradict items of information in the original interview. Overall, the level of confusional errors was surprisingly low in both of our studies, varying between 1.5 and 2.8% of the total content of protocols. Although we found that police participants included more confusional errors in their protocols than did students overall, the finding is difficult to interpret due to the very low levels of confusional errors found.

14.3.2.5 Metastatements Metastatements were defined by Stephenson et al. (1986b, p. 1115) as recalled items 'that make comment on (a) the content or organisation of the text, (b) expressions of the subject's own attitudes/ opinions towards the text, or (c) the attribution of motives/intentions to the characters that are not explicitly stated in the text'. Examples of metastatements that were fairly frequently expressed in protocols included such statements as 'I [the subject] believe the woman was hiding something,' and, 'I think the police could have been more understanding towards the woman'. Such statements are neither reproductive recall nor errors as they express the participant's sentiments on the characters in the interaction.

Stephenson et al. (1986b) found that dyads included 58% *fewer* metastatements than did individuals, and four-person groups included some 77% fewer than did individuals and 46% fewer than dyads. Clark et al. (1990) reported similar findings for their student participants, while for police participants the effect of collaboration appeared to be even more stark, with dyads including very few, if any, metastatements (dyads 87% fewer than individuals; four-person groups 81% fewer).

14.3.3 Answering questions
All participants were asked to answer a series of questions about the stimulus interview, and to rate their confidence in each answer on a four-point scale (from 'guessing' to 'certain').

14.3.3.1 Accuracy Stephenson et al. (1986b) found that student four-person groups produced 66% more correct answers than did individuals, and 25% more than dyads, while Clark et al. (1990) found student four-person groups produced 36% more correct answers than individuals, and 15% more than dyads. Similarly, police four-person groups produced 7% more correct answers than dyads, and 31% more than individuals. In addition, within each condition, police participants consistently provided more accurate answers than did students. Collaborative remembering appears to enhance the accuracy of question answering, with the amount of enhancement being dependent, at least in part, on group size.

14.3.3.2 Accuracy and confidence Our findings for the relationship between accuracy and confidence are fairly clear and consistent. First, across both police and student participants, individuals and groups were consistently able to distinguish between their accurate and inaccurate answers in terms of reported confidence — confidence in accurate answers was consistently higher than that for inaccurate answers. However, individual participants consistently made the greatest discrimination in terms of confidence between accurate and inaccurate answers. This discrimination was reduced in dyadic conditions, and reduced even further in four-person group conditions.

Although groups produced more *correct* answers than individuals, and were more confident than individuals that their correct answers were indeed correct, when their answers were actually *incorrect* groups were significantly more confident than individuals that there answers were *correct*. Although the increased confidence of groups in their correct answers may be viewed as a positive benefit of group over individual remembering, it is apparently achieved at the cost of a reduced ability by groups to distinguish between confidence in accurate and inaccurate answers overall, in other words, there is a *misplaced confidence effect*.

14.3.3.3 Recalling as an individual and as a group member The studies reviewed above employed a situation which is analogous to a police officer *either* recalling an interview on his or her own, *or* recalling it as a group member. However, it is likely that sometimes officers may either initially recall an incident on their own and then participate in a group recall or discussion of the incident, or, *vice versa*, an officer may be initially involved in a group recall or discussion of an incident, and then recall it on his or her own.

Stephenson et al. (1986a) investigated the accuracy and confidence of student participants' answers to questions: (a) when individual question answering was followed by dyadic question answering, and (b) when dyadic question answering was followed by individual question answering. Their analysis of the accuracy of answers to questions revealed that collaboration before or during question answering had no effect on overall accuracy. In other words, prior individual question answering did not enhance the accuracy of subsequent dyadic question answering.

In terms of their confidence in accurate answers, participants who initially answered questions in a dyad were significantly more confident than those who initially answered the questions individually. Moreover, their confidence only decreased marginally when they then answered questions individually. In contrast, the confidence of participants who initially answered questions individually *increased* when they subsequently answered questions in a dyad, although this increased confidence was still well below that of participants who initially answered questions in a dyad and then as individuals. Exactly the same pattern of results was also found for confidence in inaccurate answers.

Stephenson and Wagner (1989) investigated the 'misplaced confidence' in inaccurate question answering of dyads, again using students as participants. They reported that it was decision-making rather than dyadic discussion *per se* which led to the effect — participants who had earlier taken part in dyadic free recall did not display the misplaced confidence effect when they answered the questions individually, while those who free-recalled individually and then participated in dyadic recall did display the effect.

The relationship between accuracy and confidence was further clarified by Stephenson et al. (1991) using both police and student participants. The study examined three factors which they hypothesised might influence the accuracy and confidence of collaborative question answering. First, a *cognitive resources* factor was examined by comparing individual and collaborative (dyadic) performance. Secondly, an *interpersonal acquaintance* factor was examined by analysing the ratings of several independent judges of how well acquainted the participants in each recall condition would have been with each other, given their earlier association during a free-recall task. Finally, a *professional salience* factor was examined by comparing the performance of police and student participants across all conditions. It was hypothesised that the stimulus discourse (a police interrogation) would have greater professional salience to police officers than to students.

In addition to examining the measures of accuracy and confidence in question answering discussed above, Stephenson et al. (1991) also presented a more detailed analysis of accuracy and confidence. In this study, all of the questions had a 'strictly correct' answer, and it was only when individuals or dyads gave this answer that an additional point was added to their accuracy total. When an answer did not actually contradict the original but was not 'strictly correct', this would be counted as an *implicational* (or reconstructive) error. When an answer directly contradicted the original, it would be counted as a *confusional* error. This error classification system is very similar to that employed by Stephenson et al. (1986b; see 14.3.2.3). They found several significant relationships between their three factors and accuracy, error and confidence:

(a)   the greater the cognitive resources available, the greater the number of accurate answers produced (i.e., in terms of accuracy, dyads generally outperformed individuals);

(b)   the greater the interpersonal acquaintance of participants, the greater the likelihood of higher confidence in the accuracy of implicational errors (i.e., participants who had worked together previously on the free-recall task tended to be more confident in the accuracy of answers which were actually implicational errors than were those who had not worked together); and

(c)   the more professionally salient the task, the greater the risk of implicational errors being included at the expense of accurate answers, and the greater the confidence in confusional errors (i.e., police participants tended to provide more implicational errors in their answers than student participants, and also tended to be more confident in the accuracy of answers which were, in fact, confusional errors).

14.4   IS JUSTICE BEING SERVED BY THE USE OF COLLABORATIVE POLICE TESTIMONY?

Our research findings show that lawyers are justified in being concerned about the admissibility of collaborative police reports in court proceedings. The advantages of collaboration may well be outweighed by the disadvantages. Indeed, nothing in our findings suggests that we should ignore the strength of those concerns.

In reality, it is both impossible and undesirable to argue for the suppression of *all* informal discussion between police officers who are investigating the same case — such discussion is entirely normal. Our concerns focus on more formal situations when the specific purpose of collaboration is to prepare legal documents. However, we do recognise that in reality the dividing line between informal discussion of a case and the preparation of reports is often, if not always, unclear.

If collaborative police statements are to remain acceptable to the courts, our findings do suggest some changes to current practice which might maximise the advantages of collaboration whilst minimising the disadvantages. We believe that the advantages of collaboration could be enhanced by seeking to avoid any diffusion of responsibility by officers for collaboratively produced reports. One way of achieving this might be:

(a)   Initially, officers compile their own notes individually.

(b)   Officers then produce a collaborative account of an incident.

(c)   Officers then comment on any significant discrepancies between their individual notes and the collaborative report, and give reasons for such discrepancies.

(d)   The whole process should be clearly documented in writing.

Such a process would have the advantage of not losing any information recalled by individual officers, and would also provide an opportunity for prompting officers to recall additional information. The clear disadvantage would be the additional time necessary to prepare separate individual and collaborative reports, and then reconcile and comment on any differences between reports.

Finally, if collaborative accounts by police officers are to remain admissible in court, we see no reason in principle why civilian witnesses to an incident should not also be allowed to produce collaborative accounts. Indeed, in some situations, for example when several family members travelling together are involved in a car accident, it would seem to be highly unusual if they did not discuss the circumstances leading up to the incident both before and after they have made statements to the police and prior to any court hearing. Currently their testimony in court must still be given on a purely individual basis.

14.5 SUMMARY

(a)   There are both advantages and disadvantages to collaboration in terms of both the *quantity* and *quality* of what is recalled. It should be remembered that these advantages and disadvantages may only apply in situations where the motive for collaboration is to produce as accurate and complete an account of an interaction as is possible.

(b)   The *advantages* of collaboration are:

(i)   Collaboration tends to enhance the quantity of accurate information contained within a single, joint report.

(ii)   Collaboratively produced reports tend to be more consistent (or less idiosyncratic) in their contents. Such reports focus more on what is seen as 'important' facts by their authors. They tend to provide more probative information.

(iii)   Collaboration leads to the general suppression of evaluative comments within reports.

(c)   The *disadvantages* of collaboration are:

(i)   Collaboration may lead to the suppression of information which would have been included in individual reports.

(ii)   Collaboration generally leads to the introduction of more reconstructive errors in free-recall reports, and implicational errors in answers to direct questions.

(iii)   Collaboration appears to increase confidence in the accuracy of answers which are, in fact, implicational errors.

(iv)   Collaboration increases confidence in the accuracy of answers which are, in fact, confusional errors.

There therefore appear to be several reasons why collaborative reports by police officers should be treated with caution by the courts. Of particular concern are our findings that collaboration tends to increase the quantity of reconstructive errors included in free-recall reports, the quantity of implicational errors in answers to questions, and officers' generally increased confidence in the accuracy of this erroneous information. Indeed, some of our findings suggest that these effects are most pronounced when officers (and, indeed, students) attempt to construct a report consisting primarily of direct speech (i.e., as in traditional 'blow-by-blow' police notebook accounts of interactions).

Key terms
Accuracy; collaboration and accuracy; collaborative statements; collaborative testimony; confusional error; effects of collaboration; error; memory; police interrogations; police interviews; police statements; quality of recall; quantity of recall; reconstructive error; testimony.

References
Baines, P. (1987), 'Insidious collaborators', *Police Review*, vol. 95, pp. 1868–9.
Clark, N.K. (1987), *The Analysis and Prediction of Individual and Group Remembering*, unpublished doctoral thesis. University of Kent at Canterbury.
Clark, N.K., Stephenson, G.M. and Kniveton, B.H. (1987), *Getting the Gist: Individual and Collaborative Recall by Police Officers and Students*. Paper presented at Annual Conference of the British Psychological Society. Sheffield, 1987.

Clark, N.K., Stephenson, G.M. and Kniveton, B.H. (1990), 'Social remembering: quantitative aspects of individual and collaborative remembering by police officers and students', *British Journal of Psychology*, vol. 81, pp. 73–94.

Clark, N.K., Stephenson, G.M. and Rutter, D.R. (1986), 'Memory for a complex social discourse: the analysis and prediction of individual and group recall', *Journal of Memory and Language*, vol. 25, pp. 295–313.

Flavell, J.H. and Wellman, H.M. (1987), 'Metamemory', in R.V. Kail and J.H. Hagen (eds), *Perspectives on the Development of Memory and Cognition*. Hillsdale, NJ: Erlbaum.

Hartwick, J., Sheppard, B.I. and Davis, J.H. (1982), 'Group remembering: research and implications', in R.A. Guzzo (ed.), *Improving Decision Making in Organizations*. London: Academic Press, pp. 41–72.

Heaton-Armstrong, A. (1987), 'Police officers' notebooks: recent developments', *Criminal Law Review*, vol. 34, pp. 470–2.

Heaton-Armstrong, A. (1995), 'Recording and disclosing statements by witnesses — law and practice', *Medical Science and Law*, vol. 35, pp. 136–43.

Heaton-Armstrong, A. and Wolchover, D. (1993), 'Knocking heads together', *Counsel*, April, pp. 14–15.

Hollin, C.R. and Clifford, B.R. (1983), 'Eyewitness testimony: The effects of discussion on recall accuracy and agreement', *Journal of Applied Social Psychology*, vol. 13, pp. 234–44.

Stephenson, G.M. (1990), 'Should collaborative testimony be permitted in courts of law?', *Criminal Law Review*, pp. 302–14.

Stephenson, G.M., Abrams, D., Wagner, W. and Wade, G.S. (1986a), 'Partners in recall: collaborative order in the recall of police interrogation', *British Journal of Social Psychology*, vol. 25, pp. 341–3.

Stephenson, G.M., Clark, N.K. and Wade, G.S. (1986b), 'Meetings make evidence? An experimental study of collaborative and individual recall of a simulated police interrogation', *Journal of Personality and Social Psychology*, vol. 50, pp. 1113–22.

Stephenson, G.M., Kniveton, B. and Wagner, W. (1991), 'Social influences on remembering: intellectual, interpersonal and intergroup components', *European Journal of Social Psychology*, vol. 12, pp. 463–75.

Stephenson, G.M. and Wagner, W. (1989), 'Origins of the misplaced confidence effect in collaborative recall', *Applied Cognitive Psychology*, vol. 3, pp. 227–36.

Wells, G.L. and Loftus, E.R., (eds) (1984), *Eyewitness Testimony*. Cambridge: Cambridge University Press.

Recommended reading
Clark, N.K. and Stephenson, G.M., 'Social remembering: Individual and collaborative remembering for social information', in M. Hewstone and W. Strobe (eds), *European Review of Social Psychology*, vol. 7, Chichester: Wiley, 1995.

Heaton-Armstrong, A. and Wolchover, D., 'Knocking heads together', *Counsel*, April 1993, pp. 14–15.

Editors' notes

Lawyers have long argued that 'heads together in the canteen' note-making sessions by police officers lead to the corruption of the participating individuals' memories in a way that cannot, thereafter, be realistically investigated. With the benefit of this chapter, the argument has gained additional, scientific, force. We doubt whether the authors' confidence in the efficacy of their suggestion that the whole process of collaboration should be clearly documented in writing is justified. The only effective way to ensure that the individual, uncorrupted, recall of a police officer who takes part in a collaboration session is preserved is for the latter to be tape-recorded. The Northumbria Police practice is for officer witnesses to an incident to write up their notes separately and then to be interviewed about it on tape (see chapter 15).

Where collaboration sessions are incompletely recorded and it is thus impossible to isolate and test the primary recollection of the witness, an application to exclude the evidence on the basis that realistic forensic examination has been rendered unattainable — in accordance with section 78 of the Police and Criminal Evidence Act 1984 — might be considered. It has been known for this to be achieved successfully, albeit in first instance courts (who might adopt a more common-sense approach to evidential issues in preference to the outmoded and naive approach of the Court of Appeal in 1953 in *R* v *Bass*).

CHAPTER FIFTEEN

Recording witness statements

Anthony Heaton-Armstrong and David Wolchover

15.1 INTRODUCTION

It is the momentous legacy of the Police and Criminal Evidence Act 1984 (PACE) that the questioning of suspects is now hedged about with a wealth of protective formalities. These have the closely interrelated aims of mitigating the adverse effects of the 'inherently coercive nature of custodial interrogation' (*Miranda* v *Arizona* (1966) 384 US 436 per Earl Warren CJ) and ensuring precision in the recording of what suspects say to the police. Perhaps the most significant PACE innovation was audiotaping of the questioning of suspects in the police station (s. 60 of the Act) and for several years now cassette recorders have furnished an unassailable record of such questioning for the purpose of transmission to the trial court. Videotaping may eventually be adopted for the interviewing of suspects, although its use remains experimental. At present it is not the practice of the police to use pocket cassette recorders to tape the utterances of suspects outside the police station (Wolchover and Heaton-Armstrong, 1996, sects 3–120 to 3–129) and theoretically there may be circumstances when tape-recording in the police station is impracticable. Where reliance has of necessity to be placed on written records detailed rules govern their creation and much emphasis is laid on the need to give suspects the opportunity to contribute to the record-making process through inspection and endorsement of the written record and subsequent validation on tape.

The entrenchment of measures which guarantee the authenticity of evidence of statements by suspects to the police is a considerable achievement and a source of much satisfaction. But it should not be forgotten that the questioning of suspects is only one side of the investigative coin. Of comparable importance, it might be thought, is the need to preserve an exact record of the original accounts of eyewitnesses. After all, the bedrock of adversarial process is the evidence of witnesses for the prosecution, not the confession of the accused. Yet the concentration on obtaining and recording utterances by defendants contrasts very remarkably with the lack of attention paid to obtaining and taking statements from potential witnesses. By contrast with the stringent rules governing the obtaining of confession statements the process of taking witness statements is subject to few, if any, formal safeguards or regulatory constraints. Until only as recently as 1992, when the Home Office Central Planning and Training Unit issued *A Guide to Interviewing*, a manual based on the 'ethical' method of the 'cognitive interview' with its stress on the neutral search for facts, it was enhanced by little or no training. Even now it seems that there continues to be relatively little systematic training given to officers on conducting interviews, although it must be acknowledged that there has been an increasing tendency to inculcate awareness of the pitfalls of inadequate interviewing.

The statements of private eyewitnesses in criminal cases are put into writing in accordance with the provisions of s. 9 of the Criminal Justice Act 1967. Almost invariably they are compiled by police officers. Interviews in which the police take statements from witnesses are conducted in private without the keeping of any verbatim record. Hardly ever are they tape-recorded and in the absence of any independent means by which a court can determine exactly how a statement came to be made the police are relatively free to engage in the manipulation of witnesses, deliberately or inadvertently. On rare occasions there may be a risk that this will lead to the conviction of the innocent. But awful as it is to contemplate the prospect of wrongful convictions, however remote, the lack of an unchallengeable record of interviews in which witnesses give their statements to the police poses the courts with what in practice amounts to a much more serious problem. For it is frequently a direct cause of the acquittal of the guilty.

Obtaining an unassailable record of what a witness told the police during an investigation is important for another reason. It will be of critical importance if the disciplines discussed in a number of the chapters of this book are to be applied in practice. Much of the preparatory and analytical work on original witness statements that needs to be carried out in accordance with the lessons taught by those disciplines would simply not be feasible without a wholly authentic record — a tape recording — of the interview which elicited the statement. To that extent the question whether a court or jury will be in a position to make an assessment of the value of a witness's evidence in terms of any one of the disciplines reviewed in this book will very much depend on the acceptance by the authorities of the argument presented in the present chapter in favour of tape-recording and of the implementation of the proposal in practice.

15.2 ORIGINS OF PRE-TRIAL WITNESS STATEMENTS

Most officers are coy when asked how they took a witness statement. Few care to admit that the written narrative was obtained by questioning and the fiction is still perpetuated that a statement was produced by straight dictation, possibly preceded by some amount of general discussion of the issues to be covered and punctuated only by bland questions aimed at clearing up ambiguities or providing descriptive detail. Such a pretence may only be of comparatively recent origin. Centuries ago the duty of 'police' detection and inquiry rested with the investigating justice of the peace, whose statutory function was to obtain depositions from informants by way of examination. Recording such examinations was placed on a general footing by the land-mark bail and committal statutes enacted in the reign of Philip and Mary (1 & 2 P & M (1554–5), c. 13, and 2 & 3 P & M (1555), c. 10). These were the logical development of a process of evolution from rudimentary practices of summary justice in the early Middle Ages to the full-blown system of gaol delivery with its built-in delay between preliminary investigation and arraign-ment at trial. The bail statute, which required transcription of examinations where accused persons were bailed pending trial, was explicitly intended as a check against collusive release; the committal statute extended transcription to all cases of felony (Langbein, 1974).

Section 9 statements serve several purposes. They provide the basic structure governing the direction of an enquiry, the selection of defendants and the choice of offence to be charged. In furnishing an advance blueprint of the shape of the evidence they enable the case to be prosecuted and defended coherently and the trial to be supervised fairly. But chief among their functions is the preservation of original accounts and this will have three uses. First, they provide a narrative from which witnesses can refresh their memories. Secondly, they furnish a text against which consistency can be checked during the trial. Thirdly, they provide a documentary narrative which can be read at trial in lieu of live evidence in exceptional circumstances where statute permits.

15.3 USE OF STATEMENTS TO SUPPLEMENT OR QUALIFY LIVE EVIDENCE

15.3.1 Statement as a memory aid

The examination of a witness in court is not a memory test and witnesses who have made earlier statements close in time to the events to be recounted are allowed to refresh their memories from their statements. There are two possible ways in which they may be allowed to do so. Because of the lapse of time between the events and making the statement the rules of evidence may restrict refreshment to reading through the statement before the witness comes into court to give evidence. If the statement was made so soon after the event that the memory is presumed to be still fresh, the witness may be permitted to consult the statement in the witness box. The common and preferred practice in the case of civilian witnesses is for the prosecution to give them their statements to read over before they go into court but when they enter the witness box not to invite them to refer to their statements in the first instance, even though the time between the events described and the making of the statement was such that they would technically be allowed to have their statements in front of them. If they then have difficulty remembering, they may invited to consult their statements. By contrast, police officers are customarily invited to consult their notes or original statements straight away as a matter of course without waiting to see first of all if they can manage without. A few judges have been known to adopt the same practice in regard to civilian witnesses. This is evidently based on the supposition that if a police witness may be permitted to do it, so also should a private witness. The counter-argument, supporting a distinction between police and private witnesses, is that with the latter the giving of evidence is usually a once-in-a-lifetime experience and the facts of the incident are likely to remain engraved in the memory without the need to consult the aide-mémoire. By contrast, the average police officer will give evidence so frequently and about facts which so commonly repeat themselves that the memory of one case is likely to merge into that of another with no independent recall of the instant case.

15.3.2 Testing consistency
It is traditionally believed that after making all due allowance for the frailty of memory a comparison between the testimony of an eyewitness in court and a statement about the events in question uttered on a previous occasion may provide a very useful indication of the witness's veracity, accuracy and reliability. Indeed, it has been judicially asserted that 'other statements are one of the classic examples of material tending to undermine the credibility of a witness' (*R* v *Rashid* (1994) unreported CA transcript No. 89/4043/W3, judgment 17 April 1994). Of necessity, testing for consistency is dependent on restricting memory refreshment to out-of-court use of a statement, since there can hardly be any valid test of consistency if witnesses in the box have their statements in front of them in the first instance. Statements will usually have been signed months before the trial and not surprisingly differences often emerge at trial even though witnesses are given their statements to read outside the courtroom before they give evidence. Since private witnesses will usually be describing an incident completely out of their normal experience it is assumed that it will be graphically embossed on the memory and that whilst details may become fuzzy with the passage of time the essentials will tend to remain constant. Changes in the memory of such central matters are therefore supposed to furnish a useful test of reliability and it is assumed that, if conducted well, cross-examination on inconsistency will prove very illuminating.

It is not the purpose of this chapter to challenge that supposition but even assuming its validity the cogency of testing for inconsistency is often diminished by flaws in the existing system of recording witness statements. These are still almost always taken down in writing by officers involved to a greater or lesser extent in the investigation, and the content of a statement is likely to be influenced by the way in which the investigator perceives the case and receives and formulates the narrative. With the best will in the world, the way in which the story is committed to paper cannot help but reflect the officer's subjective view of the facts. Statements often owe as much to the officer's controlling hand as to the witness's actual memory. They invariably exclude the questions, which may be leading and suggestive, they can be highly selective and even quite inaccurate, and they may turn out to be seriously distorted versions of what the witness actually said. (This process has been dramatically illustrated by McLean, 1994.) At the time of telling the police their story, witnesses may be exhausted, depressed, disorientated, unwell or preoccupied. Many witnesses are insensitive to the nuances of language. So, after the officer has taken down the statement and has handed it to the witness to check and sign, crucial omissions, errors or distortions can easily be overlooked. On the other hand, the witness may simply be too tired or too timid to give voice to objections or reservations. Detailed consideration of the issue of distortion follows in 15.4.

The result may be a document which substantially, if not fundamentally, diverges from what the witness stated or intended to state. Because the content of statements is controlled by what investigators, who record them, choose to include, attempts to use a statement to test consistency often degenerate into a farce, with unresolved conflicts over just exactly what it was that the witness did say to the police. Of course, discrepancies may be genuine ones, truly showing up the witness as unreliable or even dishonest. But defending barristers have long perfected the art of exploiting inadequacies in the system of taking down statements in order to cast 'blame' on a witness for ostensible inconsistencies which may be no more than the spurious product of inherent failings in the traditional recording process. When a witness answering the prosecuting barrister's questions departs in some significant respect from an earlier statement to the police, the defending barrister in cross-examination will embark on a series of standardised entrapping questions designed to seal up escape routes. Questions tend to proceed along the following lines. Before making the statement did the witness read the printed declaration at the top of the first page indicating the importance of telling the truth? Did the witness appreciate the importance of honesty, care and accuracy? Was everything of importance included? At the conclusion of making the statement did the witness read it through before signing it or was it read back by the officer? Was the witness shown the statement before coming into court? Was it read through carefully? Did it revive memory of the facts as clearly as when the statement was made? Has the evidence in the witness box corresponded exactly with the contents of the statement?

These preliminary, ensnaring, questions are designed to prevent such attempts to evade the embarrassment of apparent self-contradiction as praying in aid the lapse of time since the events occurred. Finally the trap is sprung and the witness is confronted with the inconsistency, omission, addition, elaboration, or embellishment, as the case may be. The result is often an excruciating attempt to claim either that the officer put down something that was not said or otherwise left out something that was. If called to resolve the conflict the attesting officer will be torn between selling the witness short or admitting to inattention or error. Since such officers will usually be moved to protect their own *amour propre*, witnesses may well end up being made to look unreliable or dishonest — not the officer whose mode of interviewing and transcription may have been seriously at fault. At the very least the conflict will remain unresolved and the doubt will often be applied in favour of the undeserving accused. Using these expurgated or inaccurate versions of what the witness actually told the police in private in order to pick holes in their evidence in court hardly conduces to getting at the truth.

15.4 DISTORTION OF THE PRIVATE WITNESS'S ACCOUNT IN THE PROCESS OF ELICITATION AND TRANSCRIPTION

Broadly innocent reasons may explain why during the taking of a statement a factual assertion by a witness is omitted from the narrative text, misrecorded or misrepresented by the writer. For example, the statement maker may speak in a rambling or disconnected fashion or may suffer from poor diction or may speak in an obscure dialect or with an unfamiliar accent. This may lead to misunderstandings or omissions from the body of the statement if the statement taker is inexperienced or insufficiently vigilant to avert them, but it is liable to occur even with old hands. Again, the witness may lay insufficient emphasis on a particular point despite its potential significance, with the result that the statement taker fails to notice it amongst a mass of other more prominently voiced assertions. However, a more insidious factor than simple miscommunication is the influence of unjustified supposition. Whilst officers delegated to take a witness statement often have little or no involvement in the investigation this is usually where the witness is of marginal importance. But statements by major witnesses are usually taken by officers at the heart of an inquiry and this can lead to unconscious slanting of the narrative content. In spite of the unquestioned desirability of preserving detachment an investigator may understandably form an impassioned view of the case not warranted by the actual evidence available. From this there may stem an emotion-led tendency to assume the existence of facts conforming with the preconceived belief. The assumption by an officer of the existence of facts not actually established by available evidence may lead to their inclusion in a statement in two possible ways, one by direct impact on the witness's spoken narrative, the other affecting the recording process. By the influence of suggestion an officer with a forceful and persuasive personality may impose on an uncertain witness a belief in the existence of a particular fact. As to distortion through the recording process, ambiguities may tend to be read in favour of a particular supposition (i.e., the suspected culprit's guilt) although, objectively considered, they could equally be read to the contrary. Again, averments which, on the face of it may seem perfectly clear in their meaning may be misinterpreted in conformity with the suspect's supposed guilt. The attachment to a given belief may even cause what is said to be misheard. The consequence may be that statement takers will unconsciously rewrite what was actually said in accordance with what they believe was implied.

In contrast with innocent misquotation, distortion or corruption of the witness's original account may be the result of deliberate manipulation. Thus the process of implanting in the witness's mind a belief in a particular fact may occur quite deliberately. In adopting the belief the witness then 'dictates' it to the officer. Another approach is to misquote the witness in writing out the statement and then to procure a signature without giving the witness an adequate chance to inspect the record. (This could be achieved by reading back the statement incorrectly.) Somewhat recklessly, it may be hoped that when, months later at trial, the witness reads the statement before giving evidence its content will be adopted uncritically on the basis of the assumption that if it was in the statement it must have been believed to be true, even though there is now no actual memory of the particular fact but a wish on the part of the witness not to be obstructive, unhelpful or seen to be incompetent. Deliberate manipulation of witness or record may be motivated by zeal where the officer firmly believes a particular person to be guilty and perceives the existing evidence to be inadequate to guarantee a conviction. This is an example of what has been called 'noble cause corruption'. But less 'nobly' the motivation of the police may reflect an anxiety to cover their backs against a legitimate complaint of unlawful arrest or some other illegality or impropriety. Either way, it is instructive to quote the account by Dr Roderick Munday (1997) of having:

> . . . regularly heard stories to make the flesh creep concerning the way in which policemen have sometimes adjusted or attempted to adjust witnesses' versions of events — verging from an unsuccessful and puzzling attempt to get a member of the Bar to agree that his wife was with him in a boat on the Thames when he witnessed a rape on the towpath ('because it looks better, sir') to a student who, to his evident distress, had been politely cajoled into giving descriptions of two men who mugged him by a bank cash machine which he did not recognise but which happened to fit those of two persons apprehended that same night by the constabulary.

An important factor in rendering some witnesses vulnerable to deliberate manipulation is that involvement in a case frequently begins for an individual as a suspect. The transition to witness is often made in the belief that an escape from prosecution is being offered and that there is little choice but to cooperate. Acquiescence in these circumstances hardly conduces to willing testimony. On the other hand, the witness may be perfectly innocent and eager to help the police but suggestible, not very observant or possessed of only a mediocre memory. It is easy to see how in either sort of case people are open to manipulation by a zealous investigator or one anxious to avoid criticism for impropriety or incompetence. There will be an obvious and clearly justifiable interest for the defence in learning how the witness's statement was taken, under what blandishments and exactly what was said. It sometimes turns out with a witness who started out being questioned as a *suspect* that no PACE record was kept of the interview which led on to that person eventually signing a *witness* statement. Since it is inconceivable that such a statement will have been prompted without some amount of questioning, it follows that the officers who were secluded with the witness during that session must have committed a breach of the requirement of PACE Code C, para. 11.5(c), to tape-record it. The breach can be used not only to attack the officer's credit on other aspects of police evidence in the case, e.g., admissions attributed to a defendant, but there may be an argument for seeking exclusion of the witness's evidence *ab initio* under s. 78 of PACE on the basis that the foundation on which the witness gives evidence — the statement — was obtained through the commission of a breach of the rules.

Many investigating officers will be unaware, or, at least, only dimly aware, of the possible effect of unconscious influences emanating from a statement taker in distorting the content of a witness's statement. But few will fail to appreciate the implications where deliberate manipulation is suspected. Hence officers are invariably concerned to cultivate the impression that witness statements are the product of dictation to an indifferent amanuensis. Thus, they will usually concede that there was some generalised initial discussion on the broad outline of the subject matter and will sometimes admit the occasional interjection intended to keep the witness within the bounds of relevance, or a neutral question designed to elicit details of a description, for example. But the suggestion of any greater involvement in controlling the content of the statement will always be vehemently denied.

15.5 POLICE WITNESSES AND JOINT RECOLLECTION

The problem of suggestibility affects the police officer's note of an incident (in notebook or original statement form) wherever conferring has taken place. Since *R* v *Bass* [1953] 1 QB 680 officers have been permitted to 'pool recollections' of an incident when writing up their notes. (But in contrast with permissible police practice, David Wolchover remembers a trial in which two private witnesses had been present together when they each in turn gave eyewitness statements to a police officer and the circuit trial judge considered that this fact alone so tainted the quality of their evidence that he stopped the case: *R* v *Hickmott* (1989) unreported, Snaresbrook Crown Court, 2 February 1989, Judge Sanders.) The pooling of recollections involves officers in effect interviewing each other. Even where no concoction is in issue, the method remains inherently unsatisfactory as a means of recording accurate memory. It has been roundly and repeatedly criticised, from the perspective both of legal practice (Heaton-Armstrong, 1985, 1987) and of clinical psychology (Stephenson, 1991). It is true that conferring between witnesses about an incident at which they have both recently been present can be a useful means by which one witness may trigger the other's memory on points of detail. The danger is that the process will in reality become a smokescreen for ironing out embarrassing inconsistencies in the interests of presenting an unshakeable joint account. Officers are often asked in cross-examination if they can remember any case in which, upon conferring, they had experienced radically different recollections on crucial aspects of their accounts which were reflected in their notes. Needless to say, an affirmative reply is rare, not to say unknown.

Conferring has its benefits but is open to abuse as long as it remains a confidential process. Moreover, from the prosecution point of view it can prove to be counter-productive. Under cross-examination, officers who claim to have conferred are rarely able to give a precise account of the collaborative process consistently between them and these differences alone can often be exploited by the defence to spoil what would otherwise be a perfectly sound prosecution case. Spotlighting sessions in the police canteen may remain a hit-and-miss affair but the very vagueness of efforts to recount it furnishes a wedge to drive between the participating officers.

The forensic difficulties caused by conferring need to be illustrated. Two officers have pooled their recollections prior to and during the note-making process. Identical or neatly dovetailed accounts are the result. The officer asks permission to refer to his notebook. The defence advocate, justifiably, asks whether the officer can assure the court that the note comprises only what he as an individual could remember and does not, therefore, include material which reflects not what he but only his colleague could remember. Hardly surprisingly, the officer gives his assurance that the note contains what he could remember himself. The judge accepts this assurance and gives permission for the note to be referred to. In view of the continuing applicability of Lord Devlin's observation that it is the general habit of the police never to admit to the slightest departure from correctness (Devlin, 1960, p. 43) any cross-examination of a police officer as to whether his note truly reflects what he could personally remember when the note was made is invariably a wholly artificial exercise.

The obvious and inherent danger in the collaboration process is that hearsay, i.e., material which one officer has disclosed to a second about an incident but which the second cannot recollect personally, will creep into the account given by the second. Judicial reluctance to acknowledge what is so clear to a layperson can be significantly compared to the courts' response to other situations which risk infringement of the hearsay rule — for example, where civilians confer about the description of a vehicle or suspect (see *Jones* v *Metcalf* [1967] 1 WLR 1286; *R* v *McLean* (1968) 52 Cr App R 80).

15.6 FIRST DESCRIPTIONS IN IDENTIFICATION CASES

The problem of variation is liable to be acute in cases of identification, with descriptions often changing between statement and evidence or the degree of purported conviction in the identification intensifying with the passage of time. It hardly needs to be said how essential it is that full and accurate records are made of every description at the time that it is provided to the police. Moreover the way in which witnesses express their opinion that the defendant is the culprit may be of crucial importance. It is not unusual when witnesses who have attended an identification parade and have picked out the defendant only after some hesitation for them to make a statement concluding with something along the following lines: 'Having further considered the matter and what happened on the parade, I am now positive that the man I picked out is the man who robbed me'. The factors which have led to such an affirmation may remain a mystery and it is obviously essential to have as comprehensive a record as possible of what happened at the parade. Loftus (1979, ch. 1) gives a graphic account of how the 'firming-up' process was corrupted in the Sacco and Vanzetti case in the United States in 1920.

15.7 FIRST REPORTS OF CRIME

Hitherto we have been discussing the compilation of formal statements by civilian witnesses. But the s. 9 statement may not be a witness's first account of the incident or topic in question. The first written reference to salient facts may be in the 'crime report'. But even those details may not be written up in the crime report until a good time has elapsed since the information was given to the police. Moreover, it may have been passed on second or even third hand, with the intervention of Chinese whispers. Often the first report is imparted to another civilian, although, for present purposes, we are concerned exclusively with first notification to the authorities, since only those can be made subject to systematic recording. First reports to the police usually come about in one of three ways: by a 999 call or one to the local police station; over the counter at a police station; or to a constable in the street or some other location to which the police have been called. In the past the Crown Prosecution Service and the police were apt to give all sorts of justifications, often ingenious ones, for refusing to release details of initial complaints by witnesses as recorded on crime reports and elsewhere. These ranged from the assertion that it is 'confidential information' to claims that, if a crime report is recorded on computer, the record is data protected (see Heaton-Armstrong and Wolchover, 1992a). Alternatively, it was said that only a judge can authorise disclosure of crime reports. Guidelines issued by the Attorney-General ((1982) 74 Cr App R 302, para. 1) and practice directions issued by the Lord Chief Justice ([1986] 2 All ER 511, para. 8) appeared to have little effect but the milestone disclosure decision in *R* v *Ward* (1994) 98 Cr App R 337 followed by the Criminal Procedure and Investigations Act 1996 have largely eliminated these obstacles for the defence.

15.8 THE SOLUTION FOR EXISTING PROBLEMS: AUDIO AND VIDEO-RECORDING

15.8.1 Private witnesses

The obvious and simple solution to the problems highlighted in this chapter is at the very least to audiotape (better still video-record) the giving of witness statements in appropriate cases, including first reports of crime. If this were done there would be no need to maintain any inhibition about interviewing witnesses during the taking of the statement. Following representations by the authors in 1996 the Operational Policing Policy Unit of the Home Office Police Policy Directorate in conjunction with the department's Criminal Policy Directorate have been considering the whole issue of taping witness interviews (see Wolchover and Heaton-Armstrong, 1997). This will involve re-evaluation of the brief suggestion contained in the 1992 Home Office booklet, *A Guide to Interviewing*, that in 'more serious cases, such as a fatal road accident or a serious assault,' it may be 'beneficial' to support note-taking by tape-recording the interview. (The National Crime Faculty Manual *A Practical Guide to Investigative Interviewing* (1998) states that in certain cases it is now recognised as best practice for skilled interviewers to record witness and victim interviews on audio or videotape and that the decision to do so may be that of the senior investigating officer who with the assistance of the investigating officer will determine the interview strategy.) No one would sensibly suggest that all witness interviews should be tape-recorded and we attempt below to devise a working test for identifying statements which should be so recorded.

An excellent illustration of the immense benefit for justice which would be gained from the taping of witness statements is the dramatic outcome of a trial at the Central Criminal Court in February 1998, widely reported in the national press and broadcast media (see *The Times*, 4 and 6 February 1998). On being tried for rape two 10-year-old boys, the youngest ever to be so prosecuted, were ordered by the judge to be acquitted because the alleged victim, aged eleven, had made no rape allegation during a 45-minute video-recorded interview with a woman police officer. When the questioning appeared to be over, the officer re-entered the room, and asked a question which the judge described as 'both leading and wholly improper' and which, she observed, in effect put words into the girl's mouth. After this, it was held, the allegations of rape were tainted and it would not be proper for the charges to go before the jury. Although the case provides an interesting example of the videotaping of a witness interview, it does not support an argument specifically for video-recording because the vice which the recording exposed would have been revealed by audio-taping.

The taping of witness statements is widely practised in a number of common law jurisdictions. (It was reported that in *Kennedy-Smith*, a rape trial in Massachussets, defending counsel played a taped statement to a prosecution witness in order to demonstrate inconsistency: see *The Daily Telegraph*, 4 December 1991.) It is not wholly unknown in the British Isles. In a fraud committal on the Isle of Man civilian witnesses had made statements on tape which a police officer then purported to reduce into writing. Comparison between the tape recordings and the transcripts revealed a degree of variance which, it was argued, could only have been the result of deliberate alteration by the officer. In cross-examination of the witnesses decisive concessions were obtained from them consistent with the original tapes and all charges were dismissed (*Drake* (1991) unreported, Isle of Man Petty Sessions).

As to first reports preceding the formal statement phase, these should at the very least be accurately logged in writing and signed immediately. At best, they should be tape-recorded, an exercise which ought to present no particular problem. Telephone calls can easily be tape-recorded, as can reports of crime across the police station counter. For recording first complaints elsewhere, constables could be equipped with pocket cassette recorders, with a lapel microphone, as has been advocated for use in recording the utterances of suspects 'in the field'. The Royal Commission on Criminal Justice (1993, ch. 3, para. 11) referred to an experiment organised by the Association of Chief Police Officers in Essex.

Some police forces in England and Wales, supported by senior officers, appear to acknowledge the desirability of tape-recording interviews with witnesses. At a seminar organised jointly by the British Academy of Forensic

Sciences, the Criminal Bar Association and the Law Society in 1996, Mr David Phillips, Chief Constable of Kent and secretary of the crime committee of the Association of Chief Officers of Police (ACPO) called for the tape-recording of witness statements, saying, 'Let us remove the editorial filter of the police officer's pen. Let us introduce into the courtroom glimpses of the reality.' Following this, the National Crime Faculty at Bramshill Police College set up a working party to consider producing a manual for police forces on best practice in the investigation of crime. This was published in late 1998, using a murder investigation as a model, and had the approval of ACPO and HM Inspectorate of Constabulary. A significant aspect of its guidance is the recommendation that, according to the dictates of best practice, interviews with 'significant witnesses', at least during a murder investigation, should be tape-recorded. The practice of the Northumbria Police was reviewed in an article by Sarah Gibbons (1996) and at a seminar organised by the British Academy of Forensic Sciences was described in some detail by Gary Shaw, a Detective Inspector with the Northumbria Police and Force Interview Advisor/Co-ordinator since 1995 (Milne and Shaw, 1998). Initially, the policy in Northumbria was to concentrate on key/crucial witness interviews within serious and major crime investigations when introducing the need to consider audio tape-recording the interview. This has subsequently been extended to all types of key witness interview where the officer feels that benefit would be gained from audio-taping. Hitherto experience has shown that many of the practical problems cited by opponents of the scheme as objections to its efficacy can be easily overcome. Further, the Northumbrian practice has highlighted the following incidental benefits apart from that of ensuring a comprehensive and accurate record (Milne and Shaw, 1998). It permits the interview to flow in such a way as to facilitate the obtaining of significantly more accurate, reliable and detailed information than when the process of witness interviewing is merely recorded in the form of a narrative statement. Tape-recording permits an assessment to be made of a witness's calibre and the enhanced scrutiny of detail which it affords may be crucial if the witness later becomes a suspect and may even itself transform the witness into a suspect. It provides a vital means of screening for any questions which the officer may have omitted to ask. The quality of the statement produced from the tape assists greatly in refreshing the memory of the witness prior to any subsequent court appearance. Audio-taping tends to produce one complete statement as opposed to having to take several statements from one person. It allows more informed decision-making on prosecutions. It assists in structuring, planning and preparing interviews with suspects. It can refute allegations of police malpractice. Lastly, it can help in the identification of training needs. Chairing the BAFS seminar at which Milne and Shaw delivered their paper, Lord Justice Rose observed that he had been much impressed by Detective Inspector Shaw's contribution, that tape-recording 'must be the way forward' and that he would use his capacities to encourage this.

There is a good case in fact for video-recording the interviewing and taking of statements from witnesses. The advantages in terms of furnishing a comprehensive record of the witness's demeanour and gestures are obvious. Nuances of considerable import may well be missed from the witness's account if sound-only recording is employed. This alone may make the investment in appropriate equipment and training essential, but in fact the availability of relatively inexpensive apparatus makes this an entirely practicable proposition. Under the enlightened leadership of Mr David Phillips, the Kent Police have taken the Northumbrian practice further and officers investigating serious crimes are encouraged to video-record interviews with key witnesses. The provision of equipment sufficient for the purpose has been justified within existing budgeting arrangements because in Kent investigators often make use of the videotaped record to study the demeanour and content of witnesses' accounts for the purpose of progressing their enquiries. For example, repeated playing of the tape may occasion an intuitive leap leading to the uncovering of other evidence or the establishment of a vital evidential link. Again, scrutiny may facilitate exposure at an early stage of the witness as untruthful, unreliable or as actually involved in the crime under investigation.

It is not only the police who ought to tape-record interviews with witnesses. Such professionals as, for example, social workers and health-care workers, who in the course of their duties are likely to receive complaints of crime from victims or witnesses should be encouraged to employ tape recorders.

The Criminal Justice Act 1991 provides that interviews with child witnesses in cases involving violence, cruelty, neglect and sexual offences should be video-recorded and that the recording may in the discretion of the court be adduced as the child's evidence-in-chief. The measure had been recommended in the report of the Advisory Group on Video Evidence chaired by Judge Pigot (Home Office, 1989) on the basis of the principle that children should give evidence in surroundings and circumstances which do not intimidate or overawe them and in the presence of the smallest number of people. Pigot received professional evidence suggesting that children generally recall past events most accurately when subject to the least stress and that although the formality and solemnity of the courtroom context are often thought to promote truthfulness by witnesses, this may actually have a deleterious effect on the fullness and accuracy of children's testimony. Pigot also took account of opinion that children's memory fades more rapidly than that of mature persons and will be tainted to a greater degree by subsequent disclosure and questioning (see Spencer, 1991). The Advisory Group believed that an early video-recorded interview may counteract the loss resulting from this tendency. The 1991 Act presumes the vulnerability of child witnesses as a class. In their report, *Speaking up for Justice* (1998), the Home Office Interdepartmental Working Group on the Treatment of Vulnerable or Intimidated Witnesses in the Criminal Justice System have recommended the extension of the principle of video-recording interviews and their use as evidence-in-chief in cases of witnesses who are identified as vulnerable or intimidated within criteria defined in the report. Yet the present authors would argue that the decision as to whether a witness statement should be tape-recorded ought to depend not on the personality of the witness but rather on the importance of the witness's account in the prosecution of the crime under investigation and on whether that account is liable to be contentious.

15.8.2 Police collaboration on note-making

The process by which officers pool their recollections when writing up their notebooks may be entirely legitimate but for the reasons given in 15.5 it is open to abuse if not monitored with precision. Whilst the present regime may cause unfairness to the defence it may equally damage the prosecution case, for defence advocates are often able to score valuable points by ridiculing police claims under cross-examination that several officers shared exactly the same memory of a given incident. In the recollection of many advocates countless acquittals have followed attempts by officers to over-egg the pudding. The process of collaboration also needs to be formalised and tape-recorded and the era of repairing to the police canteen will have to end. Tape-recording would force the police to be more honest and would make them more credible.

15.9   THE ABSENT CONTENTIOUS CROWN WITNESS: IMPACT OF THE WIDER POWERS TO READ THEIR STATEMENTS

There is a particularly compelling reason why it is vital to have the best possible record of what the witness told the police. Culminating from a long gestation of judge-made and legislative principles, the Criminal Justice Act 1988 and the Criminal Investigations and Procedure Act 1996 authorise the reading of statements at trial in the absence of the maker regardless of whether their content is disputed and the maker's presence is sought by the opposing party. Part II of the Criminal Justice Act 1988 provides for the admissibility of the written statement of an absent maker as evidence of the truth of its contents in a variety of circumstances (namely, death, unfitness for attendance by reason of bodily or mental condition, fear, the consequence of being 'kept out of the way', absence abroad and impracticability of securing attendance, and whereabouts unknown and all reasonable steps taken to find the maker). It also provides for the adducement of the statement as evidence of the truth of its contents when the maker is present but does not give evidence through fear. The Act does not require the statement to have gone through the committal process but since most statements which are likely to be important in a case will have done so, to a large extent part II has been rendered otiose by the 1996 Act. The latter removes virtually all statutory conditions for the reading at trial of depositions and statements processed at committal.

The Act abolishes the concept of taking live evidence at committal in the presence of the parties. The only evidence now admissible in committal proceedings is that under new s. 5A of the Magistrates' Courts Act 1980, which restricts admissible evidence to that tendered by the prosecution and constituting written witness statements prepared in the usual statutory form, depositions falling with the new s. 5C of the 1980 Act, and certain documentary and real evidence. The taking of depositions is provided for by the new

s. 97A of the 1980 Act. This is intended to deal with the witness who is unwilling to make a written statement. A summons (or, in certain circumstances, a warrant) may be obtained to compel appearance before a magistrate, who will take the deposition in private apparently in the absence of the parties. There is no provision giving either party the right to attend, let alone to put questions.

Under s. 68 of and sch. 2 to the Criminal Investigations and Procedure Act 1996 any statement or deposition admitted in evidence at committal is admissible at trial subject to a right of objection which the judges are required to uphold or dismiss in their discretion according as the interests of justice dictate. There are no specific conditions of admissibility (such as death or unfitness to attend) and having regard to the way the provisions are drafted, it appears that the burden is on the defence to sustain the objection, although no explicit indication is given of where the burden lies. It has been observed that the section will inevitably be applied inconsistently in practice, eventually leading to judicial legislation in the form of guidance from the Court of Appeal, an unsatisfactory substitute for properly drafted Parliamentary legislation (Richardson, 1996). In the House of Lords Baroness Blatch, the Home Office minister, anticipated on behalf of the government that the courts would turn for guidance to the Criminal Justice Act 1988 (573 HL Deb, 5th ser. col. 952, Lords' consideration of Commons' amendments), but it has been pointed out that this leaves the position extremely vague (Richardson, 1996). No provision is made for the burden of proof and there are no conditions of admissibility which must exist before any question of exercising discretion comes into play. The minister gave death and illness as examples, but it would be quite impossible to read these into the legislation merely on the basis of their citation as examples.

With the abolition by the 1996 Act of the right of defendants to demand that at committal proceedings prosecution witnesses give evidence 'live' and in the presence of the defence, some contentious statements, prepared as always by the police behind closed doors, may end up being read at the trial without the defence having had any right or opportunity to test their reliability through cross-examination. Article 6(d) of the European Convention on Human Rights, declaring that everyone charged with a criminal offence has the minimum right 'to examine or have examined witnesses against him', seems to have gone by the board with this legislation. (For a useful critique see Munday (1997).) If courts are going to make increasing use of such statements, the least that we can ask for is that we have an exact recording of what the witness actually said, not what some police officer wrote down on the witness's behalf.

The Crime and Disorder Act 1998 abolishes committal proceedings for offences triable on indictment. Instead persons charged with such offences will be sent forthwith to the Crown Court for trial regardless of whether the prosecution are in possession of sufficient, or, indeed, any, evidence to sustain the charge at that stage. Since the prosecution of such offences will not now be passing through a committal process, witness statements will not be eligible to be read by virtue of the 1996 Act. Instead, it would seem that the question whether they may be read will revert to being determined by the 1988 Act.

15.10 PRACTICAL ASPECTS OF THE AUDIOTAPING OF WITNESS INTERVIEWS

Responding to a proposal by the authors the Royal Commission on Criminal Justice (1993, ch. 2, paras 14 and 15) doubted whether the proposal to tape-record witness interviews would be workable on a wide scale. They believed that it would be impracticable and costly to record all such interviews electronically. Nor was it easy for them to see how the police could predict which interviews would be likely to prove contentious and so warrant electronic recording and they did not wish any recommendation of theirs to result in more people being taken to the police station for interviews which could as readily be conducted elsewhere. The Home Office proffered three further objections:

(a)   there would need to be similar safeguards as currently apply to tape-recording interviews with suspects;
(b)   there would be resource implications in terms of equipment, including demand for copies of tapes, and man-hours;
(c)   it would be difficult to provide safeguards against allegations of tampering with the tape if the interviews were conducted outside the police station (letter from OPPU to the authors, 30 April 1997).

It is proposed to discuss these objections next.

15.10.1 Selecting which interviews must be taped

15.10.1.1 Criteria   As already observed, no one would sensibly suggest that all interviews with witnesses should be taped. What should be the criteria for deciding whether to tape-record a witness's statement? The gravity of the offence under investigation might be a general starting point. For example, the rule might be that tape-recording would be unnecessary if the offence being investigated carried no custodial penalty. If this were thought insufficiently discriminatory, a higher limit might prove more acceptable. For example, it might be deemed unnecessary unless the investigation involved an offence carrying a maximum penalty of at least six months' imprisonment. In all such cases a simple rule of thumb might apply requiring the taping of any interview with a witness who was reasonably likely to make assertions of a kind which might be disputed in subsequent proceedings. Of course, this might not catch all assertions which prove in the event to be the subject of bitter contention at trial, for the possibility of dispute may at the time have seemed too remote to be real. Whether to record a witness interview in borderline cases may have to be a matter of fine judgment on the part of the officer conducting the interview. In cases of doubt it may be wise to err on the side of caution. Arguably, it should be made compulsory for decisions to be made by an officer of at least inspector's rank. Additionally, it might be made a requirement to consult the CPS. One problem which will inevitably need to be addressed concerns the point at which an officer investigating an offence and dealing with a potential witness should start to tape-record the interview. There may be many occasions when it will be clearly appropriate to start taping at the outset, for example, when the officer already knows that the person has relevant information to give and is in no doubt about the willingness to give a statement. Thus, the officer may be visiting the witness at home by arrangement for the explicit purpose of taking a statement. (It has been pointed out that home interviews should be free from domestic interruptions and distractions, Milne and Shaw, 1998.) However, there will be other occasions when the situation is ambiguous or delicate. The officer may be feeling the way with someone who may or may not have relevant information to give or may be reluctant to give it. To initiate the interview by overtly switching on a tape recorder may instantly alienate a nervous or hostile witness. We assume that covert taping in such a case would be considered unacceptable. It may often be necessary for the officer to nudge a witness into cooperation before deciding that it is safe to bring out a tape recorder. In Northumbria investigating officers are required to consider audio-taping 'key' witnesses where it is felt benefit would be gained from so doing; examples of selected interviewees include: victims; eyewitnesses to the event; witnesses who have had a relevant conversation with the suspect after the event; hostile or potentially hostile witnesses; witness to events after the incident involving the suspect; any person who was known to be the last to have been with the victim prior to the offence being discovered; witnesses who have discovered bodies; and police officers who initially attended the scene and witnessed events or arrested the suspect; Milne and Shaw (1998).

15.10.1.2 Enforcement How might the requirement to tape-record be enforced? Section 78 of PACE would be available to exclude the live evidence of a witness where it would clearly have been desirable to tape-record the witness's statement and there was no good reason for having failed to do so. Since the decision to exclude would have to depend on whether it would be unfair to allow in the evidence, it would be necessary to devise a suitable test of unfairness. Whether the defendant was likely to suffer *actual* unfairness from the failure to tape-record could only be determined on the basis of the following three criteria:

(a)   Is there an inconsistency between the written statement and the witness's live evidence?

(b)   Is the witness claiming that there was in fact no difference between the evidence in the witness box and the account given to the police, and that the ostensible inconsistency is attributable to a written transcription error on the part of the recording officer?

(c)   Is the inconsistency a substantial and significant one which might have a real bearing on the outcome of the case?

To make admissibility of the witness's evidence as a whole dependent on these questions would mean that evidence would always have to be led and cross-examined in the first instance in the absence of the jury. In other words, in any case in which there was no tape-recording of the witness's statement and it was sought on that account to exclude the witness's evidence there would have to be a *voir dire* to determine if any inconsistencies were revealed. This would hardly be considered acceptable practice and the other option of directing the jury to disregard the testimony as 'not evidence' would be an anomalous and clearly unsatisfactory mode of applying s. 78. The only feasible test, therefore, would have to be one based on the *risk* rather than the *actuality* of unfairness. The test of potential unfairness would necessarily be restricted to a demonstration of the rather vague and imprecise possibilities (a) that the untaped written statement contains assertions which the prosecution need to prove to obtain a conviction and (b) that the evidence was of such a kind that there was a real possibility that it might be tainted by inconsistency.

15.10.2 Security
We would argue that there is very little need for anything like the level of security required in the case of interviews with suspects. The uniquely damning nature of confession evidence is such that there is an inherent motive to concoct it. In contrast, there is relatively little motive for misconduct over the tape of a witness interview. There are two conceivable ways in which a tape may be interfered with: (a) illicit editing to produce a counterfeit and (b) secret suppression or disposal of the tape of an abortive interview in favour of the tape of a replacement interview.

15.10.2.1 Counterfeiting Since it can never be known whether or how a witness's original account to the police will change when giving evidence in court there can be no question of any temptation to edit a tape illicitly in order to preserve the appearance of consistency. But what of a motive for doctoring the tape in order to make the witness's account, as ostensibly recorded, more damaging to the defendant than the disappointing version actually given? How would this benefit the police? The defence would be unlikely to introduce the tape, since they would hardly want to cite the more damaging bogus version merely in order to demonstrate inconsistency. Perhaps, the hope might be to introduce the doctored tape later under the hostile witness procedure, or alternatively to arrange the witness's disappearance and then seek adducement of the tampered tape in lieu of the witness's live evidence either under the Criminal Justice Act 1988, ss. 23–6 or under the broader provisions of the Criminal Investigations and Procedure Act 1996, s. 68. In an alternative scenario it might be hoped that a doctored tape could be used to lead a witness to believe later that its contents represent true contemporaneous memory. After some lapse of time the police will play back the counterfeit tape to the witness in the hope of somehow inducing a belief that since it at one time must have represented the witness's memory, it will be quite safe to recite in court what is believed must have been the true account, although no longer actually remembered. (It is envisaged that tape-recording would not displace the practice of taking a written statement, so that counterfeiting a tape would require complementary forgery of the statement.) In themselves these conjectures seem far-fetched but they all depend on one key element: the feasibility of editing a tape so as to foil detection by an expert. Yet, as is very well known, sophisticated modern electronics defy such an exercise.

15.10.2.2 Suppression The second conceivable mode of interference is suppression of the existence of tapes. Supposing after the conclusion of an interview during which a statement has been taken down in writing the officer listens to the tape, is embarrassed by the extent and manner of having led, fed or pressurised the witness, wishes to dispose of the tape, and decides to start the whole process again using a more neutral approach. The use of twin-deck recorders of the kind presently employed in the case of defendant interviews would not prevent such a practice. Again, supposing a police officer wishes to 'soften up' a reluctant witness before taking a statement, in order to control the content as it affects a particular suspect. This the police would always be free to do with or without the use of dedicated security recorders. Witnesses at the police station are not supervised under PACE conditions and there would be no means of comparing the interview times automatically recorded on the tape against any independent log of the time the witness was present with the officer in the interview room or elsewhere. In any event very many if not most witness statements are taken at the witness's home. There would therefore be little to prevent pre-interview manipulation. Furthermore, the use of defendant-interview machines would also not preclude interruption from going undetected. If a dishonest officer felt the need to stop the twin tapes in the middle of an interview in order to render a witness more pliable there would be little to prevent their disposal from being suppressed and a new interview started using a fresh pair of tapes.

15.10.2.3 Adequacy of standard pocket cassette recorders Our contention, then, is that there is little or no need for witness interviews to be recorded on machines of the kind used to record interviews with suspects. Standard pocket cassette tape recorders would be perfectly adequate. Importantly, their use would enable witness interviews to be conducted outside police stations and this answers the Royal Commission's original objection.

15.10.2.4 First reports Tape-recording of 999 calls and those made to the police station would presumably be inaccessible to officers involved in the particular case, who might have a motive for erasure or other interference. Recordings of reports over the counter would be less inaccessible but can presumably be kept sufficiently secure with only a modicum of technical wizardry. The security of cassettes in pocket machines in the personal possession of investigating officers might pose more of a problem, but, again, no doubt, one which is far from intractable.

15.10.3 Interview transcripts, summaries and written statements

It is envisaged that the existing process of taking a written statement would not be supplanted by tape-recording. Yet would not an *ex post facto* summary of the tape prepared by the interviewing officer in place of taking down a formal statement during the interview tend to be more accurate? For such a practice to be accommodated within, and adapted to, the existing system of preparing written statements for contingent use at trial, the summary would presumably have to be in the traditional 'section 9' form, requiring the witness's signature after preparation. This would necessitate a later session with the witness, who after the lapse of time might challenge the accuracy of the summary or might want to amend, alter or add to the original account. This might require the playing back to the witness of the original tape. Furthermore, the witness might during this process say something of importance, making it desirable to tape-record these exchanges as well. Ideally the whole validation process would require two tape recorders but even if one machine were used both for playing back the original tape and then for recording the witness's comments in validation, the whole process would require a careful feat of juggling which might well defeat even the most meticulous of officers. In Northumbria the practice is to prepare a formal statement ex-post facto following which the interviewing officer goes through the document with the witness in order to check its accuracy and to prompt recollection of additional detail (Milne and Shaw, 1998).

Preparation of the summary would require considerable time spent in addition to the interview itself. The practice of obtaining *ex post facto* validation would not only be time-consuming but would also be cumbersome. Furthermore it is by no means certain that a summary prepared from the tape after the event would be significantly more accurate than a statement made in step with the interview. But although an interview which involved writing out a statement would probably be more protracted than one in which nothing was taken down in writing, there is little doubt that the total time spent on the latter and then on preparing a summary would far exceed that of an interview in which a statement was taken. The statement would be checked and signed at the end of the interview and the system of taping would thus represent no more than a simple grafting on to the existing process of committal.

There is another very good reason for maintaining the practice of taking a written statement from the witness. Having to write out the witness's narrative is sure to impose on the officer the discipline of keeping it on track, ensuring it remains pertinent and, whilst aiming to be comprehensive and detailed, nevertheless stays free of digression and repetition. Taking down a statement in writing inherently tightens up control of the narrative.

With such a practice as this it would not normally be necessary for the police to prepare transcripts of the taped interview. In effect the written statement prepared during the interview would be its summary. It might be desirable if, at some stage after the conclusion of the witness's interview — during which the officer will have written out the witness's draft statement — the officer were to listen to the tape in order to check whether the written statement accurately reflected the defendant's account on tape. The fact and terms of any substantive variation could be endorsed in a note at the bottom of the statement. This would not need to be signed by the witness but would merely represent an indication for the guidance of the court and for all parties.

Clearly copies of any witness interview tapes would be available to the defence so that they might check whether the statement was a fair reflection of what was spoken on tape and transcribe such passages as they might predict to be in dispute. Where the original tape contained material which the police wished on proper grounds to remain confidential the rules might provide for the prosecution to obtain the consent of a judge to serve an expurgated copy.

15.10.4   Cost

15.10.4.1   Equipment   Twin-deck security recording machines with a built-in time clock cost about £700. On the other hand, pocket cassette recorders are inexpensive, good basic machines retailing for as little as £20. Even high-quality machines with a wealth of gadgetry superfluous to the limited purpose under discussion retail for not much more than £50. There will be the cost of batteries or mains adaptors. Audiotape cassettes for defendant interviews are nowadays supplied in bulk to the police at relatively little cost. This is evidenced by the fact that although, as we understand it, copies supplied to the defence remain the property of the police, their return is never sought and sets of chambers and robing rooms up and down the country are always littered with discarded cassettes. If the Crown Prosecution Service and defence solicitors and counsel were required to return both defendant interview and witness interview cassettes they could be reused at least for working copies. (But this would have to depend on trust, because it would hardly be cost-effective to chase up non-returned cassettes.)

15.10.4.2   Checking tape content and defence preparation of transcripts   Since it would be advisable for officers to check the statement against the tape this would clearly involve some additional cost in staffing terms and, again, provision would have to be made for some increase in defence solicitors' legal aid costs involved in checking tapes and preparing transcripts of any relevant portion.

15.10.4.3   Consequent savings   It is arguable that the increased expenditure involved in providing pocket tape recorders and blank cassettes and the costs of additional police duties in checking the tape against the written statement will be offset in several respects. There will be some reduction of cross-examination of witnesses in that there will no longer be any basis for blaming the attesting officer for inaccurate transcription. It follows that there will be no need, as there often is at present, to call the officer to court in order to answer the witness's claim. Again, defence counsel will not need to expend time in addressing the jury on who is to be believed, the officer or the witness, and likewise the judge will not have that point to deal with in summing up. Juries may therefore take up less time in returning verdicts.

15.10.5 The need for immediate reform in any event

Even assuming that the tape-recording of witness interviews required security measures matching those in place for the interviewing of suspects the importance of the proposal is of such magnitude that the principle at stake would justify the limited cost involved in any event. Moreover, security recorders are not so bulky that they cannot be taken to witnesses outside the police station. There would be no need for all witnesses to come to the police station to be interviewed. The risk the present practice poses of wrongful convictions and acquittals is too substantial to ignore. Furthermore, even if audiotaping on simple cassette recorders left open some risk of tampering, the fact remains that taping even on basic machines provides a form of safeguard which is not available at all under the present arrangements.

The introduction of tape-recording of interviews with suspects was delayed for many years as the result to a large extent of cost objections. Yet, if successive Home Secretaries had accorded more respect to such authorities as Professor Glanville Williams (1979) and had implemented their suggestions at an earlier stage, it might well have been that the cost of installing equipment would have been offset by the avoidance of the need to pay out enormous sums in compensation to people whose convictions were subsequently quashed as the result of doubts over the reliability of traditional methods of recording interviews. It is assumed that the present government would not resile from the view of the previous Conservative Home Secretary when in a speech at Plymouth he acknowledged the first importance of modern technology in the fight against crime (*The Times*, 26 March 1994).

15.11 COLLABORATIVE NOTING BY THE POLICE

Our observations above on security and the question of cost would apply equally to the question of requiring the tape-recording of sessions in which officers pool their recollections in writing up their notes. The Home Office noted that there might be hearsay implications. We are not sure if by this it was meant that hearsay problems might prove an impediment to our proposal. In fact, as we have previously observed (Heaton-Armstrong and Wolchover, 1992), we believe it will eliminate the risk of hidden hearsay intrusion. The obvious and inherent danger in the collaboration process is that a recollection which one officer has conveyed to a second officer about an incident but which the second cannot recall, will creep into the account given by the second. This will happen either unconsciously or else deliberately in the interests of maintaining solidarity between the officers. Tape-recording the process of collaboration will throw a spotlight on which one of two or more officers remembered exactly what facts. The practice in Northumbria where two or more officers are witness to an incident is that they write up notes of it and are then interviewed on tape (related by Shaw at the BAFS seminar in which the paper by Milne and Shaw, 1998, above, was read).

15.12 POTENTIAL IMPACT ON TRIAL PROCEDURE OF THE VIDEO-RECORDING OF WITNESS STATEMENTS

There is perhaps some irony in the fact that the installation of audio or video-recording of statements in order to enhance the fairness of using such statements under existing rules of evidence will of itself open up the possibility of streamlining the trial process so as to admit of a significantly broader use of pre-recorded narrative.

Reference has already been made to the use, by way of an exception to the hearsay rule, of the statements of absent witnesses as evidence of the truth of their content. The electronic recording of such statements will make it more difficult to resist their adducement under existing rules. But where witnesses are present there is a need to consider the extent to which and the purposes for which their pre-recorded statements in general might become admissible in evidence. Under existing rules, they can be used to refresh memory where they so qualify, they can be introduced in cross-examination to show inconsistency, introduced in re-examination to show consistency where late concoction has been alleged in cross-examination, and they can be introduced in the event of a witness turning hostile.

With an unassailable record of the making of the earlier statement it would become increasingly difficult to oppose the argument that statements should also be admissible in chief in the first instance to show consistency — the defence should not be able to have it both ways. But there is a potentially much more important issue concerning the possibility of statements being given the additional status which they currently lack, i.e., the power to prove the truth of the facts they state. This extension would be a major and radical departure, not only procedurally and evidentially, but also jurisprudentially. The more accurate and comprehensive the record of the taking of a statement the stronger the case becomes for introducing it as evidence of the facts contained in it. There is a world of difference between a conventional witness statement signed by the maker but written by a police officer and a video-recording of the interview which produced that statement.

Indeed, it might be argued that if all potentially contentious witness narratives were to be video-recorded when the memory of the facts related were fresh, live evidence-in-chief might well be dispensed with altogether in favour of playing the tape to the jury, as evidence of the facts stated in it. The witness would, of course, be present to confirm the account given on tape and to answer any questions, either by way of supplementing it or in cross-examination. Legislation has now been in force for some years empowering courts to receive such evidence in the case of child witnesses. Implementing recommendations 1 and 2 of the Pigot report on video evidence (Home Office, 1989), s. 54(2)(a) and (b) of the Criminal Justice Act 1991 provides that in cases involving violence, cruelty, neglect and sexual offences the video-recorded interview of a child witness may, in the discretion of the judge, be admissible in substitution for the child's live evidence-in-chief. In conjunction with the provision, a memorandum of good practice on the video-recording of interviews with child witnesses was issued as guidance by the Home Office and the Department of Health. Pigot further recommended that the cross-examination of the child witness should also take place on video at some stage before the trial (recommendation 4) but this has not hitherto been implemented. The recommendation has, however, been re-iterated in the Utting Report (1997). The effect would have been to eliminate altogether the live evidence of children in sanctioned cases (see McEwan, 1990 and see also Spencer, 1991). The Scottish Law Commission made a similar recommendation but stipulated that the statement, whether in written, audio or video-recorded form, would only be admissible if 'it can reasonably be inferred that it accurately and completely records what was said by the witness on the previous occasion' (1990, paras 4.45–4.66 and see Draft Bill, cl. 8).

In their report *Speaking up for Justice* the Home Office Interdepartmental Working Group on the treatment of Vulnerable or Intimidated Witnesses in the Criminal Justice System (1998) recommended the extension of the rules permitting the video-recording of interviews with child witnesses and the admissibility of such recordings in evidence in the first instance to interviews of vulnerable or intimidated witnesses by police officers, social workers or those involved in the investigation of crime or appropriate defence representatives, or both (recommendation 41; para. 8.48). The Working Group also recommends that video-recorded pre-trial cross-examination should be available for use in appropriate cases where the witness's statement has been recorded on video and could particularly benefit from cross-examination outside the courtroom (recommendation 45; para. 8.59). At the time of writing, the Youth Justice and Criminal Evidence Bill, anticipated by the Working Group's report, is being debated in Parliament. The Bill's proposal to restrict the categories of witness whose video-recorded interviews are admissible as their evidence-in-chief is unfortunate. (See Editors' note to chapter 9.)

The implications of expanding the provisions for children to witnesses in general clearly merit serious consideration. Hitherto the signs have not been encouraging even for the sanctioning of mere video-recording of pre-trial narrative, let alone using it in court as evidence in the first instance. In *R* v *Dye* (1991) (unreported, CA, *The Times*, 19 December 1991) a television company making a documentary on drug trafficking approached the Customs and Excise for cooperation. Leading counsel for the Crown was asked for his opinion and advised that it could be provided before the trial. Three prosecution witnesses were accordingly interviewed on film as though they were giving evidence-in-chief at the trial. In the view of the Court of Appeal counsel's advice was wrong. The perils which might result from what almost amounted to a dress rehearsal of their forthcoming appearances in the witness box were all too plain, even where, as in the instant case, the film was not broadcast until the trial was over. There was a further serious error in that counsel for the Crown failed to inform defence counsel about the filming of the witnesses until after the trial was over. If defence counsel had known of this they would have cross-examined those witnesses as to any differences between their filmed evidence and that in the box. In the event, the differences proved insufficiently significant to overturn the conviction and the proviso was applied. (The proviso to s. 4(1) of the Criminal Appeal Act, now repealed, allowed a conviction to stand even where the ground of appeal was upheld, if no miscarriage of justice was likely.) In contrast with this rather negative approach it is of note that one of the principal recommendations in the 11th report of the Criminal Law Revision Committee (CLRC) was the use in general of statements as evidence of the facts stated in them (1972, paras 235 and 239). Whilst stressing the particular importance of 'the preservation of the principle of orality in criminal trials', the CLRC concluded that 'the essence of the proposed scheme is to supplement oral evidence by hearsay evidence which is likely to be valuable for the ascertainment of the truth'. The proposal was incorporated into a draft Criminal Evidence Bill (cl. 3(1)). The judge could offset over-reliance by the jury on out-of-court statements by suitable directions prior to their introduction in evidence and when summing up. The current practice is that following inclusion of a statement to show (in)consistency, the jury are warned that they must not treat the statement as capable of proving the facts stated in it. Perhaps the distinction between this and the CLRC scheme is, for practical purposes, academic and unlikely to be appreciated by the average juror however carefully the attempt to explain it to them is expressed.

The CLRC chose not to spell out, in so many words, the objective behind their scheme of using statements to 'supplement' oral evidence in proof of the facts averred, apart from the rather obliquely expressed purpose that 'it was likely to be valuable in the ascertainment of the truth'. But it is tolerably clear that their intent was to enable the prosecution to rely on material incriminating of a defendant which the witness had disavowed or omitted. At present this is allowed in under the memory-refreshing procedure or the hostile witness rule. In either case the statement is not evidence of the facts contained in it, unless adopted by the witness, but goes to credibility. Under the CLRC scheme a case could presumably go to the jury on the basis of a statement in spite of retraction by the witness.

By contrast with the use of a statement to *supplement* oral evidence for this purpose, the very strength of video recording is its potential utility as a *substitute* for live evidence. The use of a video-recording as evidence-in-chief is a much more radical purpose than that conceived of by the CLRC. What in principle are the merits and the objections? If under the present regime witnesses are allowed a virtually free reign to read their statements on the strength of the fiction that they are 'refreshing their memories' why not show a tape of them giving their account when their memories really were fresh? In favour of the argument is the principle that evidence is not a memory test and playing the tape is much better than placing the documentary aide-mémoire in front of the witness. Further, rather than ousting the traditional oral principle, it may be said actually to enhance it. At present evidence is given usually on the basis of refreshment of memory outside court from a written statement made contemporaneously with the events narrated but the accuracy of which may be vitiated by inadequacies in the method of recording. So the very foundation of the oral testimony may be a statement artificially prepared. Written statements fail to disclose whether an averment was elicited by a leading question or, whilst originally expressed tentatively, became engraved in tablets of stone by the mere act of putting it into a narrative form of writing. By contrast, electronic recording is the harnessing of technology to gather oral evidence at the moment of its potentially highest value — when recollection was fresh. Additionally, it records what is recollected free of tainting by the process of repeating the account (see Sanders et al., 1996, footnote 2). As distinct from written statements video-recording reveals warts and all. This is not something that can truly be said of audiotaping because of the obvious difference that video portrays the important factors of demeanour and gesture (see Sanders et al., 1996). Finally, in inviting the witness to confirm assertions recorded on tape, it preserves the central feature of trial in open court in which the accused is confronted by his or her accuser. Witnesses may be emboldened to make false allegations in the privacy of the police station 'studio'; when required to confirm them in open court, under oath, and in the face of the defendant, their gall may desert them.

But it is on this last point that there is a cogent objection against using the video-recording as an automatic replacement for evidence-in-chief. Dishonest witnesses may find it easier to sustain a false story if they are merely required to adopt what they said on tape and be cross-examined on it, than if they actually have to start from scratch. Moreover, quite apart from the question of effrontery, it is arguable that even allowing witnesses to give evidence from an aide-mémoire, let alone allowing them to adopt a tape-recording, is to remove an important check against perjury. Honest witnesses, it can be argued, will tend to remember the salient facts without an aide-mémoire in front of them, for actual experience will impress itself on the memory far better than invention. People who make things up, so the argument goes, often forget their lines and the best way to test their honesty is to put them in the witness box without sight of a proof of any kind. On the other hand, it must be conceded, the power of retention, even in the case of an honest witness, is not to be overestimated (see Loftus, 1979).

Another important objection is that it is preferable that the jury should hear the witness's account elicited in an ordered manner by examination-in-chief designed both to present a coherent and comprehensible picture and to omit inadmissible matter. Prosecuting advocates in court should have the discretion to decide how they will present the evidence, rather than simply to act the role of glorified button-pushers on a VCR. As a result of inadequate questioning by an untrained police investigator what comes over on tape may be a rambling, confused and thoroughly confusing narrative. By the intervention of a few deftly aimed questions, this can be tidied up and made completely comprehensible to a jury. Furthermore, it has been reported (by Sanders et al., 1996) that some prosecutors take the view that using a videotape for evidence-in-chief can make the ordeal of cross-examination more difficult as the witness has not been 'warmed up' by a friendly prosecution barrister before being cross-examined.

If videotape was regularly used it might be envisaged that many would require editing. In a report by the Crown Prosecution Service Inspectorate on its thematic review of cases involving child witnesses (1998) it was found that the quality of video evidence has steadily improved, both technically and in terms of interviewing skills, but that video interviews nevertheless regularly required editing and that this had occurred in 54.3% of cases on file samples which were listed for trial and were invariably instigated by the defence or the court. The interdepartmental working group on vulnerable and intimidated witnesses have made the obvious comment (Home Office, 1998, para. 8.46) that the use of videotaped evidence in criminal proceedings is both time-consuming and costly, with time needed to arrange and tape the interview and all those involved in the process at a later stage (the CPS, defence and the judge) needing time to watch the video. Time and resources are also needed to edit when necessary and to provide transcripts.

What if the audio or video-recording reveals that a witness said things only after improper pressure was applied by the statement taker? Potential witnesses who are also potential suspects may be particularly vulnerable to threats of prosecution if they do not fall in with an investigator's theories about the case. The Scottish Law Commission concluded that if a statement was unlawfully obtained, this might affect admissibility unless, in spite of the circumstances, the witness nonetheless agreed that the contents of the statement were true (1990, paras 4-68–4.70). Their report cites only unauthorised telephone tapping as an example of what the Commission envisaged as coming into the unlawfully obtained category. Statements by witnesses in response to leading questions by investigators should, the Commission decided, relate to weight not admissibility. The dividing line between 'unlawfully obtained' and 'improperly elicited' may be rather narrow.

Key terms
Audiotape-recording; collaboration; cost; counterfeiting; distortion; inconsistency; memory refreshment; selection of witnesses; self-contradiction; summaries; suppression; videotape-recording.

References
Central Planning and Training Unit (1992), *A Guide to Interviewing*. London: Home Office.

Criminal Law Revision Committee (1972), *Eleventh Report. Evidence (General)* (Cmnd 4991). London: HMSO.

Crown Prosecution Service Inspectorate (1998), *Report on Cases Involving Child Witnesses — Thematic Report 1/98*. London: Crown Prosecution Service.

Devlin, P. (1960), *The Criminal Prosecution in England*. London: Oxford University Press.

Gibbons, S. (1996), 'Extracting the best', *Police Review*, 22 March 1996.

Heaton-Armstrong, A. (1985), 'Police officers' notebooks', *Criminal Law Review*, p. 781.

Heaton-Armstrong, A. (1987), 'Police officers' notebooks: recent developments', *Criminal Law Review*, p. 470.

Heaton-Armstrong, A. (1994), *Recording and Disclosing Statements by Witnesses: Law and Practice*, paper prepared with the assistance of D. Wolchover, presented at a seminar in London on 12 October 1994 held by the British Academy of Forensic Sciences, the Criminal Bar Association and the London Criminal Courts Solicitors Association and published in *Medicine, Science and the Law*, vol. 35, p. 136.

Heaton-Armstrong, A., and Wolchover, D. (1992a), 'Recording witness statements', *Criminal Law Review*, p. 160.

Heaton-Armstrong, A., and Wolchover, D. (1992b), 'The eyes have it', *Police Review*, 28 August 1992.

Heaton-Armstrong, A., and Wolchover, D. (1993a), 'Warts and all', *Police Review*, 5 February 1993.

Heaton-Armstrong, A. and Wolchover, D. (1993b), 'Disclosing witness statements', *Archbold News*, 26 February 1993.

Heaton-Armstrong, A. and Wolchover, D. (1993c), 'Knocking heads together', *Counsel*, April 1993.

Heaton-Armstrong, A. and Wolchover, D. (1993d), 'On the record,' *Law Society's Gazette*, 16 June 1993.

Heaton-Armstrong, A. and Wolchover, D. (1997a), 'A sounder system,' *The Independent*, 16 April 1997.

Heaton-Armstrong, A. and Wolchover, D. (1997b), 'Tape recording witness statements', *New Law Journal*, 6 June 1997 and 13 June 1997.

Home Office (1989), *Report of the Advisory Group on Video Evidence*. London: HMSO.

Home Office (1998), *Speaking up for Justice*, Report of the Interdepartmental Working Group on the Treatment of Vulnerable or Intimidated Witnesses in the Criminal Justice System. London: Home Office.

Langbein, John H. (1974), *Prosecuting Crime in the Renaissance*, Cambridge Mass: Harvard University Press.

Loftus, Elizabeth F. (1979), *Eyewitness Testimony*, Cambridge Mass: Harvard University Press.

McEwan (1990), 'In the box or on the box? The Pigot Report and child witnesses', *Criminal Law Review*, p. 363.

McLean, M. (1994), 'Quality Investigation? Police interviewing of witnesses,' paper presented at a seminar in London on 12 October 1994 held by the British Academy of Forensic Sciences, the Criminal Bar Association and the London Criminal Courts Solicitors Association and published in *Medicine, Science and the Law*, vol. 35, No. 2.

Milne, R. and Shaw, G., 'Obtaining witness statements — best practice and proposals for innovation', paper presented at a British Academy of Forensic Sciences seminar on aspects of witness testimony held in Morrison Hall, Gray's Inn, London, on 16 December 1998 (jointly sponsored by the Criminal Bar Association and the Law Society and chaired by Lord Justice Rose, Vice President of the Court of Appeal, Criminal Division).

Munday, R. (1997), 'The drafting smokescreen', *New Law Journal*, 30 May 1997 and 6 June 1997.

National Crime Faculty (1998), *A Practical Guide to Investigative Interviewing*, Bramshill: National Crime Faculty and National Police Training.

Richardson, J. (1996), 'Commentary on the Criminal Procedure and Investigations Bill', *Criminal Bar Association Newsletter*, September 1996.

Royal Commission on Criminal Justice (1993), *Report* (Cm 2263). London: HMSO.

Sanders, A., Creaton, J., Bird, S. and Webster, L. (1996), *Witnesses with Learning Disabilities — A Report to the Home Office*, unpublished.

Scottish Law Commission (1990), *Report on the Evidence of Children and Other Potentially Vulnerable Witnesses* (Report No. 125). London: HMSO.

Sharpe, S. (1989), *Electronically Recorded Evidence*. London: Fourmat.

Spencer, J.R. (1991), 'Do children forget faster?' *Criminal Law Review*, pp. 189–190.

Stephenson, G.M. (1991), 'Should collaborative testimony be permitted in courts of law?', *Criminal Law Review*, p. 302.

Utting, Sir William (1997), *People Like Us*, Report of the Review of the Safeguards for Children away from home. London: Department of Health and the Welsh Office.

Williams, G. (1979), 'The Authentication of Statements to the Police', *Criminal Law Review*, p. 6.

Wolchover, D. and Heaton-Armstrong, A. (1996), *Confession Evidence*. London: Sweet and Maxwell.

PART THREE

EVIDENTIAL ISSUES

SUMMARY

Putting the learning offered by parts 1 and 2 into effective practice at the forensic stage and acknowledging the difficulties involved in doing so as a result of what may be flawed investigation practices is fraught with further snags. This section classifies some of the complications and blind alleys that are apt to arise in preparation for, and the conduct of, litigation involving contentious witness accounts, and defines better practice for the effective analysis of testimony.

Chapter 16. The influence of witness appearance and demeanour on witness credibility. Chris Fife-Schaw
Fact-finders are influenced by witness appearance and demeanour and are encouraged to do so through training and judicial directions. Some research, however, indicates that a 'common knowledge' approach to these factors may not result in sensible and useful conclusions being drawn. Cues traditionally thought to be available to fact-finders may, in reality, be misleading. Strategies to avoid such wrong thinking, which centre on informed education drawing on psychological expertise, are discussed.

Chapter 17. Identifying anomaly in evidential text. Eric Shepherd and Anna Mortimer
This chapter explains, from the psychologists' viewpoint, the dangers inherent in inadequate or misleading interviewing and recording methods used when a witness's account is obtained and preserved. It sets out the mechanisms recommended to be employed when the text is later subjected to fine-grain analysis. The effectiveness of this will greatly depend on the integrity of the scribe's editorial approach and that of the record itself. The lessons present a challenge to advocates, whose task, if conscientiously and comprehensively undertaken, will involve very considerable and time-consuming attention to detail.

Chapter 18. The admissibility of expert psychological and psychiatric testimony. Ronald McKay, Andrew Colman and Peter Thornton QC
The rules concerning the admissibility of expert evidence in these categories may have been given an interpretation which prevents fact-finders from understanding issues relating to mental processes. Whilst these readily digestible if properly explained, the assumption that jurors, for example, are aware of the dangers of investigative processes which risk memory corruption, may not be justifiable — at least as far as the areas covered by some chapters in this book are concerned. A more liberal approach to the receipt of psychological and psychiatric expertise — both through generalised training and in individual cases — is desirable.

Chapter 19. Problematic testimony. Anthony Heaton-Armstrong, David Wolchover and Eric Shepherd
This final chapter focuses on the more pressing difficulties encountered in forensic practice which tend to prevent fact-finders seeing and hearing the whole picture. Thus the modern legislation governing disclosure of 'unused material' by prosecuting authorities and third parties is said to have become excessively restrictive and to have a tendency unjustifiably to obstruct fact-finders in their search for truth and accuracy. Lack of cooperation by witnesses in proper efforts to scrutinise their accounts, whether by prosecution authorities or defence lawyers, is subject to insufficient sanction in an accusatorial system of justice which hampers effective inquiry. There is much need for enhanced training programmes in the fields covered by the book both for professional practitioners and lay fact-finders.

CHAPTER SIXTEEN

The influence of witness appearance and demeanour on witness credibility

Chris Fife-Schaw

16.1 INTRODUCTION

Does witness demeanour influence jurors' and other fact-finders' deliberations? While most observers agree that a witness's demeanour ought not to distract jurors and fact-finders from the content of their evidence, this potential source of bias has received little research attention. This chapter draws on the Elaboration Likelihood Model of persuasion (ELM — Petty and Cacioppo, 1986) as a useful framework for understanding how and when such factors might influence jury decision-making and uses it as a guide for framing future research into courtroom practice.

To begin with I should be clear about what is intended by the term 'demeanour'. It was defined by Stone (1991, p. 822) as follows:

> 'demeanour' excludes the content of evidence, and includes every visible or audible form of self-expression manifested by a witness whether fixed or variable, voluntary or involuntary, simple or complex.

The important point for the discussion here is that the concern is with cues available to jurors about the witness that are logically, or empirically demonstrated to be, unrelated to the content, accuracy or quality of the evidence being given.

For simplicity I shall refer to juries and jurors throughout this chapter, but in principle the ideas discussed here will apply equally to any person who is in the position of fact-finder in criminal proceedings.

16.2 PAST RESEARCH

The bulk of research on juries' perceptions of witnesses has been concerned with the relationship between perceived witness confidence and the accuracy of their testimony. However, since there is a general, everyday, bias in favour of believing that more attractive people are honest (the so-called 'beautiful is good' hypothesis, Dion, Berscheid and Walster, 1972) there seems to have been surprisingly little concern that attractiveness and other demeanour cues (including confidence) might influence jurors. Eyewitness testimony is often central to a criminal case and is widely regarded by the public as amongst the most damning kind of evidence available. All too frequently, though, the apparent value of having an eyewitness overrides a consideration of the possibility, however remote, that an eyewitness has made an identification error.

A great deal of research has focused on sources of eyewitness error and there is a body of research that has looked at the relationship between perceptions of witness confidence or certainty and witness accuracy. Eyewitness certainty is particularly interesting since it has been shown that even though there seems to be no relationship between confidence and accuracy, jurors seem to believe witnesses when they appear confident and express certainty about their evidence. For example, Wells, Lindsay and Ferguson (1979) found that jurors' attributions of eyewitness confidence accounted for 50% of the variance in juror's decisions to believe witnesses, even though witness confidence was not found to be related to witness accuracy. Indeed, advocates have known for a long time that jurors rely heavily on a witness's degree of confidence as an index of the witness's accuracy and take active steps either to reinforce or to undermine perceptions of confidence in the service of their case.

Meta-analytic investigations suggest we should be very cautious when assessing the utility of confidence for predicting accuracy in real criminal cases as they find that correlations between accuracy and confidence are only in the region of $r = +0.3$. This can be interpreted to mean that less than 10% of the variation in witness accuracy is likely to be predictable from variation in apparent witness confidence. The accuracy–confidence relationship is weak under laboratory conditions, which are relatively optimal for information processing, and probably functionally useless in courtroom settings.

That people rely on apparent confidence as a guide to credibility is unremarkable since in everyday social interactions expressive confidence can be a useful guide to credibility. The question is whether we want people to use this heuristic in the courtroom where it probably does not work. Witnesses have to answer fairly direct questions with answers only allowable within a restricted range of formats. There tends not to be scope for negotiation of meanings or for the witness to ask questions of lawyers. There is the possibility of intimidation from lawyers and overt challenges to the witness's honesty or integrity which are missing from most everyday interactions. Additionally, the penalties for misleading the court are considerably more harsh and readily obvious than is the case in more mundane day-to-day interactions. Naturally, some witnesses will deal with these pressures better than others.

16.3   RESEARCH ON ATTRACTIVENESS

A substantial body of research already highlights the great importance of attractiveness in guiding everyday initial impressions of strangers. Attractiveness is very important to us even though we may not want to acknowledge it. Among many characteristics, attractive people are more likely to get hired for jobs, have their written work regarded favourably and are less likely to be regarded as psychologically disturbed or maladjusted. Much effort has gone into establishing a link between attractiveness and attributions of criminality, the hypothesis being that attractive criminals will be perceived as less guilty, and subsequently receive lighter sentencing.

The value of much research on this topic has been questioned since most of it has been conducted under artificial laboratory conditions. Whilst this does present a problem for interpretation this is a somewhat unhelpful criticism since, in England and Wales, research on real juries is currently not permitted by law. However, observational studies have established that attractiveness is predictive of both minimum and maximum sentencing in US-based research and tends to confirm the laboratory findings. Downs and Lyons (1991), for instance, had police escorts in Texas rate the attractiveness of 1,742 defendants charged with various misdemeanours. After controlling for the seriousness of the crimes, they found that the 40 judges involved set larger fines and greater bails for less attractive defendants.

Stewart (1980) had observers rate the attractiveness of defendants in real US cases and found a correlation between attractiveness and sentence length $r = -0.29$ after controlling for the seriousness of the crimes. Attractive defendants were slightly more likely to avoid incarceration when compared to unattractive defendants. Interestingly, this study provided suggestive evidence that unattractive defendants were more likely to have been charged with very serious crimes, though it is not possible to tell whether this reflects a bias on the part of the police and those bringing the prosecutions or whether unattractive criminals really do commit more serious crimes. The numbers of cases observed prevents confident generalisation though this is clearly a finding worthy of further study.

The most often cited confirmation of the 'beautiful is good' hypothesis is supplied by two studies by Dion (1972; Dion, Berscheid and Walster, 1972), who found that not only does the bias exist, but it holds across all ages including childhood. Dion and colleagues found that the transgressions of a child were more likely to be tolerated if the child was attractive than if it was unattractive. Furthermore, an attractive child's serious transgressions were evaluated less negatively than were an unattractive child's transgressions, leading to less severe punishment.

The crucial point here, of course, is that there is no evidence that attractive people are good or always tell the truth and what remains largely unresearched is the effect that witness attractiveness might have on perceptions of their credibility. Are attractive people more likely to be believed than the less attractive and if so under what sorts of conditions? Preliminary research on this topic (Bennett and Fife-Schaw, 1993; Dunne, 1994), which falls into the category of artificial laboratory-based research, suggests that more physically attractive witnesses may be believed more than unattractive ones and that this bias acts independently of perceived confidence.

Other research on witness attractiveness has conceptualised attractiveness more broadly to incorporate attractiveness of character, social status attractiveness and other non-physical characteristics. Experimental mock-jury research where attractiveness was equated with occupational status suggests higher-status witnesses are seen as more credible, though this depends on the relative attractiveness of the defendant and whether the evidence is given for the prosecution or the defence. Some studies have manipulated the 'likeableness' of witnesses by prefacing the witness testimony with brief descriptions of the character of the witness. When testifying against a defendant, likeableness increased perceptions of credibility and the degree of guilt ascribed to the defendant.

Some care in interpretation needs to be exercised when the definition of attractiveness is extended beyond physical characteristics. The imputed character of a witness in studies such as those described above is obviously a judgment reached by a third party and not the mock jurors themselves. Indeed it may be difficult to come to a judgment about, say, the boringness/liveliness of a witness (a trait often used in these sorts of study) in the context of a trial where evidence about this personality characteristic may be unavailable. Similarly, the use of occupational status may not simply be one of 'higher is better' as more general persuasion research would suggest that it is perceived similarity of status that may be important. This possibility remains unresearched.

16.4   WHY AND WHEN WILL DEMEANOUR BE IMPORTANT? A THEORETICAL FRAMEWORK

Research on the impact of demeanour cues on jurors has proceeded largely on a pragmatic rather than a theoretical basis. It has tended to be driven by the need to see whether particular cues influence jurors at all rather than the need to develop a theory of why and when these factors should be important. Whilst theories exist about the persuasive power of differing characteristics of the evidence given (e.g., structural coherence) a theoretical framework for understanding why and when demeanour cues will be influential has yet to become widely established (see Kaplan and Schersching, 1980 for an early attempt at such a model).

Jury trials in adversarial systems of justice are fundamentally arenas for persuasive communications. Competing versions of events are proposed by the prosecution and defence each attempting to persuade jurors of the validity of their account. Whilst it is hoped that this process will reveal the truth, most of the exchanges will concern the reconstruction of past events and the jury will be directed to areas of ambiguity and differing interpretation. If the trial is fundamentally about attempts to persuade, do general theories of persuasion and attitude change have anything to tell us about how demeanour cues might influence juries?

16.4.1 The Elaboration Likelihood Model of persuasion (ELM)

Research on the factors influencing the success of persuasive communications has been a central theme of social psychological research for more than 60 years. Though there have been many theories of persuasion with limited ranges of application during this time, there now exist a number of integrated theoretical frameworks that have become well established. By far the best known of these is Petty and Cacioppo's (1986) Elaboration Likelihood Model, which will be drawn upon here. Research continues into this model but thus far it has withstood the test of time and generated countless research predictions, the vast majority of which have been supported. The model is presented in figure 16.1.

The model proposes two routes to persuasion. The first, known as 'central route processing', involves the message recipient engaging in 'cognitive elaboration' on the content of the message. Cognitive elaboration is a term used to mean that the recipient will think about the content of the message and will consider this content in the light of existing message-relevant knowledge and attitudes. Should the result of this cognitive elaboration lead to a positive evaluation of the message, persuasion will take place. If the elaboration process gives rise to largely negative evaluations, no attitude change will take place or, possibly, a shift in attitude against the message will occur. Persuasion occurring as a result of central route processing is likely to be long-lasting and be more likely to lead to message-consistent behaviour in the future. It is assumed that it is this kind of processing we require of jurors.

The second route to persuasion is referred to as 'peripheral route processing'. In this mode, the recipient does not engage in elaboration of the message content but attends to peripheral (non-content) cues in the persuasive communication. To put it another way, recipients resort to simple decision-making heuristics. For instance, the recipient might regard the communicating source as expert and trustworthy and conclude that anything the source advocates must be good or right *because* the source is a trustworthy expert. The attractiveness of the source may induce persuasion as might the source's perceived confidence. Conversely, untrusted or unattractive sources might be ignored because they are unattractive or untrustworthy, irrespective of the merits of their case. This is where the 'beautiful is good' hypothesis discussed above fits within this framework. Persuasion achieved through the peripheral route is less likely to influence behaviour in the long term but in the short term may influence choices and related attitudes.

These heuristics are kinds of decision-making biases that would also include the use of more generalised social stereotypes. These might include not believing people who hold opposing political or ideological views to your own, e.g., 'There's nothing that a Conservative politician tells you that can

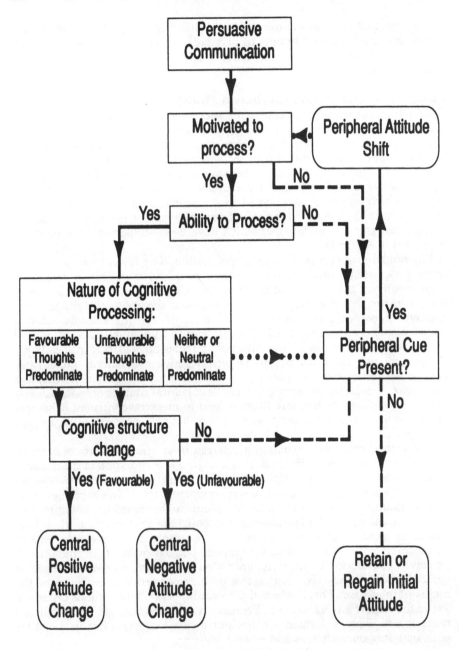

Figure 16.1 The Elaboration Likelihood Model of persuasion (adapted from Petty and Cacioppo (1986))

be worth listening to'. They might also involve racial stereotypes and prejudices, e.g., 'Blacks are always involved in crime' and therefore people from racial minorities should not be believed. The use of heuristics should not to be viewed as somehow deviant or always undesirable, however. We are bombarded with attempts to persuade us every day and we simply lack the mental resources and time to elaborate on each communication that we come across. The facility to make quick decisions about communications, based on simple heuristics, that will be good enough most of the time is clearly an aid to daily life. They are, however, undesirable in the context of a trial.

The important features relevant to making practical recommendations concern the early stages of the persuasion process and the factors that determine which route is employed. In the jargon of the model, these are the factors that determine the likelihood of elaboration, hence the name, 'elaboration likelihood model'. The two key factors are motivation to process the message and ability to process the message.

When the audience for a persuasive communication is motivated to hear it and has the ability to comprehend it, then it is likely that they will 'cognitively elaborate' on the message. They will think about the content of the message and produce their own message-relevant thoughts about it. If jurors are thinking hard about the content of a piece of evidence then it is here that factors such as the structural and logical coherence of the accounts will influence judgments. This is 'central route' processing. It does not mean that the message (here evidence or argument) will necessarily persuade, as the motivation to process the message may stem from an existing commitment to an opposing view. Recipients may be motivated by prior interest or involvement or by feelings of personal responsibility for outcomes related to the behaviours or choices advocated by the message. On the other hand, if motivation is low or the audience lacks the ability to comprehend the message, then the audience is likely to resort to peripheral cues about the message and the communicator rather than to think through the content of the message.

'Ability' as used in the ELM can refer both to relatively stable mental abilities and situation-specific variations in ability. Where people lack the necessary knowledge base to understand a communication it is unlikely to invoke coherent message-relevant thinking. Indeed, members of the Roskill Committee (Fraud Trials Committee, 1986) were concerned that juries would not be able to comprehend the evidence in complex financial fraud trials. A fear underlying the Committee's recommendations was that jurors would resort to what amounts to peripheral route processing and base their judgments on aspects of the defendants and witnesses unrelated to the nature of their evidence.

Similarly, complex trials may contain too many competing persuasive communications for jurors to deal with. If confusion and the pace of argument prevent satisfactory elaboration on particular points, jurors may resort to peripheral cues and rely on these heuristics when forming a judgment about the evidence. Obviously it is incumbent on barristers to present their cases in ways that avoid such an overload yet, of course, adding to confusion may held an opposing barrister whose case would not be helped by jurors elaborating too long on his or her own, possibly weak, arguments.

Ability to process a message may also be impaired by relatively short-term factors. Tiredness and boredom may limit people's ability (and motivation) to attend to the proceedings of the court. Distractions, noises outside the courtroom, extractor fans and disruptions in the public galleries may all serve to reduce the likelihood of jurors elaborating on the evidence under consideration. As we know from recent research, jurors take little notice of (or at least are unable to be influenced by) judges' directions to ignore inadmissible evidence or interruptions. Witnesses providing large bodies of evidence very quickly or, perhaps in a mumbled fashion, will reduce juror's ability to elaborate on the evidence.

16.4.2 Making predictions using the ELM
Assuming the ELM to be an appropriate model to use in this domain, what predictions does it make about when peripheral cues about witnesses will be important?

16.4.2.1 When peripheral witness cues will not be important   The model would suggest that highly motivating cases will encourage jurors to concentrate on the evidence given. Where the crime in question is particularly serious, noteworthy or inherently thought-provoking, jurors ought to be motivated to attend fully to the evidence. Similarly when jurors have a personal interest in the outcome, perhaps through identifying with one of the parties involved, central route processing should take place.

Where the number of arguments or interpretations of the evidence is small jurors should not become overloaded and be unable to process the evidence. If the testimony of witnesses is largely in substantive agreement, the attractiveness of any particular witness is unlikely to influence interpretations of events. If witness A is the ninth person to see the accused holding the smoking gun, A's beauty or otherwise is unlikely to influence the conclusion that the accused held a smoking gun. Some experimental evidence would already suggest that some biases and other social prejudices are less likely to influence jurors in clear-cut cases (Kaplan and Schersching, 1980).

Jurors may be motivated to attend closely to the evidence if they come to believe that they will be personally responsible for deciding the outcome of the trial. This is likely to be something about which individuals differ. Some may take comfort in being only one of 12 people charged with reaching a verdict and thus feel absolved of the responsibility of paying close attention to the proceedings. Others may feel that they cannot rely on their fellow jurors to do all the work for them. Emphasising the individual juror's personal responsibility on regular occasions is indicated.

16.4.2.2 When peripheral witness cues will be important   When the evidence in a trial requires some baseline knowledge or expertise beyond that held by the average juror then ability to elaborate on the evidence may be rapidly exceeded. As noted earlier, the Roskill Committee clearly took the view that financial fraud was probably too complicated for most people to comprehend and the ELM would suggest that peripheral witness cues might be more important in such cases. Providing expert witnesses to interpret specialist evidence in simple neutral terms for the jury's benefit is only likely to promote understanding as long as a single interpretation is offered. Cases where opposing counsel provide competing expert interpretations will presumably add to confusion. Such cases are also likely to be perceived by many people as somewhat tedious and unexciting. The outcome may be perceived (rightly or wrongly) as of no real consequence for society ('victimless crime') and of no consequence to the interests of jurors themselves. This low state of motivation should promote peripheral cue processing.

Trials involving complex evidence may overwhelm jurors' abilities by virtue of its volume even if it is readily understood. Long trials in particular may promote peripheral processing. Jurors may become bored and easily tired as the proceedings progress. Long trials, almost by definition, involve large bodies of evidence and a good degree of ambiguity and uncertainty about its proper interpretation. Jurors may come to 'take against' the defendant, the witnesses, counsel or even possibly the judge. Irritation with irrelevant peripheral cues of the main players may increase as time goes on. Experimental data suggest that delays and time-wasting by judges and lawyers promote biased and hostile decision-making by juries. Witness demeanour factors should be more influential, however, where a small number of witnesses provide a lot of complex evidence rather than in cases where many witnesses are involved, none of whom are in the witness box long enough to become especially noticeable.

Distractions of various kinds should limit jurors' ability to concentrate on the evidence and thus promote peripheral cue processing. Obvious distractors include disruptions in the public galleries, people dropping things, shuffling papers or key participants' nervous habits such as scratching or twitching. Poor-quality ventilation and temperature control may induce drowsiness as might continuous background noises such as fans or traffic noise.

Less obvious distractors would include the external lives of the jurors. Jurors may experience personal problems in their lives that may occupy their attention. Births, deaths and marriages continue to impinge on people's lives during the trial. Many (most?) will be concerned about being away from work or home and the mounting pile of work that may await them on their return. Minor health complaints may also serve as distractors, particularly ailments such as heavy colds or piles.

16.4.2.3   Summary

Factors that increase ability to focus on the evidence
Uncontested expert explanations of the meaning of evidence.
Small numbers of arguments.
Small or simple body of evidence.
Evidence confirmed or repeated by multiple witnesses.

Factors that decrease ability to focus on the evidence
Contested or multiple contradictory expert explanations of the meaning of evidence.

Long trial.
Large or complex body of evidence.
Distractions.
Poor heating and ventilation.
Events in juror's life outside the court.
Juror's minor health ailments.

Factors that increase motivation to focus on the evidence
Intrinsically interesting or compelling case.
Case where jurors are likely to identify strongly with one party.
Case where the trial outcome might have implications for the juror's own activities.
Reminders of personal responsibility as a juror.

Factors that decrease motivation to focus on the evidence
Case involving financial or highly technical irregularities.
'Victimless' crime.
'Free-riding' juror (an individual difference factor).
Long presentations of evidence from a small number of witnesses.
Poor heating and ventilation.
Events in juror's life outside court.
Juror's minor health ailments.

16.5   PRACTICAL IMPLICATIONS

The ELM allows us to make predictions about when and why peripheral cues may be important in determining trial outcomes and may also be useful in pointing the way to improving trial procedures. Working under an assumption that jurors should process the evidence via cognitive elaboration, steps should be taken to maximise motivation and ability, the two factors that determine the likelihood of this elaboration.

Many of these steps are already in place though some are not yet fully realised:

(a)   Distractions in courtrooms are already kept to a minimum but more attention could be paid to older court buildings where heating and lighting conditions are poor. A noisy air-conditioning system may not compensate for an overheated airless room.

(b)   There would certainly seem to be a case for introducing procedures that speed up trials. Not only is this in the interest of justice in the sense of promoting a wide-awake cognitively elaborating jury, but it would also save money and increase the speed with which other cases can be dealt with by the courts. It may well be that justice is not really served by allowing defendants and prosecutors lengthy periods in which to present all the evidence they have in support of their case. Since, in complex, long trials, there is often extended debate about the meaning of evidence, defence and prosecution lawyers should be encouraged jointly to identify specific areas of ambiguity before coming to court with the aim of presenting the nature of these ambiguities clearly to juries.

(c)   The role of the information provided for jurors cannot be under-estimated. Judges should continually emphasise the personal responsibilities of individual jurors for their decisions. They should explicitly warn against 'social loafing' and relying on others to do the decision-making.

McGillis (1979) suggests that warning jurors about their likely biases in orientation sessions can reduce the effects of these biases. Existing video presentations employed by some courts in the UK might be usefully extended to cover more than the basic facts about court procedures to include a recognition of these biases. Clear explanations of the likely consequences of jurors getting bored or tired would be one topic that could be easily covered by asking jurors to reflect on their state of alertness when recalling pieces of evidence. Jurors could be told about peripheral processing heuristics (in laypersons' terms) and warned against using them when deliberating on the evidence. This warning should be reinforced prior to juries retiring to consider their verdicts.

16.6   THE SPECIAL CASE OF CHILD WITNESSES

The discussion so far in this chapter has implicitly referred to the demeanour of adult witnesses. Child witnesses present a special case since it is widely believed that the essentially peripheral cue that the witness is a child, in the sense that children can tell the truth and lie just as adults can, is regarded by many as far from peripheral and indeed central to assessments of credibility. There is now widespread concern about how best to allow children to give evidence in court and much of this concern stems from a combination of factors particular to the appearance of children in court.

The first major factor giving rise to concern is that children frequently appear as witnesses in cases of abuse (violence or sexual) and are often also the victim of this abuse. In a majority of such cases they are likely to know the defendant well. This has led to a boom in research on how child witnesses should be allowed to present their evidence given the probably reasonable assumption that children will find appearing in the witness box intimidating and distressing. The relative merits of video links and the use of barriers between witnesses and defendants as means of obtaining reliable evidence from children will not concern us here though the question is dealt with elsewhere in this book (see chapter 4).

The second major factor has been the widely held belief that children, more so than adults, are suggestible and will respond inappropriately to attempts to influence their evidence. While the literature on the suggestibility of child witnesses contains many contradictory findings, reviews suggest that, given appropriate attention to the context of questioning, even quite young children can provide forensically relevant and reliable evidence (e.g., Ceci and Bruck, 1993). Despite this, recent Australian research among magistrates and judges confirms that these groups believe children to be more suggestible and therefore less credible (Cashmore and Bussey, 1996) and mock jury research indicates that child witnesses are seen as less credible when faced with leading (as opposed to non-leading) questioning (Kalra and Heath, 1997).

Though there is no clear picture emerging about global biases of jurors faced with child witnesses, there is evidence of an interesting gender interaction in that women seem more likely than men to view child witnesses as credible (e.g., Crowley, O'Callaghan and Ball, 1994). Also, there is suggestive evidence that when using video links, young boys are rated as more credible than young girls and older girls are perceived more favourably than younger girls (Westcott, Clifford and Davies, 1991). Another intriguing finding from the same study suggests that when children give evidence via a video link the nature of the framing of the camera shots can influence perceptions of credibility. Medium-range shots (as opposed to close-ups) appear to make younger children appear less credible than older children while close-up angles yield no age differences.

Though children, more so than adults, are susceptible to pressure from adults, there is no logic that says that children are *necessarily* less reliable witnesses. Certainly the literature would suggest that adults work on an assumption that children are unreliable witnesses but it would seem that this assumption needs to be tested more rigorously. The present state of the research literature, whilst still far from conclusive, would indicate that it is important for trial judges to alert jurors to the possibility that they may be assuming that child witnesses lack credibility merely because they are children. It is in such cases that neutral expert testimony on the cognitive capabilities of children may be especially useful.

16.7 SUMMARY

The research literature contains sufficient evidence suggesting that peripheral cues might influence juror's deliberations to warrant these being taken seriously when refining court procedures. The literature indicates that perceived confidence and attractiveness are both factors worthy of serious consideration. The ELM would seem to offer a framework both for making clear, testable predictions for researchers and for guiding modifications to legal procedures.

To improve the chance of a fair trial initiatives to reduce the likelihood of peripheral processing must be worthwhile. However, it would be unwise to overstate the influence of peripheral cues on juries. First, as the chapters in this book indicate, a number of factors influence jurors of which witness demeanour is only one. Secondly, there are usually 12 jurors and for witness cues to have a marked effect on the outcome of a trial a majority of jurors would have had to have been influenced in the same way. The probability of a majority simultaneously lacking motivation or the ability to concentrate on the evidence may be quite small though, of course, in the absence of research we will not know how small. Thirdly, in many cases jurors swayed by peripheral cues of witnesses may nonetheless arrive at the 'right' conclusion about the evidence. Sometimes attractive witnesses will be telling the truth. Sometimes jurors will not believe people who really should not be believed even though they may have arrived at this conclusion for somewhat spurious reasons.

Key terms
attractiveness; persuasion; witness credibility; witness demeanour.

References
Bennett, K. and Fife-Schaw, C.R. (1993), *Attractiveness, Confidence and their Relation to Eyewitness Believability*. Presentation at The British Psychological Society, Social Psychology Section Conference, Jesus College, Oxford, September 1993.

Cashmore, J. and Bussey, K. (1996), 'Judicial perceptions of child witness competence', *Law and Human Behaviour*, vol. 20, pp. 313–34.

Ceci, S. and Bruck, M. (1993), 'Suggestibility of the child witness: a historical review and synthesis', *Psychological Bulletin*, vol. 113, pp. 403–39.

Crowley, M.J., O'Callagan, M.G. and Ball, P.J. (1994), The juridical impact of psychological expert testimony in a simulated child sexual abuse trial, *Law and Human Behaviour* 18(1), 89–105.

Dion K.E. (1972), 'Physical attractiveness stereotype: is it present at childhood?' *Journal of Personality and Social Psychology*, vol. 24, pp. 207–13.

Dion K.E., Berscheid, E. and Walster, E. (1972), 'What is beautiful is good', *Journal of Personality and Social Psychology*, vol. 24, pp. 285–9.

Downs, A.C. and Lyons, P.M. (1991), 'Natural observations of the links between attractiveness and initial legal judgements', *Personality and Social Psychology Bulletin*, vol. 17, pp. 541–7.

Dunne, M. (1994), *Eyewitness Believability and Potential Jury-room Influence*. Unpublished dissertation, Department of Psychology, University of Surrey.

Fraud Trials Committee (1986), *Report*. London: HMSO.

Kalra, B. and Heath, W. (1997), 'Perceptions of a child as a witness: effects of leading questions and the type of relationship between child and defendant', *Psychological Reports*, vol. 80, pp. 979–86.

Kaplan, M.F. and Schersching, C. (1980), 'Reducing juror bias: an experimental approach', in P.D. Lipsitt and B.D. Sales (eds), *New Directions in Psycholegal Research*. New York, Van Nostrand Reinhold.

McGillis, D. (1979), 'Biases and jury decision making', in I.H. Frieze, D. Bar-Tal and J.S. Carroll, *New Approaches to Social Problems*. San Francisco: Jossey-Bass.

Petty, R.E. and Cacioppo, J.T. (1986), 'The elaboration likelihood model of persuasion', in L. Berkowitz (ed.), *Advances in Experimental Social Psychology*, vol. 19. Orlando: Academic Press.

Stewart, J.E., II (1980), 'Defendants' attractiveness as a factor in the outcome of criminal trials: an observational study', *Journal of Applied Social Psychology*, vol. 9, pp. 348–61.

Stone, M. (1991), 'Instant lie detection? Demeanour and credibility in criminal trials', *Criminal Law Review*, pp. 821–30.

Wells, G.L., Lindsay, R.C.L. and Ferguson, T.J. (1979), 'Accuracy, confidence and juror perceptions in eyewitness identification', *Journal of Applied Psychology*, vol. 64, pp. 440–8.

Westcott, H.L., Clifford, B.R. and Davies, G.M. (1991), 'Children's credibility on camera: the influence of age and production factors', *Children and Society*, vol. 5, pp. 254–65.

Recommended reading
Stephenson, G.M. (1992), *The Psychology of Criminal Justice*. Oxford: Blackwell.

Editors' notes
This chapter is of considerable importance to those who train professional and lay judges and practitioners and those who are responsible for formulating directions to lay fact-finders concerning the right approach to contentious witness testimony. Witness confidence is potentially misleading especially where there are disputes about identification (see chapters 12 and 13). The implications for training bodies such as the Judicial Studies Board are clear.

CHAPTER SEVENTEEN

Identifying anomaly in evidential text

Eric Shepherd and Anna Mortimer

'Is there any point to which you would wish to draw my attention?'
'To the curious incident of the dog in the night-time.'
'The dog did nothing in the night-time.'
'That was the curious incident.'

Sir Arthur Conan Doyle, *Memoirs of Sherlock Holmes*

17.1 INTRODUCTION

A fundamental task of a lawyer is the analysis of the fine-grain detail of written and recorded evidential text. The public assumes that lawyers, whether acting for the prosecution or defence, have as a common objective, a 'warts and all' commitment to detect and to confront anomaly, bringing this when detected to the court's attention and seeking an explanation through cross-examination.

A detailed description of how particular kinds of evidence can be analysed is provided in Ede and Shepherd (1997). In this chapter we focus on the identification of anomaly. We summarise how the character of text, how it is compiled as evidence and the psychological processes of reading, listening and observing, constitute substantial barriers to achieving this task. We review the many forms of anomaly, particularly those that defy ready detection. We argue that the solution lies in systematic methods of collating and representing evidential detail, and briefly describe some methods to achieve this. Possible explanations of identified anomaly are considered before reviewing potential barriers to implementing systematic methods for identifying anomaly in evidential text.

17.2   BARRIERS TO IDENTIFYING ANOMALY

17.2.1   The character of evidential text

Evidential text predominantly comprises written statements and other formal documentation. The advent of recording now requires lawyers to listen to and to observe interviews, which are typically translated into written text in the form of summaries of tape-recorded interviews (ROTIs) or indexes of video-recorded interviews (IVRIs), or, less commonly full transcripts.

Evidential text provides a narrative of 'what happened'. Whether written or recorded this text is a complex interweaving of *episodic* and *identity* detail:

(a)   *Episodic detail* creates for the recipient a representation of events: each event occurring at a point in space (a location or setting) and time (date, time, duration), with one or more individuals, or objects, engaged in sequences of action (including communication), thought or emotion.

(b)   *Identity detail* creates a representation of persons (e.g., physical appearance, background detail, associates), objects, locations, or rituals or routines (repeated sequences of action or procedure).

17.2.2   Writing and speech

Halliday (1987, pp. 74 and 79–80) observed:

A written text is an object; so what is represented in writing tends to be given the form of an object. But when one talks, one is doing; so when one talks about something, one happens to say that it happened or was done. . . . Speech and writing will appear, then, as different ways of meaning; speech is spun out, flowing, choreographic, oriented towards events (doing, happening, sensing, saying, being), processlike, intricate, with meanings related serially; writing is dense, structured, crystalline, oriented towards things (entities, objectified processes), product like, tight, with meanings related to components.

It is no surprise therefore that lawyers prefer written evidential text. Audio and video recordings highlight the convenience of written text. Equipment is required to process a much more demanding, and potentially frustrating, medium. Sustained attention, intent powers of concentration and close observation in multiple replays are essential to disentangle extempore conversational exchanges.

Spoken utterances have stops, starts, pauses and are often unfinished. They do not correspond to written punctuation. Syntactical connections are often opaque. Elliptical references abound. The flow of ideas is embedded with, and disrupted by, asides and commentary. Nuances of meaning are conveyed by non-verbal non-vocal communication (e.g., tone of voice, rhythm, speed, volume, pitch, pause and silence), and, in the case of video, additional non-verbal non-vocal communication (e.g., movement of the face, hands and body) (see chapter 4). Recording quality is frequently poor. With video recordings the image of the interviewee is usually so small that it is impossible to discern facial expressions or limb movements.

Interviews often appear to meander in terms of taking turns to speak, structure and *topic progression*, i.e., the change in subject matter across time. Topic changes (initiated by the questioner or the questioned) and recursions (returning to a previous topic) are frequent and often unpredictable. Furthermore when giving an account people frequently relate episodes in their 'story', the *narrative sequence*, in a different order to the sequence of events as they actually happened. Hence the listener or observer has to gather and reorder episodic detail distributed in responses across the course of the interview.

Section 9 statements (i.e., statements prepared for use under the Criminal Justice Act 1967, s. 9) prepared by officers confirm Halliday's observations about the object quality of written text. These are tight texts because their contents have been carefully selected and crafted (see chapter 9). The officers have translated the complexity of interview responses into easy-to-follow narratives. The narrative is presented chronologically, topics progress steadily and, where stated, cause-and-effect relationships and lines of reasoning are explicit.

Close reading of written text enables the identification of significant, or potentially significant, detail which is noted in memory and noted physically by sidelining, underlining, flagging (e.g., with Post-it stickers), and written notation. Increasingly lawyers are using information technology, computers and word-processing software (e.g., cell and spreadsheet formats) to collate key material.

Although less easy to work with than statements, written versions of interviews are much easier than the recordings themselves. However, if it is a summary, missing text has to be inserted freehand. Even where there is a full transcript it is still necessary to annotate instances of over-talking, interruptions, pauses and their duration, and other non-verbal behaviours.

17.2.3 Words into images
Words are often inadequate for the task of describing physical circumstances, e.g., relative positioning in a location, orientation, direction of gaze, movement, approach, entry and exit. The problem is complicated because people vary greatly in their ability to image and to think spatially. Some gloss over the inadequate words without realising that they have little or no idea in their mind's eye of the witness's representation of reality. In contrast imagination takes over some people, creating an image not portrayed in the text.

Even the most amateur sketch can assist with imaging. In the vast majority of cases, however, police officers fail to assist the court by making a sketch or by obtaining (or producing) a sketch following a requested demonstration by the witness.

17.2.4 The compilation of evidential text
The Crown Prosecution Service arranges evidential text according to the precedence assigned to individuals in a case. Each individual's statements are arranged chronologically according to the date they were signed (which may be some time after interviewing began). Interviews are organised in a similar manner.

No criticism of the CPS is intended when we say that such compilation obscures potentially important information concerning the sequence in which evidence arose or was obtained. Some lawyers inspect the totality of evidence, draw up a master chronology of statement production and interviewing, and then read or listen to the material in this identified sequence. Others do not, with obvious implications.

17.2.5 The psychology of processing text

Any text presents a reader, listener or observer with a continuous stream of information, comprising packages of detail which van Dijk and Kintsch (1983) termed *micro-propositions*. Although the recipient may hold in working memory particular propositions considered to be potentially significant and worthy of later attention, it is impossible to retain every proposition. As we read, listen or observe we unconsciously reduce the mass of detail to more manageable proportions. We create a mental framework of *macro-propositions* — key bits of information, ideas, themes or 'bullet points' — by:

(a) *deletion* — discarding irrelevant or redundant detail;
(b) *integration* — combining two or more distinct ideas into a single idea;
(c) *generalisation* — reducing two or more similar ideas into one; and
(d) *construction* — 'going beyond the evidence' by drawing inferences.

Further reduction and reconstruction generate the overall 'gist'.

These processes are economical but problematic. The recipient's frame of reference, motivation, attitudes and even factors such as tiredness, bring about premature closure, confirmation bias, ironing out, and selective synthesis, as well as errors of omission and commission (see chapter 9).

In sum there are substantial practical, procedural and psychological barriers to the identification of anomaly.

17.3 ANOMALY IN EVIDENTIAL TEXT

Anomaly is that which is incongruous. We summarise below some of the many forms of incongruity that may arise in written and recorded text.

17.3.1 Deficiencies in detail

The fundamental, forensically significant distinction between 'core', or 'central', detail and 'peripheral' detail has been mentioned in chapters 2 and 4.

There is an implicit expectation that an account will give sufficient detail, particularly core detail, to enable the reader or listener:

(a) to recreate mentally the sequence of events and descriptions reported by the witness, particularly of his or her experiences;
(b) to follow the witness's line of reasoning or logic.

A deficiency in detail where detail could be expected constitutes the 'non-barking dog' to which Sherlock Holmes drew Inspector Gregory's attention.

17.3.1.1 Deficient descriptions The witness gives a description that is lacking in some way. The deficit may be one or more items of information being unstated, stated vaguely or ambiguously.

Such shortcomings are often missed in the course of an interview. They are obscured by the processes of drafting a s. 9 statement or in the preparation of a written summary of a tape-recorded interview (ROTI) or an index of a video-recorded interview (IVRI). They can be overlooked when processing large amounts of written evidence.

Of potential significance also is the lack of non-verbal description. People commonly use hand movements which reinforce verbal descriptions, e.g., *illustrators* mimic the action being described; *batons* point in space to indicate relative location, direction of movement, orientation, or route taken from the vantage point of the person giving the description.

17.3.1.2 Failure to identify key individuals The passive voice or other oblique verbal constructions can avoid or obscure identification of a key individual, e.g., 'The knife was handed to me and I was told to stab her'.

Interviewers often fail to recognise the necessity to probe these constructions. Lawyers can also overlook their significance.

17.3.1.3 Conversational deficits The witness gives an account which is wordless, e.g., the witness describes an episode in which the alleged perpetrator enters the room, engages in a sequence of actions including the commission of an offence, and leaves the room, but there is no reference to any verbal exchange between them.

Alternatively the witness describes a one-sided conversation, e.g., what the other person said but not what the witness said.

Missing conversation is often overlooked by interviewers and later by lawyers when processing a recording or reading an IVRI or ROTI.

17.3.1.4 Sequential and logical discontinuity Certain narrative detail is, by its nature, core or central. When this is missing there is a 'jumping' effect. Examples are the absence of a step — or steps — in a narrative sequence, an outcome without a triggering cause, reason, event or set of circumstances ('Roy was in a foul temper'), or an action with the quality of being a reaction ('I decided to go for a walk').

Interviewers and lawyers often miss such discontinuities.

17.3.1.5 Empty accounts An empty account is superficial, lacking detail in each of its component episodes. Such incongruity may go unnoticed because the 'thin' account evidences narrative continuity.

17.3.1.6 Measured disclosure This occurs when the witness discloses detail reactively. There is no spontaneous initiation of a topic or introduction of detail. He or she awaits the question and gives an answer that does not go beyond the confines of the question. There is no added information, no asides, commentary, or observations that are common to unrestrained disclosure.

17.3.1.7 Lack of emotion, sensation or response People vary in the extent to which they communicate emotion or sensation. When a witness reports — or exhibits — *no* emotion this is a potentially significant deficit. Emotion is communicated by many changes in non-verbal behaviour, e.g., self-grooming hand movements, called *adaptors*; tone of voice; silence, pausing and vocal dysfluencies (Shepherd, 1996a, 1996b).

Also noteworthy is lack of reference to an expected sensation, e.g., external and internal feelings of pain or discomfort occasioned by a sexual assault. Absence of illustrators indicating the location or the 'shape' or 'direction' of pain is also potentially significant.

Similarly significant is the absence of an expected response, e.g., a reaction — verbal or physical — to an assault.

17.3.1.8 Missing statements A statement, official document or interview may directly refer, or allude, to one or more individuals materially involved in the case prior to, or as part of, the investigation. However, it may not be noticed that, curiously, there are no statements from these individuals: they are 'non-barking dogs'.

17.3.2 Anomalous contrast

17.3.2.1 Incongruous use of language Vocabulary (lexicon), sentence construction (syntax) and verbal usage are liable to be anomalous. The language used in a critical part of an account, e.g., the description of evidentially significant material actions or appearance, may contrast with language use in the remainder of the witness's statement or responses.

Indirect reported speech may involve language use which contrasts with that in the greater part of the witness's account. When the utterance is converted into direct reported speech the difference in character becomes very apparent, suggesting the words originated from someone other than the witness.

17.3.2.2 Narrative contrast Narrative contrast occurs when different stages in the narrative are characterised by varying degrees of detail. Episodes that are over or under-detailed relative to others are potentially significant.

17.3.2.3 Extraordinary detail The amount and character of the detail in a description may be extraordinary, raising concerns as to the actual source of the detail, e.g., 'It was an 8-inch knife with a serrated blade, tapering to a point, and had a black handle about 2 inches long with two brass studs'.

17.3.3 Invalid descriptions
A description is necessarily invalid if it is counter to physical or psychological reality. Similarly invalid are assertions that are logical absurdities. There is a maxim in forensic psychology and psychiatry: what could not have happened did not happen.

17.3.4 Incongruous variation and contradiction

17.3.4.1 Inconsistency 'Internal inconsistency' refers to detail failing to agree, or converge, with other detail in an account. 'External inconsistency' refers to detail in an individual's account failing to agree, or converge with, detail in other accounts — whether given by the same individual at different times or by another individual or other individuals.

The PEACE model of police interviewing (National Crime Faculty, 1996) requires the officer to include in a statement any unresolved inconsistency with earlier accounts. This is rarely done (see chapter 9).

The detection of external consistency is particularly problematic where there are multiple statements, multiple documentary sources and multiple interviews.

17.3.4.2 Evolving descriptions The representation of reality gradually changes within an account or across two or more accounts, e.g., a 'light-coloured sweater' becomes a 'reddish sweater-type top', then a 'red tank top'.

With evolving descriptions there is often an incongruous change in ability to tell: e.g., a shift from certainty or precision to uncertainty and imprecision.

17.3.4.3 Differing versions An individual may give two or more wholly incompatible versions of an incident or a description. The process of drafting a s. 9 statement all too often prevents detection of this anomaly.

Different versions are potentially identifiable in recordings. However, akin to drafted s. 9 statements, written summaries, ROTIs and IVRIs tend to present an apparently coherent single account, obscuring different versions.

Detection is all the more difficult when two or more differing versions emerge across the course of one or more interviews.

17.3.4.4 Migrating detail Migration of detail occurs when significant narrative or descriptive detail disclosed in the statement or interview of one witness crops up in an account subsequently obtained from one or more other witnesses.

Migrating detail is difficult to detect when reading straight through a body of evidence in which statements (and transcribed or summarised interviews) are arranged according to the precedence assigned to each witness. Migration is much more readily detected by breaking up the bundle and placing all statements and interview texts in chronological sequence according to the date and time the witness made the statement or was interviewed.

17.3.4.5 Ratcheting This occurs in alternating interviewing of key witnesses. For example, in initial interview A gives an account. B in a subsequent interview somewhat modifies, altering or adding to, A's account. A is re-interviewed and somewhat modifies B's account. B is then re-interviewed and modifies A's second account. A is then re-interviewed and amends B's second version, and so on.

We term this phenomenon 'ratcheting' because, just as the pawl in a ratchet prevents the cogwheel going backwards, so the repeat interviewing process never allows a return to what witness A originally said. A dramatic example of ratcheting occurred in *R* v *Miller* (1993) 97 Cr App R 90 in more than 20 statements from two key witnesses who were alternately interviewed across a 10-month period.

17.3.5 The need for systematic collation and different ways of representing detail

Absurdity could be expected to be the most readily detected anomaly. People assume oddity will be readily apparent in detail currently being registered. It may be recognised, should subsequent detail reveal earlier unremarkable detail to be incongruous, but only so long as the antecedent detail is *still accessible in working memory*.

Paradoxically many odd, invalid or even absurd representations go unrecognised. A woman described, how after a drinking session, she was raped by her sister's common-law husband on a weightlifting bench in an outside shed. Her statement described how, when both were the worse for drink:

He opened the door to the main shed which is to the front of the shed. . . . There was a weightlifting bench just inside the door. The weight part was against the far wall, with the bench pointing towards the door. There was just enough room to open and close the door.

The shed door actually opened outwards. In fact very few shed doors swing in. Alarm bells should have rung for those taking or reading her account. They did not.

Discontinuity and incongruous variation are very much more difficult to detect, particularly within and across several texts. 'Non-barking dogs' which are *not* in the text, or in the body of evidence, are even more likely to go undetected. Detection rests upon:

(a) perception and registration of material, or its absence, as potentially salient or significant, and

(b) the ability to hold in working memory an extreme amount of noted detail (or lack of detail) whilst processing other material.

Most individuals cannot perform in this manner. An item of detail that does not immediately strike as salient or significant is liable to be lost with the mass of other subsequent unremarkable detail: it may be deleted, integrated with other detail, or incorporated in a generalisation. Subtle and even fundamental gaps, changes and contradictions risk going undetected. There is no antecedent detail in working memory against which to test detail being currently read, listened to or observed.

Lack of manifest incongruity, memory limitations and biased reduction and reconstruction of information prevent lawyers from identifying the spectrum of potential anomaly. They need methods which do not rely upon salience, make no demands on memory and enable them to retain, to collate and to represent detail — even the apparently unremarkable — in ways assisting the detection of anomaly within and across one or more written or spoken texts.

17.4 METHODS FOR IDENTIFYING ANOMALY IN EVIDENTIAL TEXT

17.4.1 Recreate what is being asserted

17.4.1.1 Image then draw a picture A lawyer should *minimally* create a detailed image in his or her mind's eye of what is being asserted, akin to constructing a set in a play and actions by those on the set. The next, essential, stage is to translate this image into reality, i.e., to draw a sketch of the envisaged set.

The sketch enables identification of critical gaps and the unstated. An anomalous lack of detail becomes apparent:

(a) if so much detail is missing that it is impossible to create an image or a sketch from the information given;

(b) if imagination is necessary to fill in that which is missing from the representation in the text.

The sketch can also be tested against reality by relating and comparing it with:

(a) any photography, video recording, or sketches produced in the body of evidence;

(b) the actual location;

(c) any material object or layout similar to that described.

An example: an allegation of rape
This is a continuation of the earlier example of the alleged rape on a weightlifting bench.

The woman said:

[He] pushed me down on to the end of the bench. . . . He put his hands on my shoulders and pushed me down so my head and shoulders were on the bench. My bottom was on the bench but my legs were over the edge with my knees bent and my feet were on the ground. . . . He put his knees on top of my knees so he was still upright but leaning on my knees with his knees. . . . I was holding on to the bench with my hands to stop myself falling off. He leant over me. He had hold of his penis in his right hand and his left hand was on my shoulder.

She described the rape during which time she said he was holding her 'upper arms'.

The bench on which the alleged rape took place was about a foot wide tapering to hinged, angled backrest. Like all such benches it was at a height from the ground that allowed a reclining person to have his or her thighs extended at an angle on either side with lower legs vertical to the ground. Imagery and a sketch (with two matchstick figures) indicated the degree of incongruity within her account.

They were both the worse for drink. The bench was exceedingly narrow. He was leaning on her knees with his knees, i.e., she was supporting him. Throughout he held on to her upper arms. This would have been physically impossible had she been holding on to either side of the narrow bench: suggesting that instead she had them extended above her head, holding on to the headboard. In this configuration, any voluntary or involuntary movement or stretching of either of her legs or arms would have occasioned him, if not both of them, to fall off.

These anomalies raised doubts concerning the absence of consent.

17.4.1.2   Recreate the representation   Recreating asserted detail is a potent test of its reality. If the re-creation shows something could not have happened in the way described, this permits argument that it did not happen.

Re-creation can be assisted by the lawyer's sketch and any other illustration or visual aid, which may or may not be in the body of evidence. Conducting an experiment, or a re-enactment (role-play), is best done through physical role-play, visiting and going over the ground, and, where necessary using (or improvising) props.

An example: an allegation of sexual assault
A young man alleged that, as he walked past an alleyway, he was grabbed from the rear by a man who held a knife to his throat. Still with the knife held to his throat he was then dragged backwards some distance over allotments to a shed. The man broke into the shed, opened the door and, having pushed the young man inside, committed a number of sexual acts upon him.

Role-play (which was photographed and video-recorded) confirmed a number of anomalies, already suggested by mental imagery.

(a)   If held in the manner described, the knife would have been to the back of his neck *not* to his throat.

(b)   It is physically impossible to drag a person in such a neck hold backwards over a considerable distance, and over uneven ground.

(c)   Detail was lacking. How did the man force the shed open? Did he retain hold of the young man around the neck? If so, how was the lock on the shed broken? If he released his hold what did he say, what did the young man do, and when the man attended to the task of breaking in why did the young man not simply run away?

17.4.2   Tabulation of detail (grids)
Tabulation is a simple method for collating and representing detail from one or more texts.

17.4.2.1   The basic format   The basic format is a grid.

• One column for each description or account examined.
• Columns are placed in chronological order of interview or statement production.

- Where applicable, there is an initial *index column* with *datum cells* that specify a particular aspect or area of detail or information within the descriptions or accounts.
- The intersection of columns with rows creates cells in which the relevant text of descriptions or accounts is entered.

Reading across rows enables identification of missing detail, inconsistency, evolving descriptions, differing versions, and, where there are accounts from more than one person, migrating detail and ratcheting. Reading down columns as well as across rows reveals narrative discontinuity, narrative contrast, empty accounts, and measured disclosure (e.g., in two or more statements by one witness).

Table 17.1 illustrates the construction of a grid from three statements. (Note: the statements could be from one individual on different occasions or three individuals.) The table reveals anomalies. The three statements failed to make mention of four episodes but the omissions were not the same in each case. Where there was common mention of detail across episodes there were instances of anomalous disagreement.

	Statement 1 – date	Statement 2 – date	Statement 3 – date
Episode 1	Detail	Detail (disagrees)	
Episode 2		Detail	Detail (agrees)
Episode 3	Detail		Detail (disagrees)
Episode 4	Detail		
Episode 5		Detail	Detail
Episode 6	Detail	Detail (agrees)	
Episode 7	Detail		Detail (disagrees)
Episode 8		Detail	
Episode 9			Detail

Table 17.1   Illustration of tabulating three statements

17.4.2.2   *Examples of tabulation*

A case of alleged sexual assault or rape
A 14-year-old girl had run away from home, staying out overnight. When found and taken home the next day she told her friend but not her parents that she had been sexually assaulted and raped. Across the next week she gave accounts to friends, teachers, a general practitioner, officers called to attend, and a woman detective in a child protection unit. A week after the alleged offence a detective arrested a 14-year-old boy who attended the same school as the girl.

Table 17.2 summarises the detail of the evolving description of her assailant. Note the datum line.

Source	CD (AB's friend)	EF (AB's best friend)	GH (Tutor: AB's school)	IJ (Deputy Head: AB's school)	KL (General practitioner)
Date [ref]	Wed 15 July [UnUM – p. 5]	Wed 15 July [UnUM – p. 3]	Thurs 16 July [UnUM – p. 3]	Thurs 16 July [UnUM – p. 2]	Thurs 16 July [UnUM – p. 1]
When AB spoke to witness	Sat 11 July 1630	Mon 13 July 0900	Mon 13 July 1050	Mon 13 July 1100-1200	Mon 13 July 1315
Age	Male, 19 to 25	Man	Lad about 17–18	Youth	Man
Height	5'7"–5'8"				
Build	well built				
Colour					
Hair	•light brown/ blonde •short				
Eyes					
Accent	•London accent •'definitely not local' (West country)				
Hat	•black hat •with 'logo on the front'				
Coat/jacket	•brown coloured waist length jacket •waterproof in places •'brown patches' •writing/pattern on back				
Shirt	white				
Trousers	black 'trousers'				
Footwear	shoes				
Ability to recognise attacker again				AB says she cannot remember enough about the youth to report it to the police	

Table 17.2 Tabulation of details from a sequence of accounts

MN AB's friend)	OP (Tutor: AB's school)	WPC Q and PC R (FOAs) Log	Progress sheet [signature illegible]	Video int of AB by WDC S IVRI	DC T (Arresting officer + IO) Pocket book
Sun 19 July [UnUM – p. 2]	Thurs 16 July [UnUM – pp. 4–5]	Tues 14 July [UnUM – p. 8]	Tues 14 July [UnUM – p. 10]	Wed 15 July [CB – pp. 11-38]	Sat 18 July [UnUM – p. 11]
Tues 14 July after break	Tues 14 July afternoon	Tues 14 July about 2200	Tues 14 July	N/A	N/A
Man	Lad	No description taken!!	Youth about 17	17–18	Boy, 14
				5'6"	5'9"-5'10"
	strong			skinny	skinny
			white	white	
	•blonde •short		blonde	•'light - like blonde' •quite short	•dark brown •normal length
				•light •'maybe blue'	brown
				•Northern •London cockney accent •'not strong'	Strong local (West country)
	hat		baseball hat	•black hat •tight fitted to the head with a band turned up •with a person on it (with a red top on and wearing a hat)	No hat on arrest - search found: •black wool hat with motif (man lying down) •black wool hat with motif of man sitting up
				•tawny/fawny coloured 'coat', quite short •poss. half leather/half material, normal coat material, poss. •padded cotton on arm/back •'bomber type jacket'	•*plain* fawn bomber type jacket, single material [when arrested] •*no* other jacket [established from search]
				•blue checked •blue and white checked, poss. quite thick material	•beige [when arrested] •green shirt (from search)
			blue jeans	•black 'trousers' •quite baggy	•black jeans [when arrested] •black trousers (from search)
				poss. trainers — dark	•black trainers (when arrested) •pair of LA gear black boots (from search)
	AB says: •she does not know the lad •she would recognise him again		•AB cannot provide any further description of the youth •AB 'might only' be able to recognise him again	AB says she has never seen him before	

The police did not identify the anomalies. Hence she was not questioned about these nor did the police recognise the need to apply the final ADVOKATE criterion (see chapter 9).

A case of murder
Although not twins, two brothers were almost identical in features. One was the driver of a van, the other the front passenger. Their friend was in the back. Whilst the van was stationary a heated exchange began with three youths standing on the pavement. A car drew up behind, occupied by five young men who were friends of those on the pavement. The van and car occupants got out and an altercation took place. One of the van occupants went to the van and returned with a knife. The group scattered. One of the car occupants was pursued, stabbed and fatally wounded.

The three men drove off in the van and were subsequently arrested. The seven others gave descriptions of the appearance and actions of the van occupants, particularly the one with the knife.

Table 17.3 summarises a grid constructed from the witnesses' statements. To simplify the table, the grid does not include the actual detail.

Because the police failed to draw up a grid they were unable to compare systematically the detail of the seven witnesses' statements. A grid subsequently drawn up by the defence revealed wide divergences between their accounts and descriptions, particularly of the man who wielded the knife.

17.4.3   THEMA: thematic emergence of anomaly in interview narrative

Narratives and conversations are characterised by topic progression. The text (in the case of an interview, a question–answer exchange) focuses on a topic, perhaps covering a number of sub-topics before the topic is changed.

Following initial mention of a topic (or sub-topic), an immediate development to what has been said or any later development by recursion to the subject matter creates second and subsequent mentions. Taken together these mentions constitute a 'theme'. Tabulation of topics and their developments enables the identification of themes and emergent anomaly within these by comparing the detail of first and subsequent mentions.

We originally developed a grid method called THEMA (thematic emergence of anomaly) to conduct this form of analysis on one or more video and audio-recorded interviews. It can also be applied to transcripts.

17.4.3.1   The materials required   We find it easiest to work with a combination of recording and full interview transcript. In addition we have made a number of refinements to the basic method, harnessing the abilities of recent developments in word-processing and spreadsheet software. However, any professional wishing to detect anomaly in emergent themes in a recording, whether or not aided by a full transcript, can conduct a simple THEMA analysis, either by hand or using a word processor. We instruct police officers on advanced investigative interviewing courses how to conduct manual

	WITNESS 1	WITNESS 2	WITNESS 3	WITNESS 4	WITNESS 5	WITNESS 6	WITNESS 7
DRIVER							
Description							
Actions							
FRONT PASSENGER							
Description							
Actions							
REAR PASSENGER							
Description							
Actions							

Table 17.3   Form of tabulation of the descriptions and actions of three men given by seven witnesses

THEMA analyses of tape-recorded interviews in order to prepare for subsequent interviewing.

17.4.3.2 The basic concept   The first column represents the first mention of detail on specific topics — or sub-topics within a topic. The second column represents the second mention — development or expansion — of detail on a topic (or sub-topic), the third further mention, and so on.

The cells contain both the witness's utterances and the interviewer's, e.g., a triggering question.

There is no limit to the number of cells which can be devoted to a topic. As many cells as are thought appropriate may be opened.

Reading across cells enables detection of:

(a)   absence of detail in first and subsequent mentions;
(b)   emergent variation and contradiction;
(c)   problematic interviewer behaviour, such as:

(i)   an antecedent question, comment or assertion influencing or shaping the interviewee's response;

(ii)   misrepresentation of an interviewee's prior response, or responses.

Table 17.4 illustrates a THEMA grid. For the sake of simplicity actual text is not included.

	First mention	Second mention	Third mention	Fourth mention
Topic 1	Text	Text (same)	Text (different)	
Topic 2	Text			
Topic 3	Text	Text (different)	Text (same as second)	Text (same as first)
Topic 4	Text	Text (same)		
Topic 5	Text			
Topic 6	Text			
Topic 7	Text	Text (different)		
Topic 8	Text	Text (same)	Text (same)	Text (different)
And so on				

Table 17.4   Example of a THEMA grid

Table 17.4 shows that, as the interview progressed, the individual gave anomalously differing versions in respect of four topics.

17.4.3.3   An example   A juvenile was arrested for the indecent assault of the seven-year-old sister of one of his friends. She alleged he had been 'rude'. She was interviewed and re-interviewed several months later.

THEMA analysis of the video-recorded interviewing of the child indicated a lack of spontaneity and measuring of responses. Her accounts were relatively empty, lacked narrative continuity, lacked core narrative detail and contained no reference to any verbal exchange taking place. Despite a chaotic topic sequence, attributable in great measure to the interviewer's lack of skill, THEMA analysis revealed to the defence — and the prosecution — that the child actually gave not one but five accounts.

- Version 1: She did not know how the juvenile was 'rude'.
- Version 2: She said nothing happened.
- Version 3: She said nothing happened after the juvenile put his tongue in her mouth.
- Version 4: The juvenile engaged in cunnilingus after he put his tongue in her mouth.
- Version 5: She could not remember what happened after the juvenile put his tongue in her mouth.

Further advice on how to conduct a simple THEMA analysis on recordings or transcripts, either manually or using a word processor, is at appendix 1. You may wish to read this before proceeding to the next section.

17.4.4 SE3R: a graphic method for representing narrative detail

SE3R (S — E — three R) is used in the police service and by investigators in the public and private sectors. It represents narrative detail graphically, facilitating rapid analysis and assisting storage in memory of this detail. SE3R is a mnemonic, specifying the steps involved in achieving these two aims: skim, extract, read, review, and recall.

17.4.4.1 The basic concept SE3R has the following key features:

(a) It is applicable to written or recorded texts from one or more individuals.
(b) It translates text into an immediately grasped graphic representation. Figure 17.1 is a fragment from an SE3R, illustrating:

(i) the *event line* representing episodic detail of events in chronological order;
(ii) *identity bins*: 'index card'-like representations of information concerning people, entities, and locations.

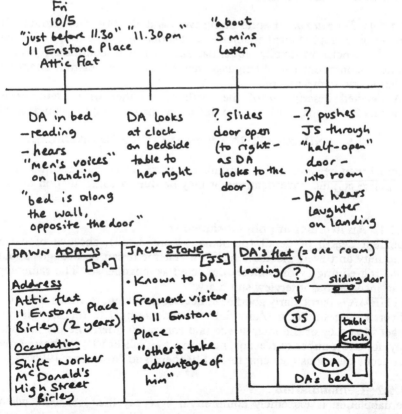

Figure 17.1 Illustration of SE3R detail

17.4.4.2 Episodic detail Figure 17.1 shows how a vertical line represents each event. Date, time and location detail is recorded above the line; episodic detail on actors, entities, actions, reactions, conversations and the like is entered below the line.

The original evidential text is subjected to five mapping rules. These facilitate the detection of anomaly whilst preserving the character of the original text:

(a) converting the first person into the third person;
(b) ensuring all pronouns are unambiguous;
(c) converting the past tense into the present;
(d) converting the passive voice into the active;
(e) converting indirect reported speech into direct.

17.4.4.3 Identity detail Figure 17.1 shows how an identity bin can contain descriptive text or a sketch, the product of the image recreated in the mind's eye of the reader, listener or observer from the detail disclosed by the witness — with the benefits described earlier in this section.

17.4.4.4 The outcome Representing event and identity detail, from multiple sources, in a graphic form enables identification of a wide range of anomaly, e.g., deficiencies in detail, sequential and logical discontinuity, empty accounts, incongruous use of language, narrative contrast, extraordinary detail, variation and contradiction.

A detailed description of the method, together with examples is in appendix 2. You may wish to read this before proceeding to the next section.

17.5 EXPLANATIONS FOR DETECTED ANOMALY

Anomaly can be explained in a number of ways: it may be a result of the way the police conduct investigations, it may be due to confabulation or deception.

17.5.1 An artefact of police behaviour

Apparent dearth of detail (particularly core detail), absence of narrative continuity and even inconsistency in a statement can be brought about by maladroit editing by the officer who acted as amanuensis. The same applies to an incongruous interview summary.

THEMA is particularly good at indicating the extent to which interviewing officers create anomaly. Many fail to listen carefully to the interviewee, or forget what they or the interviewee said earlier. Furthermore the interviewee may, for any number of reasons, not correct an officer who mishears or poses erroneous questions (see chapter 4; Shepherd and Mortimer, 1995).

17.5.2 Confabulation

Confabulation is extremely common in everyday life. It occurs when an individual says something spontaneously to fill in a gap in his or her experience. It is *not* lying, although all too many lawyers and judges view confabulation and deception as synonymous.

The appropriate response to confabulation is to confront the individual, questioning empathetically. If the individual persists with the confabulation this raises doubt about validity and reliability.

17.5.3 Deception

17.5.3.1 Missing detail Grid and THEMA analyses as well as SE3R are particularly good at highlighting the various guises of missing detail: paucity of detail, lack of narrative continuity, narrative contrast and, of course, 'non-barking dogs'.

As pointed out above missing detail may well be an artefact of police behaviour. However, where this appears not to be the case then missing detail is a potential pointer to deception, since evasion is the most common, effortless, form of lying (Ekman, 1985).

17.5.3.2 Understatement and overstatement The analyses we have described highlight understatement and overstatement, which are both potential indicators of deception. Here the individual seeks to obscure deliberately by speaking in generalities (Ekman, 1985).

17.5.3.3 Active deception Active deception involves the conscious, strategic representation of an untruth as the truth. It takes effort. The individual has to negotiate a number of hurdles:

(a) He or she must avoid wishful thinking and anticipate being questioned.

(b) An effort has to be expended in preparing a storyline whose parameters — start and finish — must cover not only the material time but also an appropriate span on either side.

(c) The constructed account must have an appropriate degree of identity and episodic detail, describing actions, thoughts, feelings, and utterances, particularly in conversations. The liar must be a good raconteur, engaging in asides, commentary and disclosing minutiae. He or she must be able to reduce the risk of narrative contrast by extending the parameters, giving detail concerning even earlier or later events.

(d) The liar must have a good memory and rehearse continuously. He or she must avoid being too pat — making minor errors concerning peripheral detail, but ensuring that he or she corrects these immediately to ensure that no anomaly is detected, pre-empting any questions and reducing the risk of suspicion.

Systematic methods of collation and representation enable detection of individuals who are likely to be falling at one of these hurdles. They highlight anomalies potentially indicative of an unprepared individual or one unable to hold the detail of his or her deception in memory.

17.6 BARRIERS TO SYSTEMATIC APPROACHES TO THE DETECTION OF ANOMALY

In addition to assisting the detection of anomaly the systematic methods we have described also facilitate preparation for, and actual, cross-examination. However, despite these attributes many lawyers will view the methods as alien. For them close reading, a practised eye and a good enough, if not good, memory are sufficient to detect anomaly.

The methods do take time: time above and beyond that devoted to normal processing of evidential text. They are objective adjuncts to analysis rather than a substitute for established approaches.

Those who practise law and administer justice place great worth upon subjective assessment of evidential text. Anomalies revealed by systematic analyses and which question the validity of subjective assessments made in ignorance of these are wholly unwanted. It is to be hoped that those who administer justice will resist dismissing the use of systematic techniques, and their outcome, as an inappropriate, counter-productive waste of time and effort.

17.7 SUMMARY

(a) Lawyers and judges are tasked with detecting anomaly in evidential text. They prefer written text but have to cope with more challenging recordings.

(b) Substantial barriers to the detection of anomaly are the nature of text, how evidence is organised, and the psychological processes underlying reading, listening and observing.

(c) Anomaly can emerge in many forms in written and recorded evidential text. These include: deficient descriptions, failure to identify key individuals, conversational deficits, sequential and logical discontinuity, empty accounts, measured disclosure, lack of emotion, sensation or response, missing statements, incongruous use of language, narrative contrast, extraordinary detail, invalid descriptions, inconsistency, evolving descriptions, differing versions, migrating detail and ratcheting.

(d) Systematic methods for collating and representing evidential detail — recreating the image, tabulation, THEMA and SE3R — enhance the likelihood of detecting such anomalies by avoiding the bias, reduction and reconstruction of conventional information processing.

(e) Anomaly may be an artefact of police behaviour or may be the product of confabulation, or a failure in one of the forms of deception — evasion, overstatement, understatement, and active lying.

(f) Systematic methods for detecting anomaly may not be entirely welcome.

Key words
Anomaly; evidential text; grids; SE3R (skim, extract, read, review, recall); tabulation; THEMA (thematic emergence of anomaly).

References

Clark, H. and Clark, E. (1997), *Psychology and Language*. New York: Harcourt Brace Jovanovich.

Ede, R., and Shepherd, E. (1997), *Active Defence*. London: Law Society.

Ekman, P. (1985), *Telling Lies*. New York: Norton.

Halliday, M. (1987), Spoken and written modes of meaning. In R. Horowitz and S. Samuels (eds), *Comprehending Oral and Written Language*. San Diego, CA: Academic Press.

National Crime Faculty (1996), *Investigative Interviewing: A Practical Guide*. Bramshill: Police Staff College.

Shepherd, E. (1996a), *Becoming Skilled*, 2nd ed.. London: Law Society.

Shepherd, E. (1996b), *A Pocket Reference*, 2nd ed.. London: Law Society.

Shepherd, E. and Mortimer, A. (1995), 'Putting testimony to the test', *Practitioners' Child Law Bulletin*, vol. 8, No. 4, pp. 44–6.

van Dijk, T. and Kintsch, W. (1983), *Strategies of Discourse Comprehension*. New York: Academic Press.

Recommended reading

Ede, R. and Shepherd, E. (1997), *Active Defence*. London: Law Society.

Editors' notes

We recommend that this chapter be read in conjunction with *Active Defence* (see under 'recommended reading'). Of all chapters this illustrates most clearly the importance of obtaining unexpurgated and complete records of investigators' interviews with witnesses which, as we argue elsewhere, can only be achieved through recording.

Two factors have a potential to affect the fine-grain analysis of a witness's recorded account provided prior to testimony: the identification of the witness's physical and psychological vulnerabilities, and the availability of relevant source material.

APPENDIX 17.A1
THEMA ANALYSIS

17.A1.1 What to put in the THEMA

17.A1.1.1 The text You need to enter the text of utterances by the interviewer as well as the interviewee. Also enter absence of replies, non-verbal behaviours (both vocal and non-vocal), and instances of overtalking and interruption.

17.A1.1.2 Keeping track You need to keep track of the material. Enter in the cell the reading of the start of the first utterance. This reading can be either the time shown on the audio-transcriber (remember to set it to zero at the outset!), on the time line on the video-recording, or (least efficient) the trip meter of a cassette player if this is the only machine you have.

If you are using a cassette player with a trip meter, do a calibration: noting how many seconds equate to a particular number of revolutions of the trip meter. With this you can convert a trip meter reading into minutes and seconds. There will be a margin of error but it will not be very great.

17.A1.2 Manual THEMA analysis

17.A1.2.1 Size of the grid The number of topics (or sub-topics) and number of mentions are necessarily unknown at the outset of the analysis. The initial size of the grid at the outset is therefore arbitrary. It should be able to extend downwards as more topics and sub-topics emerge, and it should have a sufficient number of columns to accommodate at least three or four mentions.

When conducting a manual analysis the cells should be large enough to account for varying amounts of text across a run of mentions.

An effective, flexible solution is a photocopied pro forma (A4 or A3 sheets on their side) with three or four pre-drawn columns and some four or five rows, creating conveniently large cells (see figure 17.A1.1).

Leave plenty of white space below text which you enter into a cell. If you find you are wanting to put a lot of text into a cell it is likely that the material covers more than one sub-topic. Look for where the sub-topic ends. When the next sub-topic starts simply enter this in next cell below. And so on.

Leaving 'white space' after text in the cell gives you flexibility when dealing with later mentions. If a subsequent mention generates more text on a topic or sub-topic, you will be able accommodate this. Similarly, if a subsequent mention generates material on a new sub-topic (i.e., covers matters not raised in an earlier mention), simply draw a line across beneath the text of the previous sub-topic thus creating a new row (see figure 17.A1.2). In doing this THEMA operates to highlight that in previous mentions there was no reference to this subject matter (a potential anomaly). It also creates subsequent cells able to accommodate any further mention of the sub-topic.

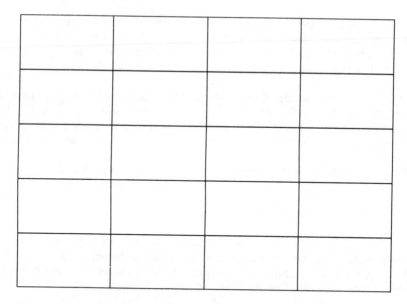

Figure 17.A1.1   THEMA pro forma

Text	Text	Text	
Text	Text		
Text	Text	Text	
Text	Text	Text	Text
		Text (new sub-topic)	Text
Text	Text		

Figure 17.A1.2   Creating a new row to accommodate text on a sub-topic raised for the first time in a later mention

When you have filled the first column of cells continue to another THEMA pro forma, and so on.

17.A1.2.2 Immediate expansion If there is an immediate expansion of a topic, e.g., the interviewer asks a probing question, enter the text in the next column in the cell adjacent to the previous mention. When the topic changes revert to the first column, entering the text in the next blank cell.

17.A1.2.3 Subsequent expansions With each mention (expansion) enter the text in the next available column — in the next available cell in the row containing material on this theme. If the text covers material on a new sub-topic, i.e., not mentioned before, then create a row in the manner described above.

When the number of mentions exceeds the column capacity of a pro forma sheet attach a blank pro forma to the side of the first sheet (with a strip of adhesive tape), thus doubling the number of columns. If further mentions occur then add another sheet, and so on.

17.A1.2.3 Reducing the size of the THEMA As with any tabulated representation, having completed the analysis the sheets can be reduced in size using a photocopier with an appropriate facility. Affixing sheets to an A1 flip chart allows a large amount of detail to be examined at once.

17.A1.3 THEMA using a word-processing program
THEMA analysis using a PC (desktop or portable) with the spreadsheet or cells option of a word-processing program is extremely easy.

17.A1.3.1 Size of grid Open up a grid with an arbitrary number of columns and rows, e.g., five by five. The depth of a cell adjusts automatically. When you reach the final cell of the first column open up more rows.

17.A1.3.2 Initial expansion Proceed to the next column, putting text in the appropriate adjacent cell.

17.A1.3.3 Subsequent expansions Create additional columns as required. Extra columns can be fitted to the page by adjusting column width and reducing font size.

If the text covers material on a new sub-topic, i.e., not mentioned before, then insert a row.

17.A1.3.4 Reducing the size of the THEMA The facility to reduce font size provides great flexibility. As indicated above, affixing reduced sheets to an A1 flip chart allows a large amount of detail to be examined at once.

17.A1.4 Working with a recording alone

17.A1.4.1 Initial processing Listen to, or observe, the recording straight through *at least once* without stopping. This will enable you to gain a coherent, overall grasp of the total narrative and a 'feel' for the progression of topics. A second play will give you an even greater grasp of material. You will find that you 'know' what is coming next, when topics change, and be able to register more since you will be listening, and looking, more intently.

This initial processing will enable you to note when key disclosures begin, i.e., the point at which you will want to start your THEMA analysis.

17.A1.4.2 Conducting the THEMA analysis Identify the point at which the first topic begins, enter the timer reading and then the text in the first cell. Press the pause button when you feel you have a comfortable amount of text in working memory and need to enter this in the cell. Do not hold too much in memory. This will tire you. Most people can hold two or three simple sentences in working memory. You will find, however, that with greater practice — doing THEMA analyses — your will develop an ability to hold increasing amounts of verbatim text in memory.

When the topic ends or a sub-topic emerges, enter the timer reading in the next cell down and then enter the text, and so on.

17.A1.5 Working with a transcript

17.A1.5.1 Initial processing Skim-read through the transcript (at slightly faster than your normal speed), without stopping. This will enable you to gain a coherent, overall grasp of the total narrative and a 'feel' for the progression of topics.

17.A1.5.2 Identifying topic progression Re-read at your normal speed. This gives the same benefits as a second replay of a recording.

Note where disclosure of evidential significance starts. Draw a short line above the text. Read on until the topic ends then draw a line below the text. Read on until the topic ends, and so on. Some people like to number topics or even give them a short keyword heading to capture the theme.

17.A1.5.3 Conducting a THEMA analysis Having marked up the topic progression, return to the beginning and conduct a manual or word-processor-assisted THEMA analysis.

17.A1.5.4 Making the task even easier If you have a computer file copy of the transcript, marking up topic progression and THEMA analysis is extremely easy. A computer file can be obtained from the individual or firm producing the transcript. Alternatively, if no file exists, one can be created by passing the transcript through an optical scanner.

Using a block (cell) facility, topics can be easily delineated, ready for transposition into a THEMA grid using copy and paste commands.

APPENDIX 17.A2
SE3R:
A METHOD FOR REPRESENTING AND ANALYSING
NARRATIVE TEXT

17.A2.1 The application of SE3R

SE3R can be applied to any narrative text, whether in the form of a written document, such as a statement or transcript, or a recording, e.g., of an interview.

Because it is extremely easy to apply SE3R to written text, it is helpful to learn, and to gain confidence, by initially practising on documents.

17.A2.2 The materials you need

You need:

(a) Blank paper, in landscape orientation. A4 photocopying paper or lined notepad on its side is convenient.

Many experienced users of SE3R use A3 size. The added space makes it easier to represent detail arising from two or more versions in one account or from two or more accounts.

However, any size of paper can be used, e.g., the authors use a spiral-bound shorthand pad to capture contemporaneously detail in SE3R format when conducting or observing an actual interview, particularly a cognitive interview.

Some investigators, particularly in the police service, use SE3R pro formas with an event line and identity bins already printed on A4 sized paper (see figure 17.A2.1).

Some investigators use A4/legal notebooks with an event line pre-drawn on every page.

(b) A notepad to record any questions or queries raised as you apply SE3R.

(c) Pens of more than one colour. This allows you to differentiate, according to colour, the detail of different versions in one account or drawn from two or more accounts. For example, black ink = first version/first account, blue = second, red = third, green = fourth, pencil = fifth.

17.A2.3 Procedural basics

(a) Put documents in chronological order. If you need to work on more than one document, identify the chronological order in which they were generated. Conduct your analyses according to this identified sequence.

(b) Apply the method to one document at a time. Resist the urge to work on more than one document at once.

(c) Enter reference detail. Put core reference information on the front sheet, e.g., in the top right corner. Typical information includes:

(i) Type of document, e.g., written statement, pocketbook entry, custody record.

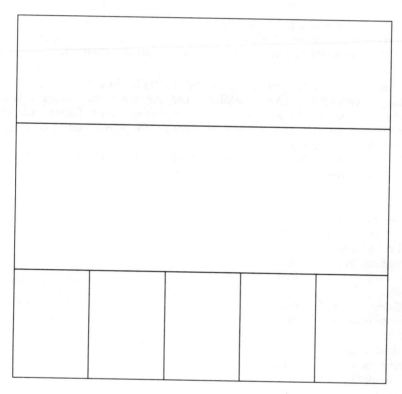

Figure 17.A2.1   SE3R pro forma

(ii)   Page numbers, i.e., those assigned by the CPS in disclosed evidence.

(iii)   Number of pages.

(iv)   Its position in terms of sequence of production if it is a second or subsequent document derived from the witness.

(v)   Provenance of the document, i.e., date, time and place the document was produced.

(vi)   Identity of the narrative giver, e.g., the person making the statement.

(vii)   Where applicable details of the amanuensis, i.e., the person who wrote down the document on behalf of the narrative giver.

(d)   Paginate each sheet.

(e)   How you lay out information in the space available to you affects your ability to grasp detail, and to commit this to — and to retrieve it from — memory.

There are many ways in which to make detail clear and memorable:

(i)   Underline surnames.

(ii)   Try not to squash in detail.
(iii) Be as neat as possible.
(iv)   Use white space, i.e., try to separate out information.

Abbreviation enables you to capture more detail, more quickly.

Many investigators, like journalists, use speed-writing systems, which commonly drop out the vowels (a - e - i - o - u) in words. Experiment with abbreviating words in this manner. Remember the word should be reliably recoverable from its abbreviated form.

Use abbreviations for high-frequency words — there is nothing to stop you devising your own (but remember to be consistent).

Examples of useful abbreviations are:

also known as	aka
appropriate adult	AA
Birmingham	Bham
daughter of	d/o
forward	fwd
left	l
officer	offr
pocketbook	pb
right	r
sexual assault	sa
somebody	sb
something	st
son of	s/o
statement	stat
victim	vm
with	w
witness	wit

Abbreviate the names of key people in the narrative, e.g.:

Beth	B
Chalky	C
Gary	G

Be careful that you do not use the same letter for two people whose names start with that letter. In such a case use two letters, e.g., first and second name.

Where a text refers to individuals who are not named assign a number to these individuals, starting at 1 for the first.

Where appropriate use symbols, e.g.:

→	to; towards; forwards
←	back; backwards
↔	back and forth; to and fro

↓   down; downwards
↑   up; upwards
↕   up and down

(f)   Qualifying utterances must always be noted.

- If the narrative giver says 'about', write 'about' e.g., 'about 2 p.m.'.
- If the narrative giver uses a form of words locating the event in time, write the actual words used, e.g., 'soon after' 'as he was leaving'.
- If the narrative giver qualifies a detail, i.e., saying he or she is 'not sure' or words to this effect, put the letters 'NS' after the qualified detail.
- If the narrative giver says he or she 'does not know' or words to this effect, use the letters 'NK' by the category of detail, e.g., 'date NK', 'loc NK', 'speaker NK'.

(g)   Highlight the manifestly incongruous. Always note anomaly, using whatever notation suits you, e.g.:

(i)   Missing detail: signified by a double question mark, ??, or a question mark in brackets, (?).

(ii)   Odd or doubtful detail: signified by a double exclamation mark !! or a exclamation mark in brackets (!).

17.A2.4   Conducting SE3R on a single written text

S — Skim
This involves a first reading of the text from beginning to end without stopping at an even, steady pace, rather quicker than your normal reading speed.
   Resist the following temptations:

(a)   to stop your flow to dwell on some details rather than others, i.e., that which strikes you as noteworthy;
(b)   to glance forward;
(c)   to look back to reread, or check, what you have just read or something earlier in the document;
(d)   to stop, in order to memorise a significant detail.

Approaching text in this manner will give you an overall awareness and coherent grasp of the content of the text. With practice you will become very proficient at getting a rapid and substantive 'feel' of the narrative and how it emerged, i.e., the key stages (and their order), key topics and themes, how these were raised and by whom.

E — Extract
This involves going back to the beginning and methodically reading through the text, registering the detail and extracting this into SE3R format.

Create an event line. If you are working with blank paper, draw a line about two thirds up the page, extending all the way from left to right across its entire width (figure 17.A2.2).

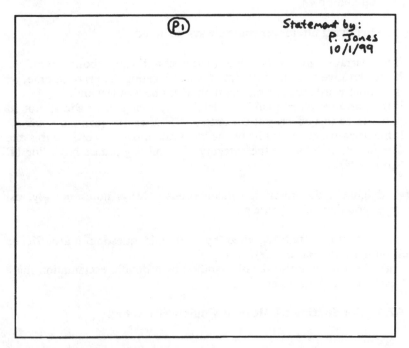

Figure 17.A2.2   Relative location of *event line* on notepad.

Map event detail. Starting at the beginning of the document:

(a)   identify each event as it appears in the narrative,
(b)   map each event chronologically on to your event line,
(c)   record episodic detail connected with the event, e.g., detail on people, entities and locations.

Mapping events
When you identify an event draw a vertical line which cuts the event line (figure 17.A2.3).
Each cutting line is an event.
You need to create some space between one cut and the next. Practice will enable you to find what spacing suits you but in the initial stages experiment with a gap of just over an inch (or about three centimetres).

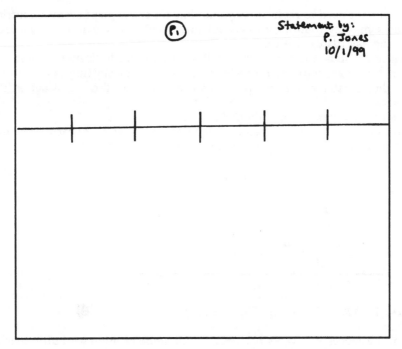

Figure 17.A2.3 Events cutting the *event line* (NB: Details of events not shown.)

Temporal and location detail
Write temporal and location details above the vertical line. Imagine you are writing the detail in a column or block of white space.

Be consistent in the order of detail. The most sensible order is descending: day, date, time, geographical location, more specific location, e.g., room (figure 17.A2.4).

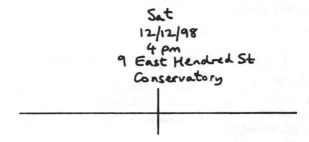

Figure 17.A2.4 Temporal and location detail

You do not need to replicate day and date for subsequent events occurring on the same day (date). Simply omit this detail but remember to indicate when the day (date) changes.

In a continuous stream of activity following an initial indication of time text does not normally indicate a time for each 'step'. Typically time is mentioned when the narrator wishes to specify this in respect of the next stage in the narrative.

Enter time phrases (e.g., 'about 11') verbatim.

Indicate duration by a bracket extending to the right towards the next event. Write above the bracket the duration (figure 17.A2.5).

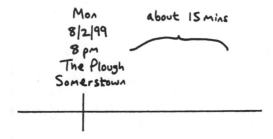

Figure 17.A2.5   Duration of an event

Indicate successive events occurring in the same location with ditto marks, i.e., ', or a simple dash or hyphen.

Episodic detail
Enter episodic detail on *actors*, *entities*, *actions* and *reactions* below the vertical line. Again imagine you are writing the detail in a column or block of white space (figure 17.A2.6).

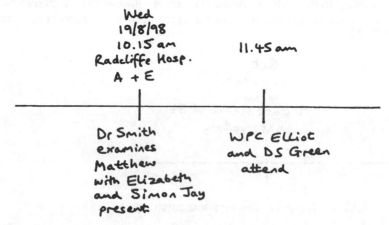

Figure 17.A2.6   Episodic detail

Apply the basic conversion rules
Apply the following rules to create a clear representation that reveals anomaly.

Rule 1. Convert the first person into third person
The aim is to present the teller's narrative as an objective clear account. Furthermore if the words 'I' and 'me' were retained, when more than one account is entered on an SE3R, it would become confusing.

Hence, in a statement by Trevor Jones any reference to 'I' becomes 'TJ' (or 'J' or 'Trevor'), and 'me' becomes 'him'. Similarly any reference to 'we' or 'us' is made clear, e.g. as 'TJ and AM', and as 'they'.

Rule 2. Ensure all pronouns are unambiguous
When the narrator uses a pronoun to refer to an individual:

(a)   make clear that you know to whom the narrator is referring;
(b)   if it is clear, spell this out in the first instance, e.g., 'they' or 'them' become 'EH and MB';
(c)   if is it not clear to you who 'they' or 'them' refers to then indicate this oddity, i.e., 'they' (??).

Rule 3. Turn the past tense into present tense
Convert text in the past tense into the present tense, e.g., in a statement by Trevor:

Text in statement:

   I saw Tracy sitting on Ian's lap.

SE3R entry:

   Trevor sees Tracy sitting on Ian's lap.

This conversion from past into present is crucial:

(a)   It coincides with our underlying mental processes, i.e., transforming a verbal image of a past occurrence into a current, visual, image (though some people may not be conscious of doing this) (Clark and Clark, 1977).
(b)   It makes the narrative more real and more memorable, i.e., an account of actions in the present time is easier to picture and therefore easier to remember.
(c)   It highlights earlier events which should be mapped on to the event line in the appropriate chronological position, e.g.,

Text in statement:

   George decided to do something about it after what we found out a couple of days earlier.

SE3R isolates two events:

   (i)   an earlier event:

      a couple of days earlier — we (??) find out (??).

   (ii) this event:

      George decides to do something having found out (??) (a couple of days earlier).

SE3R has thus highlighted potential anomalies, raising a range of questions needing to be answered:

   (1)   To whom does 'we' refer?
   (2)   What was found out?
   (3)   How? From where or from whom? When?
   (4)   What was it exactly that led George to decide to do something?

Rule 4. Turn the passive voice into the active voice
For example, in a statement by Peggy:

Text in statement:

      Lucy was comforted by me and my mum.

SE3R entry:

      Peggy and her mother comfort Lucy.

Conversion from passive to active is very helpful:

   (a)   It coincides with our underlying mental processes, i.e., we rearrange the passive into an active construction (though some people may not be conscious of doing this).
   (b)   It makes the narrative more real and more memorable, i.e., an account of actions in the present time is easier to picture and therefore easier to remember.
   (c)   The passive voice can obscure wittingly or unwittingly detail of forensic significance, e.g., in a statement by Sean:

Text in statement:

      They were all standing round the bed. He was being assaulted. Then I was pulled forward. I had to do the same as what was done to him. They threatened to kill me.

SE3R reveals:

> They are all standing round the bed.
> ?? is/are assaulting him(?).
> ?? pulls/pull Sean forward.
> Sean has to do the same (??) as ?? did to him.
> ?? threatens/threaten to kill Sean.

SE3R highlights the obscuring property of the passive and raises questions concerning:

(i)   The identity of the person/persons carrying out the assault.
(ii) The nature of the assault.
(iii) The identity of the person/persons pulling Sean forward.
(iv) The actions which Sean describes as 'the same'.
(v)   The identity of the person/persons threatening to kill Sean.

Rule 5. Turn indirect reported speech into direct reported speech
Turn indirect reported speech into direct reported speech and put quotation marks around the utterance, e.g., in Trevor's statement:

Text in statement:

> Tracy was very upset and said to me Uncle Ian had done something awful to her.

SE3R entry:

> Tracy is very upset and says to Trevor: 'Uncle Ian has done something awful to me'.

Conversion from indirect to direct reported speech is very helpful:

(a)   If the revealed use of words and phraseology appear 'out of character' with the provenance, personality and development of the person who purportedly uttered them this raises the question: where did the odd language come from?

(b)   Police officers acting in the role of amanuensis have a tendency to use 'police speak', rephrasing what the individual actually said into much more complex verbal constructions, ponderous phraseology, 'highfaluting', 'difficult' or 'long' (polysyllabic) words, as well as technical words (particularly describing the action in legal terms). Children are particularly at risk of having their accounts obscured and refined in this manner, especially their reported speech.

(c)   Some tellers use ponderous words and phraseology that they would not use in everyday conversation. Their reasons for doing this differ. The process of giving a statement may overwhelm them. They may see the statement rather like doing a piece of assessed 'school' work. They may want to avoid giving detail (for any number of innocent or guilty reasons).

The following example illustrates how applying this conversion rule reveals such anomaly:

Text in statement:

> Jennifer told me she had been sexually assaulted by Mr Piggot in his room. She said Mr Piggot fondled her repeatedly about her private parts and then asked her to fellate him.

SE3R entry:

> Jennifer tells Kylie: 'I have been sexually assaulted (??) by Mr Piggot in his room'.
> Jennifer says: 'Mr Piggot fondled me repeatedly about my private parts (??) and then asked me to fellate (??) him'.

SE3R thus brings to the fore the necessity to check exactly what Jennifer said to Kylie.

Representing simultaneous events, actions and reactions
List each simultaneous action, each action being preceded by a hyphen (figure 17.A2.7).

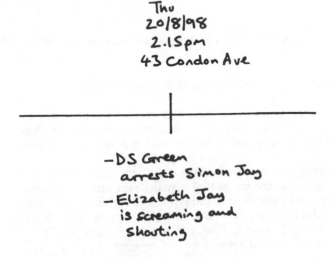

Figure 17.A2.7 Simultaneous events

If the narrative describes two (or more) events as happening in different locations, create a second event line and enter detail in exactly the same manner on this second line.

If more lines are needed, just create these in parallel. These parallel lines only need to be used as long as is necessary to include the simultaneous activity (figure 17.A2.8).

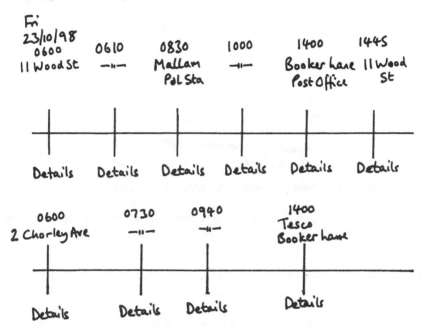

Figure 17.A2.8   Events occurring in different locations

NB: For the sake of simplicity actual details are omitted.

Representing dialogue

(a)   Dialogue occurring without other intervening actions taking place. A reported verbal exchange is represented as a continuous event, i.e., list the utterances below the vertical line (figure 17.A2.9).

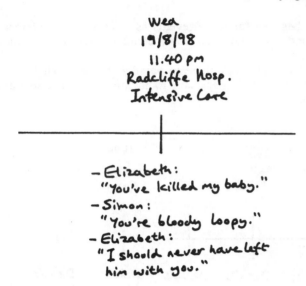

Figure 17.A2.9   Dialogue without intervening actions

(b)   Representing actions with intervening utterances. Use separate events on the event line to represent actions and intervening utterances.

Identity bins
Identity bins are located along the bottom of the page. Always draw lines round an identity bin. This ensures that:

(a)   information does not merge between bins;
(b)   the material within a bin is eye-catching and can be easily referred to later;
(c)   there is greater likelihood of detecting gaps or inconsistencies in the collated material.

Initial detail on any identity occasions the creation of a bin. Subsequent detail on the identity is entered in the appropriate bin.
Bins should be used to collate detail on:

(a)   every individual mentioned in the text;
(b)   entities, e.g., objects, locations, institutions, groups;
(c)   routines, i.e., repeated activities such as a ritualised sex 'game', cashing up a till at the end of the day.

A bin can be used to represent a visual image as conveyed in the text and conjured up in the mind's eye, e.g.:

(a)   a sketch of an entity — such as an object, feature, clothing, etc.;

(b)   a layout described in the narrative, e.g., a room, house, intersection of routes;

(c)   relative positioning and orientation of people — this enables illustration of what or who was reportedly (and was actually) visible from where and by whom.

This use of an identity bin is very useful:

(a)   Attempting to turn words into images often reveals what is obscured by the words of the narrative. The disclosed detail is in fact forensic twaddle. That which is reported does not 'add up' because it is an invalid (unreal) verbal representation that does not map on to physical reality.

(b)   It provides the basis for comparison with:

(i)   any subsequent diagram requested from the individual,
(ii)   the real entity, e.g., the actual location.

Examples of identity bins are given in figure 17.A2.10. Note the use of abbreviations, including use of single initials to reduce text in the episode detail.

LUCY GEE [LG]	WILL NUTT [WN] "Nutter"	NUTT'S VEHICLE
Address 5 Elmore Lane Bardon Town Works for Nutt (prostitution) (3½ years) One child: Samantha (2 years)	Former live-in partner of LG. Father of Samantha Lives off LG's earnings. "Does dope". Violent to LG	White Cavalier Used by LG to "do tricks" Repossessed "Late Nov 98"

Figure 17.A2.10   Examples of identity bins

In Figure 17.A2.11 and Figure 17.A2.12 there are SE3R analyses of two statements. Both analyses reveal anomalies which are not readily detectable from the statements.

More than one version contained within one account
When a second or subsequent version is detected, use different colours to record the differing representation, i.e., as a different event on the event line. If the subsequent version purportedly occurred at the same time but in a different manner, this can be represented as another event in the same way as simultaneous events (see figure 17.A2.7).

Similarly different versions of identity bin detail can be entered in a different colour.

R — Read

This constitutes an accuracy and quality check upon your extraction of detail.

Read through the document at your normal reading speed:

(a)   checking the detail of the text is accurately entered into the SE3R;

(b)   correcting any errors of omission, i.e., entering detail which was missed, or commission, i.e., inaccuracy.

R — Review

Put the document to one side.

Reviewing involves methodical examination and evaluation of your SE3R, with particular reference to the detection and highlighting of anomaly.

Be systematic in your reviewing:

(a)   Scan the event line. Look at the steps and the detail of each step with a view to identifying empty accounts, breaks in narrative continuity, narrative contrast, 'non-barking dogs' and measured disclosure, i.e., lack of detail where this could be reasonably expected.

(b)   Examine each event and discrete sequences of events (episodes) which are, or are purportedly, linked.

(c)   Note any consistencies (repetitions of disclosed detail), ambiguities, vaguenesses, inconsistencies, contradictions and any other forms of anomaly.

(d)   Apply the *forensic twaddle test* — establish in your own mind whether the event or events as described are anything other than logically sound and physically possible (e.g., being in two places at once; doing two mutually exclusive actions).

(e)   Make a note of questions raised by your review.

R — Recall

You will find that by this stage you will be very familiar with the detailed content of your SE3R and will have a good memory for this content even though you have not consciously sought to memorise it.

This is because the combination of skim reading, systematic, critical extraction using the approach to representation described above, and methodical review constitutes a sequence of effective memorial processes.

The recall step is aimed at helping you consolidate detail from your SE3R in working memory and to store it in long-term memory. Do not engage in this stage unless you feel it necessary.

If you need to memorise material be systematic:

(a)   Do it in stages — identity bin detail first, then events.

(b)   Break down the task, i.e., within each stage memorise in 'chunks'. Do not try to remember everything in one go.

Memorising identity information
Isolate the identity bins that you want to memorise. Take one bin at a time:

(a) look at the bin;
(b) scan its contents;
(c) study — look at each detail in turn;
(d) close your eyes;
(e) visualise the bin; then its individual contents;
(f) open your eyes;
(g) check — scan and study;
(h) close your eyes, visualise and so on.

Memorising event line information
Look at the event line. Memorise it in terms of gist:

(a) identify key events;
(b) isolate discrete episodes;
(c) note the number of steps (events) within an episode.

Adopt the same approach as for memorising the content of identity bins.

Checking your recall
A good method of checking your recall is:

(a) turn your SE3R sheet over so that it is face down;
(b) reproduce on another sheet the detail of your SE3R from memory.
Put in the key event and identity details in exactly the same location.

17.A2.5 Conducting SE3R on multiple written texts
To represent more than one account there are three options:

(a) Representing two accounts. A second text can be treated in the same way as a simultaneous event or two versions in the same text (see above). The event line of the second account is drawn under that of the first, with coinciding events reflected as being in the same relative position on the event line. Where there are more than two accounts this is not recommended since the amount of information is too great.

(b) Representing two or more accounts. Use a common event line and identity bins but differentiate the sources by using a different coloured pen for each account. If you are using one colour for two or more accounts you can give precision referencing:

(i)   by using the four areas of white space created by an event bisecting the event line, entering such detail as the initials of the witness and the page number of the statement;

(ii) by putting the source of the detail in brackets, e.g., beside the detail in the identity bin or opposite temporal and location details above the event line.

(c)   Convert the SE3R representation of two or more accounts into a grid. The event detail of the first account or statement is entered in the first column, that of the second account or statement in the second column, and so on.

17.A2.6   Conducting SE3R on recorded text

S — Skim
Skim here means intently listen to, and in the case of video observe, the recording, only stopping to resolve indistinct utterances or difficult-to-differentiate detail on the video recording.

E — Extract
Extracting detail is somewhat more problematic. Interviews underline the fact that the narrative sequence, i.e., the order in which an individual describes the occurrence of events, very often does not correspond to the order of actual events. This is complicated by the fact that police officers tend to change the topic rapidly and without apparent logic, and return to the topic across the course of the interview — sometimes repeatedly and endlessly.

When an event pops up out of sequence all that is necessary is to exercise a degree of decision-making. If it antedates an earlier event on the event line, place the event in the appropriate place.

If an event pops up only to be deferred to a later time in the interview for disclosure, exercise judgment and place the event some distance ahead on the yet-to-be-completed event line. If you overestimated the situation this, is easily resolved: bring the detail back into line, at the right chronological point. If you underestimated, leaving yourself with too little space between events, simply write the word INSERT above the space and open up a separate SE3R sheet to represent the events which occurred. Remember to number insert sheets, e.g., INSERT 1, INSERT 2, and so on, should you need to create more than one insert sheet.

Everything else is as for conducting an SE3R on a written text.

17.A2.7   A worked example of SE3R: a case of assault
The material for this example is a statement given by Frederick Ussher. The statement was taken down by PC 256 James Goldsworthy on Sunday, 16 December 1996. The statement says:

> I am a final year student at Trentham College. At weekends I work part-time as a barman in the Feathers public house in George Street, Purleigh. At about 10.30 p.m. on Saturday, 15 December 1996, I was serving in the public bar. Two men who are regulars and who I know to be called Jason and Ernie were standing at the left end of the bar near the doors to the women's and men's toilets. Jason is about 20 and Ernie is about 30. Jason was nearest the toilets and Ernie was to his right. They were celebrating Jason's birthday and he had been bought a drink by someone at the bar to Ernie's right. Behind them and in front of the large

round pillar by the door to the men's toilets stood a group of three men and a woman. The man nearest the men's toilets was fair-haired. He was in his early 20s and was wearing a combat jacket. Facing him, that is, towards the toilets, stood a balding man in his 40s with a Frank Zappa moustache wearing a green Army jumper. Between them with his back to Jason and Ernie was a stocky dark-haired man. I think he was wearing a dark green top. I think it was a roll-neck jumper but I am not sure. He had a strong Newcastle accent. The woman was about 18–19. She wore a fur bolero jacket and a black miniskirt. She went to the toilet. When she came out of the toilet she was tugging her miniskirt down as she walked back to her group. Jason pointed towards her with his pint glass which was nearly empty. He said very loudly in her direction that if she needed help she only had to ask. Someone in the group said something about people need to be taught to keep their eyes to themselves. The man with his back to the bar was given an empty glass and swung round towards Jason. He hit Jason's glass with his glass and jabbed the broken rim towards Jason's face. I rushed through to the Saloon Bar to get Mr Fyfe the manager. When we returned to the Public Bar the group had gone. Jason was leaning on the bar holding a bar towel to his eyes. I looked over the bar. Ernie was laying motionless face down on the floor.

The SE3R representation of this statement is figure 17.A2.11. When you read the SE3R note:

(a)   the use of abbreviations and symbols;
(b)   conversion of past tense into present;
(c)   conversion of reported speech into direct speech;
(d)   conversion of passive into active — revealing the need to investigate the identities involved;
(e)   the simple diagram derived from Ussher's verbal descriptions.

Figure 17.A2.11 SE3R of Frederick Ussher's statement

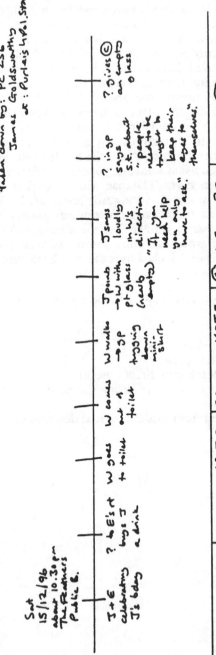

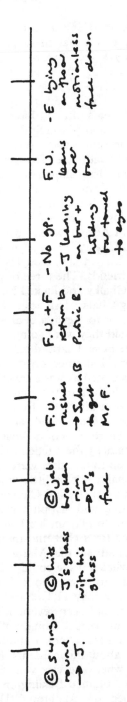

17.A2.8 A worked example of SE3R: a case of indecent assault

The material for this example is a statement given by Tracy Brand. The statement was taken down by WDC 962 Brenda Barclay on Monday, 14 October 1996. On the reverse of the statement is Tracy's address: 213 Ramage Way, Mallam MY45 6ZA.

I am Tracy Brand. I am 30 years old and have two children Kevin Brand who was born on 4 May 1983 and Maria Smith who was born on 5 August 1990. Kevin's father Charlie Brand and I divorced in 1989. My relationship with Jim Smith, Maria's father, ended the year she was born. I live with my two children at the address shown on the reverse of this statement. On Thursday 1 August 1996 I was at home with Maria and Kevin. After dinner we were in the lounge. Kevin and Maria were playing and I was sitting in the armchair reading. At about 2 o'clock Kevin's cousin Stephen Brand called with his friend Adrian White, who everyone calls 'Chalky'. Stephen is a year older and Chalky is a year younger than Kevin. Stephen is the son of my former brother-in-law, Douglas Brand. The two boys live in East Hermitage and are friends. The three boys played, while I read my book. Maria climbed over Chalky and kicked him. When he did not react she threw a tantrum kicking Chalky. I smacked her and sent her up to her bedroom. The boys then went to Kevin's bedroom. Not long after Kevin came into the lounge and said they were going to the shopping precinct. I presumed he meant all three boys. I carried on reading for a bit longer and then decided to check Maria. I stopped on the top stair. I could see that Kevin's door on the left was closed as was ours straight in front of me. The door of Maria's bedroom which is to the right of ours was a little open. Through the gap I could see a bit of the front window and the dressing table in front of it. I then heard Maria giggle and then Chalky say 'Go on'. Then I heard both of them laugh. I went downstairs to the kitchen. When I got to the bottom of the stairs by the kitchen I shouted that I didn't know what the two of them were up to and they were to come down right away. About five minutes later Chalky left. A little while after this Maria came into the kitchen. I asked her what she and Chalky were doing upstairs. She giggled. I got angry, shouting and slapping Maria. Maria said nothing happened. She then went out to play on her bike. Last Sunday 6 October my friend Mavis Long called for a chat mid-morning. Just before she left she told me that her Sharon had said that Maria had pulled her pants down and said she could lick her whatsit if she could lick Sharon's. I was shocked but Mavis said it was nothing to worry about. Little girls often show their parts to each other. Then on Friday 11 October the school telephoned in the morning to say that there had been several incidents where Maria had asked to lick other girls' private parts. I thought of the incident with Chalky and Maria. I collected Maria from school at about 3.30. On the way home Maria laughed when I asked about the incidents. I then asked her what had happened in her bedroom when she was with Chalky. She said he had licked her whatsit. After tea I phoned Ecklington Police Station. At about 7 o'clock two officers attached to Ecklington CID WPC Ann Heming and

PC Andy Gibb called. I sent Kevin and Maria into the lounge then I was asked to give details. I then called Maria from the lounge telling Kevin to stay there. Maria was then interviewed with me present beside her. The next morning at Mallam Police Station Interview Suite Maria and I were met by WDC Brenda Barclay of the Force Special Investigation Unit who is based at Mallam. She explained to Maria the routine showing her the video room. With me sitting near Maria she interviewed her on video for about three-quarters of an hour.

The SE3R representation for this statement is at Figure 17.A2.12.

Figure 17.A2:12   SE3R of Tracy Brand's
statement

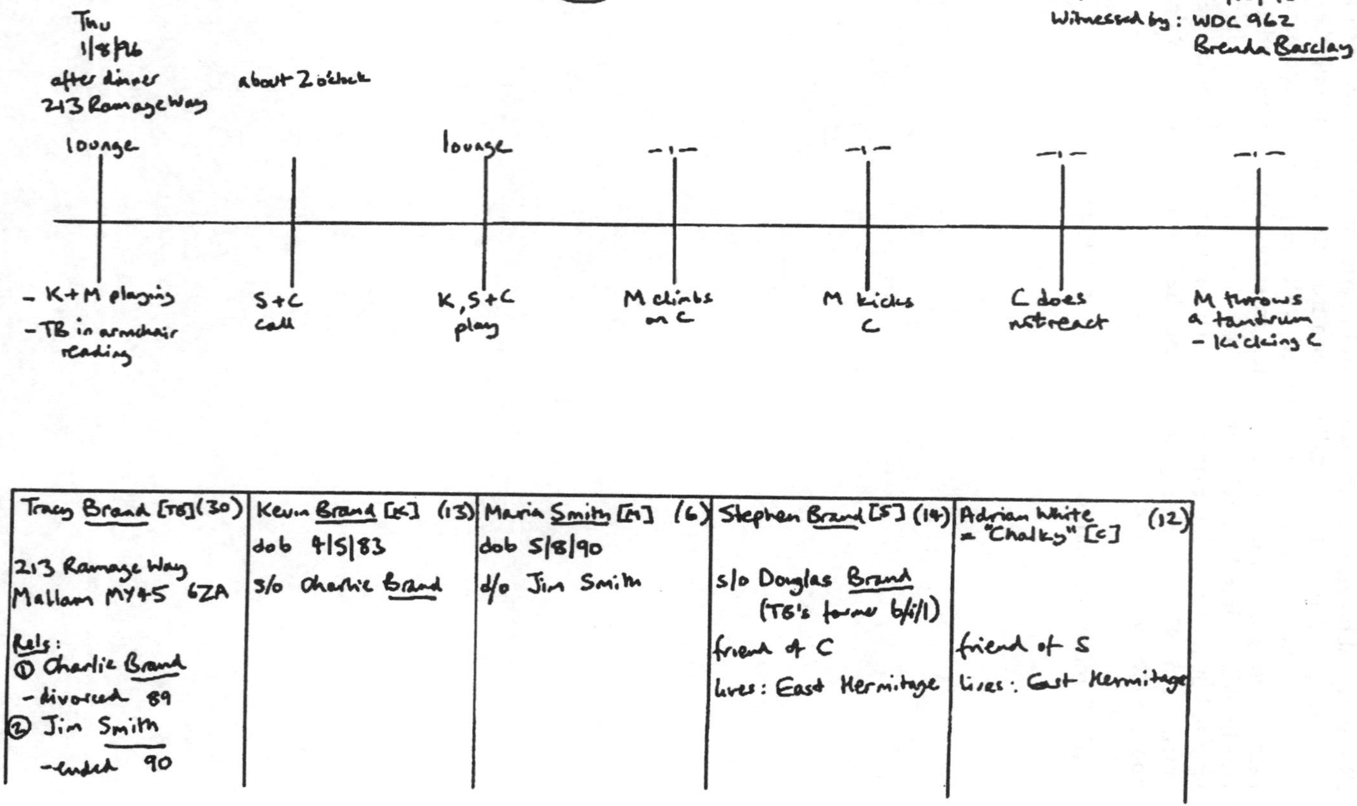

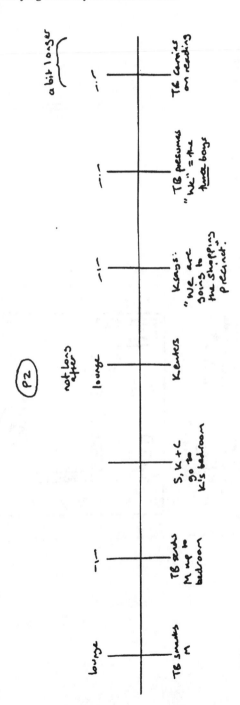

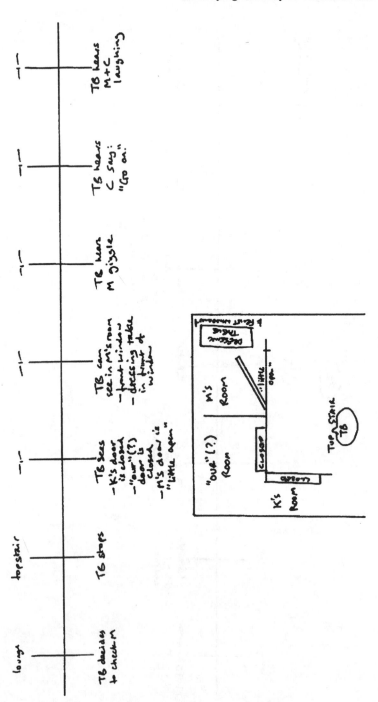

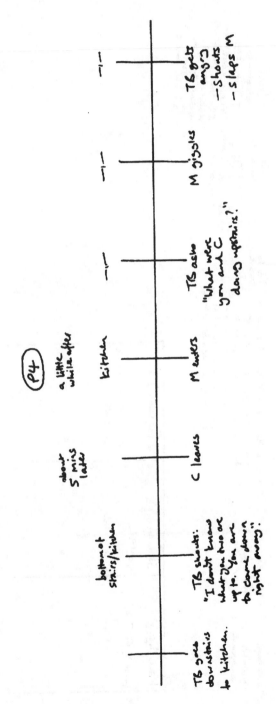

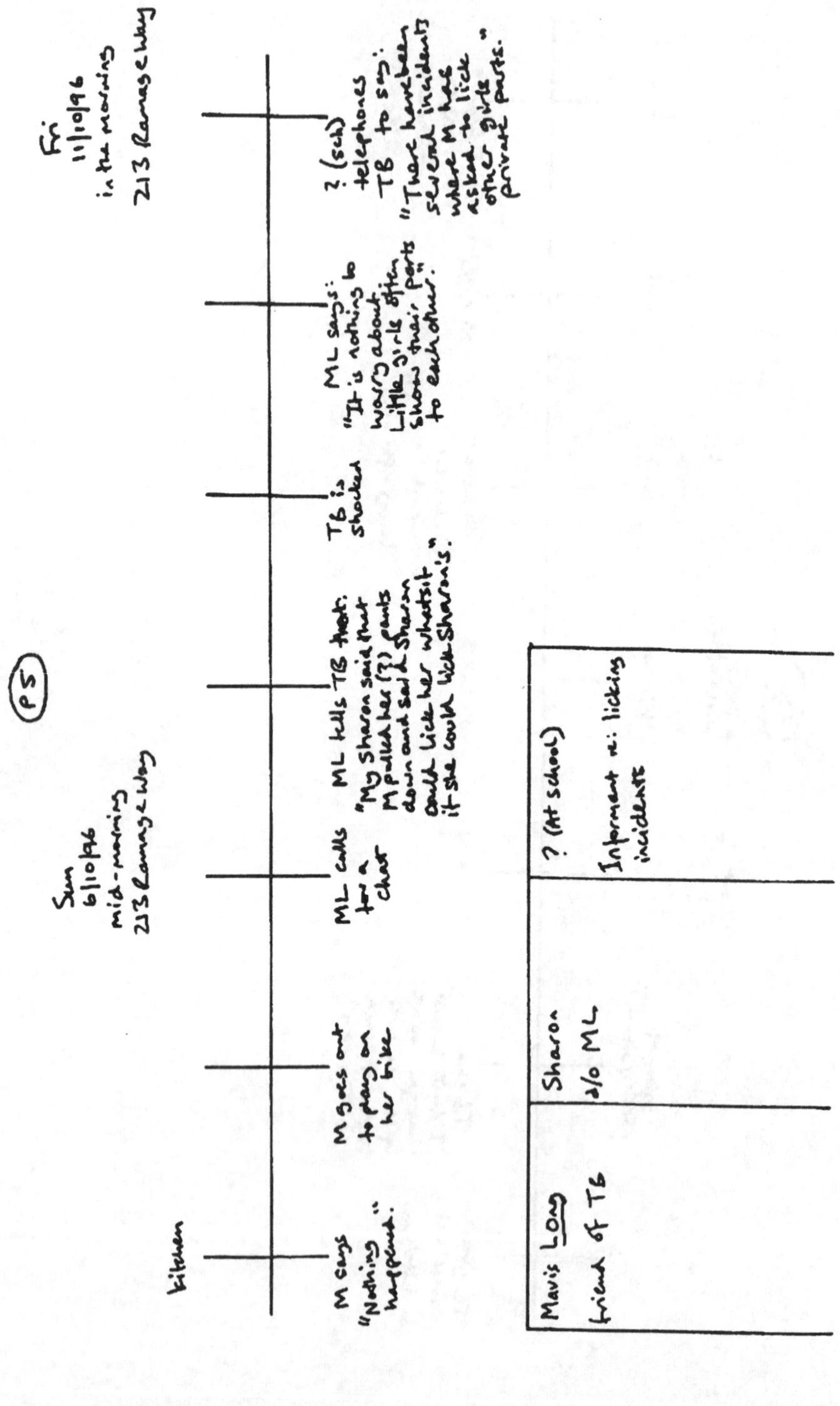

Fri
11/10/96
in the morning
213 Ramsey Way

? (sex) telephones TB to say: "There have been several incidents where M has asked to lick other girls' private parts."

ML says: "It is nothing to worry about. Little girls often show their parts to each other."

TB is shocked

ML tells TB that: "My Sharon said that M pulled her (?) pants down and said Sharon could lick her whatsit. parts. if she could lick Sharon's."

Sun
6/10/96
mid-morning
213 Ramsey Way

(PS)

ML calls for a chat

M goes out to play on her bike

M says "Nothing happened."

kitchen

Mavis Long	Sharon	? (At school)
friend of TB	d/o ML	Informant re: licking incidents

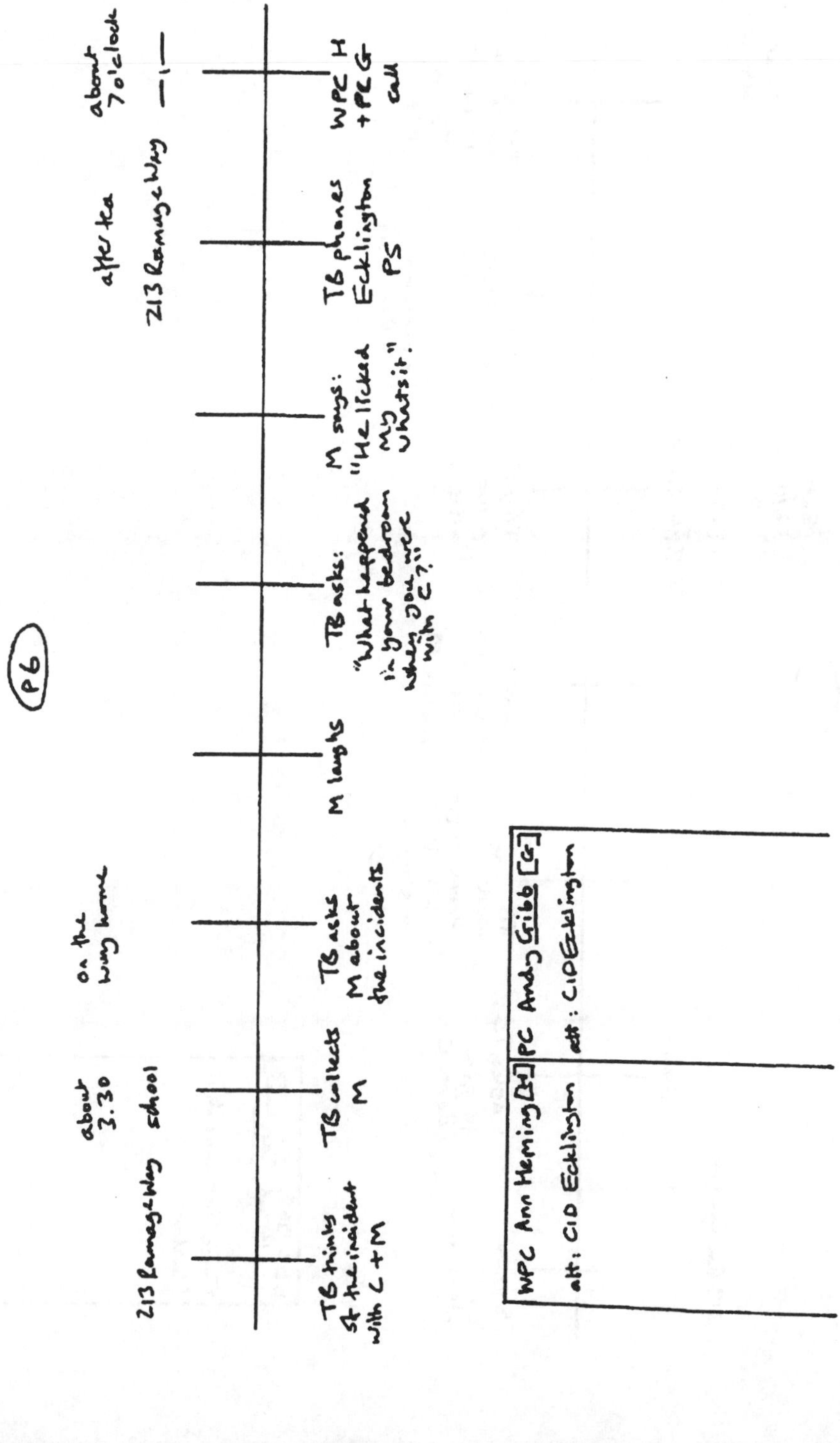

(P6)

about 3.30
213 Ramsey Way school

on the way home

after tea
213 Ramsey Way

about 7 o'clock

TB rings Sgt the incident with C + M

TB collects M

TB asks M about the incidents

M laughs

TB asks: "What happened in your bedroom when DPW were with C?"

M says: "He licked my whatsit"

TB phones Ecklington PS

WPC H + PEG call

WPC Ann Heming [DH]	PC Andy Gibb [G]
att: CID Ecklington	att: CID Ecklington

213 Ramage Way

leitham

(P7)

Sat
12/10/96
?
Mallam PS
Int. Suit

about
3/4 hour

TB sends
K+M
into lounge

? asks TB
to give
details

TB
-calls M
from lounge
-tells K
to stay in
lounge

? interviews
M with TB
present
beside M.

TB+M
meet
WDC B

WDC B
-explains
to M the
routine
-showing
video room

WDC B
interviews
M on video
-TB sits
near M

WDC 962
Brenda Barclay [B]

Force Spec. Inv. Unit.
Mallam

CHAPTER EIGHTEEN

The Admissibility of expert psychological and psychiatric testimony

R.D. Mackay, Andrew M. Colman and Peter Thornton QC

18.1 INTRODUCTION

18.1.1 Expert testimony: background

The purpose of civil and criminal trials is to decide issues of fact and of law. In England, Wales and Scotland, issues of fact in the most serious criminal trials are decided by juries and issues of law by judges. For several centuries, decisions about issues of fact, in certain cases, have been assisted by experts. As early as 1554, Saunders J remarked in the case of *Buckley* v *Rice-Thomas* (1554) 1 Plowd 118, at p. 124 (quoted in Cross and Tapper, 1995, p. 555) that:

> . . . if matters arise in our law which concern other sciences or faculties, we commonly apply for the aid of that science or faculty which it concerns. Which is an honourable and commendable thing in our law. For thereby it appears that we do not despise all other sciences but our own, but we approve of them and encourage them as things worthy of commendation.

In cases requiring abstruse or technical knowledge, experts were initially invited to serve on juries, then in the late Middle Ages they began to testify as witnesses. Testimony from experts in various fields became commonplace in England during the latter half of the eighteenth century, in parallel with the rapid development of numerous specialised branches of science and technology associated with the industrial revolution, which took place in England from about 1760 onwards. For example, in the landmark case of *Folkes* v *Chadd* (1782) 3 Doug KB 157, which we shall refer to again later, a leading engineer was called to give expert evidence about what had caused a harbour to silt up.

Expert testimony on psychological and psychiatric matters is of much more recent origin. Psychiatry, the branch of medicine concerned specifically with mental disorders, emerged only in the first half of the nineteenth century, and it was not until the 1880s that psychology began to be recognised as an independent discipline in its own right devoted to the scientific study of the nature, functions and phenomena of behaviour and mental experience, both normal and abnormal. The first psychological expert to testify anywhere in the world was probably Albert von Schrenck-Notzing, who was called as a witness in 1896 at the trial of a Munich man accused of murdering three women. His evidence focused on what has more recently come to be called the eyewitness misinformation effect — a form of memory distortion arising from confusion between what was seen or heard at the time of an event and information obtained after the event. In the United States at about the same time, Hugo Münsterberg served as a psychological consultant in two murder trials, and although his own evidence was not admitted in court he became a forceful advocate of forensic psychology in general and psychological testimony in particular.

18.1.2   Issues for psychological and psychiatric testimony
Most witnesses are permitted to testify only about facts, but expert witnesses are allowed to testify about their expert opinions as well. Typical issues on which expert psychological and psychiatric witnesses have testified include the following (adapted from Lloyd-Bostock, 1988, pp. 142–3). Did A suffer brain damage, and if so what are its likely long-term effects? Is B a fit person to have custody of her child? Is hypnosis likely to have improved witness C's memory? Is D's mental condition such as to require him to be detained under the Mental Health Act 1983 for the protection of others? Is E mentally fit to stand trial? What psychological evidence is available regarding the suggestibility of a child witness such as F when being interrogated by police officers? Is G's eyewitness identification of the accused likely to be trustworthy? Does H suffer from severe learning difficulties, and if so how is this likely to affect his future earning power? What are the likely effects of long-term alcohol abuse on J's memory? Is K's confession likely to be genuine?

The rapid growth of psychology and psychiatry since the Second World War has not been accompanied by a corresponding increase in the amount or the range of expert testimony from specialists in these fields. In England, the judiciary have maintained a sceptical and cautious attitude towards the admissibility of such evidence. This attitude crystallised in an influential decision of the Court of Appeal in the case of *R* v *Turner* [1975] QB 834, which established an important rule governing the admissibility of psychological and psychiatric evidence.

18.2   THE *TURNER* RULE

18.2.1   Background to *Turner*
The decision in *R* v *Turner* resulted in psychological testimony being ruled inadmissible in numerous cases except ones in which defendants were

affected at the time of the alleged offences by recognised mental disorders, by mental handicap, or by automatism, all of which may be thought of as abnormal mental states. In cases involving unfitness to plead or insanity, psychiatric evidence is not merely tolerated but legally required by the Criminal Procedure (Insanity and Unfitness to Plead) Act 1991, though this does not cover automatism. The ground on which the expert evidence in *Turner* was excluded was that, because no mental abnormality was involved, the proposed expert testimony dealt with matters of 'common knowledge and experience' that could be understood by a jury without the help of an expert. This criterion for the admissibility of expert psychological and psychiatric evidence has come to be called the *Turner* rule.

The defendant in *Turner* had killed his girlfriend with a hammer after she told him with a grin that she had been sleeping with two other men and that the child that she was carrying was not his. He pleaded provocation, claiming that he had been overwhelmed with blind rage and had hit her with the hammer without realising what he was doing. Although he showed no signs of any mental disorder, the defence wished to introduce psychiatric evidence to show that he had enjoyed a deep emotional relationship with the deceased, that he was likely to have experienced an explosive outburst of blind rage after her confession to him, and that after the crime his behaviour showed profound grief for what he had done, which was consistent with his defence of provocation. But after examining a psychiatric report outlining the evidence that the expert witness intended to give, the trial judge ruled the evidence inadmissible on the ground that it dealt with matters of 'common knowledge and experience' within the experience of the jury.

18.2.2 The Court of Appeal decision
The defence took the case to the Court of Appeal, arguing that the trial judge had erred in refusing to admit the expert evidence, but the appeal was dismissed. Lawton LJ justified the Court of Appeal decision as follows in *R v Turner* [1975] QB 834 at p. 841:

> If on the proven facts a judge or jury can form their own conclusions without help, then the opinion of an expert is unnecessary. In such a case if it is given dressed up in scientific jargon it may make judgment more difficult. The fact that an expert witness has impressive qualifications does not by that fact alone make his opinion on matters of human nature and behaviour within the limits of normality any more helpful than that of the jurors themselves; but there is a danger that they may think it does.

The *Turner* rule has been used to exclude expert psychological and psychiatric evidence in innumerable criminal cases since 1975 (Mackay and Colman, 1991, 1996). Following this leading case, the courts have been comparatively indulgent in their readiness to admit expert psychological and psychiatric testimony in cases involving pleas of diminished responsibility, though not where defendants have voluntarily consumed alcohol or dangerous drugs, but they have been reluctant, for a time at least, to admit such testimony in cases in which defendants pleaded provocation and those involving other issues of criminal responsibility or *mens rea*.

18.3 TRANSPARENCY OF NORMAL BEHAVIOUR

18.3.1 Assumption behind the *Turner* rule

The *Turner* rule did not fall from the sky without warning or premonition. It arose from a principle that can be traced back at least as far as the late eighteenth century, when Mansfield J ruled in *Folkes* v *Chadd* (1782) 3 Doug KB 157 that an expert's opinion is admissible only if it furnishes the court with information that is likely to lie outside the common knowledge and experience of the jury or, more generally, the trier of fact, and this principle became firmly established in the English common law. The interpretation of this principle in relation to psychological and psychiatric evidence, which became the *Turner* rule, was the assumption that human behaviour, except when it stems from some form of mental abnormality, is within the common knowledge and experience of a jury. A few years before *Turner*, in *R* v *Chard* (1971) 56 Cr App R 268, Roskill LJ had expressed this assumption as follows, at pp. 270–1:

> Where the matters in issue go outside [the jury's] experience and they are invited to deal with someone supposedly abnormal, for example, supposedly suffering from insanity or diminished responsibility, then plainly in such a case they are entitled to the benefit of expert evidence. But where, as in the present case, they are dealing with someone who by concession was on the medical evidence entirely normal, it seems to this court abundantly plain, on first principles of the admissibility of expert evidence, that it is not permissible to call a witness, whatever his personal experience, merely to tell the jury how he thinks an accused man's mind — assumedly a normal mind — operated at the time of an alleged crime.

Roskill LJ was implying by these words that normal, non-disordered behaviour is fully transparent and therefore not in need of explanation or clarification by experts. We may call this the *transparency assumption* about normal behaviour. A few years later Lawton LJ expressed this assumption more explicitly and bluntly in his *Turner* judgment, when he commented on the proposed expert testimony in relation to provocation that 'jurors do not need psychiatrists to tell them how ordinary folk who are not suffering from any mental illness are likely to react to the stresses and strains of life' (p. 841). But is the transparency assumption about normal behaviour justified?

18.3.2 Evidence against the transparency assumption

It has been argued that the application of the *Turner* rule by the courts has been inconsistent and excessively restrictive, and in particular that the underlying transparency assumption is false. There is abundant research evidence to suggest that ordinary people find many forms of normal behaviour as difficult to understand as mentally disordered behaviour (Colman and Mackay, 1993).

For example, experimental evidence has shown that, in explaining other people's behaviour, observers tend to underestimate the importance of external, situational factors, such as social pressures, and to overestimate the importance of internal, dispositional factors, such as personality traits. This powerful distortion of perception, which is sometimes called the *fundamental attribution error* or the *overattribution bias*, has been confirmed by numerous independent researchers (Webster, 1993). Since external, situational factors often play a significant role in criminal acts, it follows that jurors may not always be able to understand the causes of such conduct purely on the basis of their common knowledge and experience of human behaviour, in spite of the fact that no abnormality is involved.

A closely related example of normal, non-disordered behaviour that is far from transparent and is demonstrably outside the everyday understanding of even intelligent and well-educated people is provided by Stanley Milgram's well-known experiments on obedience to authority (Milgram, 1974). These experiments showed that approximately two-thirds of ordinary people who volunteer to take part in experiments are fully obedient to firm and insistent instructions from the experimenter to deliver apparently painful and possibly lethal electric shocks to an innocent victim who screams with pain and then appears to lose consciousness or die. The findings, which have been replicated by a number of independent researchers (Blass, 1991), are clearly beyond the common knowledge and experience of ordinary people, because people grossly underestimate the level of obedience likely to occur in the experiment, and only about one in a hundred people believe that they themselves would be fully obedient in such a situation. Furthermore, before the experiment had been published, it was described in detail to a group of 40 senior psychiatrists at a leading United States medical school, and they predicted that only about one person in a thousand would be fully obedient (Milgram, 1974, p. 30).

The research literature is replete with further examples of normal forms of human behaviour that are demonstrably opaque to common-sense understanding or intuition. In fact, empirical studies have shown that ordinary people generally have a very poor knowledge and understanding of psychological functions and phenomena (Furnham, 1992). The supposition that only mentally disordered behaviour transcends the common knowledge and experience of ordinary people is not supported by the evidence. This implies that the transparency assumption about normal behaviour, according to which the *Turner* rule has been used to exclude psychological and psychiatric evidence of non-clinical psychological phenomena on the ground that they necessarily fall within the common knowledge and experience of ordinary jurors, seems groundless. Largely for this reason, the restrictive interpretation of the *Turner* rule was not followed by the Court of Appeal in the case of *R* v *Emery* (1993) 14 Cr App R (S) 394.

18.4 DURESS, PROVOCATION, CONFESSIONS AND *MENS REA*

18.4.1 *Emery* and duress
Sally Emery was a 19-year-old unmarried mother of a child called Chanel, who died at the age of 11 months with many injuries, including fractured ribs

and a ruptured bowel, resulting from a prolonged period of severe physical abuse. In January 1992, the jury in the Peterborough Crown Court acquitted Sally Emery of occasioning actual bodily harm to her child, but found her guilty of failing to protect the child from the father, and she was sentenced to four years' detention in a young offender institution. She appealed against this sentence and it was reduced to 30 months by the Court of Appeal in November 1992.

Sally Emery pleaded that she had been acting under duress. She testified at her trial that the father, Brian Hedman, had often severely abused both her and Chanel, and that her failure to protect Chanel was due to fear. Her counsel, Helena Kennedy QC, wished to call two expert witnesses — a psychologist with many years' experience working with abused women and a psychiatrist with specialist knowledge of responses to serious trauma — to support the defence of duress. The experts were ready to testify that Sally Emery had been suffering from *battered woman syndrome*, a syndrome resulting from prolonged violence and abuse of a woman by her partner that can induce a form of 'learned helplessness' characterised by an inability to stand up to the abuser, a feeling of dependence on the abuser, and an inability to withdraw from the situation. The prosecution objected, citing the *Turner* rule, on the ground that the proposed evidence did not focus on a recognised mental disorder but on a form of normal behaviour, which was assumedly within the common knowledge and experience of a jury. The trial judge ruled the evidence admissible, his justification being that without expert help the jury might find the defendant guilty, whereas with the understanding gained from the expert evidence they might acquit her.

The case went to the Court of Appeal as *R* v *Emery* (1993) 14 Cr App R (S) 394, where a judgment given by Lord Taylor of Gosforth CJ fully endorsed the trial judge's decision and its justification. Lord Taylor commented (at p. 397) that the condition of learned helplessness that was the subject of the proposed expert testimony, though not a mental disorder, 'is complex and it is not known by the public at large. Accordingly we are quite satisfied that it was appropriate for the learned judge to decide that this evidence should be allowed.'

The *Emery* decision did not abandon the *Turner* rule altogether: expert evidence dealing with matters within the 'common knowledge and experience' of a jury remained inadmissible, but the interpretation of the rule in relation to expert psychological and psychiatric evidence was relaxed. In particular, it was no longer assumed that all forms of human behaviour apart from mental disorder, mental handicap or automatism are fully transparent, and that expert testimony regarding them was therefore invariably part of 'common knowledge and experience' and hence inadmissible. The *Emery* decision thus appeared to open the door to psychological and psychiatric evidence across a far wider range of behaviour than had been the case before 1993. In particular, the notion put forward in *R* v *Turner* [1975] QB 834 that 'jurors do not need psychiatrists to tell them how ordinary folk who are not suffering from any mental illness are likely to react to the stresses and strains of life' (p. 841) seemed, for this case at least, well and truly buried.

18.5 EVOLVING CASE LAW

18.5.1 The objective test in provocation

In a similar way the courts seemed to be adopting a more relaxed approach to the objective test in cases involving pleas of provocation. This test requires the jury to consider 'whether the provocation was sufficient to make a person of reasonable self-control in the totality of circumstances (including personal characteristics) act as the defendant did', as Lord Simon expressed it in *Director of Public Prosecutions* v *Camplin* [1978] AC 705.

It is worth noting that Lord Taylor CJ approached the issue of 'battered woman syndrome' in an analogous way in *R* v *Ahluwalia* [1992] 4 All ER 889 when he made it clear that, had evidence of this condition been before the trial judge, 'different considerations may have applied' (p. 898) as to whether the condition could amount to a 'characteristic'. That such mental conditions may constitute characteristics for the purposes of the objective test in provocation has since been more clearly endorsed by the Court of Appeal in a series of decisions, including *R* v *Humphreys* [1995] 4 All ER 1008, *R* v *Dryden* [1995] 4 All ER 987 and especially *R* v *Thornton (No. 2)* [1996] 2 All ER 1023, in which Lord Taylor CJ, in holding that battered woman syndrome could be a relevant characteristic, said that 'mental as well as physical characteristics should be taken into account' (p. 1031). In arriving at this decision his lordship followed the decision of the House of Lords in *R* v *Morhall* [1996] AC 90, but failed to mention the fact that in that case Lord Goff of Chieveley had expressed concern about the emphasis on characteristics placed by the Court of Appeal in *R* v *Newell* (1980) 71 Cr App R 331, concurring with the reservations about the 'needless complexity' of the role of characteristics within the provocation plea expressed by Cooke P in the New Zealand Court of Appeal in *R* v *McArthy* [1992] 2 NZLR 550.

Shortly after *R* v *Thornton (No. 2)* [1996] 2 All ER 1023, Lord Goff added to this criticism in his judgment in *Luc Thiet Thuan* v *R* [1996] 2 All ER 1033, when he remarked that the liberal approach in New Zealand towards 'characteristics' was likely to have been influenced by the absence of any defence of diminished responsibility in that country. Accordingly, he considered that mental infirmity impairing the defendant's power of self-control could not be attributed to the reasonable person for the purposes of the objective test, because this would have the effect of incorporating the concept of diminished responsibility 'indirectly into the law of provocation' (p. 1046). The only exception should be where the 'mental infirmity of the defendant [was] itself the subject of taunts' (p. 1046). It seems clear from Lord Goff's majority judgment that, in re-emphasising the importance of the objective test in provocation, he was at the same time endorsing the *Turner* rule in the sense that it must follow that expert medical evidence should remain inadmissible on the central issue of whether a reasonable person would have lost self-control in similar circumstances. That this is the effect of the ruling in *Luc Thiet Thuan* is made abundantly clear in the dissenting opinion of Lord Steyn when he said that to admit such evidence 'on the subjective issue whether the woman had in fact lost her self-control' while at the same time requiring the jury to ignore such evidence 'when they consider the objective issue' would leave a jury 'puzzled by such artificially compartmentalised directions' (p. 1049) and would inevitably lead to injustice.

Since the ruling in *Luc Thiet Thuan* v *R* [1996] 2 All ER 1033, in which Lord Goff was openly critical of the decisions of the Court of Appeal in *R* v *Ahluwalia* [1992] 4 All ER 889, *R* v *Humphreys* [1995] 4 All ER 1008 and *R* v *Dryden* [1995] 4 All ER 987 as being inconsistent with the objective approach to provocation as interpreted by the House of Lords in *Director of Public Prosecutions* v *Camplin* [1978] AC 705, the Court of Appeal had to decide which line of authority to follow. In *R* v *Campbell* [1997] 1 Cr App R 199, Lord Bingham of Cornhill CJ decided that it was not open to the Court of Appeal to choose between the two competing views, because the court was bound by its own previous decisions and not by Luc which, technically, as an appeal to the Privy Council from Hong Kong, was a decision outside our legal jurisdiction. Nevertheless, Lord Bingham leaned towards the less restrictive approach, as did the Court of Appeal subsequently in *R* v *Smith (Morgan James)* [1998] 4 All ER 387; [1998] Crim LR 896 (at the time of going to press, the prosecution appeal to the House of Lords is pending). It follows that mental characteristics that may have influenced a defendant's loss of self-control continue to be relevant for the objective test in provocation, as had already been made clear in *R* v *Thornton (No. 2)* [1996] 2 All ER 1023 at p. 1031. There seems little doubt that this trend towards liberalisation of the law relating to provocation will lead to a radical if gradual shift in reducing the impact of the *Turner* rule by permitting expert psychological and psychiatric evidence to assist a jury in deciding whether a reasonable person with similar mental characteristics would have lost his or her self-control. That this is the case was further demonstrated by the Court of Appeal's decisions in *R* v *Hobson* [1997] Crim LR 759; *R* v *Parker* [1997] Crim LR 790 and *R* v *Smith*, all of which follow *R* v *Campbell*.

18.5.2 The objective test in duress
While a step forward in this respect has taken place in relation to provocation, more recent cases involving pleas of duress seemed to be casting doubt on the more liberal approach adopted in *R* v *Emery* (1993) 14 Cr App R (S) 394. In that decision the Court of Appeal had accepted that the proper question for the experts to decide was 'whether a woman of reasonable firmness with the characteristics of [the defendant] would have had her will crushed' (p. 398). It seemed clear from this that the objective test in duress, which requires the jury to decide whether a person of reasonable firmness, sharing the defendant's characteristics and circumstances, would have been unable to withstand the threats in question, was being interpreted in much the same way as the analogous test in provocation.

However, it was not long before the Court of Appeal began to question this approach. First, in *R* v *Hegarty* [1994] Crim LR 353 the court made it clear that it did not consider that the Lord Chief Justice 'intended to throw any doubt on the general rule . . . that the application of the objective test is a matter for the jury and that the evidence of witnesses is inadmissible'. This approach was followed in *R v Horne* [1994] Crim LR 584, where it was made clear that for the purposes of the reasonable firmness standard, 'evidence of personal vulnerability or pliancy falling short of psychiatric illness is not relevant'. Similarly, in *R v Hurst* [1995] 1 Cr App R 82 the court upheld a refusal to admit evidence about the possible effects on the defendant of sexual abuse as a child on the following ground:

> So long as there is this objective element in the standard by which a person's reaction to duress is to be judged, we find it hard to see how the person of reasonable firmness can be invested with the characteristic of a personality which lacks reasonable firmness, and although we appreciate the difficulty involved in trying to separate personal characteristics one from another, we are bound by the formulation in the case of *R v Graham* [1982] All ER 801 at p. 806.

Finally, in *R v Bowen* [1996] 4 All ER 837, the Court of Appeal was called upon to consider whether low intelligence should be regarded as a 'characteristic' for the purposes of the objective test in duress. In arriving at his decision Stuart-Smith LJ considered (at pp. 844–5) that a number of principles could be derived from the above authorities including:

> The mere fact that the accused is more pliable, vulnerable, timid or susceptible to threats than a normal person are not characteristics with which it is legitimate to invest the reasonable/ordinary person for the purpose of considering the objective test.
>
> The defendant may be in a category of persons who the jury think less able to resist pressure than people not within that category. Obvious examples are age, where a young person may well not be so robust as a mature one; possibly sex, though many women would doubtless consider that they had as much moral courage to resist pressure as men; pregnancy, where there is added fear for the unborn child; serious physical disability, which may inhibit self-protection; recognised mental illness or psychiatric condition, such as post-traumatic stress disorder leading to learned helplessness.
>
> Psychiatric evidence may be admissible to show that the accused is suffering from some mental illness, mental impairment or a recognised psychiatric condition, provided persons generally suffering from such a condition may be more susceptible to pressure and threats, and thus to assist the jury in deciding whether a reasonable person suffering from such a condition might have been impelled to act as the defendant did. It is not admissible simply to show that in the doctor's opinion an accused, who is not suffering from such illness or condition, is especially timid, suggestible or vulnerable to pressure and threats.
>
> In most cases it is probably only the age and sex of the accused that is capable of being relevant.

In applying these principles, his lordship could not see 'how low IQ, short of mental impairment or mental defectiveness, can be said to be a characteristic that makes those who have it less able to withstand threats and pressure' (p. 845).

The impact of this decision could be viewed as reaffirming the importance of the objective test in duress as well as making it clear that the *Turner* rule continues to hold sway in this connection. However, some progress has been made in that the decision in *Emery* was approved in *Bowen*, when it was made clear that 'post-traumatic stress disorder leading to learned helplessness' can constitute a characteristic for the purposes of duress. As Smith and Hogan (1996) have pointed out, 'the acceptance of such an illness as a relevant characteristic suggests that the objective test has broken down' (p. 247). If this is so for duress, the same seems true for provocation. However, although this breakdown of the objective test will have the beneficial effect of permitting more expert testimony to be admitted, by themselves these developments do nothing to rid the law of the *Turner* rule. That this is so can be well illustrated by focusing on the issue of *mens rea* (see paragraph 18.5.4 below).

18.5.3 Confessions

A particular area in which the courts have shown some willingness to depart from the *Turner* rule has been in relation to the admissibility of confessions. In one of the Broadwater farm cases, *R* v *Raghip* 90/5920S1, *The Times*, 9 December 1991, the Court of Appeal allowed fresh evidence on appeal (evidence that would have been admissible at trial had it then been available) of the psychological and psychosocial state of the appellant, even though there was no suggestion of mental illness. The court pointed to the 'artificiality' of drawing a strict line between IQ scores of 69 and 70, as had occurred in *R* v *Masih* [1986] Crim LR 395. The evidence was admitted to provide assistance on the issue of the admissibility of the confession under s. 76(2)(b) of the Police and Criminal Evidence Act of 1984. One of the circumstances to be considered was the mental condition of the defendant. At trial that was a decision to be taken on medical evidence and not, as in this case, by the judge's own assessment of the defendant in interview or in evidence. The Court of Appeal found that information about the appellant's abnormal susceptibility to suggestion and his level of functioning — equivalent to that of a child aged nine — was highly relevant information and could not have been divined from his performance in the witness box.

Applying *Raghip*, the Court of Appeal in Northern Ireland in *R* v *Kane*, 19 December 1997, admitted evidence of a psychologist on appeal to cast doubt on the reliability of a confession. In *Kane*, one of the Casement Park murder cases, the trial judge, sitting without a jury, had formed the opinion without expert help that the defendant was 'deliberately trying at times to give an appearance of being more unintelligent than he is'. In fact, unknown to the judge, but accepted on appeal, the defendant had a modest IQ of 78 and suffered severe anxiety problems coupled with a high level of compliance.

Raghip was also followed in *R* v *Ward* [1993] 1 WLR 619. The Court of Appeal concluded 'on the authorities as they now stand' (including *Turner* and *Raghip*) that expert evidence of a psychiatrist or a psychologist that a defendant, while not suffering from a mental illness, was suffering from a personality disorder so serious as to be properly described as a mental disorder, might be admissible to demonstrate the unreliability of confessions made by that defendant, although such evidence would be admitted only on rare occasions. The conviction was quashed on this and other grounds.

In *R* v *Strudwick* (1993) 99 Cr App R 326, Farquharson LJ reflected (at p. 332) on the mood of change:

> It is not suggested here that the appellant is suffering from a mental illness, but that is not in itself conclusive against the admission of his evidence. The law is in a state of development in this area. There may well be other mental conditions [including psychological damage] about which a jury might require expert assistance in order to understand and evaluate their effect on the issues in a case.

Ironically, this modern approach was presaged 20 years earlier by Lawton LJ in *R* v *Turner* [1975] QB 834 at p. 842:

> In coming to the conclusion we have in this case we must not be taken to be discouraging the calling of psychiatric evidence in cases where such evidence can be helpful within the present rules of evidence. These rules may be too restrictive of the admissibility of opinion evidence.

Lawton LJ went on to refer to the recommendations of the Criminal Law Revision Committee (Cmnd 4991 at p. 252), of which he was a member, that an expert should be allowed to give an opinion 'on any relevant matter on which he is qualified to give expert evidence' — even on intent. However, as the following paragraphs show, the law is still a long way from having adopted such a position.

18.5.4 The *Turner* rule and *mens rea*

The courts have consistently ruled that inferences about a normal person's state of mind can be drawn from that person's conduct and the surrounding circumstances without the aid of expert evidence. This means that where the issue concerns the knowledge or intention of a normal person, the *Turner* rule must prevail, as was made clear in *R* v *Chard* (1971) 56 Cr App R 268, a murder case decided before *Turner*. Similarly, in *R* v *Coles* (1995) 1 Cr App R 157 the trial judge refused to admit expert psychological testimony in answer to a reckless arson charge on the ground that the 15-year-old defendant's mental capacity, though lower than average, did not disclose any evidence of abnormality. In upholding this decision, the Court of Appeal ruled that the evidence in question related solely to characteristics of the defendant that could be evaluated competently by a jury through reference to the facts without the assistance of expert evidence, because adolescents of varying stages of maturity and brightness were all within the common experience of jurors. This is a clear-cut application of the *Turner* rule, and it is interesting to note that while the boy's age would be a relevant characteristic for the purposes of both provocation and duress, this is not so when it comes to the fundamental issue of whether the defendant had *mens rea*. However, although age gets in as a 'characteristic' in cases of provocation and duress, it seems highly unlikely that any expert testimony would be permitted to assist a jury in its deliberations about how a reasonable 15-year-old would react to provocation or duress. In that sense the *Turner* rule is once again designed to ensure that the ruling in *Coles*, about adolescence and immaturity, will apply equally to other areas of the criminal law, as is well illustrated in *R v Davies* (1995) 94/4098/S2, a case dealing with the admissibility of expert evidence in relation to the reliability of testimony given by very young children, where the Court of Appeal had no hesitation in following the *Turner* rule, saying:

> It is fundamental that experts must not usurp the function of the jury in a criminal trial. . . . Particular circumstances arise when there are characteristics of a medical nature in the make-up of a witness, such as mental illness, which would not be apparent to the jury or the effect of which would not be known to the jury without expert assistance. These circumstances do not arise in the case of ordinary children, who are not suffering from any abnormality.

18.6 SUMMARY

The *Turner* rule continues to dominate the question of the admissibility of expert psychological and psychiatric testimony. Accordingly, if the mental processes of an accused are not claimed to be abnormal, the jurors must use their own knowledge and experience to decide the issue in question. This is well illustrated within the broad area of *mens rea*, where it is only in exceptional cases that expert evidence is permitted to assist a jury. As an example of an exceptional case, in *R v Toner* (1991) 93 Cr App R 382 it was decided that the possibility of a mild attack of hypoglycaemia lay outside the ordinary experience of jurors, in the sense that they would not be able to make a judgment about how such a medical condition might have effected the accused's mental state in relation to *mens rea* without the aid of expert evidence. However, it seems clear that such cases are exceptional.

With regard to provocation and duress, the Court of Appeal has begun to review the doctrine of 'characteristics' in relation to the relevant objective tests. In cases involving pleas of provocation, courts are beginning to allow expert evidence on the question of how a reasonable person would have reacted, but in cases involving the defence of duress, the trend still favours the *Turner* rule.

The fundamental question is whether the *Turner* rule is fatally flawed. It assumes that 'ordinary' and 'normal' are well-defined personal attributes and that the distinction between 'normal' and 'abnormal' can be clearly understood and recognised. It restricts the admissibility of psychological and psychiatric expertise to the supposedly 'abnormal', on the dubious transparency assumption according to which all 'normal' forms of behaviour are necessarily within the common knowledge and experience of a jury. The transparency assumption does not seem to accord with research evidence, and in any event, as psychology and psychiatry develop, the crude distinction between 'normal' and 'abnormal' is becoming increasingly difficult to maintain. It would be more reasonable to extend the range of expert testimony to include forms of behaviour and states of mind that fall short of mental disorders but are nonetheless poorly understood by ordinary people. In many ways this seems to be what is beginning to happen in relation to provocation, and more particularly in a number of important confession cases, and it may only be a matter of time before this trend begins to dilute the broader impact of the *Turner* rule.

Key terms
battered woman syndrome; common knowledge and experience; confession; duress; eyewitness misinformation effect; fundamental attribution error; learned helplessness; *mens rea*; objective test in duress; objective test in provocation; overattribution bias; provocation; reasonable firmness; transparency assumption; *Turner* rule.

References
Blass, T. (1991), 'Understanding behavior in the Milgram obedience experiment: the role of personality, situations, and their interactions', *Journal of Personality and Social Psychology*, vol. 60, pp. 398–413.

Colman, A.M. and Mackay, R.D. (1993), 'Legal issues surrounding the admissibility of expert psychological and psychiatric testimony', in N.K. Clark and G.M. Stephenson (eds), *Children, Evidence and Procedure* (Issues in Criminological and Legal Psychology, No. 20). Leicester: British Psychological Society, pp. 46–50.

Criminal Law Revision Committee, Eleventh Repoort (1972) Evidence (General), Cmnd 4991 (HMSO)

Cross, R. and Tapper, C. (1995), *Cross and Tapper on Evidence*, 8th ed.. London: Butterworths.

Furnham, A. (1992), 'Prospective psychology students' knowledge of psychology', *Psychological Reports*, vol. 70, pp. 375–82.

Lloyd-Bostock, S. (1988), *Law in Practice*. London: Routledge.

Mackay, R.D. and Colman, A.M. (1991), 'Excluding expert evidence: a tale of ordinary folk and common experience', *Criminal Law Review*, pp. 800–10.

Mackay, R.D. and Colman, A.M. (1996), 'Equivocal rulings on expert psychological and psychiatric evidence: turning a muddle into a nonsense', *Criminal Law Review*, pp. 88–95.

Milgram, S. (1974), *Obedience to Authority: An Experimental View*. New York: Harper and Row.

Smith, J.C. and Hogan, B. (1996), *Criminal Law*, (8th ed.). London: Butterworths.

Webster, D.M. (1993), 'Motivated augmentation and reduction of the overattribution bias', *Journal of Personality and Social Psychology*, vol. 65, pp. 261–71.

Editors' notes
The authors' suggestion that in the light of recent developments and freshly available learning the *Turner* rule requires reconsideration and relaxation is compelling. Lawyers have much to discover from psychologists and psychiatrists which would assist them and those lay fact-finders whom they direct in conducting meaningful analyses of contentious witness testimony and, as a result, coming to just and right conclusions. The Court of Appeal's more liberal approach to the admission of expert evidence concerning the workings of the mind in the areas discussed is welcome and indicates a more open-minded trend.

CHAPTER NINETEEN
Problematic testimony

Anthony Heaton-Armstrong, David Wolchover and Eric Shepherd

19.1 INTRODUCTION

This chapter has three general aims. The first is to identify factors which obscure the main incedences of witness vulnerability detailed in part 1 of this book. The second is to outline some of the problems involved in examining whether it is the methods of investigation themselves which may trigger such vulnerabilities. This exercise will draw upon the raw material referred to in part 2. The third, focusing on the trial process, is to highlight the problems involved in presenting the results of these enquiries for consideration by the fact-finding body.

The issues dealt with here, as with much of the remainder of the book's contents, tend to concern the crucial question of whether, when a witness gives incorrect or misleading testimony, this is a result of deliberate untruthfulness or of factors which lead to honest errors of perception and memory.

The examination of testimony which is provided by a mendacious witness, whilst not necessarily leading to the discovery of the truth, gives rise to comparatively few forensic problems. In contrast, the unravelling of an imagined or corrupted but honestly delivered account is likely to involve complex questions relating to the workings and intricacies of the human mind. It is in this area where problems will arise unless the judiciary are appropriately educated and professional expertise from psychiatric and psychological witnesses becomes more readily available to the fact-finding body.

A court needs to know from experts what science has established about the factors of human functioning which may give rise to problematic testimony — that which is honestly incorrect or misleading. Traditionally courts have been only allowed to learn about *abnormal* psychological functioning, from psychiatrists or clinical psychologists in evidence judged admissible. The realities of normal functioning which give rise to problematic testimony have been ruled to be within the common ken of the average layperson. This book provides ample evidence that this position is unsupportable. Scientific research has cumulatively demonstrated that the realities of normal psychological functioning which give rise to problematic testimony are either unknown to lay people or are completely at odds with common-sense understandings or beliefs. As normal lay people clearly do *not* have knowledge or have inaccurate, unfounded notions it is perverse to deny a court learning about these realities from an expert.

The first step is to inform judges of the mismatch between scientific findings and lay notions. This will bring home how untenable it is to allow courts to know about abnormal functioning whilst keeping them in the dark concerning unknown, yet empirically established facts concerning normal psychological functioning, its limitations and its fallibilities.

19.2 JUDICIAL TRAINING

Wherever the mental state of a witness providing contentious testimony is relevant in any case, an assessment of the witness's reliability must depend, if it is to have any validity, on the consideration of psychological and psychiatric issues. Here, the extent of the fact-finder's knowledge of the workings of the human mind will play an essential role. Against the background of the chapters of this book which involve specific vulnerabilities and shortfalls in investigative techniques it is important for the judges of fact to be informed about the basics of memory and its potential for corruption. Yet it is one thing to be able to call on a body of theory and research about the deficiencies of witness perception and memory. It is quite another matter to find ways by which that learning may be harnessed by the judges of fact in assessing the evidence given by witnesses. Essentially this is a problem of 'judicial training'. In this context the word 'judicial' must be given a wide meaning. It must be read to embrace all judges of fact, not merely professional judges of the High Court or Crown Court, or stipendiary magistrates. It must therefore extend to include judges with no legal qualifications, that is, lay magistrates and jurors. But judicial training will be of two different kinds, direct and indirect. For professional judges there must be formal training programmes in the relevant disciplines. Lay judges, on the other hand, will need to rely on the guidance given them by professional lawyers. It will be given by advocates through the evidence they call and the submissions they make. In jury trials it will be given by professional judges through directions to the jury. In conviction appeals to the Crown Court, it will be given by circuit judges to their lay justice colleagues sitting on what used to be called 'appeal committees'. In court-martials it will be given by the judge-advocate to the soldier-judges. In magistrates' courts it will be given by the clerk to the justices.

Training programmes for practitioners and professional judges tend to emphasise purely legal issues and to assume an acquaintance with psychology and psychiatry as these fields touch on the evidence of witnesses in trials.

Where any learning from professional 'mind' disciplines is disseminated among lawyers it is apt to be through individual cases in which experts have given psychological or psychiatric evidence. There has been something of a departure from this pattern of late in dealing with false confessions. For centuries the phenomenon has been widely known as a result of the attention given to it by a host of writers — from Maimonides in the eleventh century to the American Hugo Munsterberg in the twentieth. However, in recent years, following something of a softening of the jealous attitudes of lawyers towards expertise from other disciplines, the validity of scientific tests and expert evidence relating to confession has been acknowledged by the higher courts. Indirectly, this more liberal attitude towards the scientific validation of the phenomenon of false confession has paved the way for legislation designed to prevent it through the introduction of protective measures for suspects under custodial investigation.

It cannot be satisfactory that the judiciary and fact-finders should be exposed to such an important issue as the scientific analysis of witness testimony on an incidental and piecemeal basis. The traditional fall-back on the 'common knowledge' objection to receiving expertise from extra-legal disciplines is demonstrably outmoded when contrasted with the modern treatment by the Court of Appeal of false confession cases. The Court's attitude in such cases has moved away from the narrow view that false confession can be commonly understood as a result of a fact-finder's experience of the world, to be enlightened position that, frequently, it can only be properly understood through the evidence of scientists.

False confession by suspects forms a small, albeit significant part of what we term 'problematic testimony'. This book illustrates that there are, additionally, numerous other false evidence phenomena which can be discovered or indicated using scientific expertise. A systematic approach to the training of fact-finders and those who direct them will enhance 'common knowledge' and enable this new learning to be put into practice when difficult issues relating to contentious testimony are raised. There is a pressing need for such an approach.

The mechanics of improved training courses for professional judges or lay magistrates need not be as costly or time-consuming as might be feared. An essential starting point would be the assimilation of the basic processes covered in chapters 1 and 2. This core material provides a considerable degree of insight not currently enjoyed by judicial trainees. Once digested, it would enable them to direct lay fact-finders such as jurors (or lay colleagues on appeal committees) in a way that would facilitate sensible analysis of witness testimony. It would avoid the unhelpful and almost ubiquitous 'the witness are for you — make of them what you will' type of direction. Such an approach assumes a 'common knowledge' and an ability to dissect evidence using psychological criteria which many 'ordinary folk' simply do not have.

This generalised 'enhanced common knowledge' training really applies to all witness testimony. It could be imparted to jurors on a non-specific basis through pre-trial start instructions of the kind that are currently contained in introductory leaflets and video films and through tailor-made or Judicial Studies Board directions adapted for specific cases.

Judicial training should not stop at providing the basic core material concerning the flaws of mental processes. If injustices of the kind discovered on an ad hoc basis in the false confession cases are to be avoided, it is important that judges are made familiar with the pitfalls of perception, remembrance and proof which are set out in the other chapters. This will empower them to become more adept at disregarding, or exercising healthy scepticism, about categories of evidence which have hitherto been perceived either as 'safe' or otherwise patently inadequate or not susceptible to examination but which is admitted in evidence because of historical or expedient factors.

19.3 DISCLOSURE

19.3.1 General

Identifying the factors which may induce a witness to give wrong or misleading evidence or to succumb to influence by inappropriate investigative methods necessitates full disclosure by the prosecution in two specific areas. First, there needs to be full exposure of the background details and history of the mental and physical health of the witness. Second, it is necessary to maintain and furnish comprehensive records of the process by which investigators or quasi-investigators obtain factual accounts from witnesses. Disclosure may need to be effected by an investigator or prosecutor in a criminal case, by a third party such as the local authority employing a social worker or a medical practitioner, or on behalf of a co-defendant. In criminal cases the law relating to disclosure is principally governed by the provisions of the Criminal Procedure and Investigations Act 1996, which sets out a tightly defined process, highly dependent on the efficiency and professionalism of those to whom it is directed. We do not propose, here, to reiterate its provisions or detail the procedures intended to be followed when they are put into practice. Eric Shepherd's work *Active Defence* (co-authored with Roger Ede), and other works in our lists of recommended reading, cover this ground usefully and comprehensively. Instead, our observations will focus on some of the hurdles that will need to be surmounted in attempting to identify (a) witness vulnerabilities and (b) source material for the analysis of investigative methods. Difficulties occur either because although the relevant material exists it is not easy to discover, or because of the failure to create material such as interview records, which might afford opportunity for analysis. The primary source of information relevant to whether a witness is vulnerable because of the factors outlined in the first section of this book will be medical records and those collated by quasi-investigators such as social service workers and therapists. The holders of this type of material will be third parties to legal proceedings and may put forward specific or principled objections against disclosing it to litigants. In the face of a refusal to disclose, the only recourse is to the court itself through an application for a witness summons, endorsed in a way that enables the material sought to be located and identified. This might be followed by an application by the third party to set aside the summons, or by a claim that the material is protected under the doctrine of public interest immunity.

In an accusatorial system of justice, the defence are particularly susceptible to the accusation that an attempt to discover material which might have a bearing on the reliability of the evidence of a prosecution witness is no more than a 'fishing expedition'. The use and prevalence of this expression in the higher courts assumes that the prosecution are exclusively responsible for investigating an allegation of wrongdoing and that efforts by the defence to broaden the ambit of an investigation beyond that conducted by the prosecution are to be deprecated and discouraged. If a prosecution investigation causes information about a witness's vulnerability to be revealed, all well and good. However, if the defence are dissatisfied with the comprehensiveness of a police enquiry and seek to delve further, the system assumes that they are embarking on an illegitimate fishing expedition. Thus the law relating to disclosure by third parties is restrictive and seems almost designed to frustrate rather than to facilitate the broadening of an investigation beyond the scope deemed sufficient by the prosecution. Additionally, the attempts by prosecuting investigators to discover vulnerability factors may themselves be obstructed by third parties. However, the passage of a prosecution enquiry into the past of their own witnesses is likely to be eased by the witnesses themselves, who may be reluctant to block access to their third-party records for fear of raising suspicions about the truthfulness of their evidence.

19.3.2 Medical records

If the prosecution have sought and obtained the medical records of their witnesses, with or without their consent, and have served them on the defence, problems will rarely arise. However, there will be difficulties if, having obtained the records, the prosecution opt to decline disclosure of them under the Criminal Procedure and Investigations Act 1996. If the prosecution choose not to disclose the records the defence will need, first, to seek voluntary disclosure — likely to be feasible with the witness's consent. Failing this, the defence will have to apply for a witness summons naming the holder of the records and requiring production. If the records-holder argues that the summons should be set aside or that the records should be protected by public interest immunity, the rules relating to third-party disclosure will apply. No legal privilege arises out of the doctor–patient relationship.

19.3.3 Other third-party material

Much material attesting to a witness's vulnerability will be contained within the witness's medical records. However, other sources controlled by third parties may throw light on the physical or mental health of witnesses or illuminate aspects of their past conduct which, in suggesting the existence of a particular weakness or vulnerability, will cast doubt on their reliability. These include school records or those kept by other establishments at which a witness has been resident, for example, a prison, and notes made by non-medical health-care workers such as therapeutic counsellors.

19.3.4 Non-cooperative witnesses

As a result of information either disclosed by medical records or obtained from associates of the witness, the defence may occasionally conclude that in order to obtain a comprehensive picture it will be necessary for the witness to be examined by a doctor, psychiatrist or psychologist on behalf of the defendant. Experience has shown that requests directed to witnesses in these circumstances are usually refused. Since an unreasonable refusal may argu-ably preclude effective scrutiny of the witness's evidence this may form the basis of an application under s. 78 of the Police and Criminal Evidence Act 1984 to exclude the witness's evidence altogether. Such an application is likely to be unsuccessful if the request for an examination is perceived as being unduly speculative. This is acutely likely to be the case where, for example, it is thought that a witness's belief that she has been subjected to a sexual assault is the by-product of a narcoleptic episode or 'false memory syndrome'.

19.3.5 Third-party disclosure and the law

Much of the third party material which we envisage will need to be identified during the discovery of witness vulnerability factors comprises records made of what a witness has said during a non-investigator interview. For example, a complainant alleging sexual assault may have undergone therapy before going to the police and without previously having complained. If the therapist has maintained a record of the relevant interview sessions, it will obviously be desirable to establish, first, whether the nature of the therapy had the potential for corrupting the witness's memory, and, second, whether allega-tions made during the therapy by the complainant are consistent with later accounts and the witness's evidence in court. However, the law relating to the disclosure of witness's previous statements to third parties clearly rules out orders for non-voluntary disclosure. In *R v Cheltenham Justices, ex parte Secretary of State for Trade* [1977] 1 WLR 95, it was held that there was no right to production of documents containing previous statements by a witness to a third party which might contain a discrepancy. Subsequent decisions have confirmed this on the basis that to be disclosable the material has in itself to be admissible evidence. It will not qualify for disclosure if the basis on which it is sought is to provide material for prospective cross-examination. The fact that, following denial of a previous inconsistent statement it may in other circumstances be possible to prove the latter by adducing the document sought or by calling the person to whom the statement was made and who created the record, does not abrogate the *Cheltenham Justices* rule (*R v Derby Magistrates' Court, ex parte B* [1996] AC 487). Taken to its limits — which is, sadly, not unknown — the law precludes the discovery of what may be highly damaging statements by or to a third party, even if they are wholly contradictory to the witness's evidence. The use of the expression 'fishing expedition' to describe defence attempts to obtain such material is wholly inappropriate. However, until the appellate courts come to grips with the potential injustices which may flow from strict adherence to the rules on third-party disclosure, fact-finders will continue to be prevented from seeing significant parts of the evidential picture.

19.3.6 Disclosure by the prosecution

During the investigative process the prosecution have complete control over the creation of records of statements made to them by witnesses. The courts have long acknowledged that comparison between evidence and previous statements is the principal and classic way of testing the reliability of a witness's evidence. Moreover, Parliament through the Criminal Procedure and Investigations Act 1996 and the accompanying Code of Practice has emphasised the importance of retaining the records of police investigations. However, no proper or useful analysis of previous statements can take place when, as is invariably the case, the records of such statements do not exist, are incomplete, or fail to include the full context in which the statement was obtained, that is, the interviewer's questions. Current police practices are detailed in chapters 9 and 15. Paragraphs 5(1) and 5(4) of the CPIA Code of Practice are especially apt:

Retention of material. (a) Duty to retain material.

5(1). The prosecutor must retain material obtained in a criminal investigation which may be relevant to the investigation. This includes . . . material generated by him (*such as interview records*). . . .

5(4). The duty to retain material includes in particular the duty to retain material falling into the following categor[y]: interview records (written records, or audio or video tapes, of *interviews with actual or potential witnesses* or suspects) (emphasis added).

As we have argued elsewhere, the belief that interviews with suspects are so ripe for misconduct that huge resources are now utilised for recording them in unassailable form whereas interviews with witnesses do not pose the same risk of subornment, intimidation and improper influence is naive beyond argument. Only when witness interviews are comprehensively recorded can anyone — whether fact-finder or expert — begin to undertake any sort of realistic and effective analysis of them both for inherent frailties and consistency with evidence.

However, even assuming that investigators have tape-recorded their interviews with potential witnesses, the difficulties for the defence do not end there. There is no guarantee, under the present regime, that the prosecution will voluntarily disclose tape recordings of witness interviews because disclosure of all unused material is now a matter for their judgment and discretion. Present indications are that the practical arrangements concerning disclosure by the prosecution are inefficient and even dangerous, as was anticipated would be the case before the 1996 Act came into force. Some categories of unused material held by the prosecution should automatically be disclosable and these should, of course, include the full and unexpurgated record of interviews with witnesses concerning the subject matter of their complaint or account.

19.4 THE USE OF EXPERTS

Much valid expert evidence has been withheld from fact-finders altogether or otherwise presented in a misleading or insufficiently powerful form. The cause has often been inadequate preparation, poor drafting of reports or the failure by advocates to pick up on clues to vulnerability or a lack of reliability which are apparent in material originally before them.

19.4.1 Instructing experts

Whether it will occur to the professional practitioner to consider instructing an expert will largely depend on the extent of the practitioner's experience in the field and knowledge of the concepts referred to in this book. An expert may be useful for one or the other of two purposes. The expert may be enlisted to explain a proposition of general application in relation to a particular facet of the evidence such as the dangers inherent in inappropriate questioning of children. Alternatively, the expert may be called to give evidence concerning a witness's specific vulnerability, perhaps relating this to the way in which a pre-evidential account may have been collated. Care must be taken to ensure that the expert's observations are material and potentially admissible in evidence. Careful attention also needs to be paid to whether the expert can add to the fact-finder's common knowledge or whether, assuming that the latter has been properly and comprehensively 'trained', the report will add nothing to concepts of which the fact-finder is already aware.

19.4.2 Identifying the right expert for the task in hand

The proliferation nowadays of professional expert agencies and directories of experts advertising specialisations provides sufficient reference to enable legal practitioners to track down potential candidates. Formalised engagement should await an informed decision on whether the chosen expert possesses the experience and skills to undertake the exercise required. At the pre-employment stage it is advisable for a defending solicitor, working in liaison with the trial advocate, to ensure, through spoken contact with the provisional candidate, that the right person for the job has been selected. Once funding arrangements are in place, what ought to be exhaustive instruction can begin. Advice on these issues is detailed by Eric Shepherd and Roger Ede in *Active Defence*.

19.4.3 Presenting the expert and the expert's report to the court

Assuming that the expert's report has been suitably drafted and served in accordance with the advance disclosure rules, the next hurdle to be overcome is adducing the expert's evidence. If admissibility is an issue, the court will have to decide whether to hold a *voir dire* (that is, a 'trial within a trial' on admissibility) and, if so, at what stage in the proceedings. It may be preferable to know whether expert evidence is ruled as admissible at an early stage so that consideration can be given to alternative methods of making the fact-finding body familiar with the particular expertise. Even if ruled inadmissible per se, many reports will provide a useful resource when witnesses are cross-examined. Where an expert has been employed by an opposing party and has provided a report relevant to a contentious issue it will rarely, if ever, be advisable for its conclusions to be accepted at face value and employment of an expert for one's 'own side' is strongly urged.

The strength of an argument relating to the admissibility of psychiatric or psychological expert evidence will usually be enhanced by the provision to the court of a skeleton argument which should refer to the relevant law — summarised in chapter 18 — and any relevant learned articles or books.

It will usually be necessary for one's own expert to be present in court whilst the questionable witness and the expert from the opposing side are giving evidence and it will be essential to hold regular conferences with the 'friendly' expert during the trial in order to keep track of the way in which the evidence is unfolding.

19.4.4 References to 'common knowledge' during the trial

If the prospective evidence of an expert is ruled inadmissible on the basis that the subject matter comes within the 'common knowledge' of the fact-finder, it follows that, subject to materiality, the advocate, in the course of the closing speech or address, should be given a free rein to refer to that 'common knowledge' as expounded by the expert. The effectiveness of such submissions will depend on the advocate's familiarity with the concepts explained in the book and the extent to which the court, or judge, has been trained to understand them and as a result is receptive to them.

19.5 CONCLUSION

The treatment of witnesses and the realistic and proper analysis of things said by them have for too long been neglected fields — in stark contrast to the extensive consideration given to that of suspects. A radical new approach amongst crime investigators and lawyers is needed to ensure that what lies behind the evidential assertions of witnesses is accurately and intelligently revealed and analysed. Practices relating to the questioning of witnesses and the recording of their statements are patently anachronistic and can only be justified on the basis that the courts have allowed them to 'stand the test of time'. Judges and advocates should be required to learn about the workings of the human mind, about its faculties of sense and remembrance, about the distorting processes of perception and the corrupting influences of memory. Only a thorough grounding in this field secured through formal training courses will enable advocates to present cases effectively and judges to make rational and reliable fact-finding decisions or to direct fact-finders to do so. A more aggressive judicial approach to inadequate or incomplete investigation is needed along with a more inquisitorial approach to justice. Where evidence of a witness's vulnerability exists but is unattainable or where it is apparent that the nature of an investigation may have corrupted a witness's memory courts should be more ready to prevent cases from proceeding further. Above all, police interviews with potential witnesses should be tape-recorded.

The fallacy that 'ordinary' fact-finders do not need to be guided by psychiatric or psychological expertise in explaining complex thought and memory processes and that understanding witness testimony is a really rather simple process which requires no training whatever needs to be comprehensively debunked.

In 1952 a man called Mattan was hanged following his conviction for a murder he did not commit. In 1998, 46 years later, Lord Justice Rose, the Vice-President of the Court of Appeal Criminal Division posthumously allowed the executed man's appeal against conviction. Giving judgment, he said that it was a matter of profound regret that it had taken so long for the conviction to be shown to be unsafe and he added: 'No one associated with the criminal justice system can afford to be complacent'.

Key terms
Common knowledge; confabulation; disclosure; expert testimony; fantasy; judicial training; vulnerabilities.

Recommended reading
Corker, D. (1996), *Disclosure in Criminal Proceedings.* London: Sweet & Maxwell. ISBN: 0 421 568 100.

Gudjousson, G. and Haward, L. (1998), *Forensic Psychology: A Practitioner's Guide.* London: Routledge. ISBN: 0 415 132916.

Sprack, J., 'The Criminal Procedure and Investigations Act 1996: The Duty of Disclosure', *Criminal Law Review* [1997] 308.

Tansey, R. QC, and Keleher, P., *Disclosure,* a Practical Research Paper, London: Sweet & Maxwell.

Index